SIMONIDES
A HISTORICAL STUDY

JOHN H. MOLYNEUX

Senior Lecturer in Classics,
University of Nottingham

BOLCHAZY-CARDUCCI PUBLISHERS

Softbound cover illustration by Leandros Kokkoris
Cover designs by David Van Delinder

Copyright © 1992 Bolchazy-Carducci Publishers

All rights reserved. No part of this publication may be reproduced or transmitted in any form or by any means, electronic, mechanical, photocopying, recording, or otherwise without the written permission of the publishers.

Bolchazy-Carducci Publishers
1000 Brown Street, Unit 101
Wauconda, Illinois 60084

Printed in the United States of America

International Standard Book Number:
Hardbound 0-86516-222-0
Softbound 0-86516-223-9

Library of Congress Cataloging-in-Publication Data

Molyneux, John H.
   Simonides: a historical study / John H. Molyneux.
   p. cm.
   Includes bibliographical references and index.
   ISBN 0-86516-222-0: $39.00 — ISBN 0-86516-223-9 (pbk.): $24.00
   1. Simonides, ca. 556-467 B.C.   2. Epigrams, Greek—History and criticism.   3. Poets, Greek—Biography.   I. Title.
PA4411.Z5M64 1992
884'.01—dc20
                                                                             92-5319
                                                                                CIP

Contents

I. Introduction   1

    1. Aims of this study; selection and treatment of material.   1

    2. State of scholarship on the Simonidean epigrams; treatment of the epigrams in the present study.   6

    3. Summary of Stella's article proposing a revised Simonidean chronology   23

II. Some Early Lyric Poems   33

    1. The ode or odes for Glaucus of Carystus   33

    2. Works for Leocrates and Agatharchus   42

    3. Odes for Eretrians: Eualcides and Lysimachus.   45

    4. Epinician ode concerning Crius of Aegina   47

III. Simonides and the Pisistratids   65

    1. The evidence connecting Simonides with Hipparchus, and Stella's treatment of this evidence.   65

    2. Other topics relevant to Simonides' Pisistratid connections   68

IV.	**Some Early Epigrams**	81
	1. The epigram for Milo of Croton	81
	2. Epigrams for the events of 507/6 B.C.	84
	3. Epigrams for Aeginetans	87
V.	**Simonides in Relation to Other Poets**	97
	1. Bacchylides	97
	2. Lasus and dithyrambic contests	99
	3. Xenophanes	105
	4. "Theognis"	106
	5. Timocreon	107
VI.	**Simonides' Thessalian Period**	117
	1. Simonides' connections with the Aleuadae	118
	2. Simonides' connections with the Scopadae	121
	3. Simonides' connections with the Echecratidae	127
	4. Works for other Thessalians	129
	5. General Survey of Simonides' activity in Thessaly; dates of his association with his Thessalian patrons.	132
VII.	**Simonides in the Persian Wars I: Marathon to Artemisium**	147
	1. Marathon	148

	2. The period 490-480 B.C.	155
	3. Artemisium	156
VIII.	**Simonides in the Persian Wars II: Thermopylae to Plataea**	175
	1. Thermopylae	175
	2. Salamis	187
	3. Plataea and after	197
	4. Conclusions	202
IX.	**Simonides in Italy and Sicily**	211
	1. The Ode for Anaxilas of Rhegium	211
	2. The Ode for Astylus of Croton or Syracuse	214
	3. Simonides and Gelon	220
	4. Simonides and Hieron	224
	5. Simonides and the Emmenidae of Acragas	233
X.	**Simonides' Relations with Pindar**	247
	1. The argument based by Stella on the relationship of Simonides and Pindar; methodology of the interpretation of Pindar.	247
	2. Pindaric passages quoted as evidence by Stella: *Ol.* 2; *Isth.* 2; *Ol.* 9.	248
	3. Other evidence for the relationship of Simonides and Pindar	263
	4. Assessment of Stella's conclusions	274

XI.	**Late Simonidean Epigrams**	285
	1. The argument based by Stella on epigrams referring to events after 468/7 B.C.; the principles involved.	285
	2. The epigrams cited by Stella, and other epigrams in the same category.	288
XII.	**The Ancient Testimonia on Simonides' Dates**	307
	1. The ancient testimonia and the orthodox modern interpretation	307
	2. Stella's treatment of the ancient evidence	318
	3. A possible modification of the orthodox account	330
XIII.	**Conclusions on Stella's Revised Simonidean Chronology**	339
	Bibliography	347
	Index	355
	Index of Passages	365

SIMONIDES
A HISTORICAL STUDY

Acknowledgements

The publication of this book was aided by a generous grant from the Research Fund of the University of Sheffield; and, at an earlier stage, grants from the same Fund facilitated the research for the Sheffield PhD thesis on which the present study is ultimately based. This help is gratefully acknowledged. I also wish to thank Professors D.A. Campbell, D.E. Gerber, and G.M. Kirkwood for their valuable comments and suggestions; but this does not necessarily imply that they would agree with all I have said, and I am solely responsible for any errors or omissions which remain.

J.H. Molyneux
Nottingham
1991

Chapter 1

Introduction

1. Aims of this study; selection and treatment of material.

The principal aim of this study is to examine the public life and poetic career of Simonides from a historical or biographical standpoint. To this end the following topics are considered: the occasion and date of Simonides' poems (in cases where the evidence warrants such an enquiry); the dates of his association with various patrons; his whereabouts and movements at various stages of his poetic career; and his relationship with the communities, governments, or individuals for whom he wrote. Occasionally it will be appropriate to ask whether the evidence concerning Simonides throws any light on disputed historical questions of a more general nature. I have not attempted a biographical study in the widest sense. No attempt is made to discuss Simonides' character, beliefs, position in literary history, or contribution to ideas. Matters such as family relationships or episodes of a personal or anecdotal nature, which form the material of the ancient biographical tradition and are treated in modern studies such as those of Bell or Lefkowitz, are discussed only if they are relevant to the question of Simonides' dates or relationship with his patrons.

Within this framework I have tried to consider the revised dating of Simonides proposed by L. A. Stella, who advances arguments for dating his lifetime from c. 532/29 B.C. to about the middle of the fifth century. A re-dating of one of the major choral lyric poets by some thirty years would, if accepted, have important consequences for Greek literary history. Even if Stella's re-dating is not accepted, there remains the question, to which she rightly drew attention, of the apparent incongruity between the traditional dating of Simonides' lifetime and the presumed dates of much of his work, which appear to concentrate most of his poetic activity in his extreme old age. No study of this kind, written at the present time, could afford to ignore the questions which Stella poses.

As regards the numerous questions concerning the individual stages of Simonides' career, it will be found in many cases that the evidence does not permit any certain conclusions but points to two or more tenable alternative hypotheses or to a wide range of possible dates. In some instances it will prove necessary to reject some more or less precise dating or some confident statement about Simonides' life or career which is not adequately supported by the available evidence; some such datings or biographical statements were originally advanced as tentative suggestions but have gradually acquired strength and solidity through repetition, until they have come to be regarded as axiomatic. However on the particular question of the dates of Simonides' lifetime, I believe that the conclusion can be reached, with a fair degree of confidence, that the traditional dating is substantially correct.

It is true that one trend of current scholarly opinion deprecates the historical or biographical approach to the study of the choral lyric poets. In the case of Pindar the methods of Bundy, who explains references in Pindar's poems in the light of the conventions of choral lyric and the poet's all-pervasive aim of praising the victor, contrast sharply with those of Wilamowitz or Farnell, who explained the same references as allusions to political events or to the personal affairs of the poet or his patron. But despite the undeniable value of Bundy's contribution to the understanding of Pindar, the opinion has sometimes been expressed that he states too extreme a case; and it is possible that a compromise may be reached which will recognise the validity of both methods of approach to Pindar, provided that they are applied with discrimination. Further, Simonides' involvement with the major personalities and major events of the contemporary scene was greater than that of either Pindar or Bacchylides. There is a good deal of explicit evidence for Simonides' familiarity with leading political figures; and some of his lyric poems, and a great many of the epigrams ascribed to him, concern momentous events and prompt questions about his relationship with the individuals or communities concerned in those events. In the case of Simonides there is less extant poetry, but more evidence of a historical or biographical nature, than in the case of Pindar or Bacchylides. Therefore, even though the validity of certain current trends in Pindaric scholarship may be admitted, it does not follow that a similar approach is appropriate or even practicable in the case of Simonides.

Apart from the direct ancient testimonia to the dates of Simonides' lifetime, the material relevant to the aims of the present study consists of those poems of Simonides, or references to him in ancient authors, which can be approximately dated or which concern identifiable persons or events. Such items of evidence are of varying importance for the particular question of the dating of his lifetime which was raised by Stella. Most of the items discussed would fall within Simonides' potential working life whichever set of dates (c. 556-468, the traditional dating, or c. 532-450, Stella's dating) were adopted; nevertheless in every case it is necessary to raise the question whether or not the item of evidence under discussion provides any clue which would favour either the traditional dating or Stella's dating. More controversial are those poems or references which might be too early to allow Stella's dating or too late to allow the traditional dating; in such cases a larger proportion of my discussion of the item of evidence in question is devoted to its relevance to Stella's thesis.

The Simonidean poems discussed in this study fall into two main categories, viz. melic poems and epigrams;

and there are also a few fragments of elegies, that is, non-inscriptional elegiac poems of greater length than the epigrams. These categories do not have the same status as evidence for our enquiry.

Only a small proportion of the melic fragments (about twenty-five, rather more than one sixth of the total)[1] can be used as evidence here; the reason for this is that many of the melic fragments are quoted in isolation by our sources for some linguistic point or some odd scrap of information, so that nothing is known about the nature or occasion of the parent poem. Even in the case of the fragments which can be used as evidence, the relevant information is often to be extracted from the context where the fragment is quoted, rather than from the words of the fragment itself. But such evidence as the melic fragments do provide can normally be accepted as reliable; for the ancient ascription of melic poems to their author is usually regarded, a priori, as correct, unless there is some positive reason for suspecting an error. My discussion of the melic fragments is confined to topics relevant to the historical or biographical questions examined in this study; thus the meaning or implication of a given word or phrase (or of alternative readings) is discussed, if the question of the occasion of the poem turns on it; but other matters, such as imagery, literary antecedents, or contribution to thought, which would be relevant in an edition of Simonides, are excluded. I have referred to the "spirit" of an ode or group of poems only when this has been used by others for an assessment of the poet's age at the time of writing; I have not thought it profitable to introduce this highly subjective criterion myself.

Of the epigrams, a rather larger proportion qualify as relevant material, in that they concern identifiable persons or historical events; about forty epigrams (rather more than one third of the total) are discussed on this basis. But since in most cases both the status of the epigrams as contemporary fifth-century inscriptions and their Simonidean authorship are open to doubt, conclusions drawn from the epigrams are of a lower order of validity than those drawn from melic fragments; and, with some exceptions, my treatment of the epigrams is less detailed. The principles on which I have based my discussion of the epigrams seem to call for a separate statement, and are set out in the second section of this chapter.

Of longer elegiac poems only a small number of fragments and notices survive; sometimes it is not clear whether a few lines in elegiacs are a complete epigram or a fragment of an elegy. Of this handful, three or four are relevant to our enquiry. The ancient ascription of elegiac poems to their author is usually accepted, unless there is some special reason for suspecting an error; and I have assumed that the few fragments of Simonides' elegiac poems can be regarded as reliable evidence.

Melic fragments are quoted by the numbers of Page's *Poetae Melici Graeci*. Where possible, epigrams are quoted by the numbers of Page's *Epigrammata Graeca* and *Further Greek Epigrams*, and elegies from West's *Iambi et Elegi Graeci;* if not found in these works, they are quoted from Diehl (*Anthologia Lyrica Graeca*), or, if not found in Diehl, from Bergk (*Poetae Lyrici Graeci*).[2] As the Greek texts are so readily available, it has seemed sufficient, for purposes of this study, to quote most of these poems in translation.

The arrangement of material in this study is as follows. Of the remaining sections of this introductory chapter, Section 2 (as already noted) discusses the Simonidean epigrams, and Section 3 summarises Stella's article proposing a revised Simonidean chronology. Chapters II-XI consider the poems and references which are relevant to the aims of this study, chosen on the principles already outlined; these chapters follow a rough chronological sequence according to the stages of Simonides' career, though the necessity of giving each chapter some thematic coherence, and so avoiding the excessive fragmentation of a purely chronological list, means that there is sometimes an overlap in dating from one chapter to another. In Chapter XII the ancient testimonia to the dates of Simonides' lifetime are examined; and in the final chapter (XIII) my conclusions on Stella's revised Simonidean chronology are stated.

2. State of scholarship on the Simonidean epigrams; treatment of the epigrams in the present study.

A large number of epigrams (rather more than one hundred) are ascribed to Simonides by authorities ranging in date from Herodotus to Planudes. Very many are unmistakably cast in the form of monumental inscriptions, whether sepulchral or dedicatory, public or private, though this is not to say that they were necessarily written for a real monument; others merely narrate an event and it is not clear whether they are inscriptional pieces; a few are obviously mock inscriptions. Others have no connection (real or feigned) with monuments; they may be improvisations in a given situation, miscellaneous short poems, or riddles. It is not always clear whether a short piece is a complete epigram or a fragment of a longer elegy.

A few Simonidean epigrams dealing with events of the late sixth century and the early to mid fifth century have been proved, by their discovery on stone, to be genuine contemporary inscriptions. In some cases the actual inscription is shorter than the version handed down by literary sources; in one case[3] the inscription is longer than the literary version. Simonides' name is not found on any stone contemporary with the events which the epigram records; this is entirely in keeping with fifth-century practice.[4] In one very late prose inscription, of the fourth or fifth century A.D., which commemorates the restoration of a decayed monument and metrical inscription dating from the Persian Wars, Simonides is named as the author of the metrical inscription.[5]

Only one epigram is ascribed to Simonides by a fifth-century authority. The ascription is not, indeed, explicit, but it is to be inferred with certainty; for there can surely be no doubt that Herodotus means to ascribe the epigram on Megistias to Simonides, even though he does not actually state that Simonides wrote it.[6] In the same context Herodotus also quotes two other epigrams on Thermopylae, but makes no explicit statement about their authorship; they are ascribed to Simonides by later writers. After Herodotus, the next Simonidean ascription is made by Aristotle, the epigram in question having been quoted anonymously by Thucydides.[7] Apart from these two ascriptions by Herodotus and Aristotle, all quotations of Simonidean epigrams are anonymous in fifth and fourth-century authors (including Herodotus, Thucydides, Lycurgus, and Aristotle), the Simonidean ascriptions being made by later authorities.[8]

There is firm evidence that Simonidean epigrams were known and quoted by writers of the Alexandrian period. It is possible that Timaeus (if, for convenience, he may be included here) quoted XIV Page as Simonidean.[9] In his work on Simonides, Chamaeleon, the Peripatetic biographer of some of the lyric and dramatic poets, who flourished about the turn of the fourth and third centuries B.C., attributed to Simonides an improvised parody and two riddles.[10] It has long been thought that the inclusion of *epigrammata* in the list of Simonides' writings in the Suda is based on Callimachus' *Pinakes*.[11] Ascriptions of epigrams to Simonides are made by Aristophanes of Byzantium, by his pupil Callistratus, and by Aristodemus, a pupil of Aristarchus.[12] Meleager included Simonides in his *Garland*,[13] and most of the Simonidean epigrams in the Palatine and Planudean Anthologies are thought to have come from Meleager. In short, during the period from about 300 to about 100 B.C., the attested quotations of Simonidean epigrams always seem to be accompanied by the poet's name; and the evidence just quoted about Callimachus and Meleager suggests that they had at their disposal a fund of epigrams which were designated, whether correctly or not, as Simonidean.

After Meleager, the next writer to ascribe an epigram[14] to Simonides is Cicero. From this point onwards, some of the most important sources for Simonidean epigrams are:

Diodorus (who always quotes anonymously), Plutarch (usually anonymously), Aristides (usually anonymously), Pausanias (always as Simonidean), and Athenaeus (usually as Simonidean). The most abundant source of Simonidean epigrams is the Palatine Anthology,[15] which quotes about seventy, the vast majority of them with Simonides' name attached. Planudes quotes forty-nine Simonidean epigrams, of which all but nine are in the Palatine Anthology.

The authenticity of the Simonidean epigrams did not become a major topic for debate until after the middle of the nineteenth century. Before that time, the general assumption was that if an epigram was assigned to Simonides by any "ancient" authority (if this term may be stretched to include the world of Byzantine scholarship), it was to be regarded as his, unless there was some definite reason to the contrary. Thus Schneidewin, in his edition of Simonides, accepted the great majority of the Simonidean epigrams, whatever the source of the Simonidean ascription. However he excludes from his edition those epigrams whose subject-matter is unmistakably late; classes a small number of epigrams as *Incerta* (tentatively rejecting some of them on grounds of style); and dismisses a few others for various specific reasons, rejecting, for example, some Thermopylae epigrams on the ground that the five *stelae* at Thermopylae can be accounted for without them.[16] Schneidewin's valuable contributions to the study of the Simonidean epigrams include the shrewd observation, later confirmed by epigraphical discoveries, that some epigrams quoted in literary sources were likely to be expanded versions of originally shorter inscriptions.[17]

The work of Junghahn[18] may be said to mark the beginning of the great debate on the authenticity of the Simonidean epigrams. Many epigrams which had not been doubted before were rejected by Junghahn for reasons such as alleged historical inaccuracy, or incompatibility with sentiments expressed by Simonides in his lyric poetry, or with the linguistic usage (literary or inscriptional) of Simonides' time. He says little about the way in which epigrams which are anonymous in an early author acquired

Simonides' name in a later author, or about the significance of the earlier author's silence. He does however state (what is now generally accepted) that the Megistias epigram (VI Page) is the most surely guaranteed of all Simonidean epigrams, because Simonides' name is added by Herodotus; and he recognises the unreliability of ascriptions in the Palatine Anthology.

The line of enquiry begun by Junghahn was developed by Kaibel in two articles[19] written shortly after Junghahn's. Kaibel accepts many of the criteria laid down by Junghahn for the assessment of particular epigrams. He is more concerned than Junghahn with the process by which epigrams ascribed to Simonides in ancient sources acquired the poet's name. He emphasised two factors which have been recognised ever since as being of fundamental importance: that metrical inscriptions of the sixth and early fifth centuries were not accompanied on the stone by the poet's name, so that epigrams taken into anthologies from monuments were likely to be anonymous and might acquire an author's name by guesswork because of the anthologist's dislike of *adespota;* and that when an early author quotes an epigram anonymously, a later author as Simonidean, the earlier author's silence may imply ignorance of the authorship of the epigram, and the later author's ascription may be based not on superior knowledge but on guesswork or unreliable information. He also speculated on the date when a collection of Simonidean epigrams may have been first made, and on the reliance to be placed on any author who may be presumed to have used such a collection. Boas,[20] though criticising Kaibel for too confidently denying Simonidean authorship of epigrams merely because such authorship could not be proved, nevertheless acknowledges the importance of Kaibel's work.

Scholars reacted in different ways to the views of Junghahn and Kaibel. On the one hand, Bergk and Hauvette made what proved to be the last determined effort to defend the authenticity of a large number of Simonidean epigrams; while on the other hand the work of Wilamowitz and Boas marked a return to the scepticism of Kaibel, which has remained the dominant trend in the twentieth century.

Bergk[21] not only defends a number of individual epigrams against particular arguments of Junghahn and Kaibel, but returns to the general position that the onus of proof is on the sceptic. He doubts whether there are enough inscriptions of the appropriate date to form a criterion for the authenticity of Simonidean epigrams. He argues, against Kaibel, that the silence of an early writer on the authorship of epigrams may be due, not to ignorance, but to indifference or even to the fact that the authorship of the epigram was universally known.

Hauvette claimed that a "critical examination of the sources"[22] guaranteed the authenticity of a limited number of epigrams.[23] He then examined these "authentic" epigrams for characteristic features,[24] and, using the stylistic criteria thus obtained, he examined the epigrams whose authenticity is not guaranteed by the nature of their sources,[25] pronouncing twenty-one as probably authentic, and forty-nine as probably spurious.[26]

Both stages of this procedure are open to criticism. Firstly, Hauvette does not make out a convincing case for the authenticity of his twenty chosen epigrams. Though he recognises the anonymity of inscriptions and the unreliability of Simonidean ascriptions in authors who relied solely on the monuments, he apparently thinks that if authors who quote inscriptions as Simonidean drew them from "des recueils littéraires", their authenticity may be taken for granted.[27] However he does not make it clear how such collections of inscriptions acquired and preserved a true tradition of Simonidean authorship. Nor does he clearly indicate by what criteria it may be assumed that one author used these "reliable" collections and another did not; the use of a phrase like...

ἐν τοῖς Σιμωνίδου ἐπιγράμμασιν

...("in the Epigrams of Simonides") is said to be one indication that such a collection was used, but Aristotle, who does not use such a phrase, is presumed to have used such a collection.[28] Again, if authors who are supposed to have drawn on the collections make some obviously false ascriptions, it is difficult to see how their word on the authorship of other epigrams can be accepted without question; thus Hauvette, while recognising that Hephaestion's ascription to Simonides of an epigram on a fourth-century victor is a "certain error", claims that Hephaestion's testimony on the Simonidean authorship of the tyrannicide epigram is "unassailable".[29]

Secondly, the stylistic criteria which emerge from the study of the "authentic" epigrams are very vague. One alleged Simonidean characteristic is that the distichs of a four-line epigram are independent of each other in sense;[30] yet this is a common feature of elegiac verse, and indeed occurs in several epigrams which Hauvette himself rejects.[31] Sometimes an epigram which contains parallelisms with the wording of fifth-century inscriptions is assigned to Simonides for that reason,[32] but others with similar parallelisms are judged to be too banal for Simonides.[33] Epigrams whose phrasing is not paralleled in fifth-century inscriptions are sometimes denied to Simonides on this ground,[34] sometimes declared to be eminently worthy of the original genius of Simonides.[35]

Soon after Hauvette wrote, an essay published by Wilamowitz[36] marked a return to the scepticism of Kaibel. The essay was prompted by the recent discovery on stone of the first distich of Simonides XI Page, a discovery which confirmed Schneidewin's suggestion that genuine inscriptions were likely to be expanded in the literary tradition. A corollary of this fact, according to Wilamowitz, is that anything which is not offered by the stone, in particular the author's name, has no authority. He is however ready to admit that some genuine Simonidean epigrams existed, particularly non-inscriptional epigrams;[37] he thus hints at the important principle, which has often been enunciated since then, that non-inscriptional elegiac pieces ascribed to Simonides are more likely to be authentic than inscriptional epigrams, because, unlike the inscriptions, they may have had Simonides' name attached to them, in the literary tradition, throughout their existence.

The fundamental study of the sources of the epigrams is that of Boas, whose investigation of the nature and relationship of the sources is characterised by immense thoroughness, wide knowledge of the relevant literature, and often great ingenuity. Boas inherited from his predecessors the basic conclusion that a Simonidean collection (of doubtful reliability) had been made in the interval between the anonymous appearance of the epigrams on stone or in early authors, and the later ascribed quotations. He believes that only the three Thermopylae epigrams quoted by Herodotus can be regarded as definitely authentic, and that Aristotle's ascription of an epigram to Simonides is unreliable, in view of the silence of Thucydides.[38] He concludes, from a probable Simonidean ascription by Timaeus, that the Simonidean Collection was compiled toward the end of the fourth century, but that it was not well-known or used a great deal until parts of it were incorporated into Meleager's *Garland*, which henceforth became the chief authority for Simonidean ascriptions.[39]

Believing that an epigram should not be dismissed as spurious merely because its authenticity cannot be proved,[40] Boas pronounced a further eight epigrams (in addition, that is, to the three in Herodotus) as probably authentic. His declared method was to decide which epigrams possessed Simonidean characteristics (*Simonideam indolem atque naturam*), and this was to be done by comparing the three definitely genuine Simonidean epigrams with fifth-century metrical inscriptions;[41] but in his published work we are given only this brief description of his method and a summary of the results; the actual investigation of this matter is promised for the second part of his commentary, which never appeared.[42]

The basic conclusion which emerges from Boas' study of the sources is still the generally accepted opinion: that only the Herodotus passage provides certain proof of the authenticity of any Simonidean epigram,[43] and all epigrams ascribed elsewhere to Simonides are open to doubt, though some of them may well be genuine. His selection of eight more epigrams as probably authentic is of little significance; his claim that three genuine epigrams provide adequate tests for judging the remainder seems very precarious, and his full discussion of the matter is not available. His book remains the definitive study of the sources of the Simonidean epigrams; and if the positive conclusions that emerge from his work are not commensurate with his high standard of scholarship, the fault lies in the nature of the material.

More recently, Page has offered two brief general discussions of the transmission and the authenticity of the Simonidean epigrams, in the *Praefatio* of his *Epigrammata Graeca*[44] and in the *Introductory Note* to the commentary in his *Further Greek Epigrams*.[45] For the most part his views are in line with those developed by Kaibel, Wilamowitz, and Boas. He draws attention to the anonymity of the epigrams on stone and in early authors except Herodotus. He considers that conjecture played a large part in the Simonidean ascriptions made by later authors, and that some late compositions were deliberately circulated by their authors with a false claim to Simonidean authorship. He notes that Meleager's *Garland* included many epigrams assigned to Simonides, and thinks it likely that Meleager obtained them from a collection of epigrams which were already assigned to Simonides by name.[46] He regards the epigram on Megistias (VI Page) as the most surely attested Simonidean epigram; otherwise he is generally sceptical about the possibility of establishing Simonidean authorship, though he allows that there may be some genuine Simonidean epigrams among those whose authorship is uncertain.

As regards the formation and date of any Simonidean collection, Page's views appear to fluctuate somewhat. In *Epigrammata Graeca*, though warmly acknowledging Boas' general merits, he sternly castigates Boas for his "error" in dating the Simonidean collection to the fourth century B.C., on the ground that several epigrams assigned to Simonides are unmistakably Alexandrian in style and that there are too many of these for us to believe that their ascription to Simonides is the result of errors and confusions in the Palatine Anthology;[47] Page therefore assigns the collection to the third or preferably the second century B.C. However, in *Further Greek Epigrams*, his views on the collection seem far more flexible. He believes that a collection of early inscriptional epigrams was made and circulated under the name of Simonides; he then allows two possibilities (expressing a preference for the former): either that this collection of inscriptions was supplemented in successive editions by the inclusion of later literary compositions; or that the literary compositions were circulated, under Simonides' name, in anthologies, independently of the inscriptional collection. He dates the formation of the collection of inscriptional epigrams "quite early in the Hellenistic period"[48] or even "in the latter part of the fourth century".[49] He thus reverts, not only to Boas' view, but also to that expressed earlier in Gow and Page's own *Hellenistic Epigrams*, where it is allowed that even the absurd ascription to Simonides of an epigram on the death of Sophocles might come from a fourth-century collection.[50]

This discrepancy is perhaps not too serious. It is agreed by Gow, and by Page throughout, that there are several epigrams, ascribed in the Palatine Anthology to Simonides, which are unmistakably of late (i.e. Alexandrian) origin; and that therefore there cannot have been a fourth-century collection which contained these epigrams. The difference is that Page (in *Epigrammata Graeca*) believed that the great majority of the Simonidean epigrams in the Palatine Anthology must belong to the Simonidean collection as originally constituted, and therefore lowered the date of the collection to allow for this; whereas Gow (and Page in *Further Greek Epigrams*) is prepared to admit the existence of a fourth-century collection, to which later additions were made for reasons varying from deliberate fraud to accidental accretion. Certainly the latter hypothesis seems to account best for the observable facts.

It is possible that adjustments and refinements may be made to Boas' account of the transmission of the evidence, but it seems unlikely that a new examination of the source-material would lead to any major reappraisal, as the gap between the anonymity of the inscriptions and of most early quotations, and the late ascription of these same epigrams to Simonides, would remain. Short of some unexpected addition to our material, such as the highly unlikely discovery of Simonides' name on a contemporary inscription, there seems to be no hope of progress through further study of the sources. There are some other possible criteria for the authenticity of the epigrams; but it should be said at once that such criteria never allow any certain conclusions to be drawn, except in the obvious cases where lateness of subject-matter disproves Simonidean authorship.

Brief mention may first be made of possible criteria for deciding whether an epigram is likely to belong to the late sixth or early fifth century, when Simonides was active. Sometimes the extravagance of the ideas expressed is an almost certain indication that a poem does not belong to this period and is therefore not by Simonides; for example, the epitaph on Anacreon[51] is universally rejected. Another criterion, that of style, is of limited value only. Sheer length, and verbosity, are commonly regarded as indications of late origin,[52] but there is some disagreement on this point.[53] Again, it sometimes happens that epigrams which are not open to objection on grounds of subject-matter, or general features of style, are declared to be late compositions because they contain some particular formula or turn of phrase which is not paralleled in fifth-century inscriptions; but pronouncements of this kind are sometimes confounded by the discovery of new inscriptions.[54] There are perhaps some limited possibilities of progress in this area. For instance, more of the features which have been alleged to be incompatible with fifth-century usage might be shown to have fifth century parallels; this could occur either as a result of further examination of fifth-century inscriptions already known, or through further epigraphical discoveries. Again, it is possible that other Simonidean epigrams may be discovered on stone (without Simonides' name attached) and proved to be genuine fifth-century inscriptions.

Next, the possible criteria for deciding whether an epigram, if it does belong or could belong to the fifth century, is to be assigned to Simonides in particular, must be mentioned here, unreliable though they are, if only to clear the ground. The test of style is, I believe, quite useless for this purpose. It was perhaps a theoretically valid test for Hauvette, who believed that he had twenty definitely authentic epigrams on which to base his enquiry; though even when one has a fair number of epigrams to rely on, the test of style, in the case of very short poems on a variety of subjects, is rather dubious.[55] (It can be argued that the writers of early sepulchral epigrams deliberately adhered to an impersonal style; at least, pieces from different times and different parts of the Greek world show a certain uniformity.)[56] But when there is only one definitely genuine epigram[57] to go on, this epigram cannot be used as a basis for stylistic comparison. Similarities of thought or expression in the epigrams to those found in Simonides' lyric poems would be a theoretically valid argument in favour of Simonidean authorship, in the case of epigrams which are known, from their quotation by early writers or their discovery on stone, to have been early;[58] the Persian War period, when Simonides wrote poems of different genres on related subjects, might seem the most promising. But in fact I know of no examples where such a comparison might usefully be made.[59]

There is one more kind of test, of limited usefulness: we may ask whether Simonidean authorship of a given epigram is consistent with the known facts of Simonides' life. If, for example, an epigram was written for Athens about 468 B.C.,[60] is it likely that the Athenians sent the commission for these few lines to the aged Simonides, now living in Sicily? If Simonides can be shown to have expressed open hostility and bias against a given city, would he afterwards receive commissions for epigrams[61] from citizens of that city? If, on the other hand, Simonides is known to have written a lyric poem as a state commission for some public event, might it be reasonable to suppose that a sepulchral or dedicatory epigram on that same event[62] was also written by him? I have tried to introduce topics such as these into my discussion where they seem relevant;[63] but it is clear that no more than a modest degree of probability can be claimed for the answers given to such questions.

The study of the authenticity of the Simonidean epigrams has, it is fair to say, reached an impasse, which seems likely to be permanent. This view perhaps receives silent assent from the many scholars who, writing in recent years on the subject of fifth-century epigrams (including those assigned to Simonides), either give the question of authorship only a cursory mention, or omit it altogether, or even positively deplore speculation on the matter.

To sum up: I accept that there is only one indisputably authentic Simonidean epigram (ep. VI, on Megistias), and a great many which are certainly or probably not authentic. Many remain in limbo, their Simonidean origin neither authenticated nor disproved. It seems to me quite likely that a fair number of these (for example, from the Persian Wars) may be by Simonides, for the time-honoured reasons that he was the author of the Megistias epigram and of many lyric poems and elegies on the Persian Wars, and that the large number of epigrams assigned to him suggests a reputation in antiquity in this field. It may also be possible to trace a link between the composition of epinician odes and of epigrams for athletes' statues.[64] I should however have no confidence in making a selection of authentic epigrams or pressing the claims of any particular epigram.

It remains to explain how I have handled the epigrams in this study. On the one hand, sepulchral or dedicatory epigrams (especially if written for states or distinguished men) might seem to offer promising material for a study such as this; on the other hand, their doubtful authenticity means that no certain conclusions can be drawn from them.

It is obviously impossible to ignore them altogether; yet any discussion of them is hedged with doubts and reservations. My choice of the epigrams to be discussed is based on the same principle as the choice of lyric fragments; that is, I have selected those that certainly or probably refer to identifiable persons or events. (I have however excluded some epigrams concerning individuals, for instance certain athletic victors or artists, about whom little is known or who can be dated only in the vaguest terms.) Not all the epigrams discussed have the same bearing on my subject; and I have handled them in different ways, classifying them, for the purposes of this study, as "non-controversial" and "controversial" epigrams.

If Simonides is alleged to be the author of an epigram written for the same city and about the same event as one of his lyric poems (for example, for Athens, on Artemisium),[65] very little depends on the authenticity of the epigram; even if it could be proved to be authentic, the addition to our knowledge of Simonides' activities would be very slight. Other epigrams, if genuine, would tell us rather more; for example, epigrams for Tegea[66] in the Persian Wars would indicate an association, not attested elsewhere, with yet another Greek state; or an epigram for Gelon[67] would associate Simonides with one more Sicilian tyrant and provide that link with Sicily (before 476 B.C.) which some have found it desirable to assume in any case. The addition of such items to our knowledge would be interesting and welcome, but not startling. Epigrams of both these kinds are "non-controversial" in the sense that they do not conflict with any other evidence about Simonides, and that, in the cases where they tend to confirm facts about Simonides attested by other sources, those facts are not disputed by any modern scholar.

But there is another small group of epigrams, the question of whose authenticity has wider implications. Some of these epigrams are "controversial", for the purposes of this study, in that they confirm, or may be thought to confirm, certain items of evidence about Simonides which play a vital role in the traditional account of his dates and which have now been challenged by Stella. Would Simonidean authorship of the Archedice epigram[68] confirm the tradition (which Stella has attacked) that Simonides was once employed by Hipparchus? Is the epigram[69] which (in agreement with other sources) testifies to the date of Simonides' birth, likely to be authentic, or is it at least based on accurate information? Further epigrams which, if written by Simonides, would tend to confirm the traditional dates of his life are the epigram for Milo of Croton[70] and the epigrams for the events of 506 B.C.[71] Other epigrams are "controversial" in the sense that their attribution to Simonides conflicts, or may be thought to conflict, with evidence about him found in other sources (this evidence, too, is sometimes vital to the question of his dates). For example, is Simonidean authorship of the tyrannicide epigram[72] compatible with the tradition that he was formerly employed by Hipparchus, or with his supposed composition of the Archedice epigram? Is the composition of epigrams for Aeginetan patrons compatible with the anti-Aeginetan motivation of the Crius ode?[73] Is the composition of epigrams for Corinth in the Persian Wars compatible with the evidence that might seem to suggest ill-will between Simonides and Corinth?[74] What is the significance of the "Simonidean" epigrams which refer or may refer to events later than the traditional date of Simonides' death?[75] As long as Simonides' dates were regarded as fixed, epigrams in this last category were automatically dismissed as spurious, but now there are two unknowns — the authenticity of the epigrams and Simonides' dates.

Another factor to be considered is the extent to which inferences of various kinds may legitimately be drawn from the ascription of epigrams to Simonides. It is generally agreed that only one Simonidean epigram can be regarded as certainly authentic; and there seems to be no possibility of reaching a firm decision on any others. But occasionally it happens that a modern scholar, without committing himself on the question of the authenticity of a given epigram, will attempt to draw inferences about Simonides' life and work from the mere fact of its ascription to him. There are in fact three types of argument which trace a connection between the ascription of an epigram to a given poet and the facts of the poet's life.

Firstly, the ascription may be in harmony with facts known from other sources. For example, the ascription to Anacreon of an epigram on an inhabitant of Abdera[76] is in harmony with evidence from other sources[77] that Anacreon was once at Abdera; or again, the ascription to Simonides of the Archedice epigram[78] is in harmony with the evidence from other sources that Simonides once stayed with the Pisistratids. In such cases, one may either take the biographical facts for granted and merely speculate that knowledge of these facts may have prompted the ascription of the epigram;[79] or, looking at the matter in a slightly different way, one may begin by speculating on the reason which prompted the ascription, and use the ascription to confirm the evidence (obtained elsewhere) on the poet's life.[80] Secondly, the fact of the ascription may be used to suggest facts about the poet's life or poetic activity for which there is no evidence from other sources; for instance, the ascription to Anacreon, in the Palatine Anthology, of some epigrams for Thessalians[81] has been made the basis for suggesting that Anacreon once stayed in Thessaly,[82] for which there is no evidence elsewhere; or it has been suggested that the ascription to Simonides of some epigrams for Aeginetans[83] was prompted by the Collector's knowledge of epinician odes by Simonides (which are otherwise unknown) for these patrons.[84] Thirdly, the ascription of an epigram may clash with evidence about the poet's life obtained from other sources, and may be used in an attempt to set aside that evidence; such arguments are employed by Stella.[85]

Rather different from the examples just considered are those cases where an epigram, ascribed to Simonides, plays an essential part in an anecdote about Simonides himself. In such cases, the Simonidean ascription and the anecdote stand or fall together. They may both be rejected, of course;

but the combination of epigram and anecdote forms a firmer basis for confirming or inferring facts about the poet's life and career than does the ascription of epigrams on subjects unconnected with the poet. For example, it has been thought that the ascription to Simonides of an epigram with a Thessalian content,[86] in the context of an anecdote about Simonides, shows that a sojourn of Simonides in Thessaly was remembered.[87]

Those who draw inferences about a poet's life from the ascription of an epigram (unaccompanied by an anecdote) sometimes do so without naming the ascribing authority or discussing its reliability. They thus seem to be tacitly accepting the general principle that the ancient ascription of an epigram to Simonides, even though it may be erroneous or may be based partly on guesswork, may be presumed not to be arbitrary or due to carelessness or accident or deliberate fraud but to be based on accurate historical knowledge about Simonides and his patrons. However the examples of demonstrably false ascriptions[88] to Simonides make it clear that no such general principle can be accepted. Such claims might indeed be made in a particular case, when the credentials of the ascribing authority have been examined; but in general it is too much to assume that a writer of the Alexandrian period or later would have been incapable of transmitting the Simonidean title of an epigram without first satisfying himself, not merely that the ascription did not clash with known facts but even that it was actively supported by corroborating evidence (evidence which is now lost to us).

In this study I have adopted the following procedure for dealing with these various categories of epigram. When discussing "non-controversial" epigrams, that is, epigrams which, if authentic, would neither pose nor solve any particular problems, I have not usually thought it worthwhile to discuss the trustworthiness of the ascribing source and to speculate on whether the ascription (correct or otherwise) was prompted by accurate historical knowledge about Simonides; nor do I pronounce an opinion as to whether the epigram is or is not authentic. Instead I simply discuss the implications the epigram would have for our study if it were authentic—always in the realisation that it may not be.

The "controversial" epigrams fall, as we have seen, into two groups. Some of them support, or might be supposed to support, evidence, obtained from other sources, which has long been accepted as reliable and has been used to build up the traditional account of Simonides' life; such epigrams form an obstacle to Stella, when she attempts to dismiss the evidence in question. In these cases, although I still refrain from pronouncing on the question of authenticity, I attempt some discussion of the reliability of the ascribing sources and the likelihood that the ascription (whether or not it happens to be correct) is based on correct information about Simonides

The other group of "controversial" epigrams consists of those which certainly or possibly conflict with other evidence about Simonides; such epigrams are sometimes quoted in support by Stella, when she challenges the evidence in question. When dealing with epigrams such as these, we must consider firstly the degree of error which the Simonidean ascription of the epigram seems to involve (if the evidence which conflicts with the ascription is true); and, secondly, the reliability of the ascribing source. We must then decide whether we prefer to maintain our trust in the evidence that conflicts with Simonidean authorship of the epigram, and so to impute error to the authority who ascribes the epigram to Simonides; or to place such reliance on the general historical accuracy of the ascribing authority that the evidence which conflicts with the ascription must itself be set aside. In theory, the greater the degree of apparent error involved in the ascription of an epigram to Simonides, the less willing we should be to impute the error to the ascribing authority and the more willing to reconsider evidence that clashes with the ascription (the other variable factor is, of course, the general reliability of the ascribing authority). As a hypothetical example: if an early and good authority ascribed to Simonides an epigram on an event that occurred one year after the traditional date of the poet's death, we could accept that the authority was guilty of a slight error and retain the poet's dates without question (or alternatively, we could suppose that the transmitted date of the poet's death was approximately, but not exactly, correct); if the same authority ascribed to Simonides an epigram on an event twenty years after the supposed date of the poet's death, we might feel bound to suspect that the evidence for the poet's dates was gravely inaccurate. But if a notoriously unreliable authority like the Palatine Anthology ascribes to Simonides an epigram on an event a hundred years after the poet's death, the fact is of no significance for Simonides' dates. In fact we are never justified in setting aside evidence on Simonides' dates on the strength of the ascription of an epigram.

3. Summary of Stella's article proposing a revised Simonidean chronology

Stella argues as follows:[89]

The dates 556-468 for Simonides' life are accepted without question by modern scholars, who even base other dates on them. But the ancient chronographers are not unanimous: the Suda gives both Ol. 56 (556-3 B.C.) and Ol. 62 (532-29 B.C.) for Simonides' birth, and the same confusion appears in Eusebius, where entries on Simonides appear at Ol. 56 (556/5 B.C.), Ol. 61 (536/5 B.C.) and Ol. 73 (488/7 B.C.). The Parian Marble reports Simonides' death in 468, and records a victory of his in 477/6 without giving his age at that time. Contemporary or near-contemporary evidence for the dates of his birth and death is lacking; for although Simonides is mentioned by Theognis, Herodotus, Plato, Xenophon, and Aristophanes, no clue to the poet's age is given (Stella pp. 1-4).

Certain discrepancies appear (Stella claims) when the datable events in Simonides' life are set against the dates 556-468. Simonides, as the quasi-official poet of the Persian Wars, shows an energy and youthful spirit surprising for a man over seventy. He travelled to Sicily allegedly aged eighty, and won the confidence of Hieron and Theron to a degree that provoked the jealousy of Pindar and enabled Simonides to reconcile the tyrants. Simonides would be about fifty years older than Bacchylides, an unlikely age-gap between uncle and nephew (Stella p. 4).

The traditional chronology might seem to be firmly based on Simonides' own words in the epigram 77 Diehl (XXVIII Page). The epigram has always been accepted, and its statement that Simonides was eighty years old in 477/6 unquestioned; but why should it be exempt from the sceptical scrutiny to which other "Simonidean" epigrams are subjected? It is found only in late sources, and on examination reveals the characteristics, not of fifth-century choregic inscriptions but of those of the Roman period. It is therefore a late composition, which drew its information on Simonides' victory from a reliable source, but calculated his age on the chronology worked out by Apollodorus or some other chronographer (Stella pp. 5-10).

The datable epinician fragments belong to the period 500-470. The Persian War poems, and the recorded victories of Simonides (against Aeschylus after Marathon; and in 477/6), fall within this period. The fragments make no certain reference to any events before 500 (Stella pp. 10-12).

The result is the same (Stella continues) if one considers those contemporaries of Simonides whom he mentioned in his poems. His friendship with Themistocles belongs to the time of the Persian Wars. Scopas cannot be dated. The dirge for Antiochus son of Echecratidas (frag. 34 Bergk, 23/528 Page)[90] is usually dated 510, but should rather be dated c. 475-60. Simonides' relations with Hieron are amply attested; his migration to Sicily, and mediation between Hieron and Theron, do not suggest that he was eighty at the time, though this point is not decisive (Stella pp. 12-15).

His relations with Pindar are more illuminating. The "crows" mocked by Pindar in *Ol.* 2.87 may be

Simonides and Bacchylides. There is more reason to see an allusion to Simonides in the "mercenary Muse" of *Isth.* 2.6; and as the ode belongs to 467/6, the allusion would be pointless if 468 were the correct date of Simonides' death. There is a definite allusion to Simonides (frag. 49 Diehl, 97/602 Page) in *Ol.* 9.48;[91] this ode is to be dated 467/6, and the same argument applies. These references show that Pindar, when he wrote *Isth.* 2 and *Ol.* 9, regarded Simonides as a flourishing rival; they show that the date 468 for Simonides' death is wrong, thereby undermining completely the dating 556-468 and proving that the calculation of Apollodorus (or some other chronographer) is wrong (Stella pp. 15-17).

Therefore (Stella argues) one should consider the alternative date of birth (*Ol.* 62, 532-29 B.C.) given by the Suda. Simonides would be about sixty when Pindar replied to him in *Ol.* 9; not much over fifty when he first came to Hieron's court; less than thirty years older than his nephew Bacchylides; a decade older than Pindar; and still in his prime in the early years in Sicily (c. 475). No known date of any Simonidean fragment, no reference in the fragments to persons or events, contradicts this chronology, which is consistent with his fervent activity c. 490-470, and his youthful exuberance for the Greek cause in the Persian Wars (Stella p. 17).

The epigrams attributed to Simonides refer to no events before 506, but do refer to events after the traditional date of Simonides' death, e.g. to Tanagra (457 B.C.) (117 Diehl, XLIX Page), or even, perhaps, to the events of 449/8 (103 Diehl, XLV Page). Whoever included such epigrams in the Simonidean collection believed that he was still alive about the middle of the fifth century (Stella pp. 17-18).

Among all the accounts of Simonides' personal relationships or conflicts (with Pausanias, Xenophanes, Aeschylus, Timocreon), only one is at variance with the proposed new dating, viz. the story of his presence, with Lasus and Anacreon, at Hipparchus' court (before 514). The account dates back at least to the fourth century;

it is not a complete fiction, but results from confusion of our Simonides with his grandfather and namesake who is mentioned by the Parian Marble ep. 49 (489/8 B.C.) and who was really the Simonides at Hipparchus' court. The entry on the Marble can be accepted as it stands; formerly it was rejected or emended as being incompatible with the usual dating of Simonides' birth at 556 (Stella pp. 18-19).

If Simonides never was a friend of the tyrants, certain anomalies disappear. His composition of the tyrannicide epigram (76 Diehl, I Page), if it is genuine, at the commission of the democracy, becomes understandable, as does his status in democratic Athens during the Persian Wars, when the tyrannicides were honoured as founders of the democracy. In the anecdotes about Simonides, there is no mention of Hippias or Hipparchus or any of their circle; Lasus need be no exception, as he was in Athens until c. 500. The dates of the sojourn of Simonides in Thessaly (c. 506-490), and the idea that he fled there after the murder of Hipparchus, are modern inventions (Stella pp. 19-20).

An alteration of twenty years in Simonides' dating means (Stella concludes) that his poetry must be considered in a new light. He was a near-contemporary of Pindar and Aeschylus. His spiritual home was democratic Athens, which honoured him as its poet laureate in the Persian Wars. The Artemisium fragment (Pindar frag. 77 Snell) is probably by Simonides. There is even a hint in Xenophon's *Hieron* that Simonides may have fought at Marathon. Simonides' fortunes rose, and perhaps fell, with those of Themistocles; the accusations of covetousness levelled at Simonides may have been originated by enemies of Themistocles (for example Timocreon, a known enemy of Simonides also), and it may be significant that Simonides left Athens about the time of Themistocles' banishment (Stella pp. 21-23).

Arriving in Sicily at the height of his maturity, Simonides lived on terms of easy equality with the Sicilian tyrants. In an atmosphere conducive to literature and philosophy he would meet Aeschylus (whom he knew at Athens), and Pindar and Xenophanes (whom he may have known before). Pythagoreanism and Orphism flourished in the West. To this period may belong Simonides' poem on Orpheus (frag. 62/567 Page); at least it can be said that his poetry now became more sober and reflective. The dirge on Antiochus (frag. 34 Bergk, 23/528 Page) belongs to this period (470-60), and indicates a visit to Thessaly during these "Sicilian" years (Stella p. 23).

The date of Simonides' death cannot be fixed; but if, as is reasonable, the tradition of his longevity is accepted, he lived till about the middle of the fifth century. At any rate, he was still alive and writing c. 466 B.C., for Pindar (in *Ol.* 9) must have been replying to a Simonidean poem written not many years before. More than half his life, and nearly all his poetic activity, fell within the fifth century. He belonged to the same world as Pindar and Aeschylus; his work is far removed from that of Anacreon and Ibycus, and must be studied anew in this light (Stella pp. 23-24).

Stella's arguments, as summarised in the above paragraphs, will be considered in the following chapters as occasion arises.

References

1. There are 148 Simonidean fragments in Page's *Poetae Melici Graeci*; one or two of these entries contain miscellaneous references and testimonia, and a few more may be *apophthegmata* or fragments of elegiac poems.
2. Page excludes (a) some of the epigrams in metres other than elegiac couplets, and (b) epigrams whose existence is attested but whose text is not preserved. Neither of these categories appears in West, whose province is the elegy, apart from 17 West, which belongs to category (a). One Simonidean piece which is preserved and which could be in elegiac metre is not found in either Page or West (63 Diehl). Epigrams in category (a) are quoted from Diehl; for category (b), which Diehl does not include, recourse must be had to Bergk. Two elegiac pieces are found in both Page (eps. LXXV & LXXXVIII) and West (fr. eleg. 16 & 6); I list them under Page.

28 SIMONIDES

3. I Page.
4. See Page (1981) 120 & n. 2.
5. XVI Page.
6. Hdt. 7.228, quoting VI Page (on Megistias) and XXII (a) and (b); see below, Chapter VIII, section 1.
7. XXVI A Page.
8. See III, XVII (a), XXII (b), and XLI Page, with their testimonia; on the testimonia of III, see further below, Chapter IV, section 2.
9. On the transmission of this epigram, see the discussions of Boas (1905: 47-66) and Page (1981: ad loc., & p. 122).
10. 7 West, and 69 & 70 Diehl; Chamaeleon frags. 33-34 Wehrli.
11. Suda s.v. Σιμωνίδης 439; see Boas (1905: 46), with references.
12. See the testimonia to XLI & LXXXVIII Page and 166 Bergk.
13. See Meleager's Preface, *Anth. Pal.* 4.1.8.
14. XXII (b) Page.
15. See Boas (1905) 138-41; Page (1981) 119-22.
16. On these various points, see Schneidewin (1835) 144, 223-7, 150-2.
17. Schneidewin on ep. 158 (XII Page); see the testimonia to XI Page and 101 Diehl (= Anacreon XV Page).
18. Junghahn (1869).
19. Kaibel (1872 & 1873); see also Kaibel's later discussion (1892).
20. 1905: 31, 34.
21. Bergk (1882) pp. 426-48, and commentary on eps. 96 & 134.
22. Hauvette (1896) p. 4; "examen critique des sources", pp. 5-38.
23. His Table A (p. 39) lists twenty definitely authentic epigrams, and Table B (p. 40) eleven definitely spurious epigrams (mostly rejected for late subject-matter).
24. Pp. 41-67.
25. Pp. 69-144.
26. Table C (p. 145), probably authentic; Table D (pp. 146-7), probably spurious.

27. Pp. 6, 22.
28. Pp. 30 f., 22.
29. P. 30, on Simonides LII & I Page.
30. E.g. Hauvette no. 2, p. 46; no. 4, p. 48.
31. E.g. no. 33, pp. 91 f.; no. 81, pp. 139 ff.
32. No. 50, p. 110.
33. No. 46, p. 108; no. 57, p. 115.
34. No. 31, p. 89; no. 35, pp. 94 f.
35. No. 5, p. 50; no. 6, p. 53.
36. Wilamowitz (1897), reprinted with some modifications in Wilamowitz (1913). I cite from Wilamowitz (1913), the more accessible work.
37. On these various points, see Wilamowitz (1913) 192 ff., 202, 138, 205-6, 211-12.
38. Boas (1905) 32-3; XXII (a) & (b) and VI Page (in Herodotus); XXVI A Page (in Aristotle).
39. Pp. 69-74 (on XIV Page); 248-9.
40. P. 31.
41. P. 33:....*instituta comparatione inter epigrammata, quae Simonidem composuisse constat, tria* (viz. the three epigrams in Hdt.7.228) *et quinti saeculi inscriptiones metricas vulgares*. It seems that the phrase *inscriptiones metricas vulgares* includes inscriptional epigrams preserved only in literary sources (and ascribed there to Simonides), as well as those that are both preserved (anonymously) on stone and ascribed in literary sources to Simonides; for most of the eight additional epigrams which Boas pronounces genuine in his summary of his results (p. 250) are preserved only in literary sources.
42. Pp. VII, 32, 73 n. 50, and passim. The second part, entitled *De epigrammatum Simonideorum origine*, once existed in the form of a competitive essay (Boas p.VII), but it was never published; and investigations kindly made for me in Amsterdam by Drs. G.J. Houtman failed to reveal any trace of the manuscript.
43. But it is usually thought that only VI Page is guaranteed by Herodotus, not, as Boas thought, all three epigrams. The authenticity of even this epigram is occasionally questioned,

30 SIMONIDES

on the ground that Herodotus may not have possessed accurate information. See further below, Chapter VIII, section 1.

44. Page (1975) v-vii.

45. Page (1981) 119-23.

46. The details of the Meleagrian sections in *Anth. Pal.* are discussed by Page (1981) 121-2.

47. Boas (1905: 75) argued that many Simonidean ascriptions had arisen by error in this way.

48. Page (1981) 123.

49. P. 210, on ep. XIV (the epigram which had prompted Boas to date the collection to the fourth century).

50. Simonides LI Page; Gow & Page (1965) II 516 (this section is basically the work of Gow, though the authors state (I p. ix) that there is little that they would not both endorse).

51. LXVI Page.

52. See the remarks of Hauvette (1896: no. 59, p. 116) on the Anacreon epitaph.

53. For example, the long and verbose epigram 148 Bergk (= Antigenes I Diehl, and Page (1981); Bacchylides III Page (1975)) is sometimes accepted as early.

54. Shortly after Hauvette (no. 35, pp. 94-5; no. 72, p. 133) had rejected the epigrams XLIX Page and 101 Diehl (= Anacreon XV Page), on the ground that χαίρετε ("farewell") addressed to the dead and an address to the dedicator of the stone were not fifth-century features, these epigrams were proved to be genuine fifth-century inscriptions.

55. See Gow & Page (1965) I pp. xxxi-xxxii.

56. See Friedländer & Hoffleit (1948) 70.

57. VI Page: see n. 43 above.

58. Where no such guarantee exists, such a comparison would be quite useless, as it could be due to deliberate imitation of a lyric poem by a late composer of epigrams. For a possible instance of this (a borrowing in ep. VII Page from frag. 26/531 Page) see Hauvette (1896) no. 24, p. 76 and Boas (1905) 220.

59. An instance of the corresponding negative argument, that an epigram expressing ideas contrary to those found in Simonides'

lyric poems is unlikely to be his, was cited above from Junghahn (this Section, with n. 18).
60. XLVI Page, on the Eurymedon.
61. XXX Page and 166 Bergk, for Aeginetan patrons.
62. XXIV Page, for Athens, on Artemisium.
63. Such matters do not usually form part of the commentary in Page's *Further Greek Epigrams* (1981), which treats the Simonidean epigrams for the most part as anonymous poems.
64. See below, Chapter IV, section 1.
65. XXIV Page.
66. LIII & LIV Page.
67. XXXIV Page.
68. XXVI A Page.
69. XXVIII Page.
70. XXV Page.
71. II & III Page.
72. I Page.
73. Eps. XXX Page and 166 Bergk; frag. 2/507 Page.
74. X, XI, XII, XIII, & XIV Page.
75. XLV, XLVI, XLVII, & XLIX Page. I am not now referring to those epigrams (e.g. LI, LVIII Page) which concern events so long after Simonides' lifetime that their ascription to him is obviously absurd, whether we accept the traditional dates of Simonides or Stella's revised dates.
76. Anacreon I Page.
77. E.g. Suda s.v. Ἀνακρέων.
78. XXVI A Page.
79. So Wilamowitz (1913: 208) on the epigram of Anacreon just cited; Boas (1905: 231) on the Collector's reasons for ascribing particular epigrams to Simonides.
80. See below, Chapter III, section 2, on the Archedice epigram (XXVI A Page).

81. Anacreon VII & XIII Page.
82. Beloch (1912-27) I 2 203. Wilamowitz (1913: 107 n. 1) disagrees.
83. XXX Page and 166 Bergk.
84. Boas (1905) 231.
85. See below, Chapter XI, section 1.
86. LXXXVIII Page.
87. Wilamowitz (1913) 142 n. 3.
88. See n. 75 above, on LI and LVIII Page.
89. Stella (1946).
90. Stella (p. 13 n. 1) wrongly cites as "Fr. 6 Bergk".
91. Stella (p. 16 n. 2) cites the old line number, 74.

Chapter 2

Some Early Lyric Poems

1. The ode or odes for Glaucus of Carystus

The only source which explicitly connects the names of Simonides and Glaucus is a passage of Quintilian.[1] Quintilian is discussing the art of memory and proceeds to tell the well-known story of Simonides' achievement in this field: a victorious boxer had refused Simonides part of the fee for his victory ode, and had told him to reclaim it from the Dioscuri, whom Simonides had praised at length in the ode; the Dioscuri paid their debt, for at a feast given to celebrate the boxer's success Simonides was summoned to the door by a message from "two youths", but found no-one there; as soon as he reached the door, the hall collapsed, killing all the banqueters, whom it would have been impossible to identify, had not Simonides remembered the seating position of each. Quintilian continues: *est autem magna inter auctores dissensio, Glaucone Carystio an Leocrati an Agatharcho an Scopae scriptum sit id carmen.* Quintilian then discusses the location of the disaster, with reference to his authorities, and mentions Scopas as being among the victims. From this passage we may conclude with some confidence that Quintilian knew of an epinician ode by Simonides for Glaucus of Carystus, which contained praise of the Dioscuri.[2]

Lucian[3] refers to an epinician ode for Glaucus of Carystus, containing a reference to at least one of the Dioscuri, written by a poet whose identity is not stated. After first discussing in what terms it would be appropriate to praise certain great athletes, Lucian proceeds:

> But how did a famous poet praise Glaucus, when he said that neither the mighty Polydeuces could have lifted up[4] his hands against him nor the iron-hard son of Alcmena? You see to what sort of gods he compared him? Or rather, he actually represented him as superior to those very gods. And Glaucus himself was not annoyed at being favourably compared with the patron-gods of athletes; nor did they punish either Glaucus or the poet for impiety in connection with such praise, but both were famous and honoured by the Greeks, Glaucus for his strength and the poet for this ode above all.

Although Lucian's quotation is anonymous, his reference to "a famous poet" implies that he expected the identity of the poet to be known to his readers. It is very likely that Simonides is meant;[5] we have concluded, from the Quintilian passage just quoted, that Simonides did at some time write for Glaucus; neither Pindar nor Bacchylides is known to have done so; and the playful humour of this passage is perhaps typical of Simonides.[6] Pindaric or Bacchylidean authorship is in any case completely ruled out by the date (520 B.C.) which many accept for this ode. However if chronology were the only criterion, the range of dates which I think we must admit for the ode (from c. 520 B.C. to c. 500 B.C. or later) would just allow the authorship of Pindar or even (according to the earliest estimates of his date of birth at c. 524-1 B.C.) of Bacchylides.

It is now necessary to set out some of the evidence for the career of Glaucus. The story of Glaucus' Olympic victory is told by Pausanias.[7] Glaucus' father, impressed by his son's feat in fitting the ploughshare back into a plough with a blow of his hand, took him to Olympia to box; and when

Glaucus, despite his strength, was near to defeat through lack of experience, his father rallied him to victory by reminding him of his feat with the plough. Pausanias adds that Glaucus won two victories at the Pythian games, and eight victories each at the Nemean and Isthmian games; and that a statue of Glaucus, dedicated at Olympia by his son, was made by the sculptor Glaucias of Aegina. Other authorities[8] give a compressed version, with some variations of detail, of the story of Glaucus' Olympic victory told by Pausanias.

Pausanias' account of Glaucus' Olympic victory seems to me to make it abundantly clear that this was his first victory, and indeed his first entry, at the great games.[9] The part played by his father in the anecdote strongly suggests that this victory was in the boys' contest; Philostratus' version, in which the father has been replaced by the trainer, also suggests the same point, since greater emphasis seems to have been placed on the trainer when a boy-victor is praised by Pindar and Bacchylides.[10]

Two sources, the *Lexica Segueriana* and the *Suda*,[11] date Glaucus' Olympic victory at Ol. 25 (680 B.C.), which is obviously far too early; and they mention three Pythian and ten Isthmian victories, thus differing from Pausanias' account. This coincidence of detail between these two sources, together with certain echoes of language in their description of Glaucus' physical qualities, shows either that one of them is derived from the other or that they both go back to a common source. The *Lexica Segueriana* add that Glaucus was killed by the design of Gelon, tyrant of Syracuse. An amplified version of this last incident appears in the scholia to Aeschines,[12] where, though it is in fact attached to the name of Philammon (a fourth-century victor mentioned immediately before Glaucus in the scholia), it is clearly meant to refer to Glaucus: this version states that "Philammon" (i.e. in fact Glaucus) came to power (in Leontini, apparently) after the death of Hippocrates tyrant of Leontini, and that, having been appointed to power in Camarina by Gelon, he was condemned to death by the people of Camarina. These accounts,[13] though differing in detail, are useful in helping to establish Glaucus' date through the connection with Gelon.

It has often been assumed[14] that the passages of Quintilian and Lucian cited at the beginning of this section refer to the same ode of Simonides for Glaucus; and some of those who definitely or apparently accept this view further assume[15] that the victory celebrated in this ode was that won by Glaucus as a boy at Olympia.

These assumptions lie behind what H.J. Rose[16] calls the "orthodox doctrine" concerning Simonides' earliest fragment, according to which it is deduced, from Quintilian and Lucian and from our knowledge of Glaucus' Olympic victory in 520 B.C.,[17] that Lucian preserves a fragment of Simonides' ode in honour of this victory.[18] Rose sets out to challenge this "orthodox doctrine".

Rose accepts that Simonides at some time wrote for Glaucus, and that Lucian is quoting from a poem by Simonides for Glaucus;[19] he also thinks it possible that Simonides may have celebrated Glaucus' Olympic victory of 520. The purpose of his article is to show that, while all this may be true, the Simonidean poem to which Lucian here refers, and from which he quotes, cannot have been written for Glaucus' Olympic victory in the boys' contest in 520, but must belong to some other poem. The first reason Rose offers is that the exaggerated praise of Glaucus at the expense of Polydeuces and Heracles might be lavished on a great boxer in his prime, but would be unpardonable if applied to a boy, however powerful. This is of course purely a matter of taste; Bowra,[20] rightly in my opinion, takes the opposite view, that the danger of hybris was less if the exaggerated praise was playfully applied to a boy victor.

Rose then continues: "But we are not left to conjectures concerning the limits of good taste; Quintilian gives us a glimpse of the contents of the ode to Glaukos which he or his Greek authorities knew." Rose shows that the ode to which Quintilian refers must have contained praise of the Dioscuri, and rightly argues that it is unreasonable to equate this ode with the one quoted by Lucian, in which one of the Dioscuri was unfavourably compared with a human victor.

However Rose obviously believes that, by showing the ode quoted by Lucian and the ode mentioned by Quintilian to have been two different odes, he is confirming his main point, that Lucian does not mean the Olympic victory of 520. This conclusion surely cannot be justified. It would of course be valid, if *Quintilian's* reference were undoubtedly to the 520 Olympic victory. But Quintilian gives not the slightest hint as to which victory is meant — as indeed Rose realises, for he regards it as no more than a possibility that Simonides may have celebrated the 520 Olympic victory or that Quintilian may be referring to this victory. The "orthodox doctrine" (based on mere assumptions) ran thus: "Lucian's quotation = Quintilian's reference = the 520 victory". Rose seems to think that if "Lucian = Quintilian" is proved untrue, then "Lucian = the 520 victory" is also untrue. But clearly this would follow only if "Quintilian = the 520 victory" were an established fact. Rose wrongly imagines that by undermining part of the "orthodox doctrine" he has demolished it all; but this would be true only if it were an inter-dependent logical whole instead of a loose-knit series of unsupported (though not necessarily incorrect) assumptions.

The one fairly definite conclusion that emerges from Rose's article is that Lucian and Quintilian are not referring to the same Simonidean poem for Glaucus;[21] but this has no bearing whatsoever on his original contention that Lucian is not quoting from an ode on the 520 Olympic victory.

Bowra[22] twice discusses and rejects Rose's conclusions; but unfortunately (though perhaps understandably, if Rose's argument is faulty) he has misunderstood what Rose was trying to say. As we have seen, Rose argues (rightly) that Lucian and Quintilian refer to different Simonidean odes, and then proceeds to draw the false conclusion that the Lucian passage does not refer to an ode for the 520 Olympic victory. But it appears from Bowra's discussion that he has wrongly understood Rose to mean that *Lucian's discussion* (and Quintilian's) refers to the 520 victory but that *the poetic fragment quoted by Lucian* does not refer to that victory — so that Lucian is thinking of and discussing one poem and inadvertently quoting from another.[23] Bowra's attempted refutation of Rose is, therefore, inevitably misleading. He stresses the reliability of Lucian and the explicitness of Lucian's language here; this is true, in that Lucian's discussion and the fragment he quotes are in obvious and complete harmony, but it is irrelevant; it is supposed to defend Lucian against a charge which Rose in fact never made. Bowra also argues that the poems referred to by Lucian and by Quintilian are not the same. Again this is true but misdirected; Bowra is advancing against Rose a point which Rose himself was trying to make.

Rose's argument is accepted by Stella;[24] Page[25] appears to commend Rose's article to his readers. However, for the reasons I have given, I believe that Rose's argument cannot be allowed to stand.

It is necessary, then, to cut away ruthlessly all the dead wood of groundless assumptions and illogical refutation of those assumptions, and to see what facts have emerged so far. They are these:

1. Lucian quotes from a poem for Glaucus (probably by Simonides) in which Polydeuces is compared unfavourably to the victor. No hint is given as to which victory is meant.
2. Quintilian very probably refers to an epinician for Glaucus by Simonides, in which the Dioscuri are praised. Again no hint is given of the occasion of the victory.
3. In view of the different treatment of the Dioscuri, the poems referred to by Lucian and by Quintilian can hardly be one and the same. We therefore have evidence of two epinician odes for Glaucus by Simonides.
4. Glaucus won an Olympic victory (probably as a boy), and many victories at the other great athletic festivals.

5. Either the Quintilian passage or the Lucian passage (but not both) may refer to this Olympic victory. But it is equally possible that neither ode refers to this victory, each referring to one of Glaucus' subsequent victories. The assumption that one or both of these odes refer to the Olympic victory seems to be based principally on the fact that this victory is more prominent in the extant literature (where it provides the subject-matter for a lively anecdote) and has a date attached to it. Our sources make it clear that after his first success (at Olympia) this great athlete won many other victories which could have been honoured by an epinician ode.

If we scan our sources for further clues, it appears that Quintilian's reference is too brief to provide any additional information. But Lucian offers us a little more. "Not even Polydeuces or Heracles could have stood up to Glaucus".[26] I have expressed agreement with Bowra, against Rose, that this genial exaggeration would be applied with less hybris to a youngster than to a man in his prime. It seems likely, though, that it was said of an all-conquering youngster, who had sailed practically unscathed through the opposition (e.g. "none of his opponents could stand up to him — why, not even Polydeuces or Heracles could have done so"). But, according to Pausanias' well-known story, Glaucus was far from doing this at his Olympic victory; exhausted by his injuries and close to defeat, he was rallied by his father to a last gigantic effort which won the day. If his opponents had withstood Glaucus well and almost beaten him, it would be quite inappropriate, and would almost amount to sarcasm, to say that the heroes of old could not have stood against him. Some remarks about victory gained against heavy odds, or defeat turned to victory,[27] would have been more suitable. It seems likely that Lucian quotes from an ode written for a victor whose skill and strength had proved him invincible. One may suggest therefore with reasonable confidence that the ode quoted by Lucian did not refer to the hard-won Olympic victory; with rather less confidence (in view of Rose's opposite opinion) I would agree with Bowra that the ode was written for a *young* victor. Thus the ode may be tentatively assigned to a victory won not long after the first success at Olympia, while Glaucus was still a "boy" or a young man, at another of the festivals where he was so often crowned.

It would obviously be desirable to know the date of Glaucus' Olympic victory, of the beginning, that is, of his victorious career. Unfortunately our authorities (cited in n. 11) fail us at this point; the date which they give (Ol. 25, 680 B.C.) is far too early. Brunn[28] emended to "Ol. 65" (520 B.C.), and this date is usually accepted.[29] The emendation[30] to "Ol. 75" (480 B.C.) cannot be right. According to the papyrus list of Olympic victors, the name of the boys' boxing champion in 480, whatever it may have been, was certainly not "Glaucus".[31] And even before the discovery of the papyrus, Brunn had rejected "480" as the date of Glaucus' Olympic victory as a boy, pointing out that it is inconsistent with the story of his service under Gelon, who died in 478. Also, as Brunn remarks, Glaucus' statue at Olympia, commissioned by his son, was made by the sculptor Glaucias of Aegina, who is thought to have flourished c. 480 B.C.; this point counts further against the date "480" for an Olympic victory of Glaucus in the boys' contest.

Whether the earlier emended date (Ol. 65, 520 B.C.) is to be accepted depends on how the impossible "Ol. 25"[32] arose; and this we cannot tell. If πέμπτην ("fifth") is correct, and the other figure (εἰκοστήν, "twentieth") is a corruption to be emended, then "Ol. *sixty*-five" (520 B.C.) is, as we have just seen, the only possible answer.[33] If the figure "Ol. 25" is completely wrong,[34] the only remaining course seems to be to follow Maas[35] in reckoning backwards from Glaucus' activity under Gelon to set his Olympic victory (assumed to be in the boys' contest) somewhere between 520 and 500 B.C.[36] It seemed virtually certain that the ode quoted by Lucian, with its hyperbolical praise of Glaucus, did not refer to his hard-won Olympic victory as a boy; and reasonably probable that the genial exaggeration of the ode referred to a victory won soon afterwards while Glaucus was still quite young. If both these points are accepted, either we may admit 520 as the date of the Olympic victory and date the ode soon after 520, or we may accept Maas' dating of the Olympic victory somewhere between 520 and 500 and so assign the ode to approximately the same range of dates. If the impression that the ode was written for a young victor is not correct, it could have been written at any point in Glaucus' victorious career, that is, at any time within fifteen years or more of his Olympic victory as a boy; the possible range of dates for the ode might then extend even into the 480's B.C. As for the other Simonidean ode for Glaucus, mentioned by Quintilian, there is no clue to indicate what stage of Glaucus' career, or which victory, it referred to; it may therefore be dated at any point within the upper and lower limits mentioned in connection with the ode quoted by Lucian (between c. 520 and the 480's B.C.).

Certainly no reliance can be placed on 520 as the date of Simonides' first known ode,[37] for it is uncertain both when Glaucus' Olympic victory occurred and whether Simonides celebrated this victory. We are forced to admit that the much-sought clue to Simonides' dating eludes us here; that the wide range of dates which we must allow for Simonides' odes for Glaucus is consistent with both the traditional chronology (Simonides born 556/5 B.C.) and Stella's chronology (Simonides born c. 532-29 B.C.).

The identity and date of Glaucus of Carystus are discussed by J. Fontenrose;[38] but his approach is so utterly different from my own (and from that of the scholars whose views I have discussed above), that it seemed impracticable to interweave references to his views into my discussion; they are therefore mentioned briefly in these concluding paragraphs.

Fontenrose believes that the reading "Ol. 25" (680 B.C.), which is found in our authorities as the date of Glaucus' Olympic victory, is correct, so that the traditional date of Glaucus' victory falls within the first Olympic century; Glaucus was in fact "a hero eponym, probably the sea-god Glaukos humanized and historicized".[39] Pausanias' statement

(6.10.3) that Glaucias of Aegina (*floruit* c. 480 B.C.) made the statue of Glaucus of Carystus is said to be due to confusion with Glaucus of Corcyra, father of the Philon whose statue, made by Glaucias, is referred to by Pausanias at 6.9.9. Pausanias (ibid.) ascribes to Simonides an epigram[40] on this statue of Philon, son of Glaucus; and if Simonides had a patron called Glaucus, it was this Glaucus of Corcyra.

Fontenrose thinks that when the poet referred to by Lucian praised Glaucus, he was praising not his patron but a legendary hero Glaucus with whom his patron was being compared. This idea is totally at variance with Lucian's statement that Glaucus did not complain at being favourably compared with Polydeuces and Heracles, and that they did not punish either the poet or Glaucus himself, who went on to win further fame for his strength — a statement which can only refer to a human patron contemporary with the poet. Fontenrose actually quotes part of Lucian's statement on his next page ("Lucian says that Glaukos did not boggle at this praise"),[41] without perceiving that it invalidates his case.

Therefore, whatever the general merits of Fontenrose's study of the legends surrounding "hero-athletes", we are bound to conclude that he is mistaken in including Glaucus of Carystus among athletes "of very dubious historicity";[42] and that the traditional approach, of trying to piece together Glaucus' career on the assumption that he is a firmly historical figure, is correct.

2. Works for Leocrates and Agatharchus

The passage of Quintilian quoted above[43] in connection with Simonides' ode or odes for Glaucus of Carystus refers to two persons, Leocrates and Agatharchus, whom we may presume to have been boxers[44] and to have been celebrated by Simonides, on one or more occasions, for victories in that sport. The discussion of Leocrates and Agatharchus is therefore included at this point, after the ode for Glaucus. There is a fair possibility that Simonides' work for Leocrates is to be dated before the Persian Wars, as are the other items in this chapter.

Apart from the reference in Quintilian alluded to above, the only evidence connecting Simonides with a Leocrates is the following epigram,[45] the first couplet of which was found on an early fifth-century stone[46] in eastern Attica; the second couplet is added in the literary sources.[47]

> O Leocrates, son of Stroebus, when you dedicated this statue to Hermes, you were not unnoticed by the fair-haired Graces (lines 1-2); nor by the lovely Academy, within whose embrace I declare your benefaction to the by-passer (lines 3-4).[48]

The name Leocrates is not uncommon;[49] and in four of the other contexts where the name occurs, the Leocrates mentioned could be the same person as in our epigram. We thus have: (A) the Leocrates of our epigram, son of Stroebus; (B) Leocrates, son of Stroebus, Athenian *strategos* in the operations against Aegina about 458 B.C.;[50] (C) Leocrates, a fellow *strategos* of Aristides and Myronides at Plataea in 479 B.C.;[51] (D) the Leocrates mentioned by Quintilian, apparently a boxer, for whom Simonides wrote a lyric ode;[52] (E) the Leocrates designated as καλός ("handsome") on a black-figure vase of the second half of the sixth century.[53]

These persons are identified by modern scholars in various combinations. It is generally, and naturally, assumed that Leocrates (A) (son of Stroebus and dedicator of a Herm in the early fifth century) is to be identified with Leocrates (B) (son of Stroebus and Athenian *strategos* in 459/8), and also with Leocrates (C) (Athenian *strategos* in 479/8). There is rather more reserve about the identification of Leocrates (A) (B) (C) with Leocrates (D) (the athlete-patron of Simonides mentioned by Quintilian); those who accept this identification naturally tend to assume that the epigram (or, more usually, the first couplet only) is by Simonides; and, while no certainty can be claimed in this matter, it would not be unreasonable to accept the identification, and to suppose that the Simonidean ascription in the Palatine Anthology may have ancient authority, may originally be based on knowledge of Simonides' epinician ode or odes for Leocrates, and may even be correct. The question whether Leocrates (E) (the καλός on the vase) should be identified with one or more of (A), (B), (C), or (D), is of slight importance.

The occasion of the dedication of the epigram cannot be determined with certainty. It has been suggested[54] that the Herm was dedicated after the battle of Plataea, in which Leocrates (C) had played a part; but a personal dedication to Hermes and the Graces is surely inappropriate in such circumstances.[55] An athletic victory is a far more likely occasion; both Hermes and the Graces are said by Pindar[56] to bestow success in athletic contests.[57] If this is so, then the epigram could be connected with the victory (or one of the victories) of Leocrates celebrated by Simonides in an epinician ode.

If the epigram was dedicated for an athletic victory, it might reasonably be dated some years before 479 B.C. (in which year Leocrates was *strategos*); for although the prime of an athlete might well overlap with the minimum age for the *strategia* (thirty years), it would be more natural to regard his athletic victory as belonging to an earlier phase of his career than his appointment as *strategos*. On the assumption that the dedicator of the epigram is to be identified with the athlete-patron of Simonides mentioned by Quintilian, a tentative dating within broad limits would thus be provided for Simonides' ode or odes for Leocrates.

On the other hand, if the dedication was for some occasion other than an athletic victory, the nearest we can get to dating the epigram (assuming Simonidean authorship) is to set the *terminus ante quem* as 476 B.C., when Simonides left Athens for Sicily. In any case, the epigram is of no help in the enquiry into the dates of Simonides' life.

The epigram neither poses nor answers any questions about Simonides' connections with other leading Athenians, as nothing is known, apparently, about the political attachments of Leocrates (B) and (C).[58]

It is likely that the Agatharchus mentioned by Quintilian, together with Leocrates and other patrons of Simonides, was a boxer.[59] If this is so, there is no other known Agatharchus with whom he can be identified. A Corcyrean runner of this name, who won at Olympia in 536 B.C., is mentioned by Dionysius of Halicarnassus;[60] and if Simonides was born about 556 B.C. (the traditional date) he could have written for this Agatharchus in 536; but although it would be most useful to have a piece of evidence to decide between the traditional dating of Simonides and Stella's dating (which places Simonides' birth about 532-29), it is clear that there is no firm evidence here. The name Agatharchus is quite common;[61] and our Agatharchus remains unidentified.

3. Odes for Eretrians: Eualcides and Lysimachus.

Herodotus,[62] describing the Persian victory over the Greeks at Ephesus in 498 B.C. during the Ionian revolt, refers to Simonides' work for Eualcides (no fragments of which have been preserved):[63]

> The Persians killed many of them, including, among other notables, Eualcides the commander of the Eretrians, who had won crowns of victory in the games[64] and had been highly (or "often") praised by Simonides of Ceos.

With this Eualcides scholars[65] sometimes identify a certain Eualcidas of Elis, whose victories in the boys' boxing at Olympia are mentioned by Pausanias.[66] I see no reason to identify these persons, who come from different parts of Greece, and whose only common characteristic is that they won athletic victories; it is not even known whether the venue, event, or age-group was the same. There is then no reason to suppose that Eualcides won his victories as a boy, or at Olympia; and attempts, based on these suppositions, to date the victory-odes with some precision, such as Maas' dating of "about 516-508",[67] do not carry conviction.

It is unfortunately not possible to decide between "highly praised" and "often praised" in the reference to Simonides' celebration of Eualcides, as the adverbial πολλά is used in both ways ("much", and "often") in Herodotus.

If Herodotus meant "often", we should have to date Simonides' earliest works for Eualcides several years before 498, to allow time for several odes. If the meaning is "highly praised" (as frequency of usage might rather suggest),[68] the reference could be to many odes or to one only; though even with this meaning, it may still seem that a body of poems for Eualcides is more likely to have made this strong impression on Herodotus than a single ode.

All that can be said for certain is that Simonides' work for Eualcides belongs to some time before 498; how long before that date, depends on whether it is thought desirable to assign Eualcides' athletic career to an earlier stage of his life than his *strategia*, a question which arose in connection with Leocrates also. There is no definite clue here for or against Stella's chronology (Simonides born about 532-29); though the traditional chronology (Simonides born in 556) would allow more scope for extending Simonides' work for Eualcides back into the sixth century, for any of the reasons considered above.

It is not possible to date Simonides' work for Eualcides, with any confidence, in relation to his other known activities; for example, to place it before or after his stay with the Pisistratids or the Thessalians. We might prefer, for convenience, to date it before his Thessalian period, thus allowing that he might have stayed in Thessaly until after 498; we might also incline to date it about the time of his work for Glaucus (also of Euboea), perhaps as early as the 520's B.C. But we must resist the temptation to think that such odes must necessarily have been the work of a young or unrecognised poet spreading his wings and venturing to Euboea before going farther afield.[69] Odes for patrons from Euboea, near to his adopted Athens as well as his native Ceos, could have been written at almost any time before his departure for Sicily in 476.

The only evidence for Simonides' poem on Lysimachus[70] is a passage of Harpocration, where "Simonides in the Dirge on Lysimachus of Eretria" is cited as one of the sources of evidence for the existence of a temple of Apollo at Tamynae, a city in Eretrian territory. Nothing is known of

Lysimachus of Eretria, and there is no clue to the date of Simonides' dirge on him. Wilamowitz[71] states that any odes for Eretrians must be before 490; but as Eretria was refounded quite soon after its destruction by the Persians in 490, and was sufficiently recovered by 480 to send contingents to the battles of 480-79,[72] a date after 490 must be regarded as possible for Simonides' ode on Lysimachus. The name Lysimachus is not uncommon among Eretrian inscriptions, some belonging to the fifth century[73] and some to a later period.[74] The former cannot, as far as I know, be precisely dated before or after 490; and there seems to be no clue here (such as might have been provided by the sudden disappearance of the name Lysimachus after 490) to the date of the ode.

4. Epinician ode concerning Crius of Aegina

The evidence for this ode[75] comes from Aristophanes and his scholiasts. In *Clouds* Strepsiades, reporting Pheidippides' unreasonable behaviour, says:

> First I told him to take his lyre and sing a song of Simonides, of how the Ram was shorn (ἐπέχθη).[76]

The scholia in the main manuscripts[77] comment as follows:

> The beginning of an ode about Crius (εἰς Κριόν) of Aegina: "The Ram was shorn (ἐπέξαθ') in proper fashion". He[78] seems to have been famous and distinguished. ὡς ἐπέχθη ("how he was shorn") is equivalent to ὡς ἐκάρη ("how he was tonsured" or "...was shorn").

Other scholia[79] are fuller:

> These verses are from an epinician of Simonides: "The Ram was shorn in proper fashion". He was an Aeginetan wrestler. According to another source (ἄλλως), in the following lines the poet has combined

the phrase's connotation of the animal ("ram") with other associated meanings: "The Ram was shorn in proper fashion when he came to the glorious wooded precinct of Zeus".

Tzetzes' scholia add:

Crius was a distinguished Aeginetan wrestler, on whose victory at Olympia Simonides wrote an ode.[80]

Two widely divergent interpretations of ἐπέξατο have long been current:
1. (literally) "cut his hair" or "had his hair cut";
2. (metaphorically) "was shorn", usually though not exclusively understood as meaning that Crius suffered some reverse or defeat.

Recently Bers[81] has argued that Aristophanes, who paraphrases Simonides' ἐπέξατο by means of the passive ἐπέχθη, cannot have thought that Simonides' verb carried a middle meaning (e.g. "had himself a haircut"); Bers therefore regards ἐπέξατο as passive in sense. He does not elaborate further on Simonides' meaning; but as he cites Page's discussion[82] for the interpretation of the poem, he would presumably follow Page in understanding ἐπέξατο as "was shorn" or "was fleeced". Reviewing Bers, Koniaris[83] argues that a word-play on the name Krios ("ram") is intended, and that this excludes the meaning "comb one's hair", which he claims (citing LSJ) to be the only attested meaning of πέκομαι when properly used of humans. Koniaris argues that Simonides plays on the name Krios by using the middle voice of πέκομαι (which would normally be used of animals in the *passive*, "be sheared"), instead of the word (κείρομαι, middle) which would properly be used of humans in the sense of "cut one's hair off" or "have one's hair cut off"; and he concludes that Aristophanes' conversion of ἐπέξατο to ἐπέχθη is a joke, in which the rustic Strepsiades refers to Krios, whom Simonides jocularly treats as "semi-human",[84] as a "ram" pure and simple. Thus

Koniaris, it seems, means that Simonides has said "Krios sheared himself" or "got himself sheared" (ἐπέξατο) instead of "cut his hair off" or "had his hair cut off" (ἐκείρατο), which he would have used but for Krios' unusual name. Koniaris apparently thinks that Simonides' reference was to a literal haircut, and that it was friendly to Crius.

We are dealing here with a variety of overlapping criteria: the interpretation of Aristophanes; the linguistic usage of middle and passive; the possibilities of word-play offered by the name Krios; and the overall intention of Simonides. As regards the intentions of Aristophanes, I find Bers' approach preferable to that of Koniaris. Even though Aristophanes' audience is presumed to be generally familiar with the relevant ode of Simonides, I think it would be more characteristic of Aristophanes' technique in this play to "feed" Strepsiades with a line for him to misunderstand (as in *Nub.* 188-9), than to make the joke turn on his misunderstanding of a line that is not quoted, especially as the point at issue is a rather subtle distinction between middle and passive usage. More importantly, at this stage of the play, Aristophanes is not so much concerned with Strepsiades' stupidity as with the retribution he has brought on himself in the form of Pheidippides' unfilial behaviour. It is probable that Aristophanes intended ἐπέχθη ("was shorn") as a genuine paraphrase of ἐπέξατο.[85]

However, even if ἐπέξατο is to be taken as middle, with the two possible meanings of "Ram sheared himself" or "Ram got himself sheared", it still seems to me improbable that this denotes a man having a literal haircut and much more likely that it is meant to associate the man with the image of a shorn animal. Admittedly there are no other attested examples, as far as I am aware, of this figurative use of πέκομαι; but the cognate πεκτέω is used once in a somewhat similar way, and there is clear evidence that κείρω, which can be used literally either of cutting human hair or of shearing sheep, can be used metaphorically of human beings in the sense of "fleece", "rob", "cheat" or some such meaning.[86] Moreover, there is evidence that the

Greeks tended to pun on the name Krios; in the passage of Herodotus which is quoted below,[87] the Spartan king Cleomenes, on learning Krios' name, reacted with a grim joke about a ram being prepared for sacrifice; and an Attic sepulchral inscription contrasts the dead person's "name of a ram" (or "name of Ram") with his soul, which was that "of a most just man".[88] These instances strongly suggest that the combination of the words Κριός and ἐπέξατο would turn the hearer's thoughts to a metaphorical shearing rather than a literal haircut.

This impression is, I believe, reinforced by some points made by Page:[89] that "the victor had a splendid haircut" would be an absurd opening to an epinician ode; that its association with the subordinate clause "when he came to Nemea"[90] is equally ridiculous;[91] and that, if Simonides did mean some such thing, it has to be assumed that he was blind or indifferent to the alternative and metaphorical meaning which ἐπέξατο would be likely to suggest in combination with the name Krios, viz. "was fleeced".[92]

If it is accepted that "Krios got himself sheared" or "...was shorn" is a metaphorical phrase based on the name "Ram", what is the metaphor intended to convey? I do not find suggestions that "Crius had a hard struggle"[93] or "Crius got undressed to go wrestling"[94] at all convincing. The most likely meaning is that Crius was stripped or deprived of something, that he was left bare or defenceless, or that he suffered some kind of reverse or defeat. As the scholiast tells us that Crius was a wrestler, and as Simonides refers to "the wooded precinct of Zeus" as the scene of the incident, Crius must surely have suffered a defeat in the games. It is true that this interpretation could be at odds with the reference in the ancient scholia to the ode εἰς Κριόν, which may be intended to mean "the ode *for* Crius" (though εἰς can mean simply "about, concerning"); and also with the apparent reference, in the same scholia, to Crius as "famous and distinguished" (though, as we have seen,[95] this could refer to the ode, not to Crius); it is certainly at variance with Tzetzes' scholium, which explicitly states that Crius was the victor.[96] Wilamowitz' objection, that mockery of a loser would be contrary to the conventions of the epinician,[97] is of doubtful validity, in view of the passages in Pindar where such mockery is found;[98] to the possible objection that there are no examples of such mockery at the opening of an ode, one might reply that opening an ode with a reference to the victor's haircut is equally unparalleled. That, indeed, is how I would incline to defend the interpretation here preferred despite the admitted obstacles — by replying that the difficulties involved in the "haircut" version are far greater.

As a further argument in support of the view that the ode was hostile to Crius, it may be observed, from the passage of Aristophanes quoted above, that the ode became so popular at Athens that it was still learnt by young Athenians, and sung by request, late in the fifth century. In view of the persistent hostility between Athens and Aegina, the popularity of the song at Athens would be hard to explain if it were written in honour of an Aeginetan, but is readily understandable if it mocked an Aeginetan for his defeat. No doubt it was this public animosity between the two states, rather than a purely private attitude of vindictiveness on the part of his patron, who had presumably defeated Crius in the games,[99] that led Simonides to compose the ode in the first place. We may therefore reasonably assume that his patron was an Athenian. The common identification of Crius the Aeginetan wrestler, whose discomfiture was sung of in Athens, with Crius the Aeginetan statesman and enemy of Athens, is as good as certain.[100]

It is now necessary to consider the evidence for the date of the ode. What little we know of the personal history of Crius the statesman comes from Herodotus' account of the relations between Athens and Aegina. About 491 B.C., when the Aeginetans gave Darius earth and water, Athens urged Sparta to take action against Aegina. Cleomenes was sent to seize the Aeginetans responsible, but was thwarted by Crius, among others; on learning Crius' name, he remarked:

"now tip your horns with bronze, ram (ὦ κριέ), to meet the great misfortune in store for you".[101] Soon afterwards Cleomenes returned to Aegina and sent Crius with nine other leading Aeginetans into custody at Athens.[102] After Cleomenes' death the Athenians refused the demand of the Aeginetans, who were supported by Leotychidas, for the return of the hostages.[103] Nothing more is heard of Crius and the other hostages. After the Athenian refusal to return the hostages, the Aeginetans succeeded in capturing an Athenian sacred vessel on its way to a festival at Sunium, and took prisoner many leading Athenians who were on board.[104] The account of Athenian-Aeginetan hostility then continues from chapter 88 to chapter 93.

Herodotus' transition at 6.94.1 seems to imply that all these events occurred before Marathon; and some modern scholars accept this dating in its entirety.[105] It is usually maintained, however, that the series of events mentioned by Herodotus from chapter 85 onwards (viz. the death of Cleomenes, the rejected Aeginetan demand for the return of the hostages, and the ensuing hostilities between Athens and Aegina) should be dated after Marathon, i.e. c. 487 B.C.[106] Page[107] apparently extends this revision of Herodotus' dating to the seizure of the hostages and their removal to Athens, which he dates "at some time between the battles of Marathon and Salamis"; but I know of no other scholar[108] who dates the seizure of the hostages after Marathon; the reason for such an action, after the threat from Persia had receded, would remain obscure,[109] and in this discussion I shall assume that the prevailing view, which dates the seizure of the hostages before Marathon, is correct.[110]

It is difficult to be certain whether the date of the removal of the hostages to Athens should be regarded as the *terminus ante quem* for Crius' athletic defeat and Simonides' ode.[111] After the Athenian refusal to return the hostages, nothing more is heard of them; and Herodotus' narrative might seem to imply that they were never returned but were left to a lingering death in captivity in Athens. But it has been plausibly suggested[112] that they were returned in exchange for the leading Athenians captured by the Aeginetans in their seizure of the Athenian sacred vessel. If this suggestion is correct, there is at least a possibility that the athletic defeat of Crius and the Simonidean ode are to be dated after the return of the hostages to Aegina; but how real we admit this possibility to be will depend on the date of their return. The Aeginetan seizure of the Athenian sacred vessel, though dated before Marathon by Hammond and others, in accordance with Herodotus' narrative, is usually dated c. 487-6 B.C., in accordance with the re-dating of some of the events in Herodotus' narrative already referred to. The later the supposed restoration of the Aeginetan hostages is dated, the less plausible does the dating of Crius' athletic defeat after that event become, for two reasons: firstly, Crius, whose son distinguished himself at Salamis,[113] would be in or approaching middle age in the mid to late 480's, so that participation in athletic contests becomes progressively less likely; and secondly, a long period of captivity would militate against the resumption of a competitive athletic career on release. Thus, if Hammond's dates for the taking of the hostages (491) and the seizure of the sacred vessel (490) are correct, acceptance of the theory that the hostages were returned to Aegina would render the dating of Crius' athletic defeat to the early 480's a real possibility. If however the usual dating both of the seizure of the hostages (c. 491) and the capture of the sacred vessel (c. 487 or later) is accepted, then acceptance of the theory of the return of the hostages will not substantially weaken the case for the choice of c. 491 as the likely *terminus ante quem* for Crius' athletic defeat and Simonides' ode. In view of the weight of opinion in favour of dating the seizure of the sacred vessel some years after Marathon and the uncertainty as to whether the hostages were ever released or not, it seems on balance that this *terminus ante quem* should be accepted.

The *terminus post quem* is more difficult to determine; but a reasonable guiding principle would be to date the ode to a period when enmity between Athens and Aegina had become sufficiently pronounced to explain the hostility to

54   SIMONIDES

Crius (and so to Aegina) which marked Simonides' ode. It is presumably on this principle that Page tends (as we have seen) to set the *terminus post quem* c. 491, that is, at the time when the Aeginetan submission to Darius had provoked Athenian anger. It seems desirable, however, to allow that the ode may have been rather earlier than this;[114] hatred between Athens and Aegina had probably been smouldering since Aegina's raid on the Attic coast in the "unheralded war",[115] which is usually dated c. 506/5; and it is even possible that ill-feeling from the "ancient feud"[116] between the two cities existed before 506, though it would be hazardous to speculate whether it was sufficiently crystallised to provoke lampoons of individual Aeginetans at Athens.

Thus the possible range of dates for the ode extends from about the last decade of the sixth century to the later 490's (or, just possibly, the early 480's). This range of dates overlaps with the possible dates of Simonides' Thessalian period; and we may perhaps prefer to take Simonides to Thessaly first, and to date the Crius ode rather nearer to the time of Crius' known antagonism to the Athenians (c. 491) and of Simonides' known association with democratic Athens (at the time of Marathon). The date of this ode is compatible with both the traditional dating of Simonides (date of birth c. 556) and Stella's revised dating (date of birth c. 532-29).

References

1. *Inst. Or.* 11.2.11-16; the passage is quoted, with other sources, by Page, Simonides 5/510.

2. Quintilian's words might appear to suggest that there was *one* Simonidean ode containing praise of the Dioscuri and written for an unidentified patron, who might have been either Glaucus or Leocrates or Agatharchus or Scopas; but it seems much more probable that Quintilian means that there were *four* such odes (one for each of the four patrons named) all containing praise of the Dioscuri, and that Quintilian's authorities merely disagreed as to which of these

four odes earned for Simonides the gratitude of the Dioscuri. For a defence of this position, and citation of some opinions on either side, see Molyneux (1971) 203 & n. 22 (in which article the Quintilian passage and related passages are discussed); and to those who think that only one ode was meant, add Huxley (1978) 237.

3. *Pro Imag.* 19 (498-9); Simonides 4/509 Page.

4. "Could lift up" is possible here but less likely: see n. 26 below.

5. The quotation was assigned to Pindar by some eighteenth-century scholars. The credit for assigning it to Simonides apparently belongs to Boeckh (1811-21: II 2 558).

6. Cf. Bowra (1961) 312.

7. 6.10.1-3.

8. Philostratus *Gym.* 34; Suda s.v. Γλαῦκος Καρύστιος 281.

9. But Klee (1918: 77, 88, 99) apparently thinks that this was not so; and Moretti (1957: p. 75, no. 134) seems ready to follow Klee. Their reason, which is not given, may be the a priori assumption (reasonable in itself) that a first victory is unlikely to have been at Olympia; but it seems preferable to follow the clear indication given by Pausanias, and the authorities who echo him, that the Olympic victory *was* Glaucus' first.

10. Most modern scholars agree that Glaucus' Olympic victory was in the boys' contest; but Klee (1918: 77) is non-committal, and Moretti (loc. cit.) assigns Glaucus' Olympic victory to the men's contest. I owe to Professor D.E. Gerber the point about the trainer's role in Pindar and Bacchylides.

11. *Lexica Segueriana,* Λέξεις Ῥητορικαί ("Rhetorical Glossary"), *Anecd. Graec.* Bekker I 232; Suda s.v. Γλαυκός 280.

12. Schol. Aeschin. 3.189 (p. 347 Schultz).

13. Glaucus' association with Gelon is usually accepted as a fact: e.g. by Kirchner (*RE* "Glaukos" VII 1 (1910) 1417.37 ff.), who follows the account of the *Lexica Segueriana*; by Freeman (1891-4: II 130, 498), who follows the scholia to Aeschines; and by Niese (*RE* "Gelon" VII 1 (1910) 1007.64 ff.), who tries to combine the two accounts.

14. First, apparently, by A.Meineke, *De Euphorionis Chalcidensis Vita et Scriptis* (Gedani 1823) 82.

15. Rutgers (1862) 26; Förster (1891-2) no. 137.
16. 1933: 165.
17. In these pages I use phrases like "the 520 Olympic victory" to refer to the Olympic victory won by Glaucus (probably as a boy) and commonly dated to 520; this does not mean that I accept 520 as the date.
18. Rose states that this argument is due to Meineke; but in fact Meineke, though he thinks that Quintilian and Lucian refer to the same victory, does not say which victory is meant.
19. Rose (1933) 166.
20. 1936: 326.
21. Though the same point, similarly based on the different treatment of the Dioscuri in the two passages, had already been made by Buttmann (1829: p. 271 note) in reply to Meineke (above, n. 14).
22. 1936: 311-12; 1961: 325-6.
23. Bowra expresses it as follows (1936: 325): "H.J.Rose therefore concludes that the quotation is not from the poem on Glaucus but from a different poem of later date. In other words Lucian has muddled his authorities and applied to Glaucus some words that really belonged to the Dioscuri."
24. 1946: 10 n. 1.
25. On Simonides 4/509.
26. I would prefer (in agreement with Edmonds, Simonides fragment 39) to interpret Lucian's φήσας ἀνατείνασθαι ἄν ("saying that he would have lifted up" or "...that he would lift up") as representing aorist indicative with ἄν of the oratio recta and so as referring to a past performance of Glaucus (viz. his performance in the victory which prompted the ode), rather than aorist optative with ἄν (preferred by most editors of Simonides), which would refer to future contests. The impression of hybris is less, I think, if an actual performance in a past event is being referred to.
27. As perhaps in Pindar Ol. 10.15 f.
28. H.Brunn, *Geschichte der Griechischen Künstler* (Braunschweig 1853) I 83.
29. E.g. by Förster (1891-2: no. 137); Klee, apparently (1918: 77); Moretti (1957: p. 75 no. 134).

30. This emendation was proposed by K.Siebelis, *Pausanias* (Lipsiae 1822-8) vol. III adnott. p. 38. As far as I am aware, it has been accepted only by Edmonds (Simonides fragment 39).

31. *P.Oxy.* II (1899) CCXXII, col.1, line 3 (p. 88): [...]φανης ηραιευς παιδ πυξ ("[...]phanes of Heraea in the boys' boxing"). Admittedly it is not certain that Glaucus' Olympic victory was in the boys' contest; but we also have the name of the victor in the men's boxing at Olympia in the same year, which again was not "Glaucus" but Theagenes (Paus. 6.6.5). (The papyrus, which names the boys' champion, shows by elimination that Pausanias must be referring to the men's champion.)

32. πέμπτην καὶ εἰκοστὴν Ὀλυμπιάδα ("[in] the twenty-fifth Olympic festival") in the *Lexica Segueriana*; the same figure in abbreviated notation in the Suda (locc. citt., n. 11 above).

33. And a corruption of ἑξηκοστήν ("sixtieth") to εἰκοστήν ("twentieth") is quite likely.

34. For instance, it is possible that ἑκατοστῇ πέμπτῃ Ὀλυμπιάδι ("in the hundred and fifth Olympic festival") (Ol. 105, 360 B.C.), the date of a victory of Philammon (schol. Aeschin. 3.189), was at some stage accidentally attached to Glaucus, and then altered to εἰκοστῇ πέμπτῃ ("twenty-fifth") to produce an early (but far too early) date for Γλαῦκον τὸν παλαιὸν ἐκεῖνον πύκτην ("Glaucus that famous boxer of old") (Aeschin. 3.189). (Some interchange of facts between Glaucus and Philammon in schol. Aeschin. (above, n. 12) has already been observed.)

35. *RE* "Simonides" III A 1 (1927) 186.65 ff.

36. It might be possible to allow a date a little earlier than 520 by following the same procedure as Maas but reckoning back a little further from Glaucus' activity under Gelon c. 480 B.C. Klee (1918: 77, 88 f., 99) dates Glaucus' victories c. 525-510; these dates are apparently arrived at (p. 77) by accepting 520 as the date of the Olympic victory, and clustering the other victories, at appropriate intervals, around this date. This is not, in my view, a legitimate means of reckoning, for I think there can be no doubt that Glaucus' Olympic victory was his first.

37. Stella (1946: 10 n. 1) rightly rejects the date "520", but for the wrong reason; as we have seen, she accepts Rose's argument, which I believe to be fallacious.

38. "The Hero as Athlete", *CSCA* 1 (1968) 73-104 (see especially pp. 89, 91, 99-103 for his discussion of Glaucus).

39. P. 89.

40. XXIX Page.

41. P. 102.

42. P. 91.

43. Quintil. 11.2.11-16, quoted in Section 1 of this chapter.

44. See Molyneux (1971) 204 n. 25.

45. Simonides 101 Diehl (= Anacreon XV Page).

46. *IG* I² 821.

47. *Anth. Pal.* 6.144 (in an Anacreontean series), with the formula τοῦ αὐτοῦ ("by the same author"), which apparently refers to Anacreon (though Bergk and Stadtmüller argue that, as there is a lacuna before this epigram, τοῦ αὐτοῦ refers to the unknown author of the lost poem). The epigram is assigned to Simonides (again by τοῦ αὐτοῦ) after *Anth. Pal.* 6.213, though Boas (1905: 154 ff.) argues that it was originally assigned to Anacreon there also.

48. For a discussion of the relationship between the inscriptional and literary versions, see Page ad loc. Page points out that the imagined speaker is probably the Herm itself.

49. There are fifteen examples in Kirchner, *Prosop. Att.* s.v.

50. Thuc. 1.105.2 etc.

51. Plut. *Vit. Aristid.* 20.1 (331 a).

52. The ode does not have a separate fragment number in the editions; see Simonides frag. 5/510 Page.

53. Kirchner *Prosop. Att.* no. 9082; the vase is now in Beazley, *ABV* p. 337 no. 24.

54. By Obst in *RE* "Leokrates" XII 2 (1925) 2001.52 ff.

55. Friedländer and Hoffleit (1948: no. 119, p. 113) rightly reject this suggestion.

56. *Pyth.* 2.10 (Hermes ἐναγώνιος, "who presides over the games"); *Ol.* 2.50 (the Graces).

57. Page (ad loc.) points out that Hermes and the Graces were linked in cult both with each other and with the Academy

(so that Hermes was probably patron of the gymnasium situated there); but that the reference to the Academy, by the late author of the second couplet, cannot be taken as a guarantee that the stone was originally dedicated there.

58. See Obst in *RE* "Leokrates" XII 2 (1925) 2002.37 ff.

59. See n. 44 above.

60. 4.41.1.

61. See Pape-Benseler *Griech. Eigennamen* and *RE*, s.v.

62. 5.102.3.

63. 13/518 Page.

64. στεφανηφόρους ἀγῶνας ἀναραιρηκότα. στεφανηφόρος (= στεφανίτης), "with a crown as prize", refers especially to the four great Panhellenic festivals, but apparently may include other festivals: see Gardiner (1930: 36, 111) and Harris (1964: 36).

65. Schneidewin (frag. 23); tentatively Kirchner (*RE* "Eualkidas" VI 1 (1907) 837.55-7) and Maas (*RE* "Simonides" III A 1 (1927) 187.6 f.).

66. 6.16.6.

67. Maas, in *RE* loc. cit. The date 508 is presumably arrived at by reckoning back a decade from 498; but from boy victor to *strategos* in ten years would be a meteoric rise. The period 516-508 perhaps represents the maximum number of Olympiads (three) in which Eualcides could have competed as a boy; though the classification into boys (twelve to sixteen years?) and *ageneioi* (sixteen to twenty years?), which would allow this, is not attested for Olympia: see Gardiner (1930: 41) and Harris (1964: 154-5).

68. There are thirteen other examples of adverbial πολλά in Herodotus. In six (1.90.1; 1.208; 2.135.6; 3.37.2 & 3; 8.124.3) the sense demands the meaning "greatly" and excludes "often"; in two (2.155.1; 6.136.2) "often" is required and "greatly" excluded; in the remainder the meaning is not so certain, but it is probably "greatly" in four passages (3.36.2; 4.115.2; 5.103.1; 9.66.1) and "often" in one (7.214.3).

69. Schmid (1929: 506-7, 507 n. 1) tends to class thus the odes for the Euboeans Glaucus, Eualcides, and Lysimachus, as well as the ode, 2/507 Page, which Schmid (wrongly, in my view) supposes to have been written *for* Crius of Aegina. Wilamowitz (1913: 139) expresses a similar view.

70. 25/530 Page; Harpocr. 174.15.

71. Loc. cit.

72. Hdt. 6.99 ff. & 119; 8.46.1; 9.28.

73. *IG* XII 9 56.122 & 257.

74. Ib. 249 A.145, B.6, B.291.

75. 2/507 Page.

76. *Nubes* 1355-6.

77. Schol. R (I 267 Rutherford); similarly schol. V (Starkie, *Clouds* ad loc.).

78. The subject here (of the verb φαίνεται) is sometimes taken to be "the ode".

79. Schol. LB, Harl.5 (Dindorf, *Aristoph.* IV 1 p. 573). (LB = Leidensis 34 (XVIII 61. C), Harl. 5 = Harleianus 5725: see White, *CPh* 1 (1906) 13, 10.)

80. *Schol. in Aristoph.* IV II, D.Holwerda (Groningen & Amsterdam 1960); similarly, and derived from Tzetzes, cod. Reg. (Dübner, *Schol. Aristoph.* p. 448). (Cod. Reg. = Parisinus Gr. 2821: White p. 11.)

81. V.Bers, *Greek Poetic Syntax in the Classical Age* (New Haven & London 1984) 105.

82. Page: 1951, 140-2. Page's discussion is also cited with approval by Huxley (1978: 240 & n. 51).

83. G.L. Koniaris, *CPh* 81 (1986) 347-8.

84. Or (Koniaris 348 n. 4) "Simonides bestializes Κριός".

85. Among recent editors of *Clouds*, A.H. Sommerstein (Warminster 1982: on line 1356) translates Aristophanes' ἐπέχθη and Simonides' ἐπέξατο in identical fashion (as "Sir Ram was shorn"); and K.J. Dover (Oxford 1968, ad loc.), who translates Aristophanes as "was shorn" and quotes Simonides in Greek, gives no hint that he sees any discrepancy between the two versions.

86. Thus, while the scholiast's equation of ὡς ἐπέχθη with ὡς ἐκάρη does not point unambiguously towards a metaphorical shearing rather than a literal haircut, it is certainly consistent with the former. The instance of πεκτέω in Ar. *Lys.* 685 in the context of a threatened physical assault, though metaphorical in the sense that it is used of men instead of

sheep, may be intended to suggest the literal plucking or tearing of hair. The examples of the metaphorical use of κείρω are: τὴν μάμμην κείρει, Herodas 3.39 ("fleeces", J.A. Nairn ad loc.; "eats out of house and home", W. Headlam & A.D. Knox ad loc.; "fleece, plunder", *LSJ* s.v., I.3); and τοὺς παχεῖς τῶν ἀνθρώπων ἀποκείροντες, Luc. *Alex.* 6 ("trimming the fatheads", A.M. Harmon ad loc.; "cheat", *LSJ* s.v., I.2). The Latin *tondeo* is similarly used (Plaut. *Merc.* 526 etc.).

87. In the present section (with n. 101).

88. *IG* II-III² 11912 (c. 400 B.C.): "This man who lies here has the name of a ram (or: "of Ram") (κριοῦ/Κριοῦ), but he had the soul of a most just man."

89. Page: 1951, 140 ff.

90. Simonides' phrase "the wooded precinct of Zeus" would suit either Olympia or Nemea. Some scholars doubt between these venues; Page and Wilamowitz opt for Nemea without discussing the point.

91. Wilamowitz offered, at different times, two different versions of the "haircut" interpretation (both friendly to Crius): (i) "had his hair cut" meaning "had a fine coiffure" ("hatte sich schön frisirt") (1913: 145 n. 1); (ii) "had his hair cut", now meaning "had to sacrifice his fine coiffure" in order to wrestle (1922: 118 n. 1). Possibly the second of these is slightly easier to imagine in combination with "when he came to Nemea". Cf. also n. 97 below. (Podlecki [1984: 184-5] favours an interpretation akin to the first of those cited from Wilamowitz.)

92. Page further argues that the "beautiful curls" of the "haircut" version are incompatible with the realities of the wrestling ring. But the relationship between length of hair and the ethos of manly sports was (as it still is) a matter of fluctuating taste: see W.W. Hyde, *Olympic Victor Monuments...* (Washington 1921) 50-3 on "The athletic hair fashion".

93. Fränkel (1962: 495), on the assumption that the ode is friendly to Crius. The sequence of hard struggle followed by victory does not seem to fit the image of a shorn animal.

94. Kegel (1962: 70). This seems far too banal, especially in conjunction with the participial phrase "having come to Nemea". Kegel's alternative suggestion ("spent all his money

(stripped himself bare) by entertaining over-generously") has rather more to commend it.

95. See n. 78 above.

96. See above, this Section, with n. 80. This scholium, though quoted by Edmonds (Simonides frag. 38), is ignored in most discussions of the Crius ode; it is left out of account (perhaps deliberately) by Page, when he states (1951: 141) that the scholia contain no evidence of the result or other details of the contest. Scholia should not be dismissed simply because they are found only in Tzetzes, as he sometimes preserves the best versions of genuine ancient scholia (see Koster, *Schol. in Aristoph.* IV 1 1960 XLIII f.); but I believe that this particular scholium should be rejected, because of the difficulties of supposing that Simonides' ode concerned a victory of Crius.

97. This was one of the reasons which prompted Wilamowitz (locc. citt., n. 91 above) to switch to the "haircut" interpretation and to the view that the ode was friendly to Crius. He had earlier (1893: II 284 n. 4) interpreted ἐπέχθη as "was shorn or fleeced" and regarded the ode as hostile to Crius.

98. *Ol.* 8.69; *Pyth.* 8.86 f.

99. I am here assuming that the ode was an epinician (which seems to be the usual assumption, irrespective of whether the ode is regarded as friendly or hostile to Crius). But perhaps it may have been a generally satirical poem (of unidentifiable genre) which opened with a reference to Crius' athletic defeat. That it was written for an Athenian patron or public would still be a reasonable assumption.

100. Cf. Eustathius' reference to Crius (n. 101 below).

101. Hdt. 6.49-50. The story is repeated by Eustathius (*in Dionys. Perieget.*, Müller *GGM* II pp. 313-4), who describes Crius as ἀνὴρ γενναῖος ἀθλητής ("a nobleman and athlete"), thus identifying Crius the statesman with Crius the athlete.

102. Hdt. 6.73.

103. Ib. 85-6.

104. Ib. 87.

105. N.G.L.Hammond, *Historia* 4 (1955) 406 ff.; L.H.Jeffery, *AJPh* 83 (1962) 44, 52-4.

106. Wilamowitz (1893) II 284-5; R.W.Macan, *Herodotus IV-VI* on Hdt. 6.87 (and Appendix VIII, vol.II, pp. 114-5); Beloch (1912-27) II 1 25 & n. 3, II 2 57; Walker, *CAH* IV 261; and others.

107. 1951: 141.

108. Except perhaps Bowra (1961: 314), who states that Crius was a leading figure in Aegina in the years between Marathon and Salamis.

109. Page's dating may be simply a slip, rather than a considered rejection of the common consensus of historians.

110. Sometimes a more or less exact date is proposed for the seizure of the hostages: e.g. September 491, Hammond op. cit. (above, n. 105) 410; "before the winter of 491/0", Macan on Hdt. 6.73.

111. This is apparently the view of Page (1951: 142) who inclines to date the ode to "the period between c. 491 B.C. and the removal of the Aeginetan hostages to Athens". This would be a period of a few years according to Page's dating of the latter event to the 480's, but hardly any time at all according to the usual dating (before Marathon).

112. Macan, App. VIII (see n. 106 above) 115; A. Andrewes, *Annual of the British School at Athens* 37 (1936-7) 6-7. Cf. Walker, *CAH* IV 263.

113. Hdt. 8.92.

114. Thus Page seems ready to accept that the ode may belong to the earlier years of the fifth century or even to the sixth century. Wilamowitz (1913: 145 n. 1) said that the ode certainly belonged to the sixth century, but gave no reason.

115. The πόλεμος ἀκήρυκτος (Hdt. 5.81.2-3).

116. Hdt. 5.81.2; 88 ff. Occasionally the historicity of the "ancient feud" and the "unheralded war", or the dating of the latter c. 506, is questioned; but this is contrary to accepted opinion.

Chapter 3

Simonides and the Pisistratids

1. The evidence connecting Simonides with Hipparchus, and Stella's treatment of this evidence.

The tradition that Simonides lived at Athens at the court of Hippias and Hipparchus at some time between 527 and 514 B.C. (and perhaps at the court of Hippias after 514) is one of the main obstacles to Stella's chronology, as she herself acknowledges.[1]

Simonides' name is linked with Hipparchus by Aristotle in his *Constitution of Athens*, and by the author of the *Hipparchus* (which is ascribed to Plato). Aristotle, after briefly characterising Hippias and stating that the real power resided in his hands, proceeds:[2]

> But Hipparchus was fond of boys and amorous and cultured (φιλόμουσος); and he was the one who sent for Anacreon and Simonides and their company,[3] and the other poets.

The relevant passage of the *Hipparchus*,[4] after crediting Hipparchus with introducing recitations of Homer to the Panathenaea and with bringing Anacreon to Athens, continues:

And he always kept Simonides of Ceos in his company, inducing him with large rewards and gifts; he did this through a wish to educate the citizens.

It is of the utmost importance for us to decide whether we can accept this information on Simonides as authentic; but there are difficulties which hamper a confident decision. Athenian beliefs about the facts of the Pisistratids' rule, and Athenian valuations of the merits of the tyrants or the tyrannicides, present a complex and changing picture;[5] and there have been doubts about the authenticity and date of the *Constitution of Athens* and the *Hipparchus*, though there is a strong body of opinion which regards the former as the work of Aristotle himself. Perhaps a few points may be made without venturing too far into this territory.

It is true that the *Hipparchus* gives a highly idealised character-sketch of Hipparchus and uses Simonides' connections with him to reinforce this picture; so that this account is not wholly disinterested. But the case of the *Constitution of Athens* is different. Admittedly this work represents, to some extent, that rehabilitation of the tyrants' name that we see in Thucydides, as against the popular image of them as veritable "tyrants".[6] But the picture which it draws of Hipparchus himself is not very flattering; he is παιδιώδης ("fond of amusements") and ἐρωτικός ("amorous"), as well as φιλόμουσος ("cultured"), while the picture of Thessalus, who is θρασύς ("arrogant") and ὑβριστής ("insolent"), is even less so. Aristotle is not, then, using Simonides' presence at the Pisistratids' court to further his own argument; he mentions it almost casually, and, indeed, as if it were a universally known fact.

Stella[7] thinks that the *Constitution of Athens* and the *Hipparchus* go back to a single source for their account of Simonides' attendance on Hipparchus (the tradition is easier to dispose of, if it is not supported by two independent witnesses). Wilamowitz[8] is wary of postulating a specific common source for the content of the two accounts; he believes that the tradition of Hipparchus' *philomousia* was based on references in Simonides' and Anacreon's verse. As Aristotle is so confident on our particular point, whereas on other points he is careful to mention various alternative versions,[9] we might suppose a unanimity of tradition about Simonides' presence at the tyrants' court, with perhaps some doubt or disagreement about who sent for him.[10]

Some kind of association between Hipparchus and at least one literary figure, Lasus of Hermione, was known to Herodotus,[11] so the tradition of Hipparchus' *philomousia* cannot simply be ascribed to later whitewashing. And as Herodotus mentions Lasus only in the context of his revelation to Hipparchus of Onomacritus' forgeries, and is not offering an account of Hipparchus' cultural interests as such, his failure to mention Simonides need not be significant.

On the evidence considered up to now, we should probably feel disposed to accept the tradition. Stella admits that her "common source" of the accounts in the *Constitution of Athens* and the *Hipparchus* is comparatively early (fourth century, of course, at the latest) and cannot be ignored. She does not dismiss the tradition out of hand, but tries to explain it as a misunderstanding. Her explanation[12] is based on an entry (ep. 49) on the Parian Marble, belonging to the year 489/8. The relevant part of this entry runs as follows:

> Since Simonides, the grandfather of Simonides the poet, being a poet himself also, was victorious at Athens...226 years, in the archonship of Aristides at Athens.

It has generally been considered impossible to accept this entry at its face value, as a reference to the grandfather of our Simonides, because it is utterly at variance with the traditional dates of Simonides' life; if Simonides was born c. 556 B.C., his grandfather, even allowing the smallest possible difference in age between grandfather and grandson, would be some years over a hundred at the time of his reported victory in 489/8. Stella however accepts the entry as consistent with her chronology[13] (if Simonides was born c. 532/29, his grandfather might have been about eighty in 489/8), and she suggests that it was this grandfather of our Simonides who was really entertained by Hipparchus and who has been replaced, in the tradition connecting Hipparchus and "Simonides", by his more famous grandson and namesake.

This entry has always been a thorn in the flesh; it could not be accepted at its face value, and no explanation or emendation has yet proved fully convincing. May we now say, then, that Stella at one stroke has reinstated the entry as historically accurate, finding in it both support for her own chronology and an explanation of the one Simonidean tradition (the relationship with Hipparchus) which ruled out that chronology?

Unfortunately we may not. This entry (ep. 49) was rejected by scholars because it clashed with traditional Simonidean chronology not merely as obtained from other sources but also as found on the Parian Marble itself a few entries later, in ep. 57, which records Simonides' death in 468/7, having lived (βιούς) ninety years. Clearly there is some error, some inconsistency, in the Parian Marble itself, and Stella is not justified in quoting ep. 49 as a genuine piece of information, without discussing its relationship to ep. 57. Commonly favoured solutions are either that ep. 49 is intended to refer to our Simonides, perhaps to his victory over Aeschylus for the Marathon poem;[14] or that it was meant to contain a reference to some other relative of his, for example his grandson,[15] which was corrupted to "grandfather" by some kind of error.[16] Incredible though it may seem, Stella appears unaware that the Parian Marble, by giving Simonides' date of death and life-span, and so in effect date of birth, confirms each point of the traditional chronology against her own.[17]

2. Other topics relevant to Simonides' Pisistratid connections

Another argument advanced by Stella against the tradition of Simonides' association with the Pisistratids is that, among the many anecdotes about Simonides' relationships and verbal exchanges with his patrons and acquaintances, none[18] concern Hippias and Hipparchus. This fact is certainly consistent with Stella's position, but the weight of her argument from silence can only be slight; there is a similar lack of anecdotes about the Pisistratids and Anacreon, but the tradition of his presence at the court is usually accepted.

If a similar argument were to be based on the apparent lack of Simonidean lyric for the Pisistratids, the argument from silence would again be of little value, in view of the fragmentary state of lyric. On the other hand, the tradition would be confirmed if any remains of such poems could be identified. It is possible that traces of one such poem are to be found in the following papyrus fragment of an ancient commentary, probably on Pindar, which was published by Zuntz:[19]

> "Neither axes nor Siren": this is directed at (or "refers to"?) Simonides (ταῦτα πρὸς Σιμωνίδην), since he in one of his lyric poems represented Pisistratus as a "Siren".

Zuntz shows that Pindar, like Simonides, must have used the word "Siren" in connection with Pisistratus; he interprets "axes" as a hostile allusion to the tyrant's power, and "Siren" as an allusion to his seductive eloquence, and convincingly restores the sense of the Pindaric passage as being that neither executioners' axes nor seductive eloquence could move or terrify some resolute opponent of the tyrant.

The word "Siren" is, as Bowra[20] points out, double-edged, connoting either pleasing charms or fatal enticement. Bowra tends to think that Simonides' use of the term to refer to Pisistratus was uncomplimentary; but the usage of the word elsewhere rather seems to support the opposite conclusion.[21] Bowra would presumably interpret πρὸς Σιμωνίδην as "referring to, echoing the words of, Simonides", but the more natural meaning seems to be "against, in reply to, Simonides".[22] Thus, as Pindar's reference to Pisistratus was certainly hostile, it seems likely that, as Zuntz believed, Simonides' reference was complimentary.

It would be reasonable to suppose that, if Simonides is criticising Pisistratus, the poem was not written for the Pisistratids; but that if he is praising Pisistratus, it may well have been written for them. On the whole, then, this fragment lends some slight support to the tradition of Simonides' association with the Pisistratids; but we must concede to Stella[23] that we cannot base too much on the fragment.

Finally there are some aspects of Simonides' activity at a somewhat later stage of his career which must be taken into account in any evaluation of the tradition of his association with the Pisistratids.

Stella[24] argues that Simonides' status in democratic Athens as the "poet laureate" of the Persian Wars, at a time when the tyrannicides were honoured as founders of the democracy, confirms her view that Simonides was never at the Pisistratids' court. To the same end, she argues further that if the epigram on the tyrannicides[25] is genuinely by Simonides, as she is inclined to believe, it would have been a strange act of fickleness on the part of the Athenians to employ, for the purpose of praising Hipparchus' assassins, Hipparchus' former guest, as well as an act of disloyalty by Simonides himself to accept the commission. The other relevant item is Simonides' supposed composition of the epitaph on Archedice,[26] daughter of Hippias, which Stella does not mention.

We must first ask, therefore, whether there is any incongruity in the fact that Simonides became the poet of the victory at Marathon, won from the Persians who were accompanied by the ex-tyrant Hippias,[27] if he himself had been a guest at the court of Hippias and Hipparchus. Here we may consider the dual role of Hippias at Marathon — he was at the same time the representative of tyranny and of Persian conquest. If the issue at Marathon had merely been between the principles of monarchy and democracy,

Simonides' position might have been somewhat equivocal. But the tyranny Hippias was coming to impose was far different from the regime Athens had known when Simonides is said to have been entertained at court, before the murder of Hipparchus. The tyranny then was not oppressive (the tyrannicides' motive had been private),[28] but to men's minds at the time of Marathon, "tyranny" meant the oppression of the last years of Hippias' rule. Formerly the tyranny had been the rule of Greeks by Greeks; now it would mean subjection to the barbarian power. We need not assume any duplicity on the part of Simonides, or a short memory on the part of the Athenians, in order to believe that the poet who had accepted hospitality from the comparatively enlightened rulers of 514 should be chosen (twenty-four years later) to celebrate a victory over one of those rulers who had in the meantime (514-10) proved himself a veritable "tyrant" and was now prepared to buy his return at the price of his city's enslavement to Persia. Simonides' position as "poet laureate" of the Persian Wars is not, I think, a strong argument against his Pisistratid connections.

In support of this position it may be in order to compare the past record of Miltiades, the *strategos* at Marathon. Miltiades had served as archon under the Pisistratids in 524/3 B.C., though their murder of his father Cimon would make him their bitter enemy hereafter and may have been the factor which led the Athenians to trust him at the time of Marathon.[29] Miltiades had also served on the Scythian expedition of Darius c. 514/3, though according to Herodotus[30] he had urged that Darius' bridge across the Ister should be destroyed. This latter incident has been regarded by some scholars as a Philaid invention designed to show Miltiades in a more favourable light, though others reject this theory and accept Herodotus' account. As even Miltiades had in the past been involved in some degree both with the Pisistratids and with the Persians, it can surely be argued that an earlier association with the Pisistratids would not be incompatible with Simonides' high standing in the Persian Wars.

A more serious problem is posed by the tyrannicide epigram. The single couplet of this which is quoted by our literary source (Hephaestion) runs as follows:

> Surely a great light dawned for the Athenians, when Aristogeiton and Harmodius killed Hipparchus.

An inscription containing what are almost certainly fragments of a two-couplet version of this epigram was found in 1936; all that remains of the second couplet is "they made their native land...", which is conjecturally supplemented by "free and equal" (ἰσόνομον).

It is uncertain when the lines were composed. There is general agreement that the epigram must be associated with a tyrannicide group; but there has been much debate as to whether it was originally written for the earlier group of Antenor (usually dated c. 510/9[31] and later removed by the Persians) and was recopied for the later group of Critius and Nesiotes in 477/6; or whether it was first composed in 477/6 for the later group. The development of the tyrannicide cult as a challenge to Alcmeonid claims to have freed Athens is discussed by Page, who argues that the epigram's exaggerated claims about the achievements of the tyrannicides would not have been possible in 510, so early after the actual events, and who therefore dates the composition of the epigram to 477.[32]

Would it, as Stella suggests, have been an act of fickleness on the part of the Athenians (or rather, a faction of the Athenians) to commission the former associate of the tyrant house to compose such an epigram? It might be possible to argue that the best available poet would be employed irrespective of his past; a former association with the Pisistratids would not have been any hindrance, we have argued, to his employment by Athens to celebrate the victory of Marathon. Our answer must depend to some extent on the date of the epigram (510/9, or 477/6). Simonidean authorship is certainly easier to accept if a thirty-five year interval had passed since his association with Hipparchus, a time which had seen the identification of Simonides with the democracy in its triumphs over the Persians, both in 490 (when they were accompanied by the ex-tyrant Hippias) and in 480/79. What then of Simonides' personal position? Would it have been an act of disloyalty for him to celebrate the murderers of his former patron? This question inevitably arouses some disquiet; and one has to ask whether this is the result of giving too much weight to one's own prejudices and preconceptions, and disregarding the conditions under which the professional poet wrote in ancient times — disregarding, that is, his "diplomatic immunity", his ability to celebrate mutually hostile parties without becoming personally involved in their cause. Or, on the other hand, might it be said that something of a personal relationship existed between a tyrant and his court-poet, so that the ties between *xenoi*[33] might have had some influence? It must be admitted that the general opinion of modern scholars is that it would have been a despicable act for Simonides to celebrate the murder of his former patron; but the opposite opinion is sometimes expressed, that the change of front carries no reproach.[34]

It is, at any rate, possible to argue that Simonides' employment by Hipparchus, and Simonidean authorship of the tyrannicide epigram, are reconcilable, on the ground either that no question of disloyalty arises in the case of impersonal commissions undertaken by a professional poet, or that, if such disloyalty was involved, Simonides could have been guilty of it. If they are reconcilable, the question of the authenticity of the epigram has no bearing on the acceptance or rejection of the tradition connecting Simonides with Hipparchus. If however, as Stella seems to think, they are not reconcilable, we must resolve the conflict between the Simonidean ascription of the epigram, and the evidence connecting Simonides with Hipparchus, and decide which of these we prefer to rely on. In discussing the reliability of the ascribing authority, we shall discuss not so much the question whether or not the ascription happens to be correct, but rather whether we may assume that the ascription (even if incorrect) was based on and supported by the facts of

Simonides' career as they were known to the ascribing authority.³⁵

The authority who ascribes the epigram to Simonides is Hephaestion. If we assume for the sake of argument that the tradition connecting Simonides and Hipparchus is true, how great is the error committed by Hephaestion in ascribing this epigram to Simonides? The error would in fact consist merely of failing to correlate two phases of Simonides' activity (phases which one trend of modern opinion has pronounced irreconcilable) — that is, of failing to perceive that Simonidean authorship of the epigram is excluded by Simonides' former association with Hipparchus. We next ask how reliable Hephaestion is in such matters; and we observe that the only other Simonidean ascription found in Hephaestion is demonstrably false.³⁶ We then have to decide between two courses; either we can place our trust in Hephaestion, pronounce him incapable of failing to take Simonides' past career into account, assume that he can have known nothing of any connections between Simonides and the Pisistratids, and reject the evidence for such connections; or we can accept the evidence for such connections, and conclude that Hephaestion, in ascribing the epigram to Simonides, has failed to notice the clash of loyalties which the ascription involves. It seems clear that the latter course is the correct one. The evidence connecting Simonides with Hipparchus is far more weighty than any assumptions we may care to make about the code of conduct of the professional poet in relation to his employers and about the historical reliability of Hephaestion.

The last item of evidence in this category is the epigram on Archedice, which is quoted anonymously by Thucydides in the following passage:³⁷

> After this (sc. the murder of Hipparchus) Hippias gave his daughter Archedice to Aiantides, the son of Hippoclus tyrant of Lampsacus (an Athenian to a Lampsacene!³⁸), perceiving that they had great influence with King Darius. Her tomb is at Lampsacus, with the following inscription:

"This dust conceals Archedice, daughter of
Hippias, who was the noblest man of his time
in Greece; she, though her father, husband,
brothers, and sons were tyrants, did not show
arrogance of spirit."

The epigram is assigned to Simonides by Aristotle, who quotes only the third line.[39]

This is an interesting example of the process whereby an epigram which is anonymous in one author is ascribed to Simonides by a later author. Here it is enough to note that some scholars,[40] allowing greater weight to the testimony of Aristotle in such matters than they would allow to later and less reliable authors, count this epigram as indisputably authentic.

How far is Simonidean authorship of this epigram, written for the tyrant house and warmly praising Hippias, consistent with Simonides' known role in democratic Athens? The statement that Hippias "was the noblest man of his time in Greece" can only mean that Hippias is now dead; so the lines were written after Marathon.[41] One might feel some doubt whether Simonides is likely both to have celebrated the achievement of the Marathon dead and later to have lauded as "the noblest man in Greece" Hippias, who brought the Persians against them; but such doubts are perhaps not enough to condemn the epigram as certainly spurious. One might also wonder whether, after praising Hippias in this way, he was likely to retain the favour of the Athenians, as he apparently did until at least 476, when, after winning his last dithyrambic victory, he left Athens for Sicily; the epigram would presumably have been written before he left Athens, not sent from Sicily to Lampsacus. But one cannot be sure when it was composed, or whether the Athenians would know or care about this commission from the Lampsacene tyrant house. Aristotle apparently felt none of these doubts.

It seems impossible to accept the authenticity of both the Archedice epigram and the tyrannicide epigram, that is, to believe that in the years following the fall of the tyranny

Simonides warmly praised both Hippias and the assassins of Hipparchus. Of the two, acceptance of the Archedice epigram causes the less serious problems concerning Simonides' loyalties, and is supported by the more trustworthy authority. All in all, however, it might be simpler if neither the Archedice epigram nor the tyrannicide epigram were Simonidean, the ascription to him of the Archedice epigram being due to his former associations with the Pisistratids, and the ascription of the tyrannicide epigram being due to his later connection with the democracy.

If the Archedice epigram is genuinely Simonidean, it tends to confirm that there was an earlier association between Simonides and the Pisistratid family; one feels that Stella should have taken it into account. Even if it is not genuine, we shall at least tend to assume that an ascription made by Aristotle is not based merely on guesswork but is at least consistent with or prompted by historical facts, i.e. that the ascription suggests that Aristotle knew of an association between Simonides and the Pisistratids. Of course, if the *Constitution of Athens*, which is quite explicit about such an association, is in fact by Aristotle, this conclusion has no independent value. It seems fair to say, then, that this epigram counts to a limited extent in favour of Simonides' Pisistratid connections and so against Stella's revised chronology, which denies such connections.

In short, we must admit that the tradition of Simonides' association with the Pisistratids is not very securely based, either on any contemporary evidence or any definitely identifiable fragments. But neither Stella's argument that the tradition is erroneous nor her explanation of how the "error" arose is fully convincing. In the final weighing of arguments to decide which Simonidean chronology to accept, we shall tend to assume that the tradition of his Pisistratid connections is true.

References

1. Stella (1946) 18.
2. *Ath. Pol.* 18.1-2.

3. τοὺς περὶ Ἀνακρέοντα καὶ Σιμωνίδην (though οἱ περί τινα ["those around someone"] is sometimes virtually equivalent to the proper name alone: see J.E. Sandys, *Ath. Pol.* ed. 2 (1912) ad loc.).

4. [Plato] *Hipparch.* 228 b-c. This passage is reproduced with some changes by Aelian (*VH* 8.2), citing the author of the *Hipparchus* as his authority.

5. For recent discussions, see Podlecki (1966) 129-41; C.W. Fornara, *Historia* 17 (1968) 400-24.

6. See Wilamowitz (1893) I 120.

7. 1946: 18.

8. 1893: I 118-20.

9. Cf. ὁ λεγόμενος λόγος ("the current story"), *Ath. Pol.* 18.4; the versions of οἱ δημοτικοί ("the democrats") and ἔνιοι ("some people"), 18.5.

10. οὗτος (sc. Hipparchus) ἦν ὁ μεταπεμπόμενος ("this man [i.e. Hipparchus] was the one who sent for [them]"), 18.1.

11. 7.3.6; on Lasus, see below, Chapter V, section 2.

12. Stella (1946) 18-9.

13. Stella accepts a reading according to which the Marble records that the Simonides in question *died* at Athens; but "was victorious at Athens" would also be compatible with Stella's chronology.

14. Jacoby (1902) 202 n. 9, 203 & n. 10. Some early scholars (mentioned by Boeckh, *CIG* II p. 319) also referred this entry to our Simonides.

15. A grandson of our Simonides (no. 8 in *FGrH* I p. 158 f.) is said by the Suda (s.v. Σιμωνίδης 442) to have written genealogies.

16. Flach (1883-4) II 612 n. 1; id., *Chronicon Parium* (Tubingae 1884) p. 23; Wilamowitz (1913) 139 n. 2; Maas, *RE* "Simonides" III A 1 (1927) 186.32 ff.; Jacoby on second thoughts, *FGrH* II C-BD p. 693.

17. See further below, Chapter XII, section 2.

18. The reference, in the passage of the *Hipparchus* quoted in Section 1 above, to Hipparchus' keeping Simonides at court "with large rewards and gifts" perhaps hardly qualifies as an anecdote.

78 SIMONIDES

19. *Pap. Berol.* 13875 (Simonides 102/607 Page; Pindar frag. 339 Snell-Maehler); Zuntz (1935) 4-7. Zuntz is quite confident that the commentary is on Pindar; Page is inclined to agree ("ut vid[etur]"); Snell-Maehler, however, class the fragment under *dubia.* Bowra (frag. 160) and Turyn (frag. 291) include the fragment in their editions of Pindar. The question of the authorship of the "Pindaric" fragment is of marginal relevance to the present discussion of Simonides and the Pisistratids, but is of greater importance for the question of Simonides' relations with Pindar (see below, Chapter 10, section 3, with n. 88).

20. 1961: 322.

21. Bowra cites two passages (Alcm. fr.1 Diehl (1 Page) 96-7; Pind. fr. 84.10-1 Bowra (94b 13 ff. Snell)) where maiden-choirs are compared to the Sirens, and two (Soph. fr. 861 Radt; Eur. *Hel.* 169) where they symbolise death. Comparisons between the Sirens and the persuasive powers of men might be more helpful; among the examples of this kind quoted by *LSJ*, there are five complimentary references (to a man's eloquence, Plut. *Vit. Mar.* 44.6; to the power of philosophy, Philodem. *Rhet.* II p. 145 Sudhaus; to the charms of writers and poets, Alex. Aet. fr.7.3, p. 126 Powell; Jul. *Or.* 2.52 d; *IG* XIV 1183.5) and two uncomplimentary references (to deceitful women, Eur. *Andr.* 936; to an orator, Aeschin. 3.228).

22. πρός followed by a name often means "against" in titles of works by Alexandrian scholars (R.Pfeiffer, *History of Classical Scholarship* (Oxford 1968) 133, 135, 248 n. 1), but it is sometimes ambiguous (ib. 133).

23. 1946: 18 n. 3.

24. 1946: 19-20.

25. I Page.

26. XXVI A Page.

27. Hdt. 6.107.

28. Thuc. 6.54 & 56.

29. Cf. N.G.L. Hammond, *CQ* N.S. 6 (1956) 119.

30. 4.137.

31. For suggestions of a later dating, perhaps c. 488, see Podlecki (1966) 137 n. 52, 138 n. 56, with references.

32. Page (1981) ad loc. (ep. I); but earlier (1975: ad loc.) Page had thought that the epigram was recopied from the 510 group.
33. Pindar (*Pyth.* 3.69; ib. 10.64) and Bacchylides (5.11; 13.224) at least affect to regard themselves as bound to their patrons by ties of *xenia*.
34. Podlecki (1966: 135-6), who believes that Simonides wrote the epigram c. 477/6, sees no moral objection to Simonidean authorship at an interval of thirty-odd years after the death of Hipparchus. He thinks that Simonidean authorship of the epigram is confirmed by the fact that references to Simonides' dithyrambic victory and to the setting-up of the tyrannicide statues are juxtaposed, under the year 477/6, on the Parian Marble (ep. 54). But it is doubtful whether this juxtaposition could be taken to indicate the Parian chronicler's belief in Simonidean authorship of the tyrannicide epigram; even if it could, the evidence of this third-century compiler would be insufficient to confirm Simonidean authorship.
35. The principles involved here are outlined above, Chapter I, section 2. Stella (1946: 19-20) does not in fact commit herself to the belief that the tyrannicide epigram is Simonidean. Nor does she, in this case, explicitly credit the ascribing authority with having made the ascription in full knowledge and awareness of the facts of Simonides' career; but she does do this elsewhere, in the case of epigrams which she uses in a similar way to dispute generally accepted facts about Simonides (see below, Chapter XI, section 1); and the argument of hers which we are now considering, about the tyrannicide epigram, does depend on the reliance we place on the ascribing authority. For these reasons I try to discuss the ascription fully here.
36. LII Page.
37. XXVI A Page; Thuc. 6.59.3.
38. So C.F. Smith effectively renders the juxtaposition of gentile adjectives here.
39. *Rhet.* 1.9, 1367 b 20; the third line is "though her father, husband, and brothers were tyrants".
40. Including Kaibel (1873: 453), who is usually sceptical about the reliability of ascriptions.
41. Hippias, who accompanied the Persians at Marathon, is said to have died either in the battle or very soon afterwards (references in *RE* "Hippias" VIII 2 (1913) 1704.53 ff.).

Chapter 4

Some Early Epigrams

In this chapter a number of epigrams are discussed which certainly or possibly belong to the period before the Persian Wars.

1. The epigram for Milo of Croton

This epigram, which is quoted only by Planudes,[1] runs as follows:

> This is the noble statue of noble Milo, who in former days conquered seven times (?) at Pisa without sinking to his knees.

Siebelis' emendation ἑξάκι ("six times") for ἑπτάκι ("seven times") is usually accepted. Our authorities[2] state that Milo was victorious in wrestling six times at Olympia; numerous victories at the other main athletic festivals are also mentioned. Pausanias adds that one of Milo's six Olympic victories was won in the boys' contest; and that Milo was defeated on his seventh appearance at Olympia. Page originally appeared to accept the emendation;[3] but later he preferred to retain "seven times", suggesting that the epigram may refer to the story that Milo once appeared at the games but found no opponents and was therefore declared the winner,[4] thus obtaining what might be said (if the anecdote refers to Olympia) to constitute a seventh Olympic victory; in that case, the epigram could not be a genuine inscription, as it would clash with the official record of six victories. But as the epigram relating the anecdote does not specify Olympia, it seems preferable to accept the emendation ἑξάκι ("six times"), in accordance with general opinion.[5]

The date of Milo's Olympic victory as a boy is given as 540 B.C. (Ol. 60) by the scholiast on Theocritus.[6] Africanus dates one of Milo's victories to 532 B.C. (Ol. 62); as there is no indication to the contrary, this must have been in the men's contest. Rutgers[7] pointed out that it is probable that Africanus is here singling out either Milo's first or his last victory in the men's contest; if this is so, the reference to a boys' victory in 540 shows that the victory in 532 must have been his first men's victory.[8] Rutgers assigned Milo's other men's victories to the immediately following Olympiads, from 528 to 516 B.C. (Ols. 63-66); this seems reasonable, as it is hard to imagine Milo's athletic prime as extending over an even longer period. Rutgers' dating of Milo's victorious Olympic career (540 in the boys' contest, 532-516 in the men's) has won general acceptance. Thus Stella is obviously wrong in stating that there are no allusions in the Simonidean epigrams to events before 506 B.C.[9]

The statue of Milo at Olympia is referred to by Pausanias and Philostratus.[10] It is said by Pausanias to have been carried into the Altis by Milo himself, and was presumably erected on the occasion of one of his victories, which, if our epigram (with the emendation ἑξάκι, "six times") really relates to this statue, would have been his sixth and last victory. The reference to Pisa in the text of the epigram does not rule out the supposition that it may have been inscribed on the base of a statue erected at Olympia itself, as its author may have intended it not merely to serve the immediate purpose of identifying a statue, but to be remembered and circulated as a tribute to Milo; and the word ποτε ("once [upon a time]") need not exclude such a contemporary reference,[11] as it may have been intended to anticipate the point of view of an onlooker in the future, looking back on the events referred to. On the other hand, it remains possible that a statue of so famous an athlete as Milo could have been erected some time after his death.

Simonidean authorship of the epigram would be consistent with other evidence about Simonides' career. We have seen[12] that Simonides may have written an ode for an Olympic victor, Glaucus of Carystus, round about 520 B.C.; and the composition of an epigram to be inscribed on a victor's statue at Olympia would be a closely related activity. It is possible to speculate that this may have been Simonides' first commission for an inscriptional epigram, and even that he may have been launched on his career as an epigrammatist as a direct result of his activities as a composer of epinicians, with the Olympic festival providing the link.

If the epigram could be assigned with confidence to Simonides, it would strongly confirm the traditional dating of his life (born c. 556 B.C.) as against Stella's dating (born c. 532-29). Stella's dating could be admitted only on one of two assumptions: either Milo's run of successes in the men's contest, which included the year 532, contained one or two gaps and can be extended beyond 516 to 512 or 508,[13] by which time Simonides might have been just old enough to be commissioned; or the statue was dedicated at Olympia at a date later than the actual victories.[14]

However, the Simonidean ascription, though it may be correct, is found only in the unreliable Planudean Anthology, and so cannot be accepted with any confidence. Nor is it possible to argue that the ascription, even if it happens to be incorrect, must at least have been prompted by a knowledge that Simonides was active about this date,[15] for the ascription could be due to carelessness or accident. This epigram thus carries little weight in the debate on the dates of Simonides' life.

2. Epigrams for the events of 507/6 B.C.

Herodotus, narrating the Athenian operations of 507/6 B.C. against the Spartans, Boeotians, and Chalcidians, describes the separate Athenian victories over the Boeotians and Chalcidians, and the eventual ransoming of the Boeotian and Chalcidian prisoners, whose fetters were hung up on the Acropolis and could still be seen in Herodotus' time. He adds that the Athenians used a tithe of the prisoners' ransom to dedicate a bronze four-horse chariot, which stood at the left-hand entrance of the Propylaea, its base inscribed with the following lines:[16]

> The sons of the Athenians, having conquered the tribes of the Boeotians and Chalcidians, quenched their insolence in grievous iron bonds; as a tithe from (the ransom of) these men, they dedicated these horses to Pallas.

The epigram is found in other literary sources,[17] and fragments of it appear in two inscriptions dated by their lettering to the late sixth and the mid fifth century.[18] It is generally assumed that the sixth-century inscription comes from the base of the original monument; that the latter was destroyed or carried off by the Persians in 480; and that the second inscription, which was seen by Herodotus, belongs to a Periclean restoration effected perhaps at the time of Pericles' conquest of Euboea in 446/5,[19] or, as some believe, after the victory over the Boeotians at Oenophyta in 457.[20] The sixth-century inscription opened with a reference to the shackling of the prisoners, which was presumably prominent in the Athenians' minds at the time of the actual events; in the fifth-century inscription and all the literary sources, the two hexameters have been interchanged, so that the epigram opens with a reference to the conquest of the Boeotians and Chalcidians, thus emphasising an aspect which was more relevant to the presumed circumstances of the restored dedication.[21] The original dedication of the chariot and inscription is probably to be dated within a year or so of the victories, that is about 506/5 B.C.[22]

Page states bluntly that the epigram is never ascribed to Simonides or any other author; but it is not certain that this is so. For one thing, there has been some dispute about the intention of Aristides in the passage cited. At para. 60 (Keil's text) he quotes Simonides 14 West,[23] attributing it to Simonides; then at paras. 63-66 he goes on to quote six more epigrams,[24] including our epigram. It was once thought (for example, by Bergk ad locc.) that Aristides meant to ascribe these six epigrams to Simonides; but this has generally (and, I believe, rightly) been denied by scholars writing after Bergk. More importantly, evidence has now been published which suggests that the epigram was in fact assigned to Simonides in antiquity. A scrap of papyrus[25] from the late first century A.D. contains parts of our epigram, preceded a few lines earlier by the letters].μωνι ("Simonides"?), which seems to suggest that Simonides was named as the author. (It is possible, as Turner says, that the full text denied Simonidean authorship; but this kind of negative statement is far less likely.) The layout of the text is that of a *hypomnema* or commentary, a fact which, as Turner points out, implies that the epigram was included in an Alexandrian edition, whether this was a collection of Simonidean epigrams or of historical epigrams.

Another epigram, which is found only in the Planudean Anthology and is there ascribed to Simonides,[26] may belong to the same historical context:

> We were overwhelmed (slain) beneath a glen of Mount Dirphys, and a grave-mound has been heaped over us near the Euripus by our community; quite rightly, for we lost our lovely youth in abiding the harsh storm-cloud of war.

The references to the Euripus and to Mount Dirphys, the high mountain in central Euboea, have led to the conjecture that this epigram, like the previous one, is concerned with the Athenian defeat of Chalcis. It is usually assumed that, if this is so, it is the epitaph of the Athenian dead. Page, however, argues that ἐδμήθημεν (line 1 of the epigram) must refer to the fate of the defeated side, viz. the Chalcidians, and comments that a phrase which comes so close to an admission of defeat is unusually frank for a public epitaph; but surely the word, in such a context, most naturally means "we were overwhelmed, slain", which could refer equally well to the victorious Athenians. If the lines are a genuine inscription for this event, they must have been carved on the grave monument very soon after the actual battle; so this epigram may slightly antedate ep. III, which followed the ransoming of the prisoners and the dedication of the chariot.

According to Stella's chronology,[27] Simonides in 506 B.C. would only be about twenty-six or less, rather young to be receiving commissions from the Athenian state. If on the other hand the traditional date of his birth and the accounts of his association with Hipparchus are accepted, the employment of Simonides by Athens in 506 would mean that the democracy was willing to overlook his connections with the tyrants quite soon after the fall of the latter; but this is by no means improbable. It seems then that any genuine Simonidean epigrams commissioned by Athens at this time would tend (and one cannot claim any more than this) to favour the traditional dates of Simonides.

Simonidean authorship of an epigram for the Chalcidians might not in itself be improbable, in view of his "Euboean connection" as shown by odes for Glaucus of Carystus, and for Eualcides and Lysimachus of Eretria;[28] but it would be hard to imagine Simonides, despite his skill in exploiting the lyric poet's "diplomatic immunity" by remaining in contact with mutually hostile parties, actually writing simultaneously for opposing sides in the same battle; it would therefore be preferable to accept an interpretation of ep. II Page which, if it is connected at all with the events of 507/6, associates it with the Athenian side.

There are reasonable grounds for believing that III Page, which definitely concerns the events of 506 B.C., was ascribed to Simonides by an Alexandrian commentator. But we cannot put such trust in this anonymous commentator as to accept his ascription without reserve; nor can we even be sure that the ascription (even if it happens to be incorrect) must at least have been prompted by the knowledge that Simonides was active in Athens at about this time. This applies a fortiori to II Page, as it is not even certain which events it refers to, and it is ascribed to Simonides only by the notoriously unreliable Planudean Anthology.

3. Epigrams for Aeginetans

The first of the two epigrams considered in this section probably belongs, like the epigrams discussed in the preceding sections, to the period before the Persian Wars. The second is probably to be dated after the Persian Wars, but it is included here, as the two epigrams must be discussed together.

The first epigram[29] is attested by the following passage of the Pindaric scholia:[30]

> But Aristodemus the pupil of Aristarchus offers a better explanation,[31] that Sogenes was born to Thearion late in life when he was almost too old, after he had prayed to the goddess, and that the birth of his son was a kind of favour from Eileithyia.[32] Therefore because of the particular circumstances (τὴν ἰδιότητα) of the athlete's birth, he (Pindar) addressed his invocation to this goddess. This was confirmed by reference to an epigram of Simonides.

The victory of Sogenes of Aegina in the boys' pentathlon is celebrated by Pindar in *Nemean 7*, in the opening lines of which Eileithyia is invoked as the divinity responsible for Sogenes' victory, perhaps because, as the scholium just quoted explains, Sogenes was born to Thearion late in life.

The text of the Simonidean epigram is not preserved; but the wording of the scholium naturally seems to suggest, and until recently it has been universally assumed,[33] that the epigram told of the exceptional circumstances of Sogenes' birth; a further natural assumption is that the epigram was written, or purported to have been written, on the occasion of his victory.

However these assumptions have been challenged by D. C. Young,[34] who argues that the name Sogenes conjured up before Aristodemus the commonplace literary image of the long-awaited son who saves the line from extinction, and that this image, coupled with the occurrence of the name Eileithyia in Pindar, prompted him to invent the historical details of Sogenes' birth; Aristodemus then adduced the Simonidean epigram, not as a historical source for the biography of Sogenes, but as a "literary parallel for the kind of onomastic pun that he has just attributed to Pindar". The epigram referred to, Young argues, is not lost but is in fact Simonides 161 Diehl:[35]

> Sosos and Soso, o saviour (σῶτερ), dedicated this to you, Sosos because he was saved (σωθείς) and Soso because Sosos was saved (ἐσώθη).

I find this argument unconvincing. It seems to me that the interpretation of the scholium which was universally accepted until challenged by Young is the obviously correct one, both on first sight and on re-examination. "This" (τοῦτο) in the last sentence of the scholium must surely refer to the fact of the "particular circumstances of the athlete's birth" mentioned in the preceding sentence; and "was confirmed by reference to an epigram of Simonides" (ἐπιστοῦτο ἐξ ἐπιγράμματος Σιμωνίδου) must surely mean that the epigram contained the relevant information. I cannot accept that Aristodemus, even if he invented the details of Sogenes' birth as Young suggests, was "attributing an onomastic pun" to Pindar. Aristodemus explains the Pindaric passage by saying that Sogenes was born late in his father's life; according to this explanation — whether or not Aristodemus invented it — Pindar invoked Eileithyia because Sogenes was born late, not merely because he was called "Sogenes". Pindar might well have seen a connection between Sogenes' name and his late and welcome birth; but any "pun" is to be attributed to Sogenes' father, who gave him that name, rather than to the poet.

Young could be right in denying that the reference to the Simonidean epigram provides any reliable confirmation of the biographical details about Sogenes' birth. It might, for instance, be possible that the writer of the epigram invented the details of Sogenes' birth in the manner suggested by Young for Aristodemus, that is, on the basis of Pindar's reference to Eileithyia and the name Sogenes. But there can surely be no doubt that the writer of the scholium or his source knew of, or believed in, the existence of an epigram which included the biographical details quoted in the scholium.

The date of Sogenes' victory is given by the Pindaric scholiasts as Nemead 14 (547 B.C.) or Nemead 24 (527 B.C.). Emendations have been proposed which produce dates of 493 B.C.,[36] 487,[37] and 467 (or 461).[38] As only a minority of the solutions proposed result in a date for Sogenes' victory later than 468/7 (the traditional date of Simonides' death), there is no need to class the epigram on Sogenes among the "late" epigrams whose ascription to Simonides is at variance with the traditional dates of his lifetime.

The other Simonidean epigram on an Aeginetan is the following, which is quoted only by the Planudean Anthology, where it is ascribed to Simonides:[39]

> Know that you have looked upon Theognetus, the boy victor at Olympia, skilled exponent of wrestling, fair to look upon and with a prowess matching his handsome form, who has crowned the city of his noble fathers.

The name "Theognetus" was restored (from the corrupt manuscript version "Theocritus") from a passage of Pausanias,[40] where we learn that Theognetus of Aegina was victorious in the boys' wrestling-match at Olympia, his statue being made by Ptolichus of Aegina. The epigram is obviously meant to belong to a statue.

Theognetus is mentioned by Pindar[41] as the uncle of his patron Aristomenes of Aegina, whose own victory is dated by the scholiasts[42] to Pythiad 35, i.e. 446 B.C., a dating which is generally accepted by modern scholars. Theognetus' own victory is perhaps to be dated to 476, by Grenfell and Hunt's tentative restoration of [θεογνητος αιγι]νητης παιδ παλην ("[Theognetos the Aegi]netan in the boys' wrestling") opposite the year 476.[43] This date would only just allow Simonidean authorship of the epigram, for Simonides had apparently gone to Sicily before Pindar wrote the second *Olympian* ode, which celebrates a victory in this same Olympic festival of 476, and it seems unlikely that a private citizen of Aegina would have sent to Sicily to commission Simonides for an epigram which was to be inscribed at Olympia.[44]

These epigrams must be considered as part of the whole question of Simonides' relations with Aegina. It seemed very probable that the Crius ode[45] is hostile to Crius, and almost certain that the motive for Simonides' mockery was political — that it was directed against Crius as an Aeginetan (not merely as a beaten competitor) to please an Athenian patron and public. If this is correct, Simonides must have departed here from his normal practice of remaining on good terms with mutually hostile parties. The "diplomatic immunity" enjoyed by the choral lyric poet might enable him to praise rival parties alternately without incurring the hostility of either, but obviously not to indulge in jibes of this kind without so doing. I find it hard to accept, therefore, either that Simonides wrote these epigrams for Aeginetans, or that any ancient scholar was prompted to ascribe them to him by positive evidence such as the existence of Simonidean epinician odes for these particular patrons (as Boas suggests),[46] or Simonidean odes for other Aeginetan patrons, or even by an anecdotal tradition of friendly relations between Simonides and Aegina. In thus suggesting that Simonides, having attacked a leading figure of a state in order to gratify a rival power, would be unlikely to write later for individual patrons from that state, are we ignoring the possibility of various parties and shifting opinions? Not, I think, in this case; hostility to Athens was probably a sentiment common to most Aeginetans throughout the period which concerns us, viz. from the beginning of the fifth century to Simonides' death. It is true that a faction of dissident Aeginetan democrats received aid from Athens about 487 B.C.,[47] but this hardly constitutes a serious exception to the general picture of Aeginetan hostility to Athens; and in any case, Aeginetan patrons of the status and means to commission Simonides for epinician odes are unlikely to have belonged to the disaffected democratic faction.

I think, then, that there is some incompatibility between Simonidean authorship of these epigrams and the conclusions about Simonides' relations with Aegina that we drew from other sources (viz. from the Crius ode). We must now briefly consider the degree of error which the ascription of these epigrams to Simonides seems to involve, and the reliability of the ascribing sources.

We have suggested that the ascription to Simonides is wrong; but the error involved in the ascription would not be a serious blunder, such as a gross misdating, but would merely consist of a failure to take into account the evidence (which we think we have discerned in the Crius ode) of Simonides' hostile attitude to Aegina. Ep. XXX Page owes its Simonidean title to the unreliable Planudean Anthology, ep.166 Bergk to a better source, viz. Aristodemus, an Alexandrian commentator on Pindar; Boas[48] thinks that both epigrams were in the Collector's *Sylloge Simonidea*. It is quite easy to believe that Aristodemus or Boas' Collector might have ascribed epigrams to Simonides without scrupulously scanning Simonides' career to ensure that there were no discrepancies or to produce positive confirmatory evidence. On the whole, I would rather accept our conclusions (drawn from the Crius ode) about Simonides' hostility to Aegina, reject these epigrams, and so impute a comparatively small error to Aristodemus or the Collector, than follow Boas in postulating melic poems for Aeginetans as a reason for the ascription of the epigrams and so reject the conclusions we drew from the Crius ode.

References

1. XXV Page; *Anth. Plan.* 24, where it is ascribed to Simonides by the formula τοῦ αὐτοῦ ("by the same author").
2. Diod. Sic. 12.9.6; Paus. 6.14.5; Africanus ap. Euseb. I 202 Schoene.
3. Page (1975) ad loc.
4. Page (1981) ad loc.; the anecdote is found in *Anth. Pal.* 11.316.
5. Page, however, confidently associates the anecdote with Olympia. He rejects the emendation "six times" in our epigram on the ground that a corruption of "six" to "seven" would be unaccountable, as Milo's six victories were common knowledge; but it could perhaps have arisen through a reminiscence of his seven Olympic appearances.
6. Ms. K of schol. Theocr. Arg. *Idyll.* 4 d (p. 135 Wendel).
7. 1862: 23 n. 4.
8. Rutgers, who did not have access to manuscript evidence for the date 540 in the Theocritean scholia, reached this same conclusion by noting that Milo was still flourishing some twenty years after the 532 victory, viz. c. 512-509 B.C. (Ol. 67), when he played a leading part in the war of Croton against Sybaris (Diod. Sic. 12.9.5-6). Rutgers also conjecturally restored 540 (Ol. 60) for the boys' victory, in place of the corrupt Ol. 7, in the mss. of Theocritus which were known to him.
9. Stella (1946) 17.
10. Paus. 6.14.5 f.; Philostr. *Vit. Apoll.* 4.28.
11. See Boas (1905) 205 & n. 161; D.C.Young, *HSCP* 87 (1983) 31-48, especially pp. 35-42.
12. See Chapter II, section 1.
13. This seems unlikely; it is improbable that even a wrestler would remain at the height of his powers for more than five Olympiads; moreover the wording of the epigram ("did not sink to his knees") implies a succession of victories unbroken by defeat.

14. This would be inconsistent with Pausanias' anecdote associating Milo himself, in his prime, with the dedication of his statue.

15. On the general principles involved, see Chapter I, section 2.

16. III Page; Hdt. 5.74-7.

17. Diod. Sic. 10.24.3; Aristid. Or. 28.64 (II 162 Keil); Anth. Pal. 6.343.

18. These are, respectively, IG I² 394 II & I.

19. References in Page's commentary ad loc.

20. A.E.Raubitschek, *Dedications from the Athenian Akropolis* (Cambridge Mass. 1949) 203, following Hauvette.

21. See Page's commentary for a full discussion with references.

22. Raubitschek (op. cit., p. 193) extends the range of dates, somewhat improbably, to c. 500.

23. 146 Bergk, 78 Diehl; not in Page (1975 & 1981).

24. Simonides XXI, XXXVIII, XLV, III, XXII (a), and XII Page. Three of these (XXII (a), XII, XLV) are ascribed to Simonides by other ancient sources; and perhaps the same can now be said of our epigram (III Page).

25. P.Oxy. 2535 (vol. XXXI (1966) pp. 14-6), with commentary by E.G. Turner and restorations by E.Lobel. (This papyrus was first reported by Turner in 1962: see *Proceedings of the Classical Association* 59 (1962) 21-2.)

26. II Page; Anth. Plan. 26.

27. The only allusion made by Stella to these epigrams is a brief reference to ep. III Page (Stella (1946) 17 & n. 1); she regards the dating of this epigram to 506 B.C. as "very doubtful".

28. Frags. 4/509, 13/518, 25/530 Page.

29. 166 Bergk; not in Diehl, West, or Page.

30. Schol. Pind. Nem. 7.1a (III p. 117.12 Drachmann).

31. Sc. for Pindar's invocation of Eileithyia.

32. The oratio obliqua construction, by which the scholiast introduces Aristodemus' explanation, ends at this point.

33. By Pindaric scholars, for the most part. The epigram is little discussed by the commentators on Simonides, presumably because its text does not survive.
34. *TAPA* 101 (1970) 635-7.
35. 168 Bergk (not in West or Page). Brussich (1975-6: 124) interestingly suggests that this epigram, with its plethora of sigmas, was intended as a parody, in reverse, of Lasus' asigmatic poetry, so that it could reflect Simonides' supposed rivalry with Lasus (on which, see below, Chapter V, section 2).
36. Nemead 41, Gaspar (1900) 40.
37. Nemead 44, Wilamowitz (1922) 160 & n. 2. As Wilamowitz accepts 573 as the date of the first Nemean festival, Nemead 44 should represent 487 B.C.; but Wilamowitz wrongly equates his emendation with 485 B.C.
38. Hermann (ap. Dissen in Boeckh's *Pindar* II 2 416) proposed Nemead 54, by which he probably meant 461 B.C., in accordance with the tendency of most early scholars to date the first Nemean festival to 567. W.Christ (*Pindari Carmina*, Leipzig 1896, 284) followed by Boas (1905: 132 & n. 97), accepts "Nemead 54" from Hermann, but equates this with 467 B.C., in accordance with the modern dating of the first Nemead to 573.
39. XXX Page; *Anth. Plan.* 2.
40. 6.9.1.
41. *Pyth.* 8.35-6.
42. Schol. *Pyth.* 8, Inscr., II 206 Drachmann.
43. *P.Oxy.* no. CCXXII col. I line 15 (vol. II 1899, pp. 88 & 91).
44. Admittedly I allow that Gelon of Syracuse may, while Simonides was still in Greece, have commissioned him for a dedication at Delphi, but the circumstances in that instance are rather different: see below, Chapter IX, section 3.
45. On the Crius ode (2/507 Page), see above, Chapter II, section 4.
46. Boas (1905) 231. Boas does not explain how Simonidean authorship of an ode for Theognetus for a victory in a Nemean festival dated by Boas to 467 is to be reconciled with the traditional date of Simonides' death in 468/7, which Boas apparently accepts. (The Nemean festival would have occurred in the summer of 467, at the very end of Olympiad 78.1, which is the year 468/7.)

47. Hdt. 6.88-92.
48. 1905: 132.

Chapter 5

Simonides in Relation to Other Poets

1. Bacchylides

The degree of kinship between Simonides and Bacchylides has sometimes been brought to bear on the question of the relative dating of the two poets.

Some sources[1] state that Bacchylides was the nephew (ἀδελφιδοῦς) of Simonides, though another version[2] merely states that he was Simonides' relative (συγγενής). The name of Bacchylides' father was Meidylus,[3] whose father was Bacchylides "the athlete";[4] and the name of Simonides' father was Leoprepes.[5] Therefore Simonides and Meidylus cannot have been brothers. The usual and most natural assumption[6] is that Bacchylides was the son of a sister of Simonides by Meidylus (though nothing more is known of this sister). Another possibility is suggested by Taccone,[7] that Simonides and Meidylus may have been half-brothers, their mother having married first Bacchylides the athlete and then Leoprepes (or vice versa).

Stella, obviously assuming with most scholars that Bacchylides was a son of Simonides' sister, uses this relationship to argue for her later dating of Simonides.[8] Dating Bacchylides' birth about 503 B.C., she states that the traditional dates of Simonides mean that there was an age-gap of at least fifty years between uncle and nephew, a gap which would be surprisingly large, especially in antiquity when girls married at an early age.

Stella is too dogmatic in her novel use of this point, which, as will appear, is not itself a new one. A fifty year gap would indeed be surprising but far from impossible, and appears to cause no misgivings at all to Jebb, who suggests[9] that if Bacchylides was born c. 512-505, his mother may have been about fifteen or twenty years younger than her brother Simonides. This would mean that she bore Bacchylides when aged about thirty or thirty-five. This is entirely credible; it would be difficult to prove that because women married young they were unlikely to bear children at the age of thirty or above.

Secondly, Stella's assumption that the gap would be at least fifty years is too confident; for the date of Bacchylides' birth is quite uncertain. Körte[10] dates it c. 516, Severyns[11] c. 518/7. It is true that in each case their main reason for choosing a date earlier than that usually accepted[12] is the fifty year age-gap between uncle and nephew which the usual date implies. But it should be noted that neither Körte nor Severyns is so sceptical as Stella about the possibility of such an age-gap between uncle and nephew; and that each has other arguments also for the earlier date of Bacchylides' birth. Bowra even allows that the date implied by the *Chronicon Paschale,* viz. 521/0, may be correct;[13] but few, I think, will be willing to date Bacchylides' birth some years before Pindar's. However there is at least a fair possibility that Körte and Severyns are right and that the age-gap was about forty, not fifty, years.

If we choose to accept Taccone's slight revision of the family-tree, the age-gap, even if it was fifty years, becomes easier to accept; we merely have to suppose that Meidylus, ten years younger than his half-brother Simonides, became the father of Bacchylides at the age of forty.

Thus the difficulty which the relationship of the two poets may at first seem to cause in the acceptance of the traditional dating of Simonides can be shown to be very slight. There is not much support for Stella here, though her argument might carry some little weight as part of a cumulative body of evidence.

2. Lasus and dithyrambic contests

In the following passage (*Vesp.* 1409 ff.), Aristophanes names Simonides and Lasus as rivals in a literary contest:

> Listen now, and see if you think this is a good story. Lasus once contended for the poet's prize (ἀντεδίδασκε) with Simonides; then Lasus said "I don't really mind."

Aristophanes can only be referring to a dithyrambic contest. Lasus is said by the Suda to have introduced dithyrambic contests; and there is firm evidence for Simonides' dithyrambs.[14]

The introduction of men's dithyrambic contests, and the victory in such a contest of one Hypodicus of Chalcis, is mentioned by the Parian Marble in an entry which is to be dated somewhere within the years 510/507 B.C. It seems reasonable to assume that the Marble is referring to the introduction of such contests by Lasus, which is thus dated c. 510/507; confirmation of this may be sought in the fact that the Suda (s.v. Λάσος) dates Lasus' birth at Ol. 58 (548-5 B.C.), which is consistent with the introduction of the contests by Lasus c. 508 B.C., the usual forty years being allowed between birth and acme.[15] The date 510/507 would then provide a rough *terminus post quem* for contests between Lasus and Simonides. As far as Simonides is concerned, the only further clue is the *terminus ante quem* provided by the occasion of his last dithyrambic victory and his departure for Sicily in 476. As regards Lasus, we can only say that, if he was indeed Pindar's teacher,[16] he must have been active about 500 B.C. (presumably in Athens, where Pindar was sent for training),[17] and perhaps after this.

Lasus is known to have been associated with Hipparchus.[18] The opinion is sometimes expressed that he was not in Athens after the fall of the tyrants[19] and that there is some incongruity between the ascription to Lasus of the first dithyrambic contest (the Suda) and the dating of this event after 510 (Parian Marble). So Pickard-Cambridge suggests in explanation that the entry on the Marble may refer "to the first victory at the Dionysia as organized under the democracy, and as distinct from such contests as may have been arranged by the tyrants with the assistance of Lasos". Schmid, who thinks it likely that Lasus was no longer in Athens in 508 (his date for *Marm. Par.* ep. 46), even suggests that Lasus was now in Chalcis, from where he sent Hypodicus (the Chalcidian victor named in *Marm. Par.* ep. 46) to Athens to supervise the performance of one of his (Lasus') dithyrambs. Bowra also takes this attitude, stating that "dithyrambic performances or competitions" were inaugurated by Lasus "under the patronage of the Peisistratids". The underlying assumption (made explicit by Brussich, among others) is that if Lasus was in Athens under the Pisistratids, he is unlikely to have remained in Athens after they fell;[20] but surely we are not obliged to make such an assumption.[21] Privitera[22] allows that Lasus could have remained at Athens after the fall of the Pisistratids; but he too claims that Lasus' introduction of dithyrambic contests must predate their fall. He argues that Lasus could not have been remembered as having introduced such contests c. 509/508 B.C. unless he had also been the victor in that year, and that as the recorded victor was Hypodicus of Chalcis, Lasus' introduction of the contests must have been earlier; but it is doubtful whether so close a link need be assumed between organisation of the contest, and personal participation and victory on the same occasion. Stella is right, then, in claiming that Simonides' rivalry with Lasus is no proof that both poets were in Athens under the Pisistratids.[23] This does not mean, of course, that we are obliged to place absolute faith in the Marble's dating of the introduction of the contests c. 510, or deny the possibility that they may have been introduced earlier.

Can any reliance be placed on the tradition of rivalry between Simonides and Lasus which the Aristophanic passage seems to reflect? Some assume that Aristophanes is referring to an actual event.[24] Others suppose that the incident is fictitious; thus Wehrli suggests that the competition between Simonides and Lasus is an invention, based on the reputation of both poets for *apophthegmata* of the kind uttered by Lasus in this instance, while Privitera argues that Aristophanes is mocking the *topos* of a confrontation between *sophoi* by attributing to Lasus, who had a reputation for *sophia*, a particularly banal response to his defeat.[25] It is no doubt true that the anecdote of Lasus' response to defeat by Simonides on a particular occasion is apocryphal; but it is extremely likely that Simonides and Lasus, both exponents of the dithyramb, did meet in dithyrambic competitions at Athens.[26] The anecdote in Aristophanes hints that Simonides' victory over Lasus was a foregone conclusion, and that Lasus was aware of, and avowedly indifferent to, this fact. Such an anecdote might be based simply on Simonides' large number of victories, and presumably formidable reputation, in this field; but it could indicate that a more specific memory of the overall superiority of Simonides in competitions between these two major figures was preserved, and also, perhaps, that Aristophanes looked on Simonides as at least Lasus' contemporary and equal (Simonides born c. 556, Lasus c. 548), rather than his junior (Lasus born c. 548, Simonides c. 532), thus providing a slight clue in favour of the traditional dates of Simonides.

There are three points, which, if substantiated, would invalidate the suggestion just advanced. Firstly, it is stated by Pickard-Cambridge[27] that there was a tradition that Lasus was Simonides' teacher; but I have not been able to find any ancient statement to this effect. Secondly, the Aristophanic scholia[28] on the line which quotes Lasus' dictum (ὀλίγον μοι μέλει) comment ἀντὶ τοῦ οὐδέν μοι μέλει τοῦ Σιμωνίδου. Christ[29] concludes from this that there was a version of the story in which the roles of Simonides and

Lasus were exactly reversed, with Simonides commenting on *his* defeat by Lasus; but it seems more likely that the scholiast has extracted this Simonidean dictum from some unspecified context unconnected with Lasus.[30] Thirdly, Privitera notes that Lasus' date of birth, viz. Ol.58 (548-5 B.C.) is linked in the Suda (s.v. Λᾶσος) with that of Darius, in agreement with Herodotus' dating of Darius, but that an alternative date of birth for Darius (557 B.C.) is given by Ctesias;[31] he therefore suggests that there may have been a synchronism which put Lasus' date of birth, with that of Darius, at 557, which is also the approximate traditional date of Simonides' birth. But as it is difficult to see any intrinsic connection between Lasus and Darius, any synchronism between them would have been quite arbitrary; and it seems preferable to accept the connection, as already noted, between Lasus' acme c. 508 (the alleged date of the introduction of dithyrambic contests) and his birth c. 548. We may therefore accept the slender clue on Simonidean chronology which the Aristophanic passage seemed to offer.

Finally it is necessary to consider what conclusions can be drawn about Simonides' dates and the pattern of his career, if the evidence of the epigram XXVII Page about his fifty-six dithyrambic victories is accepted as reliable.[32] The wording of the epigram is:

> You won fifty-six bulls and tripods, Simonides, before dedicating this tablet; and so many times, having trained the fair chorus of men, did you mount the glorious chariot of victory.

This epigram is accepted by some scholars[33] who are normally sceptical about Simonidean ascriptions; though Page (on ep. XXVIII) regards the address to Simonides in the first line of our epigram as proof that it is a literary exercise, probably by an author who had ep. XXVIII in front of him. Even if the epigram itself is a late composition, it may still preserve an authentic tradition of Simonides' fifty-six victories.[34] The lines do not state the date and circumstances of the supposed dedication; but it is reasonable to say that the epigram sums up Simonides' achievements in dithyrambic contests and refers to his last victory,[35] won in 477/6 B.C. just before his departure for Sicily and recorded in ep. 54 of the Parian Marble and in ep. XXVIII Page.

The number of victories is very large for one man. We should like to know the minimum number of years into which we could fit these victories (reckoning back from 476); but this is a very difficult calculation to make. The epigram specifies men's choruses; but the number of possible occasions would be greater, and it would be easier to fit a large number of victories into a limited period, if boys' choruses were included in the total, and it may indeed be legitimate to do so; Wilamowitz[36] rejects the second couplet, which contains the phrase χορὸν ἀνδρῶν ("the chorus of men"), on the ground that Simonides is unlikely to have written for men only or to have excluded from the total his victories with boys or maidens,[37] while Page suggests that ἀνδρῶν ("of men") was copied from ep. XXVIII and does not properly fit its context in ep. XXVII.

It is probably true that "bulls and tripods" could be won in dithyrambic competitions outside Athens[38] (perhaps including those at non-Dionysiac festivals?); and it is perhaps uncertain how many festivals[39] at Athens itself could be counted as possible occasions for these victories. Pickard-Cambridge, doubting whether all Simonides' fifty-six victories can have been won at Athens "even when all possible occasions of dithyrambic performances are taken into the reckoning", unfortunately does not say which festivals he would include or over how many years he would spread the victories.

Suppose we take as a starting point the year 508 (or thereabouts) when dithyrambic contests are said to have been instituted at Athens. It is possible that all Simonides' fifty-six victories could have been won in the period 508-476 (a thirty-two year period from which we may deduct an uncertain number of years for his visit to Thessaly), though it is true than an average of something like two to three victories a year for a period of twenty to thirty years would be a remarkable record. If the dithyrambs, then, go back no further than 508, they can be fitted into either Stella's chronology or the traditional chronology (Simonides born c. 532, or c. 556, respectively).

We would certainly prefer a little more time over which to spread these victories. The period before 508 may be taken into account if there were dithyrambic contests of some kind at Athens before 508 (despite *Marm. Par.* ep. 46) as some believe, or if there were dithyrambic contests, to which the epigram might refer, at other places (e.g. Corinth?) before this date. If either of these conditions can be allowed, we shall prefer to take some of Simonides' victories back beyond 508 and consequently to accept the traditional date of Simonides' birth rather than Stella's. And there are in fact one or two slender clues which perhaps point to Simonides' participation in dithyrambic competitions before 508. Firstly, it has been suggested that the date "Ol. 62" (532/1 B.C.) in the Suda's entry on Simonides may have marked a significant event in Simonides' career, viz. his first competition.[40] Secondly, Syrian, when quoting the epigram XXVIII Page on Simonides' dithyrambic victory in 477/6 aged eighty, states that Simonides won victories in the competitions at Athens from his youth until the age of eighty, "as the epigram makes clear".[41] In fact the epigram only refers to the one victory, at the age of eighty. Syrian's reference to Simonides' victories won from youth upwards may be a mere rhetorical flourish on the notice of one victory at the age of eighty; or it may be based on the tradition of Simonides' fifty-six victories (ep. XXVII), which seemed to Syrian to need spreading over the best part of a lifetime; but it may possibly mean that Syrian was aware of evidence for Simonidean victories extending back into the period before 508 and covering a larger proportion of his lifetime than the thirty-two year period between the supposed introduction of dithyrambic competitions in 508 and his victory of 476.

3. Xenophanes

The following scholium on a passage of *Peace*,[42] where Aristophanes hints that Sophocles shares with Simonides the vice of covetousness, is the only piece of evidence which explicitly connects Simonides and Xenophanes:[43]

> Simonides had been reproached for covetousness; and so Sophocles is said to be like Simonides because of his covetousness; and it is said that he made money out of his generalship in Samos. And for the same reason he (Aristophanes) very wittily ridiculed (Simonides)...and mentions that he was penurious. Hence Xenophanes calls him a skinflint (κίμβιξ).

Part of this scholium appears as a fragment of Xenophanes in Diels-Kranz, but they do not quote enough of it to make it readily intelligible.[44] The gap indicated above after the words "ridiculed (Simonides)" in fact contains the words β' τοῦ ἰαμβοποιοῦ, which cannot be explained as they stand but may have originated in one of two ways. Either they were meant to identify Simonides as the iambographer, and therefore should be deleted (as in Diels-Kranz), on the ground that it was Simonides the lyric poet who was reputed to be covetous; or they indicate that Aristophanes is quoting from some iambic poet[45] who had attacked our Simonides for covetousness.

There can be no doubt that it is our Simonides to whom Aristophanes and his scholiast are alluding.[46] Apart from the many other ancient references to his alleged covetousness, the same word (κίμβιξ) is used of him by Chamaeleon,[47] who was presumably drawing on Xenophanes; and indeed it is usually assumed, no doubt rightly, that the Aristophanic scholium derives its quotation of Xenophanes from Chamaeleon.[48] The reason for Xenophanes' gibe, and indeed for Simonides' general reputation for covetousness, may lie partly in Simonides' role as a professional poet charging fees, in contrast to Xenophanes' claim of the status of a detached and disinterested *sophos*.[49] In another fragment[50]

Xenophanes appears to be reproaching someone for meanness, and it is possible that Diels-Kranz are right in suggesting that Simonides may be the target here also; but since Xenophanes distributed his attacks so widely, the suggestion can be accepted only with hesitation. We are not compelled to assume that Simonides and Xenophanes actually met each other; but Jacoby may well be right in suggesting that there was a tradition of their being together at Hieron's court.[51] Another possible meeting place is Athens, perhaps at the time when Lasus was active there.[52]

There is no evidence for Simonides' dates here. The exact dates of Xenophanes' life are uncertain; but both the commonly accepted dating of Xenophanes[53] and the recently proposed lower dating[54] would allow him to have known Simonides (by acquaintance or repute) whether the latter was born c. 556 or c. 532-29 (Stella's date).

4. "Theognis"

Three passages in the *Theognidea*[55] are addressed to a Simonides who is not further identified. Bowra[56] once advanced the following reasons for thinking that our Simonides could be meant: the first passage seems to echo some of Simonides' words in a lyric poem;[57] references in the second passage to a redistribution of land could (if the author is a Parian) refer to the establishment of a democracy in Paros, which might have taken place when Themistocles, a friend of Simonides, arrived at Paros with a fleet in 480 B.C.;[58] and the third passage might reasonably be directed at one who, like Simonides, addressed Eros as σχέτλιε ("cruel one").[59] Bowra suggested that the author of the three passages, which "are clearly written by one man", could be the elder Euenus of Paros,[60] who could, as a young man, have known Simonides.

The tenuous nature of this case is at once apparent; and Bowra himself later came to believe[61] that Aristotle[62] was probably referring to the younger and better known

Euenus,[63] who was a member of the Socratic circle and could not have known Simonides; Bowra therefore now doubts whether our Simonides was the addressee. (He rejects the view of J. Carrière[64] that the younger Euenus may have addressed poems to our Simonides after his death.) Some others who accept that the younger Euenus is the author of the lines (or of some of them) do not discuss the identity of the Simonides who is addressed;[65] they presumably do not suppose that our Simonides is meant. Another approach is simply to regard the lines as anonymous pieces by different authors;[66] in this case "Simonides" still remains unidentified.

As there is complete uncertainty about the authorship of the lines and the identity of the Simonides addressed, it is clear that no conclusions about the relationships and date of our Simonides can be drawn from these passages of the *Theognidea*.

5. Timocreon

The few explicit references to the relationship of Simonides and Timocreon all indicate that it was unfriendly. A fragment of Aristotle's *Poetics*, quoted by Diogenes Laertius, states:[67]

> A certain Antilochus of Lemnos was a rival of Socrates, according to Aristotle in the third book of the *Poetics*, just as...Timocreon was of Simonides.

A mock epitaph on Timocreon (ascribed to Simonides in the Palatine Anthology) is quoted by Athenaeus:[68]

> Timocreon the Rhodian poet and pentathlete used to eat and drink too much, as the inscription on his tomb shows:
> > "I Timocreon of Rhodes lie here, having eaten a lot, drunk a lot, and slandered people a lot."

The Suda's entry on Timocreon includes the following:

108   SIMONIDES

> He quarrelled with Simonides the melic poet and Themistocles the Athenian, and composed a lampoon (ψόγον) against the latter in the form of a melic poem. And he wrote a "comedy" (κωμῳδίαν)[69] against the same Themistocles and against Simonides the melic poet.

The following epigram is attributed to Timocreon:[70]

> The Cean nonsense has reached me, unwilling though I am.

This epigram repeats the same words in two metrical forms (dactylic hexameter and trochaic tetrameter). The "Cean nonsense" clearly refers to Simonides; Timocreon is perhaps replying to Simonides' mock epitaph on him.[71]

The Suda passage just quoted also mentions a quarrel between Timocreon and Themistocles. The Suda does not state (though it seems to imply) that Timocreon's quarrel with Simonides was connected with his quarrel with Themistocles. Nor does any other ancient authority make such a statement; the abundant evidence for the association of Simonides and Themistocles contains no mention of Timocreon; and similarly, in the evidence for the hostility of Timocreon and Themistocles, there is no mention of Simonides, except in the Suda passage. Nevertheless it is generally assumed by modern commentators that Simonides' quarrel with Timocreon was due to his taking Themistocles' side against Timocreon. I shall assume that this view is correct; but it is not beyond doubt, as the passages quoted seem to provide some evidence of sparring between Simonides and Timocreon on literary matters. If Simonides' quarrel with Timocreon was unconnected with Themistocles, it would be useless to speculate about its occasion or date; very little is known of Timocreon's life or poetry apart from his quarrel with Themistocles, and his dates are only approximately known, his *floruit* being assigned to the period of the quarrel and related events.

The most important source of information on Timocreon and Themistocles is Plutarch's *Life of Themistocles*.[72] After describing how Themistocles (in 480, after Salamis) toured the islands exacting money, and quoting from Herodotus the famous story of the "two gods" with which Themistocles threatened the Andrians, Plutarch states that Timocreon in a lyric poem attacked Themistocles for negotiating the return of some exiles for money but betraying his guest-friend Timocreon for gain; the relevant ode (Timocreon 1/727 Page), which Plutarch quotes in full, elaborates this charge, alleging that "Themistocles, swayed by ill-gotten gains, made no move to restore his guest-friend Timocreon[73] to Ialysus, but accepted three talents of silver and sailed off to the devil, restoring some unjustly, expelling others, and killing others..." Plutarch then adds that, after Themistocles had been exiled and condemned for medism, Timocreon, in whose own sentence of exile for medism Themistocles was said to have had a hand, attacked Themistocles much more bitterly in another poem,[74] the fragments of which, quoted by Plutarch, point out that others besides Timocreon swore oaths with the Medes.

If our assumption is correct, that Simonides' quarrel with Timocreon was due to his siding with Themistocles against Timocreon, the *terminus post quem* for that quarrel is obviously the alienation of Timocreon from Themistocles, which was brought about by Themistocles' failure to restore Timocreon to Ialysus; but modern historians cannot agree as to when Themistocles was in a position to restore, or refuse to restore, a Rhodian exile.[75] Some accept the implication of Plutarch's narrative, that the episode is to be dated to the autumn of 480,[76] when Themistocles toured the islands of the Aegean after the battle of Salamis. However, since Herodotus[77] implies that on this occasion Themistocles went no further than Andros, and there is doubt as to whether a Greek fleet could have operated in the eastern Aegean so early, others prefer to date the incident at some point after the battle of Mycale,[78] perhaps at the time of Pausanias' expedition to Cyprus and Byzantium in summer 478,[79] or perhaps after the foundation of the Delian League in 478/7,[80] possibly as late as 475.[81]

The date of Timocreon's first poem against Themistocles[82] is sometimes treated as a separate question from the date of Themistocles' offence against Timocreon. Thus Wilamowitz and Bowra,[83] who date Themistocles' action to 480, date the poem to 478/7. Podlecki, who assigns the incident loosely to the period after 479, dates the poem c. 470, associating the poem's description of Themistocles as "traitor" with the charge of *prodosia* brought against Themistocles in his absence;[84] but this date for the poem cannot be accepted, as Plutarch explicitly distinguishes the occasion of this poem from that of the next two fragments which do belong to the time of Themistocles' exile. If Timocreon's first poem was substantially later than the incident which provoked it, we cannot be certain that Simonides' quarrel with Timocreon was still in active progress at the time when the poem was composed. This would however be confirmed, if we were to accept the attractive suggestion of Bell,[85] that Simonides' mock epitaph on Timocreon's gluttony is a response to the poem's charge against Themistocles of parsimonious entertaining at the Isthmus.[86]

The *terminus ante quem* for Simonides' quarrel with Timocreon is presumably Simonides' departure from Athens for Sicily in 476; so that the alienation of Themistocles and Timocreon, which put Simonides at odds with Timocreon, must also be before that date. We ought not, then, to follow Beloch in allowing a date as low as 475 for Themistocles' activity at Ialysus.[87]

Simonides' feud with Timocreon is thus to be dated somewhere between 480 and 476; but as we cannot date it precisely, and as we know nothing of its length or intensity, we can hardly use it to argue that Simonides' activity at any given time during the period from c. 480 B.C. was too intense for Simonides to have been as old as the traditional dating represents him.

References

1. Strabo 10.5.6 (486), followed by Stephanus of Byzantium s.v. Ἰουλίς.
2. Suda s.v. Βακχυλίδης.
3. *Et. Mag.* 582.20. The Suda (loc. cit.) gives the form "Medon".
4. Suda loc. cit.
5. Simonides ep. XXVIII Page; Hdt. 7.228.4; *Marm. Par.* ep. 54; and several other references.
6. So, for example, Jebb (1905) p. 1 n. 3; Severyns (1933) 16-7, with a stemma.
7. A. Taccone, *RFC* 36 (1908) 385-8.
8. Stella (1946) 4.
9. Loc. cit. (above, n. 6).
10. A. Körte, *Hermes* 53 (1918) 141-2.
11. 1933: 27 ff.
12. Circa 507-505: see Körte (op. cit. 140-1) for references.
13. Bowra, *Oxford Classical Dictionary*[2] s.v. "Bacchylides"; *Chron. Pasch.* I 304 Dindorf, where Bacchylides' acme is dated Ol. 74,4 (481/0), implying a date of birth (forty years before acme) at 521/0. Severyns (1933: 24 f.) seems to me to demonstrate that the date given by the *Chronicon Paschale* is an error.
14. See the Suda s.v. Λᾶσος. As regards Simonides, fragment 34/539 Page names the title of one of his dithyrambs; ep. XXVIII Page refers to a dithyrambic victory of his; and ep. XXVII credits him with fifty-six such victories.
15. *Marm. Par.* ep. 46; for the text and date of this entry, see Jacoby, *FGrH* II B p. 999 & II C-BD p. 692. On the forty-year interval between Lasus' birth and acme, see Jacoby (1904) 174.
16. Eustathius *Prooem.*, III 296.19-20 & 300.1 Drachmann (cf. *Vita Thomana*, I 4.14-15 Drachmann). Notices of such pupil-teacher relationships are of course very unreliable.
17. References in *RE* "Pindaros" XX 2 (1950) 1611.21 ff.
18. Hdt. 7.6.3.
19. Schwenn in *RE* ib. 1611.61 ff.; Schmid (1929) 544 n. 5.
20. Pickard-Cambridge (1962) 15; Schmid (loc. cit.); Bowra (1961) 318; Brussich (1975-6) 121.

21. See Podlecki (1984) 183.
22. 1965: 20, 87-8.
23. Stella (1946) 20. However Stella is wrong in claiming that we *know* that Lasus was in Athens until c.500.
24. Schmid (1929) 507, 544; Bowra (1961) 318; Pickard-Cambridge (1962) 13.
25. Wehrli (1969) pp. 81-2 (commentary on Chamaeleon frag. 30, from Chamaeleon's περὶ Λάσου, "On Lasus"); Privitera (1965) 48-9, 102. Cf. also Brussich (1975-6) 123.
26. For arguments in support of a general rivalry between Simonides and Lasus, see Brussich (1975-6) 123-4. Cf. also Chapter IV n. 35, above.
27. 1962: 14. Pickard-Cambridge has perhaps been confused by the fact that Pindar is said to have been taught by both Lasus (above, n. 16) and Simonides (Eustath. *Prooem.*, III 297.13-4 Drachmann, and *Vit. Thom.*, I 7.13 Drachmann).
28. Schol. Aristoph. *Vesp.* 1411.
29. 1941: 69.
30. The above remarks depend on the assumption that Christ has at least translated the text of the Aristophanic scholium correctly. He obviously understands the words ἀντὶ τοῦ οὐδέν μοι μέλει τοῦ Σιμωνίδου to mean "instead of Simonides' dictum 'I don't care at all' " (i.e. the scholiast is connecting Lasus' dictum with a similar saying of Simonides). But others (Privitera, loc. cit. [above, n. 25]; Brussich [1975-6: p. 89, A3]) take the words to mean "equivalent in meaning to 'I don't care at all for Simonides' " (i.e. the scholiast is expanding on the meaning of Lasus' dictum as quoted by Aristophanes).
31. Privitera (1965: 19), citing Hdt. 1.209 & 214 and Ctesias, *FGrH* 688 F 13, 19.
32. *Anth. Pal.* 6.213, ascribed to Simonides by the formula τοῦ αὐτοῦ ("by the same author"). A reference to Simonides as glorying in *fifty-five* victories is found in Tzetzes, *Chil.* 4.487; and an apocryphal epitaph on Simonides, apparently modelled on XXVII Page, at *Chil.* 1.636-9.
33. Wilamowitz (1913: 138 & n. 2), who accepts only the first couplet; Geffcken, *RE* "Simonides" III A 1 (1927) 194.27 ff.
34. Though Page doubts even this. (Page's view that the epigram claims *fifty-seven* victories for Simonides seems to be based

on an odd interpretation of the epigram's reference to fifty-six victories "before dedicating this tablet".)

35. So Bergk, Wilamowitz (1913: 138), Diehl, Pickard-Cambridge (1962: 15-16).

36. 1913: 138 n. 2.

37. It is not known, apparently, when boys' contests were introduced at the Dionysia (see Pickard-Cambridge (1962) 16). "Doric partheneia" are attributed to Simonides (Ps. Plut. *Mus.* 17 (1136 f), = Bacchyl. frag. 13A Snell-Maehler; wanting in Page's *PMG* under Simonides); though contests of maiden-choirs did not form part of the Dionysia.

38. Pickard-Cambridge allows this (1962: pp. 15-6; cf. p. 2, p. 36 n. 4, and his index p. 319 s.v. "Dithyramb: at Argos..." etc). Wilamowitz (1913: 138 n. 2) is non-committal. For dithyrambs at non-Dionysiac festivals outside Athens, see Pickard-Cambridge (1962) 3-4.

39. See Pickard-Cambridge (1962) 4 & 35-8, where (besides the Dionysia) the Thargelia, Lesser Panathenaea, Prometheia, Hephaesteia, and Anthesteria, are mentioned in connection with dithyrambs (though Reisch, *RE* Χορικοὶ ἀγῶνες III (1899) 2433.22 ff., implies that such contests may not have been held at the Prometheia or Hephaesteia before the Peloponnesian War).

40. Rohde (1878) 187. An alternative suggestion is that this date represents a synchronism with Anacreon (Rohde 188 n. 1; Jacoby (1902) 203). (Ol. 62 is actually quoted by the Suda, s.v. Σιμωνίδης 439, as an alternative date of birth, but this is usually regarded as an error for the *floruit*; see below, Chapter XII, section 1.)

41. The passage of Syrian is quoted below (Chapter XII, section 1, with n. 1).

42. *Pax* 696-7, with schol.

43. I do not count the notice of Eusebius (II 99 Schoene) which dates their *floruit* to the same period (c. 540-35 B.C.).

44. Xenoph. B 21, I 134 Diels-Kranz (who omit the section translated above as "and so Sophocles...in Samos"). The fragment is assigned by Diels-Kranz to the *Silloi*, as there is testimony (A 22, I 116 D.-K.) that Xenophanes in this work attacked all philosophers and poets; but West (Xenoph. frag. 21) thinks it may belong to Xenophanes' elegies.

45. Cf. van Leeuwen on Aristophanes ad loc. (*Pax* 697-9).

46. However the spelling Σιμωνίδης ("Simonides") in schol. Aristoph. is not in itself proof that our Simonides is meant; for, despite the distinction drawn by Choeroboscus (*Et. Mag.* 713.17 ff.) in the spelling of the names Simonides and Semonides, Σιμωνίδης is usual in the mss. even when the iambographer is meant.

47. Ap. Athen. 14.656 d, Cham. fr. 33 Wehrli (from Chamaeleon's περὶ Σιμωνίδου, "On Simonides").

48. Zuntz (1935: 5 n. 14) further postulates Didymus as an intermediate source between Chamaeleon and the Aristophanic scholium.

49. See Bell (1978: 34-7) for a useful discussion and further suggestions.

50. B 6, I 130 D.-K.

51. Jacoby (1902) 209; so also Bell (1978) 34. For Xenophanes at Hieron's court, see Plut. *Reg. et imp. apophtheg.* 175 c (= Xenoph. A 11, I 115 D.-K.).

52. For an anecdote of a personal encounter between Xenophanes and Lasus, see Plut. *De vit. pud.* 5 (530 e-f) (= Xenoph. A 16, I 115 D.-K.).

53. Born c. 570 or c. 565: still alive c. 478 or 473 (see P. Steinmetz, *Rhein. Mus.* 109 (1966) 13-34, with the references at p. 13 n. 2). L.Woodbury (*Phoenix* 15 (1961) 134-55) supports this dating but arrives at it by a circuitous route, arguing that Apollodorus dated Xenophanes c. 620-530, but then rejecting Apollodorus' dates.

54. I.e. c. 540-440 (H.Thesleff, *On Dating Xenophanes* (Helsinki 1957) passim); approved, with qualifications, by Kerferd in *CR* N.S. 9 (1959) 72.

55. 1.467-96; 1.667-82; 2.1345-50.

56. C.M.Bowra, "Simonides in the *Theognidea*", *CR* 48 (1934) 2-4.

57. 37/542 Page (4 Diehl).

58. Hdt. 8.112.

59. 70/575 Page (24 Diehl).

60. Line 472 (from the first passage) is quoted with a slight textual variation by Aristotle (*Metaph.* 4.5, 1015 a & *Eth. Eud.* 2.7,

1223 a) and ascribed to a Euenus who is not further identified. The very existence of the elder Euenus, whose *floruit* is dated by Eusebius c. 460 B.C., is sometimes doubted: see Reitzenstein, *RE* "Euenos" VI 1 (1907) 976.30 ff.

61. Bowra (1961) 358 & n. 3. Cf. M.Vetta, *Teognide, Elegie, Libro Secondo* (Rome 1980) 121-123.

62. Locc. citt. (n. 60 above).

63. References in Bowra (1961) loc. cit. and *RE* "Euenos" no. 7.

64. *Théognis* (Paris 1948) p. 110.

65. T.Hudson-Williams, *The Elegies of Theognis* (London 1910) 34, who assigns all three passages to Euenus; Reitzenstein *RE* (above, n. 60) 976.22 ff., who thinks the first passage is by Euenus but is doubtful about the second and third.

66. F.Wendorff (*Die aristokratischen Sprecher der Theognis-Sammlung* (Göttingen 1909) pp. 70-1: cf. also p. 26) distinguishes "die alten Aristokraten", the authors of the first two passages, from "der erotische Sprecher" of the third; he thinks that the Σιμωνίδη ("O Simonides!") of line 1349 has been borrowed, as a convenient vocative form, from the first two passages (lines 469 & 667).

67. Aristot. frag. 75 Rose, ap. Diog. Laert. 2.46.

68. Simonides XXXVII Page; Athen. 10.415 f.; *Anth. Pal.* 7.348. It is agreed that Athenaeus is mistaken in referring to the lines as a genuine epitaph.

69. By this term the Suda, which wrongly describes Timocreon as a writer of Old Comedy, must mean some satirical poem.

70. Timocreon 10 West (*Anth. Pal.* 13.31); not in Page.

71. So Bowra (1961) 357-8, followed by Podlecki (1975) 54. With this suggestion Bowra combines the view, held by Bergk and others, that Timocreon is also replying to a Simonidean epigram (17 West) in the same dual metrical form, which itself may have been intended as a skit on the metrical shapelessness of Timocreon's verse.

72. 21.1-7 (122 c-f).

73. N.Robertson (*AJPh* 101 (1980) 64, 67) argues that ξεῖνον ἐόντα in line 5 of the poem means "being a stranger abroad (refugee)" (not "being his guest-friend") and so does not indicate any personal ties between Timocreon and

Themistocles. He even suggests that Timocreon may not really have been a refugee at all, but may have been assuming a role in order to highlight Themistocles' misconduct.

74. Timocreon frags. 2/728 & 3/729 Page, which appear (so Bowra, 1961: 355) to be from a single poem.

75. See Fornara (1966: 257-61) and Podlecki (1975: 51-4) for a discussion of the various possibilities.

76. Wilamowitz (1893) I 138 n. 27; Bowra (1961) 352 ff.; Meritt, Wade-Gery, & McGregor in *ATL* III 185 & n. 10, 191 & n. 26.

77. 8.111-2.

78. Podlecki (1975) 52.

79. Meiggs (1972) 415.

80. Beloch (1912-27) II 2 144 n. 1; Hignett (1963) 277 n. 7; Fornara (1966) 261.

81. Beloch loc. cit.

82. 1/727 Page.

83. Above, n. 76.

84. Podlecki (1975) 52-3; similarly Robertson, op. cit. (above, n. 73) 69.

85. 1978: 41.

86. Timocreon 1/727.10-12. The identification and date of the incident at the Isthmus are discussed by the various commentators cited above.

87. In this connection, we may note that Podlecki (*Rivista storica dell' antichità* 5 (1975) 18-19, 22) suggests that Simonides' poem on Theseus (45/550 Page) may have been written for a refurbishment of the Oschophoria (a festival commemorating Theseus) by Themistocles, as a response by Themistocles to Cimon's foundation of the Theseia after his "discovery" of the bones of Theseus c. 474. This would prolong the working relationship of Simonides and Themistocles beyond the traditional date of Simonides' departure for Sicily; and Podlecki elsewhere challenges the usual view that Simonides remained in Sicily from c. 476 until his death (see below, Chapter IX, n. 127).

Chapter 6

Simonides' Thessalian Period

Simonides was for some time under the patronage of the leading noble houses of Thessaly. The evidence for the poet's own activity is, as usual, confined to a few fragments and references; but the picture of this phase of his life is further obscured by a similar lack of evidence for contemporary Thessalian history. Little is known of the persons with whom Simonides dealt, of their dates, positions of power, and relationships with each other; Thessaly, indeed, remains in the "Dark Ages"[1] until the close of the fifth century. To balance the lack of facts there is an abundance of conflicting theories.

The only honest aim of a study of Simonides' Thessalian period is a modest one — to set out the evidence for Simonides' relationships with the main Thessalian houses, distinguishing known facts from conjecture; to draw some tentative conclusions when the evidence is strong enough; and (perhaps most important) to decide whether the evidence of dating suggests acceptance or rejection of Stella's Simonidean chronology.

1. Simonides' connections with the Aleuadae

Among Simonides' Thessalian patrons were the Aleuadae, "sons (or descendants) of Aleuas", who were in historical times one of the most powerful and influential houses of the Thessalian feudal aristocracy. The seat of the Aleuadae was Larissa, in the tetrad or tetrarchy of Pelasgiotis. Their influence extended at times over a wider area of Pelasgiotis and over the Perrhaebi to the north. At times, also, the family held the office of *tagos*, the commander of the *koinon* or Thessalian national state which was formed in times of emergency by a union of the tetrarchies.[2]

Simonides' connections with the Aleuadae are firmly, if sparsely, attested.[3] Theocritus[4] refers to the wealth of various noble houses of Thessaly in the form of the large number of serfs living "in the halls of Antiochus and king Aleuas", and the large herds belonging to the Scopadae and Creondae; he adds that they had no enjoyment of this wealth after their death, and would have lain forgotten, if Simonides had not made them famous; their horses, who won victories for them at the games, also won their share of honour. It is thus clear that in alluding to Simonidean poems for Antiochus, Aleuas, and the Scopadae, Theocritus is thinking primarily of epinicians for chariot- or horse-racing. Neither Theocritus' text nor the scholia[5] on the passage show whether more than one epinician for each of the families was known. No other poems for Aleuas are known; it is not clear whether the reference to dirges, in the scholium on line 44, concerns Aleuas, as well as Antiochus and Scopas, for whom dirges are known. The allusion to the serfs and cattle owned by these families may be based on Simonides' poems,[6] or may be made by Theocritus on his own authority.

Whether we know anything further about Simonides' patron Aleuas, described by Theocritus' scholiast as "son of Simus", depends on his possible identification with the person or persons named as "Aleuas" by various ancient authors.

In the tenth *Pythian* ode, Pindar refers to his hosts, who include Thorax, as "sons of Aleuas".[7] Pindar's language[8] suggests that Thorax and his brothers hold a position in Thessaly comparable to that of the Spartan kings, and Thorax is usually assumed to have been *tagos* at least as early as 498 B.C. (the date of *Pythian* 10).[9] Herodotus[10] refers to the Aleuadae as "kings of Thessaly" (one of them no doubt being *tagos*), and makes Mardonius address Thorax and his brothers as "sons of Aleuas";[11] Thorax was presumably still *tagos* in 480-79. It seems reasonable to identify Simonides' patron, Aleuas son of Simus, with Aleuas father of Thorax, as no other historical Aleuas is known who could have been Simonides' patron. Aleuas presumably died before 498, by which time his son Thorax held the *tageia*.

We hear of an early Aleuas designated as "the Red" (ὁ Πυρρός), who played an important part in the political and military organisation of Thessaly;[12] his accession to power is described romantically by Plutarch,[13] who adds that he advanced his race to great fame and power. It is presumably Aleuas the Red who is regarded as the ancestor of the house[14] and described as "descendant of Heracles",[15] who appears on the fourth-century Aleuas-coin,[16] and of whom a fanciful story is told by Aelian.[17] Opinions differ as to whether Aleuas the Red is a historical personage,[18] to be dated in the latter part of the seventh century,[19] or a wholly mythical ancestor.[20] Aleuas the Red has occasionally been identified with Aleuas son of Simus, as early as Boeckh[21] and as recently as Sordi, who argues for a vigorous *tageia* of Aleuas the Red, son of Simus, succeeding an equally vigorous joint *tageia* of Scopas and Antiochus.[22] On the other hand, this identification was rejected as early as Buttmann[23] and is not generally accepted (Sordi's views were doubtfully received by reviewers).[24] I feel that the nature of the stories surrounding Aleuas the Red sets him earlier in time than circa 500 B.C. (whether he was a historical figure embellished with legend or a complete myth); further, the distinctive (though not incompatible) titles Aleuas the Red and Aleuas son of Simus rather suggest two persons; and I shall assume that Aleuas the Red has nothing to do with Simonides.

The question whether the various Thessalian patrons of Simonides held the office of *tagos* is relevant to our enquiry, for we have to ask whether *tagoi*-lists are of use for determining their dates. However there is doubt about the position and power of Simonides' patron Aleuas. Theocritus' phrase[25] ἄναξ Ἀλεύας ("king Aleuas") does not prove that he was *tagos*, as ἄναξ Θεσσαλίας ("king of Thessaly") would have done, and Meyer[26] rightly leaves this question open.

Ovid[27] refers to an Aleuas of Larissa who was clearly the victim of a conspiracy:

> quosque putas fidos, ut Larissaeus Aleuas,
>   vulnere non fidos experiare tuo.

The identification[28] of this Aleuas with Simonides' patron is plausible, for the story is hardly compatible with the veneration of Aleuas the Red, and no other *Larissaeus Aleuas* is known.[29] If Aleuas son of Simus, father of Thorax, *was* murdered by conspiracy, it is somewhat sinister to find his sons shortly afterwards in full control of Thessaly. Sordi[30] suggests that the conspirators were only a minority in Thessaly and that the Aleuad house remained powerful enough for Aleuas' sons to hold the *tageia*; certainly *quosque putas fidos* would apply to any internal conspiracy, and need not imply that the sons were involved; but we can only guess at the answer.

We cannot tell whether Thorax and his brothers, on coming to power, continued to employ Simonides, the poet employed by their father. Relevant in this connection is a passage of Sozomenus, who, in flattery of Theodosius, states that his generosity towards his clients outstrips the treatment of Homer by the Cretans, of Simonides by the Aleuadae, of Plato by Dionysius, and of Theopompus by Philip of Macedon.[31] Different interpretations have been placed on the passage. Firstly, how did the "Aleuadae" here mentioned treat Simonides? Sozomenus is certainly comparing them unfavourably with Theodosius, who is said to excel all the ancients in generosity. Schneidewin[32] thinks the reference to the Aleuadae is disparaging, the passage meaning that they did not reward Simonides as they ought. But Sozomenus surely means that Theodosius was even more generous (if less ostentatious) than the Aleuadae and the other patrons named,[33] so that there is no suggestion here of any friction between Simonides and the Aleuadae. Secondly, who are the "Aleuadae" referred to? The most likely answer is that the term means "the Aleuad family", so that Sozomenus could be referring to Simonides' employment (already attested by Theocritus) by Aleuas son of Simus. It is not necessary to suppose that Sozomenus meant "sons of Aleuas" or thought that Simonides was employed by Thorax and his brothers, the "sons of Aleuas" and patrons of Pindar,[34] though this remains a possibility.

Evidence that Simonides wrote for Hippocleas, for whose victory in the *diaulos* the sons of Aleuas commissioned Pindar to write *Pythian* 10, has been sought in the scholia on that poem,[35] which say that Hippocleas was also at the same time victor in the *stadion* (which Pindar does not mention); the conclusion has been drawn that the *stadion*-victory was celebrated by another poet, namely Simonides;[36] but this can only be regarded as speculative.

There is thus no firm evidence that Simonides wrote for the sons of his patron Aleuas; that is, we cannot tell whether, after the succession of Thorax, Simonides was replaced by Pindar in the service of the Aleuadae or employed by them simultaneously with Pindar. In either case, the situation contains the seeds of potential rivalry between the two poets.

2. Simonides' connections with the Scopadae

We have much more evidence for Simonides' relations with the Scopadae. Theocritus attests epinicians written for the Scopadae or Creondae;[37] Cicero and Quintilian refer to an ode to Scopas praising the Dioscuri,[38] which may well be one of the epinicians mentioned by Theocritus. The famous poem on the nature of *arete*, quoted by Plato, was written for Scopas.[39] The scholia on Theocritus[40] state that Scopas and his family were mentioned in Simonides' dirges, and Stobaeus quotes from a dirge in which Simonides laments the destruction of the Scopadae.[41]

The seat of the Scopadae is given as Crannon by several sources. The Scopadae may have had connections with Pharsalus; the name of the mother of Scopas, Echecrateia, is similar to that of the ruling house of Pharsalus, the Echecratidae, and it is usually assumed that the two houses were connected by marriage; further, the majority of Quintilian's sources[42] put the Scopad disaster at Pharsalus. It is quite likely, then, that the Scopadae had a second seat here.[43] The power of the Echecratidae, both c. 500 and in the fifth century, as well as the probable marriage-tie, make it likely that the connection was one of goodwill or mutual interest, not a dominance by Crannon over Pharsalus.

Simonides' patron, son of Creon and Echecrateia, may be identified with virtual certainty as the Scopas, son of Creon and grandson of Scopas the Elder, whose bibulous habits are mentioned by Phaenias of Eresus in his work *The Destruction of Tyrants by Vengeance*.[44] With Scopas the Elder (ὁ παλαιός), grandfather of our Scopas and clearly a historical figure, we are on firmer ground than with Aleuas the Red. He is usually identified with the person referred to in Xenophon's statement[45] that the amount of tribute laid on the subordinate Perioeci was fixed in the time of Scopas (ἐπὶ Σκόπα); and he is conjecturally dated to the earlier half of the sixth century and given the title of *tagos*.[46] If this is correct, the family once held the leading position in Thessaly, and had fulfilled a role in the early organisation of Thessaly comparable to that claimed by the Aleuadae for Aleuas the Red; but this tells us nothing about the status of Simonides' patron.

But may Xenophon's Scopas be the son of Creon, patron of Simonides? This view, occasionally advanced in the past,[47] is revived and argued with considerable verve and eloquence by Sordi.[48] According to her, Scopas son of Creon, a military commander of genius exercising jointly with Antiochus a vigorous *tageia* c. 510-506, subdued and imposed tribute on the Perioeci. This is quite opposed to the usual opinion of historians, according to which the Perioeci were subdued early in the sixth century, whereas the latter part of the sixth century saw a decline in Thessalian fortunes.[49] Sordi's view, which is of some interest to a study of Simonides' relationships but not of vital importance except as concerns the date of his patrons, has not yet been tested by time, though the first reviews were rather sceptical.[50] Sordi's arguments concern the historical development of the Thessalian *koinon* and Thessaly's relations with Athens, Sparta, and especially the Delphic Amphictyony — topics which lie beyond the scope of this study and on which I am not competent to pronounce. I venture only one or two points, not calling for expert knowledge, which seem to weigh against Sordi's view. Sordi rightly says Xenophon assumed that his readers would not doubt which Scopas was meant. She argues that Scopas son of Creon was the Scopas famous in Xenophon's time; and it is true that there are more references to him in both Greek and Latin authors than to Scopas the Elder. However the fact that Simonides' patron is particularised in our earliest sources[51] as "son of Creon", whereas his grandfather is adequately designated as "the Elder" (ὁ παλαιός) suggests that the latter was better known (his fame perhaps comparable to that of Aleuas the Red) and that he is *the* Scopas to whom Xenophon refers. Secondly Sordi admits that we hear much of Scopas' riches, his bibulous and convivial habits, and his sudden extinction, but nothing of the military genius which is a vital part of Sordi's case. The simplest conclusion is that nothing was known of him as a military genius. It seems wisest to follow the conventional view that the role Xenophon allots to "Scopas", and the position of power in Thessaly which this implies, belong to Scopas the Elder, not to Simonides' patron.

There is no firm evidence, then, that our Scopas was *tagos* of Thessaly (so that *tagoi*-lists are probably of no help in determining his date). He seems to have been designated as τύραννος ("absolute ruler") by Phaenias,[52] but this, like ἄναξ Ἀλεύας ("king Aleuas"), falls short[53] of titles like Θεσσαλίας βασιλεύς ("king of Thessaly").

He was fond of drinking and conviviality, and vain displays of luxury.[54] He won victories with horse-teams; but because of his position as *tyrannos* (and his convivial habits?) it is unlikely that he entered boxing contests;[55] this cannot, however, be completely ruled out. The petty refusal of a request by a certain "Scopas the Thessalian"[56] would not be inconsistent with a usual lavish and ostentatious hospitality, but the identification with our Scopas is quite uncertain. The petulant withholding of Simonides' fee described by Cicero and Quintilian would not be out of character for a normally generous but capricious autocrat; but I suggest elsewhere[57] that this story may have been wrongly attached to Scopas.

Scopas was most famous or notorious in antiquity for the manner of his death; he was said to have perished with most of his family in the collapse of a banqueting hall, from which Simonides is reported to have had a narrow escape. The story is alluded to by Callimachus, told at length by Cicero and Quintilian (who cites Apollodorus, Eratosthenes, and Euphorion), and echoed by several later authors.[58] These accounts are almost certainly based originally on a dirge in which, according to Favorinus, Simonides "describes the mass destruction of the Scopadae".[59]

Most modern historians have been ready to accept that some such collective disaster overtook the family of the Scopadae. There have been occasional dissentient voices; it was once suggested that the story of the collapse of the hall arose from the literal interpretation of a figurative statement, a view which has recently been revived;[60] indeed it seems to be the current fashion to reject almost the whole of the Greek biographical tradition as fictional variations on literary *topoi*. However, it seems excessively sceptical to dismiss as fiction the mass extinction of a notable ruling house, within the historical period, when the events were attested for our authorities by the surviving works of a contemporary poet,[61] probably in the form of a dirge written specially for the occasion; and the preservation by Quintilian of some odd snippets of information about the identity of the victims lends credence to the account.[62] Whether Simonides' escape from his host's fate is fictional or (in some degree) historical is a more open question; but it is quite possible that this aspect of the incident (without the supernatural element of the intervention of the Dioscuri) featured in Simonides' poem on the disaster.

It might seem a reasonable deduction, from the title of the work of Phaenias in which Scopas was mentioned (*The Destruction of Tyrants by Vengeance*), that the collapse of the house, if it is accepted as historical, was due to a political plot.[63] However Phaenias, even if he did attribute the disaster to a conspiracy, may not have claimed to possess any evidence, but may have been candidly indulging in conjecture. He may have been discussing *tyrannoi* and their death by violence, and remarked that in the case of the Scopadae no such action was necessary, the gods having put an effective end to the house. The reason for thus evading the simplest conclusion from Phaenias' title is the sheer difficulty of imagining such a collapse being successfully engineered by plotters armed only with the technical resources of 500 B.C., especially if they are supposed to have timed the collapse accurately enough to effect Simonides' rescue.[64] It is simpler to assume that the collapse was an accident, due to a structural failure or earth tremor.

Some attention has been focussed on the son of Scopas' sister who is mentioned by Quintilian as one of the victims. It has been suggested[65] that Antiochus, ruler of Pharsalus, is meant, his mother Dyseris thus being the sister of Scopas; and that the dirge in which Simonides laments the Scopadae is his dirge on Antiochus.[66] This view has some attraction at first sight: the Echecratid and Scopad houses were probably connected by one marriage (between Echecrateia and Creon, father of Scopas), and there could have been another; Antiochus died comparatively young, for Simonides' ode shows the grief of Dyseris his mother; the disaster may have occurred at Pharsalus, the seat of Antiochus; and, if the sister's son is Antiochus, this "would account for Quintilian singling him out" (Morrison). But there are considerable drawbacks. Antiochus' death is mentioned twice[67] and no reference is made to the disaster. The disaster is mentioned several times in connection with Scopas but never with Antiochus. The failure of writers to connect the disaster with Antiochus would be surprising; it could not have been due to ignorance, as the dirge to Antiochus was still extant in Aristides' time, and his death in the disaster would have been common knowledge. It is probable that the anonymous "son of Scopas' sister" is someone less prominent than Antiochus, ruler of Pharsalus and *tagos* of Thessaly. He is perhaps singled out by Quintilian as being (on his father's side) outside the family of the Scopadae, and may have belonged to one or other of the noble houses of Thessaly.

Ovid refers to the collapse of the house, and Simonides' escape, in these lines (*Ibis* 511-12):

> lapsuramque domum subeas, ut sanguis Aleuae,
>   stella Leoprepidae cum fuit aequa viro.

Some have concluded from these lines that the Scopadae and Aleuadae were akin.[68] Others[69] maintain that Ovid is mistaken, and has confused the Aleuadae and Scopadae in his recollection of the story (this is not difficult to accept, as he has mentioned Aleuas shortly before).[70] With our knowledge it is almost impossible to decide. It might be possible to acquit Ovid of error, and at the same time to accept the usual view of the Aleuadae and Scopadae as separate and perhaps rival[71] houses, if the Scopadae, like the Aleuadae and perhaps other Thessalian houses, claimed to be Heracleidae,[72] and if *sanguis Aleuae* could express this. The question is relevant, though not vital, to our study of Simonides; if the Scopadae and the Aleuadae were alien and rival houses, we have an early and minor example of Simonides' "diplomatic immunity" or ability to work for mutually hostile parties.

3. Simonides' connections with the Echecratidae

First the evidence for Simonides' employment by the Echecratidae may be cited. Theocritus shows that Simonides wrote epinicians, for victories in chariot- or horse-racing, for an Antiochus who is mentioned in the same breath as Aleuas and the Scopadae; and the scholiast on the passage,[73] citing Simonides, says that Antiochus was the son of Echecratidas and Dyseris. Aristides mentions a lament by Dyseris over the dead Antiochus; this is almost certainly a reference to a dirge of Simonides,[74] for Aristides has mentioned Simonides a line or two earlier, and we know that the poet wrote for Antiochus himself.

Next, some evidence for the history of this family. An epigram from the Anthology refers to an offering to Dionysus by Echecratidas, described as Θεσσαλίας ἀρχός ("ruler of Thessaly") and so presumably *tagos*, who may be the father of Antiochus. Another epigram refers to the dedication of a robe by a Dyseris; no clue to her identity is given, but she may be the mother of Antiochus.[75] Thucydides[76] mentions a second Echecratidas,[77] Θεσσαλῶν βασιλεύς ("king of the Thessalians") and so apparently *tagos*; his son Orestes, being banished, sought help from the Athenians, who made an abortive attempt to restore him to Thessaly (c. 457 B.C.). Echecratidas II could well be the son of Antiochus and grandson of Echecratidas I.[78]

The name of Antiochus himself occurs in two passages in connection with the well-known Milesian hetaera Thargelia. The first passage cites a fragment of Aeschines Socraticus:[79]

> Aeschines the disciple of Socrates...did not hesitate to speak like Gorgias in his dialogue on Thargelia, for he says something like this: "Thargelia of Miletus came to Thessaly and associated (ξυνῆν) with Antiochus of Thessaly, who was king of all the Thessalians".

The second passage is found in the anonymous treatise *On Women*:[80]

> Thargelia of Miletus. They say that when Antiochus was king of the Thessalians she arrived in Thessaly and married Antiochus, and that after his death she ruled Thessaly for thirty years, and that when the Persian king was leading his expedition against Greece, she received him and having proved herself in no way inferior to him[81] she sent him on his way.

There are also a number of sources which mention Thargelia alone; common themes are her beauty, intelligence, resource, and frequent marriages or liaisons; in Hesychius[82] this last theme appears in the statement that she "commanded cities and potentates" and "married very many distinguished men". Some individual items of additional information are that she was killed by an Argive whom she had imprisoned;[83] and that she won over to the Great King all those who associated with her, and, as these were men of great power and influence, spread medism through the Greek cities.[84]

The phrase "king of (all) the Thessalians", in the first two passages cited, is fair evidence that Antiochus was *tagos* of Thessaly, so that *tagoi*-lists may be used as evidence for his date. The fact that his mother Dyseris lived to lament him suggests that he died comparatively young, in the prime of life, but not necessarily in early youth. When Antiochus held the *tageia*, his father Echecratidas I, who may himself have been *tagos*, was probably dead; but this could not be inferred from the fact that Aristides mentions only the laments of his mother Dyseris, as Costanzi[85] seems to suggest. As Antiochus may have died fairly young, and the *tageia* was soon in the hands of the Aleuadae, Echecratidas II may still have been a minor at Antiochus' death.[86]

For the sake of simplicity and clarity I have accepted the view that this family ruled at Pharsalus as a separate aristocratic house, usually called the "Echecratidae", though as a generic the name has no ancient authority. The only real evidence for this is that the Athenian expedition attempting to restore Orestes laid siege to Pharsalus,[87] which is therefore assumed to be the seat of the family. Historians often assume rivalry between the Aleuadae of Larissa and the Echecratidae of Pharsalus.[88] Another view is that the "Echecratidae" were really Aleuadae, their home being the Aleuad stronghold of Larissa; Theocritus' line[89] "in the halls of Antiochus and king Aleuas" is sometimes quoted as evidence that Antiochus and Aleuas were akin and their *domoi* one,[90] but the line seems to me to prove nothing of the kind. Of more weight is Pausanias' notice[91] that the first offering at Delphi was made by "Echecratides a man of Larissa", whom some regard as the grandfather of Echecratidas I (father of Antiochus); but he is a very remote and shadowy figure, and on the whole it seems best to follow the clue provided by Thucydides' reference to the siege of Pharsalus. A third view is that the "Echecratidae" were simply Scopadae;[92] this is a possible conclusion from the name of Scopas' mother (Echecrateia) and the Scopad connections with Pharsalus.

There are no anecdotes about Simonides' relations with the Echecratidae, who remain little more than names to us. We cannot tell whether his employment by the family ended with his dirge on Antiochus. There is some possibility that he may have met Anacreon[93] at Pharsalus.

4. Works for other Thessalians

The only firm piece of evidence for Simonides' employment by any other Thessalian patrons is some papyrus fragments of an epinician for a victory in the horse-race, written for the "sons of Aeatius".[94] The papyrus does not name Simonides; but the fragments are confidently assigned to him because the title "for the horse-race" (κέλητι) resembles other titles of Simonides' epinicians[95] and is different from the titles of the epinicians of Pindar and Bacchylides. The mention of Zeus and Apollo in the first fragment seems to refer respectively to victories in the Olympian (or Nemean) and the Pythian games. In the second fragment, references to appointing someone "king with full authority (βασιλῆα τελεσφόρον) over those that dwell around" and to "happiness for the whole people (or every people: παντὶ δάμωι) of the Thessalians" may indicate that the family held the office of *tagos*. It is of course possible that the words quoted refer to mythical events; but even so, the most likely use of such a myth would be as a paradigm for a contemporary situation.

The name Aiatios is not found elsewhere; but various forms of a name closely resembling it (e.g. Aiatos) are attached in a number of sources to a member of the legendary Heraclid family to which Thessalus, the eponymous ancestor of the Thessali, belonged, the line of descent being: Heracles, Thessalus, Pheidippus, Aeat(i)us, Thessalus.[96] This Aeatius (Aiatos in our sources) is said to have campaigned against the Boeotians who formerly lived in Thessaly. Lobel's proposal to restore the name Aiatios (Aeatius), from the papyrus, in all the relevant sources has won general approval.

Gentili,[97] rightly noting that the Aleuadae of Larissa claimed to be Heraclids, seems to imply that Aeatius and his sons must have been Aleuadae also. This is a little too precise; for it is extremely likely, and is accepted by many commentators, that other noble Thessalian families claimed descent from Thessalus, the eponymous Heraclid ancestor of the Thessali. We ought to be content to say that the poem was written for some noble Thessalian family, which apparently at some time held the *tageia*.

Finally, there are two epigrams which may possibly belong to Simonides' Thessalian period. The first of these is quoted from Callistratus' *Miscellanies* (Σύμμικτα) by Athenaeus in connection with an anecdote about Simonides;[98] it was said that while Simonides was dining "with some people", his wine was served without the cooling snow which the other guests received and that he improvised the following epigram requesting some:

> Of that with which the swift north wind, rising from Thrace, covered the flanks of Olympus, and which chilled the hearts of men without cloaks and was buried alive, wrapping itself in Pierian earth,[99] let someone pour me a share; for it is not right to drink a friend's health with warm wine.

Wilamowitz remarked[100] that the epigram's mention of Olympus as the source of the wine-cooling snow shows that the hosts are Thessalian princes (only princes being able to command this luxury); and while not insisting that the verses must be genuine, he thinks they show that a sojourn of Simonides in Thessaly was remembered. We might add that if the epigram's reference to Mt. Olympus as the source of the snow is taken at face value, the seeming impossibility of carrying unmelted snow from Olympus to the seats of Simonides' known Thessalian patrons in the Thessalian plain (Larissa, Crannon, and Pharsalus) might suggest that the anecdote linked Simonides with some noble house of northern Thessaly, for example at Gonnus just south of Olympus. Gonnus may have been the seat of Cineas, who was *tagos* about 511 B.C.;[101] so the epigram and anecdote may perhaps reflect a memory of an association of Simonides with the apparently powerful, but otherwise unknown, Cineas.

Page is more sceptical than Wilamowitz about the origin of the epigram, regarding it as one of a number of "fictitious epigrams designed by the author of an anecdotal biography to add substance and colour to his narrative". The epigram, with its accompanying anecdote, is in similar vein to the parody of Homer improvised, according to Chamaeleon, by Simonides at Hieron's court when a dish failed to reach him;[102] and it is possible that Callistratus' source for our epigram was either similar to that used by Chamaeleon or Chamaeleon himself.[103] Our epigram also has features of the riddle, but with the localised and personal element lacking in some of the riddles (probably of popular origin)[104] which are ascribed to Simonides. Episodes of this type, representing the *sophos* at court, are discussed by Bell[105] in the context of the anecdotal tradition. The epigram's claims to authenticity are thus not generally rated very highly; but perhaps one should not entirely exclude the possibility that it may belong to the category of non-inscriptional elegiac poems (sometimes short, personal, and occasional pieces) which are agreed to have been preserved with a genuine tradition of authorship, as in the case of Archilochus and others.

The other relevant epigram is quoted by Pollux:[106]

> Simonides made famous the Thessalian Lycas, by composing the following *epigramma* for the hound's grave:
>
> "Even though you are dead, I think that the wild beasts still tremble at your white bones in this tomb, huntress Lycas; lofty Pelion knows your worth, and far-seen Ossa, and the lonely heights of Cithaeron."

Page is ready to follow Peek in supposing that this epigram may be a copy of an actual inscription, but does not accept Peek's dating of the epigram to the fifth century; he firmly assigns it to the Hellenistic period on grounds of tone and linguistic forms.

If the epigram is a genuine inscription, the combination of Thessalian place-names with the reference to Cithaeron must somehow be accounted for; by supposing, for instance, that the hound served different owners in different localities, or by taking the lines to mean that its fame spread from Thessaly as far as Cithaeron, or (somewhat desperately) by trying to reconcile the apparent reference to the Boeotian Cithaeron with a Thessalian provenance.[107] An alternative approach is to suppose that the piece is a literary composition by some writer who simply threw the names of three mountains together without regard for geography. In any case the epigram tells us nothing further about Simonides' activities in Thessaly, though its ascription to him may help to confirm that his Thessalian period was remembered as a significant phase of his career.

5. General Survey of Simonides' activity in Thessaly; dates of his association with his Thessalian patrons.

What brought Simonides to Thessaly? The usual view, that he left an Athens made uncongenial by the murder of his host Hipparchus[108] or by the expulsion of Hippias[109] in order to seek refuge with the Thessalians (whose affinities with the tyrants of Athens are well-known), may be correct but cannot be proved; it depends, of course, on the acceptance of the traditional chronology of Simonides' life. If Stella's revised chronology, which denies his Pisistratid connections, were accepted in broad outline,[110] Simonides would have come to Thessaly as a young poet, seeking experience in a comparatively remote area, perhaps after some initial successes nearer home, before achieving his greatest fame at Athens or Syracuse. Our meagre knowledge of the poet's activity in Thessaly provides only one slender clue to his age at the time, viz. that the poem for Scopas does not sound like the work of a young man;[111] and the wide range of dates which we must allow for Simonides' work for Scopas means that this clue is of no help in determining the poet's date of birth.

Would Simonides find Thessaly congenial? The reference to ungenerous treatment by his host, Scopas, might be taken as evidence of Thessalian boorishness; but the story of Scopas' insult is probably mistaken. Be that as it may, the general reputation of Thessaly as a backward area is well established.[112] Political and urban development lagged far behind the rest of Greece. The Thessalians were noted for garish extravagance, primitive superstition, and treachery. The anecdote about Simonides' description of the Thessalians as "too ignorant to be deceived by me", whether true or not, and whatever the meaning of "deceive" here, shows a belief in antiquity in the Thessalians' intellectual inferiority.[113] The entertainment of poets by the noble houses of Thessaly might be nothing but a token of ostentatious patronage, a "veneer of fictitious appreciation of the arts".[114] Yet the presence, at some time, of each of the three great choral lyric poets in Thessaly suggests that the Thessalians were able to provide choirs to perform the complexities of choral lyric — a feature that is strangely at variance with the general picture of Thessalian backwardness. It is not known why Simonides left Thessaly.

Smyth's suggestion that he was prompted to leave by Thessalian medism[115] could be right, but is not supported by any evidence.

The date of Simonides' visit to Thessaly is vital to the whole question of Simonidean chronology raised by Stella. Works of reference frequently offer dates (which vary widely) for the *floruit* of Simonides' patrons, or for his stay in Thessaly; sometimes reasons for these dates are given, sometimes not. It is necessary to clear the ground, and either to confess ignorance or to accept only dates based on some ancient authority.

If the identification of Aleuas Simonides' patron with Aleuas father of Thorax is correct, a *terminus ante quem* for any odes for Aleuas is supplied by Pindar's tenth *Pythian*, dated 498. This ode strongly suggests that Thorax and his brothers are now in control of Thessaly, and it is virtually certain that their father Aleuas is no longer alive, though we cannot tell how long it is since they succeeded Aleuas at Larissa. On this basis, Simonides' odes for Aleuas could belong to any time within the two or three decades before 498. It is uncertain whether Aleuas was *tagos*; but if he was, the question of date is complicated by attempts to compile *tagoi*-lists. It seems clear that a certain Cineas, described as the *basileus* of the Thessalians, was *tagos* in 511, the usually accepted date of the Thessalian expedition to Athens commanded by him.[116] Aleuas' *tageia* would therefore have to begin and end either before or after 511. It is not of course suggested that Aleuas could have entertained Simonides only while *tagos*; but the date of the end of his *tageia* might reasonably be presumed to be the date of his death.

The families of the Scopadae and Echecratidae were apparently, as we have seen, connected by marriage; and attempts are sometimes made to fix the relative dating of members of these families (especially Scopas and Antiochus) by the degree of kinship between them. However such attempts should be ignored, as the degree of kinship is purely conjectural; Scopas has been variously assumed to be the nephew, the uncle, or the cousin of Antiochus.[117]

A clue to the date of Antiochus is provided by the notice on Thargelia from *Paradoxographoi*,[118] where it is stated that Thargelia ruled Thessaly for thirty years after Antiochus' death and received "the Persian king" when he marched against Greece. Her "rule" over Thessaly presumably consisted in marriages to Antiochus' successors in the *tageia*. The Persian king said to have been received by a Thessalian potentate during an expedition against Greece can only have been Xerxes.[119] The text of the notice implies that Thargelia did not "rule Thessaly" for *more* than thirty years (so Antiochus' death cannot have occurred more than thirty years before her entertainment of Xerxes, i.e. not before 510); but the notice need not imply that her thirty-year rule was at its close c. 480 (so Antiochus' death could be placed some years after 510). As Thorax was *tagos* by 498, Antiochus' death, and vacation of the *tageia*, would thus be between 510 and 498. And as Cineas was *tagos* in 511, Antiochus' accession to the *tageia* must have been after that date, so that his whole period of office must be placed somewhere between 510 and 498.[120]

I see no hope of reaching a more accurate date. It must be admitted that the authorities who supply the clue of Thargelia's thirty-year reign are by no means reliable; but if we are willing to accept the clue, the twelve-year period (510-498) need not be doubted. Earlier dates for Antiochus' reign have been advanced, but are based on even flimsier evidence. Beloch,[121] having first correctly deduced the date of 510 or later for Antiochus' death from the story about Thargelia, then virtually rejects his own conclusions by arguing that, if Cineas was *tagos* in 511, Antiochus must have died before this. In his table of *tagoi* Beloch actually dates Antiochus c. 515. His reason (which he does not explain) for dating Antiochus' death before 511 seems to be that there is hardly time between 511 (Cineas *tagos*) and 498 (Thorax *tagos*) for a *tageia* of Antiochus;[122] but we need not insist that Antiochus held office for several years nor demand a list of equidistant *tagoi*; indeed, it seems that

Antiochus died prematurely. Beloch's tentative *terminus post quem* (520 B.C.) for the beginning of Antiochus' *tageia* rests on the doubtful assumption that this is the likely date of Anacreon's connections with Antiochus' father Echecratidas, who may have preceded his son in the *tageia*.

Meyer's dating of Antiochus[123] is no better supported. From the notices on Thargelia, he rightly sets Antiochus before Xerxes and so before Thorax (who was *tagos* from at least 498 to at least the time of Xerxes) and so in the sixth century. He then proceeds to date Antiochus' reign c. 530-520. His reason is not explicitly stated, but seems to lie in his list of *tagoi*. He accepts a *tageia* of Cineas in 511, and thinks that Aleuas son of Simus may have been *tagos* (before the *tageia* of Thorax, 498). He assumes that Scopas son of Creon was *tagos* (referring to the title of Phaenias' work on the *Destruction of Tyrants*), and that his office followed that of Antiochus (Scopas being supposed to be Antiochus' nephew and the younger man). Antiochus and Scopas are then dated before Cineas, presumably on the reasonable ground that there is scarcely time for three *tagoi* (Antiochus, Scopas, and Aleuas) between 511 and 498. But this list of *tagoi* is conjectural; there is no firm evidence that either Scopas or Aleuas son of Simus was *tagos*, nor that Scopas' mother Echecrateia was sister of Antiochus, and Scopas younger than Antiochus. Meyer's upper limit of 530 for Antiochus' reign may be based on (or at least it coincides with) his establishment of this date as a vague *terminus post quem*, calculated from the traditional date of Simonides' birth (556), for Simonides' Thessalian poems.

Stella,[124] identifying the Persian king entertained by Thargelia as Artaxerxes, dates Thargelia's supposed part in the intrigues of Artaxerxes in Greece to the period c. 470-60. She then proceeds to argue that at this time, if 510 were the correct date of Antiochus' death, Thargelia would be about sixty when she entertained Artaxerxes, which is absurd; therefore Antiochus' death, and Simonides' dirge on him, should be dated much later, c. 475-60; the consequent redating of Simonides' Thessalian activity[125] is adduced in support of Stella's revised Simonidean chronology. This chain of reasoning is easily refuted. The dating of Thargelia's intrigues is based on the false identification of Artaxerxes as the king in question. The argument based on Thargelia's age, which denies the possibility of a long interval between Antiochus' death and the association of Thargelia with the Persian king, is very weak, as there is no reason to suppose that Thargelia entertained the king qua hetaera.

The date of Scopas is the vaguest of all. Beloch,[126] assuming that Simonides was no longer young when he wrote the famous poem for Scopas,[127] dates the poem after 520, and argues from this that the Scopad disaster cannot have been long before 510; though it may, he says, have been ten to twenty years later. Meyer[128] dates the Scopad disaster c. 515; but as we saw in connection with Antiochus, his dates for Scopas are based on some unproved assumptions; Swoboda follows Meyer, and Westlake follows Swoboda, without discussing the matter.[129] Sordi's date of c. 510-506 for Scopas' *tageia* depends on the assumption that Scopas subdued the Perioeci (so after 514, when according to Sordi the Perioeci must have been still independent), and that he was *tagos* after Cineas (who, according to Sordi, was *tagos* in 512) and before Aleuas (whose *tageia* was over by 498 and may therefore have begun c. 506)[130] — all of these very controversial points. Morrison dates the disaster "towards the end of the sixth century", Kahrstedt "a few years" before the beginning of the fifth century; neither offers any reason.[131]

If Scopas was *tagos*, the *terminus ante quem* for the disaster is 498 (when Thorax was already *tagos*); Scopas' *tageia* may then have been either before or after Cineas (511). If Scopas was not *tagos*, the latest date for the disaster is perhaps c. 490, as Simonides was in Athens about the time of Marathon. The earliest possible date is very hard to decide; there is almost no reliable criterion, so that we might postulate almost any date within the last two or three decades of the sixth century. If it is thought[132] that the rise of the rival Aleuadae to the *tageia*, in succession to the related

Scopad and Echecratid houses, is best explained by a disaster to the Scopad house (and if this is made to apply even if Scopas was not *tagos*), then we shall prefer to date the disaster before 498.

Our tentative conclusions on the dates of these various Thessalian patrons may now be summarised. The death of Aleuas is to be dated either c. 498 or an indeterminable number of years before that. The *tageia* and death of Antiochus probably occurred between 510 and 498. The disaster to the Scopads could have occurred at almost any time in the thirty (or more) years before 490.

The essential fact that emerges is this: though the usually accepted dates[133] for Simonides' Thessalian period allow a more comfortable space for his activities in Thessaly than does Stella's Simonidean chronology, there is no definite proof that any of his Thessalian odes must have been written before 500 B.C. Without prejudice to any conclusions we may draw from other sources, Stella (despite flaws in certain of her arguments) is right in maintaining that there is in Simonides' Thessalian activity no positive support for the traditional chronology of his life and no insurmountable objection to Stella's revised chronology.

References

1. Westlake (1935) p. V.
2. On the Aleuadae, and the organisation of Thessaly, see Buttmann (1829) 246-93; Toepffer, *RE* "Aleuadai" I (1894) 1372-4; Kahrstedt (1924) 129, 136; Westlake (1935) 8-9, 14-16, 22-8, 31-2, 36.
3. Stella (1946: 20) and Podlecki (1980: 386) wrongly deny that there is any evidence.
4. 16.34-47.
5. Some items from the relevant scholia (pp. 327-9 Wendel; 24/529 Page) are: (16.34/35a) "...their wealth would have been of no avail for their present reputation, if they had not been sung by Simonides... Euphorion has given a full account of

Aleuas the son of Simus...and Antiochus was the son of Echecratidas and Dyseris, as Simonides says; (16.36/7) Crannon is a city in Thessaly, from which came Scopas of Crannon, the son of Creon and Echecrateia; so Simonides in the Dirges; (16.44) the Cean: he means Simonides, in that he wrote epinicians and dirges for the aforementioned famous men of Thessaly".

6. Podlecki (1980) 383.

7. *Pyth.* 10.5 & 64.

8. Ib. 1-5, 69 ff.

9. I assume that the modern dating of the first Pythiad at 582, and the dating of this ode at 498, is correct. However the old dating of the first Pythiad at 586, which would result in the date of 502 for this ode, is defended by H.C.Bennett, *HSCP* 62 (1957) 61-78, and by S.G. Miller, *CSCA* 11 (1979) 127-58. A.A. Mosshammer (*GRBS* 23 (1982) 15-30) replies in defence of the 582 dating.

10. 7.6.2.

11. 9.58.2.

12. Aristot. frags. 497-8 Rose; Westlake (1935) 25 & n. 1, 26.

13. *De Frat. Am.* 21 (492a-b).

14. Suda s.v. Ἀλευάδαι; Meyer (1909) 238 & n. 3.

15. Ulpian ad Demosth. 1.15.18.

16. Meyer (1909) 239 & n. 1; cf. Westlake (1935) 115, 146-7.

17. *NA* 8.11.

18. So Westlake (1935) 25.

19. Morrison (1942) 61.

20. Buttmann (1829) 252-4,267; Meyer (1909) 238; Wade-Gery, *JHS* 44 (1924) 60.

21. 1811-21: II 2 p. 332.

22. Sordi (1958) 61-8.

23. 1829: 252.

24. See Cawkwell, *JHS* 80 (1960) 223; Westlake, *CR* N.S. 10 (1960) 55-6.

25. 16.34.

26. 1909: 240, 245 n. 1, 249.
27. *Ibis* 323-4.
28. So Buttmann (1829) 281-2; Hiller von Gaertringen (1890) 3; Sordi (1958) 71 n. 6, 83.
29. We may disregard the obscure gymnasiarch at Larissa (219 B.C.) (*RE* "Aleuas" no. 2, I (1894) 1374.49).
30. 1958: 83.
31. Sozomenus, *Hist. Eccles., Praef.* 5, p. 2 Bidez. Cf. especially: οἷον δὲ σεαυτὸν περὶ τοὺς λέγοντας παρέχεις, οὐ τοιοῦτοι... Ἀλευάδαι περὶ Σιμωνίδην.
32. 1835: X-XI.
33. So de Boissi (1788) 20-1, 21 n. 1.
34. De Boissi (ibid.) seems to think that Sozomenus meant this.
35. Schol. *Pyth.* 10 Inscr., II 241-2 Drachmann.
36. Gaspar (1900) 35-6; Severyns (1933) 36. This suggestion is rejected by Wilamowitz (1922) 123 n. 2.
37. It is disputed whether *Kreondai* (Theocr. 16.39) is synonymous with Scopadae, or means "sons of Creon", i.e. Scopas and his brothers (of whom nothing further is known).
38. Cic. *De Orat.* 2.351-3; Quintil. 11.2.11-6; Simonides 5/510 Page. See above, Chapter II, section 1, with nn. 1 & 2.
39. 37/542 Page.
40. Schol. Theocr. 16.36/7 (see n. 5 above).
41. 16/521 Page.
42. Quintil. 11.2.14.
43. See Swoboda, *RE* "Skopadai" III A 1 (1927) 568.1 ff.
44. Phaenias frag. 14 Wehrli, in the Τυράννων ἀναίρεσις ἐκ τιμωρίας.
45. *Hist. Graec.* 6.1.19.
46. Beloch (1912-27) I 2 201-2; Wade-Gery, *JHS* 44 (1924) 57, 60; Swoboda, *RE* "Skopadai" III A 1 (1927) 568.26-39.
47. Hiller von Gaertringen (1890) 4.
48. 1958: 61-5.
49. References in Sordi (1958) 63 n. 1. See also Westlake (1935) 29.

50. See n. 24 above.
51. Plato *Prot.* 339 a; Phaenias frag. 14 Wehrli (see n. 44 above).
52. Ibid.
53. So do the phrases of Cicero (*fortunatum hominem et nobilem, De Orat.* 2.352) and Quintilian (*nobilem Thessalum*, 11.2.15) (cf. Beloch, 1912-27: I 2 202; Swoboda, *RE* "Skopadai" III A 1 (1927) 568.50-6); but too much should not be made of this.
54. Phaenias loc. cit. (above, n. 44); cf. Theocr. 16.39.
55. See Molyneux (1971) 198-200, 204 f., for Quintilian's apparent suggestion that he did so.
56. Plut. *De Cupid. Divit.* 8 (527 c), *Vit. Cat. Mai.* 18 (346 f — 347 a).
57. 1971: 203 f.
58. Most of these authorities are cited by Page, Simonides 5/510.
59. Favorinus quoted by Stobaeus, Simonides 16/521 Page.
60. Flach (1883-4) II 613 n. 3, followed by Busolt (1885-1904) II 283 n. 4; again advanced by Slater (1972: 238), apparently in the belief that it is original, and echoed by Lefkowitz (1981) 55.
61. Lefkowitz (1981: 56) wrongly implies that Quintilian could find no reference to the entire story in Simonides' poems; on the contrary, Quintilian indicates (11.2.14) that Simonides did refer to the disaster. What Quintilian was unable to find (11.2.16) in Simonides' poems was any reference to the intervention of the Dioscuri.
62. The imprecise nature of Quintilian's identification (11.2.15), and the absence of any role for these victims in the story, strengthens the impression of veracity; a fictional account would have been tidier, and would have chosen the victims for some moral or dramatic purpose.
63. Schneidewin (1835) p. XV, followed by Hiller von Gaertringen (1890) 4 n.1, Oates (1932) 14 n. 35, and (tentatively) Morrison (1942) 61 and Huxley (1978) 238. Wehrli's suggestion (1969: p. 32, commentary on Phaenias frag.14) that Phaenias or his source attributed Scopas' death to the vengeance of Simonides for the refusal of his fee, indicates that he has no high opinion of Phaenias' judgement.
64. This too is part of Schneidewin's suggestion.

65. Morrison (1942: 60), followed by Sordi (1958: 64 & n. 3) and Podlecki (1980: 385); cf. also Huxley (1978) 236 n. 36, 237 n. 41.
66. Simonides 16/521 Page (on the Scopadae) and 23/528 (on Antiochus).
67. See below, Section 3 of this chapter, with nn. 74 & 80.
68. Toepffer, *RE* "Aleuadai" I (1894) 1372.63-6; Morrison (1942) 60.
69. Meyer (1909) 240 n. 4.
70. See n. 27 above.
71. Swoboda, *RE* "Skopadai" III A 1 (1927) 568.12 f.; Westlake (1935) 30.
72. Busolt (1885-1904) II 474 n. 2; Sordi (1958) 64.
73. The relevant passage of Theocritus (16.34 ff.) is cited in Section 1 above (with n. 4), and the scholia in n. 5 above.
74. 23/528 Page; Aristid. 31.2, II 212 Keil.
75. The epigrams are Anacreon XIII & VII Page.
76. 1.111.1.
77. He is almost certainly to be distinguished from Echecratidas I, father of Antiochus; see below, Section 5 & n. 120.
78. Beloch (1912-27) I 2 204.
79. Aeschin. Socrat. frag. 22 Dittmar (ap. Philostr. *Epist.* 73, II 257 Kayser); also quoted by Diels-Kranz II 279 A 35, apropos of Gorgias.
80. *Anonymi Tractatus de Mulieribus* XI (A. Westermann, ΠΑΡΑΔΟΞΟΓΡΑΦΟΙ, *Scriptores Rerum Mirabilium Graeci* (Brunsvigae 1839) p. 217).
81. Or "having dealt with him on terms of equality" (μηδὲν ἐλαττωθεῖσαν).
82. S.v. Θαργηλία (II 301 Schmidt).
83. Suda s.v. Θαργηλία. The statement that she ruled the Thessalians for thirty years occurs here also.
84. Plut. *Vit. Pericl.* 24 (165 b). The common themes referred to above occur also in Hippias frag. 4, II 331 Diels-Kranz.
85. 1906-7: p. 76 (= 79).

86. Costanzi (1906-7) 77-8 (=80-1).
87. Thuc. loc. cit. (n. 76 above).
88. Swoboda, RE "Skopadai" III A 1 (1927) 568.1-15; Westlake (1935) 30-4. Cf. Hiller von Gaertringen (1890: 7-8) who sees the death of Antiochus as helping the Aleuads' rise to prominence.
89. 16.34: see above, Section 1, with n. 4.
90. Toepffer, RE "Aleuadai" I (1894) 1372.63-5; Morrison (1942) 60; Sordi (1958) 67.
91. 10.16.8.
92. Busolt (1885-1904) II 474 n. 2.
93. See above, this Section, with n. 75.
94. 6/511 Page, fr.1 (a) & (b); ed. Lobel, P.Oxy. XXV (1959) no. 2431 fr.1 (a) & (b) pp. 88-90.
95. See the titles to 1/506 & 3/508 Page.
96. See Polyaen. Strat. 8.44 (pp. 406-7 Melber); Charax frag. 6 (FGrH II A pp. 484-5); Pausan. Attic. frag. 204 Schwabe; Iliad 2.678-9; Apollod. 2.7.8 (2.166 Wagner); also Schachermeyr RE "Thessalos" VI A 1 (1937) 163.63-164.1; Lobel (P.Oxy. ad loc.); Gentili (1960) 118 ff.
97. 1960: 120, 122.
98. Simonides LXXXVIII Page, 6 West; Callistr. frag. 3 (FGrH III B p. 211) ap. Athen. 3.125 c-d.
99. I.e. the snow, still unmelted, was stored in underground cellars: see Page's commentary.
100. 1913: 142 n. 3.
101. Reference is made in Section 5 below to the *tageia* of Cineas, who is described by Herodotus (5.63.3) as ἄνδρα Κονιαῖον. This appellation cannot be explained in terms of known Thessalian place-names, and the emendation Γονναῖον (of Gonnus or Gonni) has been proposed.
102. Simonides 7 West, quoted by Chamaeleon (frag. 33 Wehrli) ap. Athen. 14.656 c.
103. Boas (1905) 116; Wehrli (1969) 83.
104. Wehrli (1969) 83, on Chamaeleon fr.34 (Simonides 69 & 70 Diehl).

105. 1978: 30-1, 75-6.
106. LXIX Page; Pollux 5.47-8.
107. Thus Wilamowitz (1897: 332 n. 1) speculates on the possibility of a Thessalian homonym of the Boeotian Mt. Cithaeron; as an alternative he toys with the Thessalian names Titaresios (a river) and Titaros (a mountain) without actually proposing an emendation.
108. Schmid (1929) 508.
109. Smyth (1904) 302; Bowra (1961) 323.
110. I.e. if Stella's date for Simonides' birth (c. 532/29) were accepted but the usually accepted approximate dating for his Thessalian period (c. 500) were retained. Stella in fact dates Simonides' activity in Thessaly c. 475-60: see below (this Section, with nn. 124-5).
111. 37/542 Page: see below (this Section, with n. 126).
112. See Westlake (1935) 40 ff.
113. Plut. *De Aud. Poet.* 1 (15 c-d). Simonides was supposedly replying to the question "why are the Thessalians the only ones you do not deceive?". The word "deceive" (ἐξαπατᾶν) has been interpreted here as "beguile by the charm of poetry" (in accordance with Plutarch's context) or "cheat" (which implies that Plutarch has wrongly transferred the Simonidean apophthegm from the realm of dishonest dealings to that of poetic beguilement).
114. Smyth (1904) 302.
115. Smyth ibid. On Thessalian medism, see Westlake *JHS* 56 (1936) 12 ff.; contrast P.A.Brunt, *Historia* 2 (1953/4) 162-3.
116. Hdt. 5.63.3; see above, Section 4 & n. 101.
117. For divergent views on this matter, see Meyer (1909) 244; Morrison (1942) 60; Beloch (1912-27) I 2 202.
118. See above, Section 3 & n. 80; cf. also n. 83 for a similar statement in the Suda.
119. This is universally assumed, the only exceptions known to me being Fiehn (*RE* "Thargelia" V A 2 (1934) 1304.39 ff.) who thinks Darius is meant, and Stella, whose assumption that Artaxerxes is the king in question is discussed below.
120. Acceptance of these dates for Antiochus would mean that Echecratidas I father of Antiochus should almost certainly

be distinguished from Echecratidas II, who ruled at Pharsalus after the Persian Wars and whose son Orestes sought help from Athens c. 457 (see above, Section 3 & n. 76-78). This is the view now held by almost all scholars (contrast however Page (1981) on Anacreon XIII).

121. 1912-27: I 2 203-4, 206, 210.

122. At least, Beloch explicitly advances this argument against a *tageia* of Aleuas son of Simus.

123. Meyer (1909) 242-4, 249.

124. 1946: 13 & n. 2, 23.

125. Stella offers no dates for any of Simonides' other Thessalian poems; she says (pp. 3, 12) that Scopas cannot be dated, and, as already noted, she overlooks the evidence for Simonides' connections with Aleuas.

126. 1912-27: I 2 202.

127. 37/542 Page.

128. 1909: 249.

129. Swoboda *RE* "Skopadai" III A 1 (1927) 569.14 ff.; Westlake, *JHS* 56 (1936) 13 & n. 8.

130. Sordi (1958) 61-5, 83.

131. Kahrstedt (1924) 128; Morrison (1942) 61.

132. So Swoboda *RE* "Skopadai" III A 1 (1927) 569.18-23; Meyer (1909) 244.

133. E.g. c. 509-490, Wilamowitz (1913: 142-3), though he does not think Simonides remained in Thessaly for the entire period; from the fall of the Pisistratids to the medising of the Thessalians, Smyth (1904: 302); from 514 onwards, Schmid (1929: 508); from the fall of the Pisistratids until c. 500, Bowra (1936: 335, 355) or perhaps until c. 490 (id. (1961) 323, 340). These dates have become so canonised for Gentili (1960: 121) that he refers to the "Simonidean period" of Thessalian history ("il periodo per così dire simonideo, che comprende gli anni 510-490").

Chapter 7

Simonides in the Persian Wars I: Marathon to Artemisium

The prominent status of Simonides during the Persian Wars is beyond question, but the number of poems allowed to him varies with the judgement of individual scholars; for a fair proportion[1] of the Simonidean epigrams concerns the events of the Persian Wars. They include the single indisputably authentic epigram, VI Page (on Megistias). The authenticity of the others is open to doubt, though some of them may be authentic; if Simonides is known to have written lyric poems for a given city in commemoration of events in the Persian Wars, it would not be unreasonable to believe that inscriptions for the same city, commemorating the same or related events, may also have been written by him. Most of the Persian War epigrams are "non-controversial"[2] in that they neither conflict with other data on Simonides nor have any direct bearing on the question of his dates. Those few which might be considered "controversial" do not affect the question of his dates, although they are relevant to our account of Simonides' life and work in that they concern his relationship with certain cities; thus the ascription to Simonides of the Corinthian epigrams (X-XIV Page) might appear to clash with evidence which has been thought to indicate hostility between Simonides and Corinth.

1. Marathon

There are several items of evidence which connect Simonides with Marathon, or have been interpreted as so doing. These may first be listed:

(A) Vit. Aesch. p. 332.5 ff. Page (Aeschylus, OCT)

> He (Aeschylus) went away to stay with Hieron; according to some accounts, this was because he had been offended by the Athenians and defeated by the young Sophocles, but according to others because he had been defeated by Simonides in the matter of the *elegeion* on those who died at Marathon; for the *elegeion* tends to be marked by a subtle expression of sympathetic feeling, which, as we have said, is foreign to Aeschylus.

(B) The "Marathon epigrams", Simonides XX (a) and (b) Page

These two fragmentary inscriptions, in lettering of the early fifth century, belong to the same stone, though the epigraphical evidence indicates that (b) was carved after the monument was erected. The text of epigram (a) is supplemented from a fourth-century inscription which is almost certainly a copy of this same epigram. The surviving fragments (with the supplementation) yield sense on the following lines:

> (a) The glory of these men's valour will be imperishable always...the gods may allot; for as infantrymen and on the swift ships they saved the whole of Greece from seeing the day of slavery.

(b) These men had (hearts?) of adamant...when they planted their spear in defence of the gates...having turned back by force (the might? the champions?) of the Persians (who planned?) to burn the city near the sea.

There has been a great variety of opinion on the events referred to in the two epigrams, and on the reason for the appearance of the two epigrams (one carved later than the other) on the same stone.[3] Epigram (a) has been assigned to Marathon;[4] Salamis (with Psyttaleia); Salamis and Plataea; or all the battles of 490-79 or 480-79; and epigram (b) to Marathon; the Plataeans and slaves at Marathon; the encampment at Cynosarges after Marathon;[5] an engagement at Phaleron after Marathon;[6] or Thermopylae and Salamis. The commonest views are that both epigrams refer to Marathon; or that (b) refers to Marathon and (a) to some other events (as specified above). As the only evidence for these epigrams is inscriptional, they are not explicitly linked with Simonides' name; but they must be taken into account in any discussion of Simonides' association with Marathon.

(C) Plut. Quaest. Conviv. 1.10.3 (628 d-e) (= Aeschyl. Test. 12, Radt TGF, and fr. eleg. 1 West)

> Glaucias the rhetorician says that the right wing in the line of battle at Marathon was assigned to the Aiantidae, basing his statement on the elegiac poem (ταῖς ἐλεγείαις) on the battle of Marathon[7] written by Aeschylus, who fought with distinction in this battle.

This passage does not mention Simonides, but its reference to Aeschylus' poem makes it relevant to passage (A).

(D) Marm. Par. ep. 49

> Since Simonides the grandfather (?) of Simonides the poet, being a poet himself also, was victorious at Athens...226 years, in the archonship of Aristides at Athens (489/8 B.C.).[8]

(E) Simonides XXI Page; Lycurg. In Leocr. 109

> So there is accurate testimony to their valour, inscribed on their tombs[9] for all the Greeks to see, for those (the Spartans) [Simon. XXII (b) Page], and for your ancestors:
>
>> "The Athenians, fighting as champions of the Greeks at Marathon, laid low the might of the gold-clad Medes."

The lines are also quoted by Aristides, the scholia to Aristides, and the Suda.[10] The scholia and the Suda quote anonymously, and it is now generally agreed that Aristides does not mean to ascribe the lines to Simonides;[11] so there is probably no ancient authority for their ascription to him.

(F) Simonides 9 West (62 Diehl);[12] Aristoph. Pax 736 ff. and scholia

> (Aristophanes): If then it is right, o daughter of Zeus, to honour one who has proved the best and most famous comic poet, our poet says that he is worthy of great praise.
>
> (Scholia): This is based on the *elegeia* of Simonides:
>
>> "If (it is right?),[13] o daughter of Zeus, to honour whoever is best, I the Athenian people accomplished this alone."

There is no explicit reference to Marathon here, but the wording of the last clause is certainly appropriate to Marathon.

(G) Simonides 63 Diehl;[14] schol. ad Greg. Naz. in Iulian. or. 2 p. 169 d (ed. Piccolomini, Hermes 6, 1872, 489)

> Infallibility, he says, is beyond us mortals. But to recover and correct oneself after making a small error is a characteristic of noble men. Simonides (one of the

nine lyric poets), in an *epigramma* composed for the Athenians who fell at Marathon, has written the following line:

> "To make no mistake and succeed in all things is the mark of a god."

This line is also quoted by Demosthenes[15] as part of the epitaph on the Chaeronea dead. Two interpretations have been placed on this: either the author of the Chaeronea epitaph borrowed the line from a poem on Marathon; or Gregory's scholiast, in assigning the line to Simonides and associating it with Marathon, has mistaken both author and event. There is a corresponding divergence of opinion as to whether the pessimistic tone of the line can be explained in terms of the loss of life which even the triumph of Marathon involved.

(H) Simonides V Page; Anth. Plan. 232 (Σιμωνίδου) ("by Simonides")

> Miltiades set up this statue of me, the goat-footed Pan, the Arcadian, who opposed the Medes and sided with the Athenians.

We may begin with (A), a passage which implies that there was some kind of competition between Aeschylus and Simonides for a poem on the Marathon dead. This anecdote, appearing in a late biographical notice of uncertain pedigree, must obviously be treated with some reserve;[16] but many scholars have been willing to see at least a kernel of truth in it. Among those who accept it, there are two main schools of thought. One of these holds that the relevant poems of Simonides and Aeschylus were elegies.[17] Simonides' elegy has been identified with (F) above, and Aeschylus' elegy with (C) above.[18] A. Barigazzi[19] assigns (F) and (G) to Simonides' elegy. Schmid[20] accepts the story and believes that an elegy is meant; he denies that (F) & (G) belong to this elegy, but makes no positive suggestion for identifying fragments from it. The other school of thought holds that epigrams (i.e. inscriptions) are meant. This is the view of E. Hiller,[21] who tends to believe that passage (E) may be the winning poem of Simonides. Another suggestion that has won a fair amount of support is that the winning and losing epigrams of Simonides and Aeschylus can be identified respectively with (B) (a) and (B) (b) above.[22] To account for the fact that the second epigram ((B) (b)) is carved by a different hand, Oliver suggests that the winning epigram of Simonides was inscribed first, the losing epigram of Aeschylus being added later to quieten criticism of the choice of a "foreigner" (Simonides) for the commission. Of course, the identification of (B) (a) and (b) with the *elegeia* implied by the Aeschylean *Life* (passage (A) above) requires that (B) (a) and (b) should both refer to Marathon; but many of the opinions expressed about the occasion of these inscriptions automatically exclude the double identification of (B) (a) and (b) with the winning and losing poems of Simonides and Aeschylus; and the authors of these opinions rarely discuss the question of the authorship of the inscriptions. Nevertheless, any theory which associates at least one of the inscriptions (it does not matter which) with Marathon and dates its composition near the actual date of the battle, would at least allow the speculation that the inscription might be the winning poem of Simonides.[23]

If Simonides did write on Marathon for the Athenians, it would be reasonable to suppose, with Bowra,[24] that he was acquainted with Miltiades the victor of Marathon. This acquaintance would be confirmed if Miltiades' supposed dedicatory epigram to Pan (item (H) above) were genuinely by Simonides, as Bowra is inclined to believe; but of course the date and authenticity of the couplet are disputed. Bowra further sees the skolion quoted by Athenaeus, and variously attributed to Simonides and Epicharmus,[25] as a further possible indication of Simonides' relationship with the aristocratic circle of Miltiades; but Bowra claims no certainty for this suggestion.

Thus, none of the items of evidence discussed is, by itself, very strong. Passages (A) and (G) explicitly associate

Simonides with Marathon; but the authority of (A) is not beyond question, and there is at least a possibility that in (G) Marathon has been confused with another battle. It is not certain that either (B) (a) or (B) (b) refers to Marathon, and there is no explicit evidence linking either inscription with Simonides. In (D) both the identity of the Simonides referred to, and the nature of the victory, are uncertain. (E) definitely refers to Marathon, but there is perhaps no ancient authority for ascribing it to Simonides. (F) is explicitly ascribed to Simonides, but it is not certain that it refers to Marathon. (H) is explicitly ascribed to Simonides, and names Miltiades, the victor of Marathon, and Pan, who was part of the Marathon legend; but the source is the unreliable Planudean Anthology. Nevertheless, to reject all these items of evidence would be to carry scepticism too far. The cumulative body of evidence does suggest that Simonides wrote on Marathon for the Athenians, even though the precise nature of the poem or poems cannot be definitely determined nor any fragments from them unmistakably identified.

The conclusion that Simonides probably celebrated the battle of Marathon prompts consideration of one or two related issues. A point raised by Stella may be briefly mentioned, only to be dismissed. She thinks she detects in Xenophon's *Hieron* a tradition, which ancient and modern biographers have failed to observe, of Simonides' participation "ad una guerra nelle file di un libero esercito greco"; and she suggests that Simonides, like Aeschylus, may have fought at Marathon.[26] If this were true, it would, of course, support Stella's date of birth for Simonides (c. 532-29) against the traditional date (c. 556). In the passage in question, Hieron compares the anxiety of the despot to that of men on active service. It is true that certain phrases have an air of referring to personal experiences of Simonides; yet the worthlessness of this passage for biographical details about Simonides scarcely needs demonstrating. It is generally agreed that the *Hieron* does not attempt to portray either the historical Hieron or the historical Simonides; that the Hieron of the dialogue is merely a typical despot of the better type and Simonides little more than a mouthpiece for Xenophon himself.

The question whether Simonides would have been employed by the democracy to celebrate Marathon if he had formerly been a guest at the Pisistratids' court was considered above,[27] and the conclusion drawn that there is not necessarily any incompatibility between these two phases of his activity. Similar questions can be raised concerning his relationship with rival figures on the Athenian political scene in the days of the democracy. It is sometimes thought that his relationship with certain individuals was close enough to exclude any contact with political rivals of his patrons, or even to involve him personally in the rise or fall of his patrons in public favour. Thus Bowra, commenting on Simonides' presumed association with Miltiades at the time of Marathon, and his certain association with Themistocles at a later stage of the Persian Wars, comments: "just as in 490 [Simonides] had followed Miltiades, so now he followed the new leader, Themistocles"; and he sees Simonides' departure for Sicily in 476 as associated with the decline in Themistocles' fortunes.[28]

However, I believe that we ought not to think of Simonides as being exclusively dependent at any given time on one individual or party at Athens. For one thing, Simonides seems to have exploited with great skill the choral lyric poet's privilege of "diplomatic immunity", that is of writing for and remaining on good terms with mutually hostile parties, whether rival politicians in the same city, rival cities, or warring tyrants. For another thing, it is now generally agreed that Athenian politics in the 490's and 480's B.C. do not reveal a rigid party structure or permanent loyalties or enmities, but rather a shifting pattern of temporary alliances in which individual ambition or momentary opportunism played a large part.[29] For example, Miltiades and Themistocles appear to have joined forces in 493/2 in the face of pressure from the Alcmeonids, an alliance which Themistocles seems to have dropped by 489/8 (when Miltiades was again impeached) as no longer expedient to himself;[30] and the tradition, variously regarded by modern scholars, that Miltiades opposed Themistocles' naval policy,[31] is quite compatible with their former temporary alliance. It is no doubt true that rivalry between the Philaid and Alcmeonid families was a rather more permanent feature of Athenian politics, though McGregor[32] argues that even this breach was sometimes closed by a common foreign policy. If the politicians thus made and broke attachments as expediency dictated, they can hardly have expected exclusive loyalty from the professional poet.

The realisation that Simonides is unlikely to have formed exclusive loyalties in the welter of Athenian politics has two consequences for our discussion of his activities in the Persian Wars. Firstly, we cannot use his known or presumed connections with one person or party to exclude the possibility that he was employed by another; for instance, we should allow that he could have been employed (perhaps simultaneously) by both Miltiades and Themistocles, or by both Miltiades and the Alcmeonid Megacles.[33] Secondly, our knowledge or presumed knowledge of Simonides' connections with prominent politicians cannot be used to help to settle disputed historical questions concerning the relationship between those politicians; thus if Simonides was employed by both Miltiades and Themistocles, that is no argument against accepting the tradition of their clash over naval policy.

2. The period 490-480 B.C.

It is possible that Simonides was in Athens for some time during these years. It would be natural to suppose that some of the many dithyrambic victories which he won at Athens belong to this period; and the same may be true of the lines on the death of a certain Megacles:

> Whenever I see the tomb of the dead Megacles, I pity you, unhappy Callias, for what you have suffered.[34]

Megacles and Callias cannot be positively identified. Schneidewin[35] and Wilamowitz state that the names indicate an Attic source; but like Page, they make no attempt to identify Megacles or Callias or to define their relationship.[36] Bergk[37] and Hauvette[38] do not identify Megacles or Callias with any known figure; but they assume, without discussion, that Megacles is Callias' son. Edmonds[39] tentatively accepts this relationship, and further suggests that Callias may be the Olympic victor and Marathon-fighter,[40] son of Hipponicus Ammon;[41] but I am not aware of any evidence that this Callias had a son called Megacles.[42] Even if Edmonds is right, there is no means of dating the poem — except, of course, that as the poem is addressed to Callias, his death (soon after 446/5?) provides the *terminus ante quem*. The only reason for including it at this point in our discussion is Bowra's assumption[43] that this is the Alcmeonid Megacles (son of Hippocrates) who was ostracised in 487/6, whose victory in the Pythian games in 486 was celebrated by Pindar in *Pythian* 7, and who may have died, Bowra believes, soon afterwards.[44] Bowra assumes Callias to be the Callias just mentioned (son of Hipponicus Ammon); and sees in this poem evidence for the personal friendship of these two men (for whose relationship, friendly or otherwise, I know of no other evidence elsewhere). This identification is as tenuous as the others that have been proposed; the most that can be said is that, in view of the lyric poet's "diplomatic immunity", Simonides' presumed association with Miltiades, the enemy of the Alcmeonids, is no argument against either Bowra's identification of Megacles or Simonidean authorship of the lines.

3. Artemisium

According to Plutarch, the following inscription appeared on a column which was set up (presumably by the Athenians) at the temple of Artemis at Artemisium:

> The sons of the Athenians, having once on this sea
> conquered in a sea-fight the races of all kinds of men

from the land of Asia, dedicated these tokens to the maiden Artemis, when the host of the Medes had perished.[45]

Plutarch quotes the epigram anonymously; but it is claimed for Simonides by Schneidewin and Bergk.[46] They have indeed good reason to do so, as it was Simonides who was chosen to compose the melic poem on Artemisium.

It is virtually impossible that the inscription could belong to the period immediately following the battles of Artemisium. Within hours of the third and final engagement at Artemisium, the Greek fleet received the news of the disaster at Thermopylae earlier that day; on receipt of this news the fleet withdrew from Artemisium. The area of Artemisium must have fallen at once under the control of the Persian fleet; and the Athenians' attention was now concentrated on the evacuation of Attica. If the Athenians returned to Athens[47] in the interval between Salamis (September 480) and the reoccupation of Attica by Mardonius (June 479), as is implied by Herodotus' account,[48] and if the Persians lost control of Euboea after Salamis,[49] this period provides the first possible opportunity for the dedication of the *stele* at Artemisium. But a date after Plataea is more likely. Artemisium may have remained inaccessible for the erection of monuments as long as the Persians were operating in Thessaly; and the wording of the inscription ("when the host of the Medes had perished"), though it might with some exaggeration refer to Artemisium,[50] more naturally implies that the final triumph had been won.

Another epigram which may possibly be associated with Artemisium is the following:

> I am the mightiest of beasts, but the mightiest of mortals was he whom I now guard, standing in stone effigy on this tomb.

The following lines may belong to the same epigram:

> But if Leon had not had my spirit and my name, I would not have set my feet on this tomb.[51]

Bergk makes the interesting suggestion that the epigram could have been written by Simonides for Leon of Troezen, who was killed by the Persians after being captured from a look-out vessel off Sciathos before the battle of Artemisium. However, the epigram is sometimes associated with Thermopylae.[52]

Simonides' melic poem on Artemisium[53] is one of the few Simonidean poems for which a precise occasion and a fairly precise date have been postulated. The full title of the poem, *The Sea-Fight at Artemisium*, appears in a passage of Priscian, who quotes a couple of phrases in isolation for metrical purposes; these are too short to reveal anything significant about the content, but are enough to show that the Suda's description of the poem as elegiac is incorrect. The following passage from the scholia on Apollonius Rhodius is more informative:

> Simonides says that Oreithyia was snatched from Brilissos and carried off to the Sarpedonian rock in Thrace...Oreithyia was the daughter of Erechtheus, whom Boreas snatched from Attica and took to Thrace; and having united with her there, he begat Zetes and Calais, as Simonides tells in *The Sea-Fight*.

The identification of *The Sea-Fight* mentioned here, in which Simonides told the story of Boreas and Oreithyia, with *The Sea-Fight at Artemisium* (mentioned by Priscian), is beyond reasonable doubt. The connection between Boreas and the battle of Artemisium is made clear by a passage of Herodotus,[54] where we are told that the Athenians, in gratitude for the help given them by Boreas in scattering the Persian fleet, dedicated a shrine to him on the Ilissus. Clearly, if Simonides were writing a poem to celebrate the battle of Artemisium, it would be natural for him to mention the help given by Boreas, and to emphasise Boreas' relationship to the Athenians by narrating a suitable myth. There is also some probability that an address by Simonides to the wind, to which the following passages of Himerius bear witness, belongs to this same poem:

(A) A song shall loose the cables of the ship, the song which the Athenians sing in holy chorus, calling the wind to the vessel, and bidding it to be present and to fly along with the sacred craft.[55] And the wind, no doubt recognising its own song which Simonides sang to it after the events at sea[56](?), immediately obeys the music, and blowing strongly and favourably from the stern drives on the ship before the breeze.

(B) For now, wishing to call on the wind in poetic vein, but being unable to utter poetic words, I would address the wind according to the Cean muse[57]...and spreading gently over the waves cleave thou[58] the waves that gleam about the prow; ...for in no search after evil desires does he[59] yearn to sail thy sea, but wishing rather to initiate all Ionians into the holy mysteries of righteousness...[60]

Finally, a scholium to Apollonius informs us that Simonides mentions Sciathos; and it is natural to assume, with Schneidewin and others, that this is another allusion to *The Sea-Fight at Artemisium*. The island features in the story of the Persian Wars; the capture of some look-out vessels (which led to the death of Leon of Troezen, as already mentioned) was reported to the Greeks at Artemisium by means of fire signals from Sciathos.[61]

The suggestion of Wilamowitz,[62] that *The Sea-Fight at Artemisium* was performed in Boreas' honour at the founding of his shrine on the Ilissus, has met with wide approval. Two interrelated topics are relevant to a judgement on this matter: Simonides' location of the scene of the rape of Oreithyia; and the reason for the Athenians' choice of the Ilissus as the site for Boreas' shrine.

Early accounts show some variation as regards the scene of the rape, Acusilaus perhaps naming the Acropolis, Pherecydes perhaps naming the Ilissus,[63] and Choerilus naming the source of the Cephissus.[64] Simonides, according to the main manuscript of the scholia to Apollonius, located the rape at "Brilissos"; but no such place is known. The emendation to "Ilissus", which was once proposed, coincides with the reading of an inferior manuscript; but Naeke's emendation to "Brilessus", which is the name of a mountain in Attica, has been almost universally accepted; it is palaeographically far preferable as the *lectio difficilior*, which could have easily been corrupted to "Brilissos" through itacism. Simonides' account might then agree with that of Choerilus, as "Brilessus" and "the source of the Cephissus" can well be the same place.[65] Later accounts agree in naming the Ilissus as the site of the rape;[66] as Wilamowitz points out, this was natural after a shrine was dedicated there to Boreas, for a permanent physical memorial to him on the Ilissus would mean that his name would afterwards be inevitably associated with that particular spot.

The reason for the Athenians' choice of the Ilissus as the site of Boreas' shrine must surely be that the Ilissus was already connected in legend with the story of the rape before the foundation of the shrine; it seems certain that this was the reason assumed by Plato,[67] who in the same breath mentions the legend connected with the spot and the altar sited there. Most commentators indicate, with a brevity that shows they regard the point as too obvious to need discussion, that they accept this explanation; though a few scholars are non-committal, merely admitting the possibility that the legend may have been connected with the Ilissus before the siting of the shrine.

There might seem to be some contradiction between Simonides' location of the rape (in a poem written for the Athenians) at Brilessus, and the Athenians' preference of the Ilissus version in their choice of a site for the shrine; but it may be that the Ilissus version was one of several versions then current at Athens, and was followed, when it came to the choice of a site, simply for reasons of practical convenience. However, this potential contradiction becomes real and acute if considered in the context of Wilamowitz' theory of the precise occasion of the poem. It would surely be most natural for Simonides, if he was telling the myth of Boreas at the foundation-ceremony on the Ilissus, to adopt the version which set the rape of Oreithyia on the Ilissus;

any other version, on such an occasion, would be quite out of place. Wilamowitz, who says nothing about the reason for the Athenians' choice of the site on the Ilissus, enthusiastically accepts the emendation "Brilessus" for Simonides' location of the rape; but this reading is the one factor which might count against his theory of the occasion of the poem. One might still wish to suppose that the poem was addressed specifically to Boreas in gratitude for his help at Artemisium, but that the occasion was different from, and perhaps earlier than, the actual foundation-ceremony of the shrine on the Ilissus.

The widely-accepted view that the passages of Himerius quoted above allude to the same poem also stands to the credit of Wilamowitz. *The Sea-Fight at Artemisium* clearly stressed the part played by Boreas; the Himerius passages show that in the ode in question Simonides summoned the wind to blow favourably. It seems entirely in order to assume that a poem addressed to Boreas and describing his destruction of the Persian ships might contain a plea to blow gently whenever the Athenians themselves should need a fair wind. The ship to which the wind is being called in passage (A) of Himerius is the Panathenaic ship; it may be that the references in passage (B) to the wind cleaving the waves about the prow would be too great a fiction to apply to the Panathenaic ship, but this need not mean that (A) and (B) refer to different poems; merely that the ode contained both these graphic references to the action of the wind at sea[68] and a more general appeal to the wind to blow favourably, in terms which might be used to call it to the Panathenaic ship.

The phrase "after the events at sea" (μετὰ τὴν θάλατταν) in passage (A) shows that the original ode was prompted by events other than the Panathenaic festival; but the possibility remains that it may have been originally sung at the Panathenaea. This is the view of Bowra, who identifies the ode with Simonides' poem *The Sea-Fight at Salamis*,[69] and suggests that it was a *prosodion*, which mentioned the part played by the wind in the battle of Salamis and which was sung in the Panathenaic procession when the Panathenaea was revived after the Persian withdrawal from Attica. The association of the ode with Salamis should probably be rejected; Himerius' statement in passage (A) that the wind "recognises the song (or: its own song), which Simonides sang to it" seems to indicate that the ode was actually addressed to the wind; and the part played by the wind in the battle of Salamis seems to have been insufficient to justify such an exclusive dedication.[70] That part of Bowra's theory which postulates the Panathenaea as the occasion of the original performance could still be retained, even if Himerius' ode is to be identified with *The Sea-Fight at Artemisium*;[71] but I do not think that there is any obligation thus to identify the original occasion of performance with the occasion of the revival of the ode as described by Himerius. Whatever the occasion of the original ode may have been, much of its content must have been irrelevant to the subsequent occasion; and the revival of the ode must have involved either a process of editing and selection of generalising passages addressed to the wind, or (if the whole ode was sung) a willingness to tolerate the no longer relevant topicalities of Simonides' narrative.

In short, it seems on balance that Wilamowitz' identification of the ode mentioned by Himerius with *The Sea-Fight at Artemisium* should be accepted. We have however expressed certain reservations about his theory of the occasion of this poem (that it was performed at the founding of Boreas' shrine on the Ilissus). The occasion could perhaps have been the Panathenaea, which is the occasion of the revival of the ode in Himerius; but it may have been some quite different occasion, on which one could do no more than speculate.

As regards the date of the poem, Wilamowitz[72] is surely right to insist that there can have been no celebration, or performance of choral poems, during the hasty retreat which followed Artemisium.[73] What, then, of the period between Salamis and Plataea? The Athenians are said to have celebrated Salamis by a paean of victory in which the young

Sophocles took part; our source[74] implies that this celebration was held almost immediately after the battle (presumably on the island of Salamis); and it is possible, though it seems unlikely, that the Athenians celebrated the earlier and less decisive campaign of Artemisium at the same time. The next possible opportunity would be after the return of the Athenians to Athens (if they did return), between September 480 and June 479, but again this seems an unlikely occasion; the Athenians, confronted by the ruins of their city, tempted by Mardonius, and abandoned (as they felt) by their allies, are not likely to have had either the time or the inclination for festivities.

It is most probable that the poem was not performed until after the battle of Plataea[75]; and this must certainly be the case if the occasion was (as Wilamowitz believed) the dedication to Boreas of a newly-constructed shrine. The Athenians' first task after Plataea was the rebuilding of their city walls and their ruined city. In addition, a large part of their energy (and citizen-body) was engaged in the reduction of Sestos well into, and probably throughout, the winter of 479-8.[76] The spring of 478 is the earliest likely date for the poem.

The connection between Simonides' poem on Artemisium and Herodotus' account of events may now be considered rather more closely. According to Herodotus,[77] the Athenians had called upon the aid of their "son-in-law" Boreas (whose wife was Oreithyia daughter of Erechtheus) in response to an oracle; and the act of Boreas which earned their gratitude was his destruction of a large part of the Persian fleet in the storm off the Magnesian coast[78] (which we will call storm A), before the first engagement at Artemisium.[79] Herodotus has two further descriptions of the effects of stormy weather on the Persians in the Artemisium campaign: on the night after the first engagement at Artemisium, a violent storm of rain and thunder (which we will call storm B) demoralised the Persians at Aphetae,[80] while on the same night[81] a storm totally destroyed the Persian squadron sailing round the south of Euboea (this we will call, for convenience, storm

C, though it is regarded by Herodotus as simultaneous with, and apparently as part of the same phenomena as, storm B). There is no reference to any effect of the wind in Herodotus' description of the first engagement[82] (Day 18), or the second and third engagements[83] (Days 19 & 20).

Among modern commentators on Simonides, Wilamowitz[84] notes that Herodotus cannot precisely time the Athenians' appeal to Boreas ("when they realised the storm was rising or even before this"),[85] and therefore concludes that the story of the appeal to Boreas (and so, presumably, of the oracle which prompted that appeal) is a fiction, based on the fact of the aid given by Boreas and the subsequent thank-offering; he thinks (though he does not *discuss* this point) that the storm which prompted the thank-offering was storm C. Podlecki[86] also sees chronological difficulties in the sequence of Herodotus' narrative, arguing that it is strange that Herodotus should report the Athenians' prayer to Boreas and the answering of that prayer in 7.189, yet describe the "Athenians"[87] as learning only later, from Scyllias, of the disaster to the Persians in storm A (8.8.3-8.9); he therefore connects the Athenians' appeal to Boreas[88] with the "second storm" (= storms B & C).

A full discussion of these points would involve a re-examination, on a scale quite beyond the scope of this study, of the whole question of Herodotus' accuracy in his account of the Artemisium campaign. For instance, some would regard the Athenians' alleged presence at Chalcis (where, according to Herodotus, they issued the appeal to Boreas) as simply a facet of the almost universally acknowledged error of Herodotus[89] in reporting the whole Greek fleet as withdrawing from Artemisium to Chalcis; others accept that an Athenian detachment, perhaps the fifty-three Athenian ships which join the main fleet at Artemisium,[90] had been sent to block the southern channel of the Euripus against a Persian encirclement.[91] Some accept that a Persian squadron was destroyed in storm C, while circumnavigating Euboea; others accept that this did happen, but that it happened earlier than Herodotus says, storm C really being the same as storm A; others deny the whole story of an attempted Persian circumnavigation of Euboea, so that the effects of storm C are wholly fictitious.[92] In a study of this kind, the proper course seems to be simply to indicate what relevance these controversial issues may have to our study of Simonides.

If an appeal to Boreas (perhaps at the prompting of an oracle) was made by the Athenians before the destruction of the Persian ships in the storm, the identification of Boreas as the divine agent responsible would have been more certain than if no such appeal had been made, and the motivation for the dedication of a shrine and the composition of an ode to Boreas correspondingly stronger; nevertheless, it was clearly open to the Athenians, even if no such appeal was made, to identify the destructive wind as their "son-in-law" Boreas. Again, the postulated appeal by Simonides to Boreas to blow favourably for the Athenians in the future would be all the more forceful, if he could appeal, in traditional hymn style, to the precedent of an earlier invocation ("you heard our appeal at Artemisium; so help us in the future"); but an appeal to the precedent of an unsolicited provision of aid ("you helped us at Artemisium; do so in the future") would also be effective. Thus, acceptance of the story of the Athenians' prior appeal to Boreas at Artemisium may add colour and conviction to the above account of the circumstances and content of Simonides' ode; but it is not a necessary condition for the credibility of that account.

The question at what stage of the campaign the appeal may have been made is of more interest to the structure of Herodotus' narrative than to Simonides' poem; for even if, as Podlecki thinks, the appeal was made on the occasion of the *second* storm, the agency of Boreas would be seen, in retrospect, in the first storm also; and the destruction wrought by the first storm would no doubt be included in an ode of commemoration.[93]

We have mentioned that there is no reference to any effect of the wind in Herodotus' account of the actual fighting. Podlecki[94] argues that the prominence of Boreas in Simonides' poem must mean that Simonides thought of Boreas' help as operating, not only during the first shipwreck, but "during the actual battle as well". But if this is so, then either Herodotus has failed to mention the effects of the wind during the engagements (which seems unlikely, in view of the stress which he places on its effects between engagements); or Simonides has painted an inaccurate picture of the battles (which is unlikely in an ode written for the combatants and their compatriots soon after the event). It is true that an account of the actual engagements must have been included in Simonides' poem;[95] but as Boreas' destruction of a large part of the Persian fleet inevitably had its effect on the whole Artemisium campaign, an account of the actual engagements could properly have been included in an ode in his honour even if he was inactive during those engagements.

Simonides' authorship of the poem or poems on Artemisium can no doubt be classed among the many items of evidence which point to an association between Simonides and Themistocles; for it is probable that a fair share of the credit which the rather limited success at Artemisium brought to the Greeks was due to Themistocles. Diodorus credits Themistocles with initiating certain successful manoeuvres at Artemisium;[96] and Hignett[97] is inclined to accept Grundy's suggestion that Themistocles was responsible for the choice of Artemisium as the station for the Greek fleet. (Herodotus' story[98] of the bribery of Themistocles by the Euboeans, and of Eurybiadas by Themistocles, is now generally rejected.) The general question whether Simonides was closely dependent on Themistocles or other political figures was discussed above.[99]

Simonides' poems on Artemisium would seem to indicate his presence in Athens at some time after the battle of Plataea. That he was at Athens actually at the time of Artemisium, or that he accompanied the Athenians into exile before Salamis, cannot be ascertained, but it might be a reasonable conjecture in view of his connections with Athens and with Themistocles.

References

1. About twenty, rather more than one sixth of the total. The number varies according to whether one includes poems which may be fragments of elegies or those which do not unmistakably concern the Persian Wars.

2. For the definition of what I have called "controversial" and "non-controversial" epigrams and for the bearing of these categories of epigrams on this study, see Chapter I, section 2 above.

3. For sources, text, and some incidental mention of previous opinions, see Page (ad loc.), whose own view is that (b) refers to Marathon (recopied from a Marathon monument at Athens destroyed by the Persians), and (a) to the whole war of 480-79 (or possibly to Salamis and Psyttaleia). For bibliography on these epigrams, see Jacoby (1945) 161 nn. 19 & 20; SEG 10 (1949) 404, 19 (1963) 38, 22 (1967) 63, 25 (1971) 55; Meiggs-Lewis (1969) no. 26; and to the items listed in these places add Bowra (1961) 340-1. Forty is a conservative estimate of the number of discussions of these epigrams that can be traced from the references given.

4. The reference to the "swift ships", which depends on the supplementation from the fourth-century stone, has been explained, not very convincingly, as an allusion to the fight round the Persian ships at Marathon.

5. Hdt. 6.116.

6. An engagement not attested but inferred from Hdt. loc. cit.

7. The mention of Marathon at this point as part of the "title" of Aeschylus' poem depends on Bergk's emendation εἰς τὴν Μαραθωνίαν (μάχην) ("on the (battle) of Marathon") for the inexplicable τὴν μεθορίαν ("the border country"?) of the mss. (Bergk, Zeitschrift für die Alterthumswissenschaft 2 (1835) 952 & PLG II 240). It is of course clear from Plutarch's context that Aeschylus' poem, whatever its title, gave detailed information on the battle of Marathon.

8. The text of this entry is suspect, and it is possible that a reference to our Simonides, not his grandfather, was intended: see Chapter III, section 1 (with nn. 14-16).

9. "Tombs" depends on the emendation ἐπὶ τοῖς ἠρίοις ("on the tombs") for the unintelligible ὁρίοις τοῦ βίου ("on the boundaries of life"?) of the mss.

10. Aristid. *Or.* 28.63 (II 161 f. Keil); schol. ad loc. (p. 289 Frommel); Suda s.v. Ποικίλη.
11. See above, Chapter IV, section 2, & n. 24.
12. Not in Page (1975 & 1981).
13. The first line of this couplet runs: εἰ δ' ἄρα τιμῆσαι, θύγατερ Διός, ὅστις ἄριστος ("but if to honour, o daughter of Zeus, whoever is best"). Opinions are divided as to whether supplements to complete the sense should be understood from the lost lines that preceded, or whether it should be assumed that two or more lines have been lost between the hexameter and the pentameter.
14. Not in Page or West.
15. 18.289 & 290.
16. It is regarded with some scepticism by Wilamowitz (1913: 143-4) and confidently rejected by Jacoby (1945: 179 ff.), followed by Page (on Simonides XX (a) & (b)). In an earlier work Jacoby was less sceptical: see above, Chapter III, section 1 & n. 14.
17. Schneidewin (1835) frag. 58; Kierdorf (1966) 16 n. 2.
18. Bergk (Simonides frag. 81; Aeschyl. ad. loc., *PLG* II 240); tentatively Maas (*RE* "Simonides" III A 1 (1927) 191.35 ff.).
19. 1963: 61-3.
20. 1929: 509 & n. 4.
21. *Philologus* 48 (1889) 240-1. So Meiggs (1972: 273) accepts the idea of a competition with Aeschylus and believes Simonides' poem was an epitaph (he does not identify it further).
22. J.H.Oliver (*Hesperia* 2 (1933) 488-94); J.L.Myres (*Antiquity* 8 (1934) 176-8); Bowra (1961: 340-1).
23. Similarly, if one of the inscriptions refers to Salamis, Plataea, or Thermopylae (for all of which battles Simonides is known to have written), there is a possibility (and one cannot claim any more) that Simonides was the author.
24. 1961: 386, 391.
25. *Carm. Conviv.* 7/890 Page.
26. Stella (1946: 22), referring to Xen. *Hieron* 6.7 ff. A similar conclusion (though without specifying any particular battle) was drawn from the *Hieron*, and subsequently refuted, during the eighteenth century.

27. Chapter III, section 2.
28. Bowra (1936) 358; (1961) 342, 358-9.
29. See M.F.McGregor, *HSCP* Suppl. I (1940) 71-95; A.W.Gomme, *AJPh* 65 (1944) 321-31; Sealey (1976) 187.
30. McGregor op. cit. 87, 95. However Sealey (1976: 185-6) rejects the idea of a political link between Miltiades and Themistocles.
31. Plut. *Vit. Them.* 4.5 (113 e).
32. Op. cit. 91, 94-5.
33. See Section 2 of this chapter, with nn. 43-44.
34. LXXV Page; *Anth. Pal.* 7.511, assigned to Simonides by the formula τοῦ αὐτοῦ ("by the same author"). If the lines are not an inscription, but a fragment of an elegy, as many (including Page) believe, there is a greater probability, despite Page's denial, that the ascription to Simonides is authentic.
35. Frag. 173.
36. Wilamowitz (1913: 212) says that the names are too common for an identification to be sought. (The name Megacles occurs sixteen times, and Callias ninety-four times, in Kirchner, *Prosop. Att.* s.vv.)
37. Frag. 113.
38. 1896: no. 41, pp. 101-2.
39. Simonides frag. 141.
40. Kallias no. 2 in *RE* X 2 (1919) 1615-8; no. 7825 in Kirchner *Prosop. Att.*
41. These suggestions were briefly revived by P.J.Bicknell (*Mnemosyne* Series 4, 22 (1969) 425); he later proposed an alternative identification of Callias as Kallias Kratiou named as an "ostracism candidate" on sherds of the 480's B.C., who may, Bicknell thinks, have been an Alcmeonid and the father of a Megacles (*Historia Einzelschr.* 19 (1972) 64-76).
42. His only known son was Hipponicus.
43. 1961: 341-2.
44. I am not aware of any evidence for the date of the death of this Megacles (= Megakles no. 4 in *RE* XV 1 (1931) 126.35).
45. XXIV Page; Plut. *Vit. Them.* 8.5 (116 a) & *Herod. mal.* 34 (867 f).

46. Schneidewin frag. 192; Bergk frag. 135.

47. This idea is rejected by Munro (*CAH* IV 318) but apparently accepted by Hignett (1963: 281). Burn (1962: 488, 556) thinks that only the able-bodied men returned.

48. 8.109.4; 9.6.

49. So Hignett (1963) 266.

50. Page thinks that the exaggeration would be so absurd that the clause cannot refer to Artemisium; but he agrees that the epigram exaggerates in another way, by claiming the success of Artemisium exclusively for the Athenians. See also Chapter VIII n. 74.

51. LXXXIII (a) & (b) Page, 110 Bergk. The first couplet is assigned to Simonides in *Anth. Pal.* 7.344, with the lemma "on a certain Leon, whom a marble lion guarded". The second couplet appears after *Anth. Pal.* 7.350, ascribed to Callimachus, and with the lemma "on a certain Leon, whom a stone lion guarded over his coffin". In *Anth. Plan.* the couplets appear in succession but as separate epigrams.

52. See below, Chapter VIII, section 1, with nn. 19-21.

53. References to the fragments of this poem quoted here are: Simonides 27/532 (Suda s.v. Σιμωνίδης 439); 28/533 (Priscian *de metr. Terent.* 24); 29/534 (schol. Ap. Rhod. 1.211-15c); 30/535 (Himerius, *Or.* 47.14 & 12.32-3); 130/635 (schol. Ap. Rhod. 1.583-84a).

54. Hdt. 7.189. This connection was pointed out by A. F. Naeke (*Choerili Samii Quae Supersunt* (Lipsiae 1817) p. 154), and has been acknowledged ever since.

55. Viz. the ship towed in the Panathenaic procession. Himerius' oration is entitled, in the mss., "To Basileios, at the Panathenaea, at the beginning of spring".

56. Himerius' phrase μετὰ τὴν θάλατταν (literally "after the sea") is paraphrased by Schmid (1929: 509 n. 5) as "after the storm at sea" and by Wilamowitz (1913: 208) as "after Boreas had shown his favour on the sea". The brachylogic use of μετά ("after") seems to be well attested by other examples at least as striking as this (see W. Schmid, *Der Atticismus in seinen Hauptvertretern...*, Stuttgart 1887-97, III 285-6). However, some prefer to emend to a phrase meaning "after the sea-fight" (cf. Page ad loc., frag. 30/535).

57. The reference to the "Cean muse" here depends on Wernsdorf's universally accepted emendation Κείας ("Cean") for the ms. reading οἰκείας, "my own muse" (which would contradict Himerius' denial of his own poetic ability).

58. The imperative here depends on the emendation σχίζε ("cleave!") for σχίζει, which would mean "it (the wind) cleaves" and is thus inconsonant with "thy sea".

59. The subject is Flavianus, to whom Himerius' valedictory oration is addressed.

60. The dotted lines indicate gaps in Himerius' text.

61. Hdt. 7.182-183.1.

62. 1913: 206-8.

63. Acus. frag. 30, *FGrH* I p. 55 (schol. Hom. *Od.* 14.533); Pher. frag. 145, *FGrH* I p. 97 (schol. Ap. Rhod. 1.211-15c). It is not certain how much of the stories told by the scholiasts in these places is to be ascribed to Acusilaus and Pherecydes respectively (see Jacoby's commentary, *FGrH* I pp. 381 & 425).

64. Choer. frag. 5 Kinkel, frag. 7 Bernabé (schol. Ap. Rhod. 1.211-15c).

65. Cf. *RE* "Kephisos" XI 1 (1921) 244.18 ff.

66. Plato *Phaedr.* 229 b-d; Ap. Rhod. 1.211-17; Apollod. 3.199 Wagner (= 3.15.2); Paus. 1.19.5; Tzetz. *Chil.* 8.254 f.

67. Loc. cit.

68. Podlecki (1968: 265) makes the attractive and imaginative suggestion that at this point in the poem the chorus pictured itself as returning to the scene of the battle.

69. Bowra (1961) 343-4; Simonides 31/536 Page.

70. As Podlecki (1968: 265) rightly points out.

71. Though many scholars follow Wilamowitz' suggestion that the occasion of this poem was the founding of Boreas' shrine on the Ilissus.

72. 1913: 207. Wilamowitz dates the dedication of the shrine and the performance of the poem "bald nach 479".

73. Herodotus' account (7.189) implies that the Athenians erected the shrine to Boreas shortly after their return from Artemisium. He must surely be wrong on this point; and there are other difficulties in the chronology of his account, which is discussed later in this section of the present chapter.

74. *Vit. Soph.* 3.

75. Diodorus (11.33.3) implies that the Athenians resumed such ceremonies only after Plataea.

76. Cf. Hdt. 9.114-8 & 121; and especially Thuc. 1.89.2, and Poppo & Stahl and Gomme ad loc.

77. 7.189: brief mention of this passage has already been made (see nn. 54 & 73 above).

78. 7.188.

79. 8.11.

80. 8.12.

81. 8.13-4.

82. 8.11.

83. 8.14 & 15-18.

84. 1913: 207.

85. 7.189.2.

86. 1968: 263-4.

87. So Podlecki: Herodotus says "the Greeks".

88. Unlike Wilamowitz, Podlecki (1968: 262 n. 27) accepts the historicity of the oracle to the Athenians.

89. 7.183.1.

90. 8.14.1.

91. For a discussion of this controversy, with references, see Hignett (1963) 163-6.

92. See Hignett (1963) 173-4, 386-92.

93. If Herodotus' account of the oracle to the Athenians is accepted, the natural occasion for the appeal (made in obedience to the oracle) would be at the very beginning of the campaign, rather than (as Podlecki supposes) at the actual onset of a given storm. The words of Herodotus already quoted ("when they realised the storm was rising or even before this") may perhaps indicate a conflation of two accounts: one, in which the appeal was prompted, without any oracle, by the onset of a storm and the realisation of the disastrous consequences for the Persians if the storm persisted; and another, in which they were prompted by an oracle and issued their appeal at the opening of the campaign.

94. 1968: 264.

95. If this had not been so, the poem would not have acquired the title *The Sea-Fight at Artemisium*. If the reference to Sciathos (above, this Section, with nn. 53 & 61) belongs to our poem, as seemed likely, Simonides' account was full enough to include the preliminary reconnoitring.

96. Diod. Sic. 11.12.5. f.; accepted by Burn (1962) 397.

97. 1963: 153 & n. 3.

98. 8.4-5.

99. In Section 1 of this chapter, with nn. 28, 30-31.

Chapter 8

Simonides in the Persian Wars II: Thermopylae to Plataea

1. Thermopylae

Several epigrams on Thermopylae are ascribed to Simonides. The passage of Herodotus, in which three of these epigrams are quoted, has already been mentioned in connection with the general question of the authenticity of the Simonidean epigrams.[1] It runs as follows:

> For these, who were buried where they fell, and for those who died before the departure of those who were sent away by Leonidas, these lines have been inscribed:
>
>> "Once four thousand from Peloponnese fought here against three million". (Simonides XXII (a) Page)
>
> That is the inscription for the army as a whole; but for the Spartans separately there is:
>
>> "Stranger, tell the Spartans that we lie here, obedient to their commands". (Simonides XXII (b) Page)

That is for the Spartans; but for the seer there is the following:

> "This is the memorial of famed Megistias, whom once the Medes killed after crossing the river Spercheius; a seer who, though he was then aware of the approaching Fates, could not bring himself to desert Sparta's leaders". (Simonides VI Page)

Herodotus then continues:

> ἐπιγράμμασι μέν νυν καὶ στήλῃσι, ἔξω ἢ τὸ τοῦ μάντιος ἐπίγραμμα, Ἀμφικτύονές εἰσί σφεας οἱ ἐπικοσμήσαντες· τὸ δὲ τοῦ μάντιος Μεγιστίεω Σιμωνίδης ὁ Λεωπρέπεός ἐστι κατὰ ξεινίην ὁ ἐπιγράψας.

> "The Amphictyons are the ones who honoured them with inscriptions and gravestones, except for the inscription for the seer. But Simonides the son of Leoprepes is the one who inscribed the inscription for the seer Megistias for friendship's sake" (or "...who had the inscription for the seer inscribed").

The essential question is whether Simonides' name can be linked with all three epigrams, or only with the Megistias epigram.

It is reasonably clear what the Amphictyons did in the case of the first two monuments. They must have decided that memorials should be erected to the army in general and the Spartans in particular, arranged for stones to be provided, commissioned someone to compose the epigrams, had the inscriptions carved, and financed the entire operation. Simonides' role (defined by the term ὁ ἐπιγράψας, "the one who inscribed") in the case of the Megistias memorial, is less clear; and the Amphictyons may be involved here as well, for Herodotus' words, if strictly interpreted, seem to associate the Amphictyons with all three gravestones and with the first two inscriptions, and Simonides with only the inscription (not the gravestone) of Megistias.

If, as Page once believed,[2] *epigrapsas* here means only "wrote the inscription" and not (in this context) "had the inscription inscribed", then Page would be correct in concluding, from the antithesis of Herodotus' sentence,[3] that Herodotus means that Simonides did *not* compose the other two epigrams.

Later Page[4] reverted (rightly, in my opinion) to the view of Boas,[5] that *epigrapsas* does not in itself denote the author of the epigram, but (in some sense) the person responsible for the fact that the inscription was carved. (Page and Boas also agree that Simonides was in fact the author of the Megistias epigram.) But from this point on, Page and Boas part company. Page continues to insist that Simonidean authorship of the other two epigrams is "quite ruled out by the context" (i.e. by the contrast between the contribution of the Amphictyons and of Simonides); but surely, with Page's revised interpretation of *epigrapsas*, this no longer follows; if the only explicit contrast between the Amphictyons and Simonides is that they were responsible for the provision of the first two inscriptions and he was similarly responsible for the provision of the Megistias inscription, this surely does not exclude the possibility that he may have composed the first two inscriptions. Boas, quite rightly, draws no such conclusion. Kaibel drew the more modest conclusion that Herodotus did not know who composed these two inscriptions;[6] if that were Herodotus' position, Kaibel's further inference, that Simonides was probably not the author, would reasonably follow. But again, I feel that if *epigrapsas* does not amount to an explicit statement that Simonides wrote the Megistias epigram, Herodotus' omission to name the author of the other two inscriptions does not necessarily mean that he lacked the relevant information.

As regards the meaning of *epigrapsas*, Page and Boas, though agreeing that the word denotes the person responsible for the inscription, develop this basic view in quite different directions. The difficulty lies in the "division of labour" between the Amphictyons and Simonides over the Megistias memorial, if in fact (as Page and Boas agree) the Amphictyons are responsible for all three gravestones and two inscriptions, and Simonides for the one inscription. Page[7] defines Simonides' role by stating that the subject (of *epigrapsas*) "made arrangement for, and paid the cost of, the composition and the inscribing" of the lines for Megistias,[8] while the Amphictyons "were responsible for" or "provided" or "contributed" the gravestone for Megistias. But Page does not make it clear how this division of responsibility operated or what initiative was taken by each party.

Boas[9] believes that the Amphictyons decided on the erection of all three memorials, provided the necessary gravestones, and commissioned Simonides to compose all three inscriptions; but that in the case of the inscription for Megistias, Simonides waived the fee due to him, so becoming the person responsible for the inscription (ὁ ἐπιγράψας); thus Boas confidently claims all three epigrams for Simonides. This is at least a clear and logical solution to the problem, which Herodotus' text seems to pose, of the "division of labour" between the Amphictyons and Simonides; but it is unacceptable in terms of general probability. It is surely impossible to believe that Herodotus found it worthwhile to single out for special mention, as Simonides' act of piety towards his friend, the fact that he forebore to claim his fee. Herodotus must surely mean that, had it not been for Simonides, Megistias would not have had his own separate gravestone and inscription at all.

If it is necessary to insist that the Amphictyons provided everything but the *inscription* to Megistias, an obvious explanation is that, while Simonides took the decision that the monument should be erected, and provided for the carving of an inscription, the Amphictyons supplied him with the actual stone.[10] But I think it could be argued that Herodotus intended *epigrapsas* to refer to the entire process of dedicating an inscribed monument; that his sentence "the Amphictyons were the ones who honoured them with inscriptions and gravestones apart from the inscription to the seer" means "...apart from the inscription and the gravestone which carried it"; and that it would have been superfluous, and indeed pedantic, to express the latter phrase in full. Thus the curious problem of the division of labour in the case of Megistias' memorial would be an unreal one, Simonides being responsible for both gravestone and inscription;[11] though the Amphictyons would still have co-operated with Simonides in the sense of granting him permission to erect a personal monument on the Thermopylae battlefield.

However that may be, the interpretation which we have preferred, that Simonides was responsible for the decision to erect a separate gravestone to Megistias, means that he was not commissioned by the Amphictyons to write the Megistias epigram. But as it is inconceivable that he himself commissioned another poet to write the inscription for him, his authorship of the Megistias epigram is virtually certain. Simonidean authorship of the other two epigrams, which was an intrinsic part of Boas' theory, cannot be regarded as certain; and it must therefore be acknowledged that the Megistias epigram is the only definitely authentic Simonidean epigram. However, the interpretation we have accepted shows Simonides writing the inscription for one monument at Thermopylae and co-operating closely with, or perhaps actively subsidised by, the Amphictyons in the erection of the monument itself. The assumption that he wrote the epigrams for the other two monuments erected there by the Amphictyons at the same time would be very reasonable.

The only other matter concerning these three epigrams which might warrant further comment here is the extraordinary suggestion that the phrase ῥήμασι πειθόμενοι in the epitaph on the Spartans means not only "obedient to their words" (or "commands" or "laws") but also "trusting in their words", and carries a reproach to the Spartan government for failing to send reinforcements to Thermopylae.[12] That no such double meaning was perceived by the Greeks themselves can be inferred from the following facts: no ancient authority gives any hint that he saw any such double meaning; the reading ῥήμασι πειθόμενοι was eventually displaced, in one stream of the literary tradition, by πειθόμενοι νομίμοις ("obeying their laws"), an unequivocal phrase which would have been unlikely to oust ῥήμασι πειθόμενοι if the latter phrase had been felt to carry a double meaning; and the inscription was allowed to stand on the Thermopylae monument, whereas the Spartans, had they read a reproach into Simonides' words, would surely have erased the offending lines, as they erased Pausanias' couplet from the Delphic monument.[13] Moreover if the Thermopylae encomium[14] was written as an official commission for Sparta, acceptance of the theory would involve the belief that Simonides accepted the commission for the encomium from the Spartan authorities, while nursing and concealing feelings of resentment against them. The theory must surely be rejected.

An upper limit on the number of epigrams which can be accepted as genuine inscriptions at the site of the battle is imposed by Strabo's statement that there were five στῆλαι ("gravestones", "memorial stones") at Thermopylae, including one for the Locrians.[15] However, the number of inscriptions contemporary with the events could possibly be less than five, for there is some dispute as to whether Strabo's five memorials were all original monuments from the time of the Persian War (or at least copies of such original monuments), or whether one or more of them were erected at a later date to reassert the claims of certain communities to have participated in the campaign.[16] The fact that Herodotus mentions only three inscriptions is not generally regarded as a limiting factor on the total number of inscriptions at Thermopylae, as it is considered likely that his account is based not on personal inspection of the site but on Spartan sources which failed to mention inscriptions for non-Peloponnesians; but this does seem to mean that the number of Thermopylae inscriptions on Spartans and Peloponnesians must be limited to the three quoted by Herodotus. The inscription on Megistias, even though it was written for an individual, not a community, should probably be included among the five memorials mentioned by Strabo.[17] The question of which two inscriptions may have made up the total from Herodotus' three to Strabo's five is affected by the following factors: the existence of a number of epigrams which have been preserved, and have been assigned to Thermopylae by ancient authority or modern conjecture; and the supposition that certain states are likely to have had inscriptions at Thermopylae, even though no epigrams for them have been preserved.

The Palatine Anthology quotes what purports to be an inscription *in situ* on those who died at Thermopylae with Leonidas:[18]

> The earth conceals the famous men who died here with you, Leonidas, king of broad Sparta, having endured the might of the many bows and swift horses of the Medes.

There seems to be no compelling reason why some such epitaph, on the dead of all the cities which took part, could not have stood at Thermopylae. Page's comment that there is no room for such an epitaph among Strabo's five is perhaps too dogmatic, in view of the conflicting claims of epigrams for inclusion in this number; somewhat stronger (though hardly conclusive, in view of the subjectivity of such matters) is his argument that the clumsy phrasing of this particular epigram marks it out as a late composition.

Schneidewin associates the first couplet of the epigram LXXXIII Page (which was quoted above[19] in connection with Artemisium) with the stone lion which, according to Herodotus, "now stands in honour of Leonidas" (at Thermopylae).[20] It is sometimes stated or implied that this stone lion was not erected at Thermopylae until later in the fifth century;[21] this view seems to depend on nothing more than Herodotus' statement that the lion "now stands" there, a phrase which, as Macan remarks in his commentary, does not point to any precise date, and which therefore seems to permit the assumption that the lion was erected soon after the battle. However, any supposition that a Simonidean epigram for Leonidas could have been carved on any monument at Thermopylae seems to be adequately refuted by Bergk, who points out that, according to Pausanias, no commemorative poems for Spartan royalty had ever been written, except the anonymous epigram for Cynisca daughter of Archidamus and Simonides' epigram for Pausanias of Sparta.[22]

The epigram on the Locrians, which according to Strabo stood on one of the five memorials at Thermopylae,[23] states:

> Opus, the mother-city of the Locrians with their just laws, laments these men who died fighting the Medes on behalf of Greece.

On the basis of their conduct at Thermopylae, the Locrians, who fought with Leonidas but were among those sent away before the last stand in the pass, could be said to have earned a memorial there. However Page considers that the Locrians would not have been allowed a memorial at the time of the events, in view of the fact that they went over to the Persian side after the battle;[24] he therefore thinks it likely that, if a memorial with the above inscription stood at Thermopylae, it was erected long after the battle. This argument carries some weight: the Locrians are missing from the Delphic serpent-column,[25] as are the Phocians (who fled from the fighting and after some initial resistance went over to the Persian side),[26] and also a number of the states which supplied ships to the Persians.[27] At the same time the Locrians' defection after the fall of Thermopylae could be regarded as a simple consequence of their geographical position; they were presumably among those Greek states whose performance on the Persian side at Plataea was deliberately half-hearted,[28] and their absence from the serpent-column has been judged "unaccountable";[29] and participation on the Persian side did not in all cases mean exclusion from memorials, as the Tenians, who had supplied ships to the Persians,[30] appear on the serpent-column. Thus any judgement on the likelihood of the Locrians' exclusion from the Thermopylae memorials is a highly subjective matter; and the onus of proof seems to lie with those who reject Strabo's testimony to the memorial of the Locrians, which he obviously regarded as ancient. Strabo does not name the author of the epigram, which is ascribed to Simonides by Schneidewin and Bergk;[31] if the epigram is accepted as ancient, Simonidean authorship would seem to be quite probable, in view of his composition of the Megistias epigram and (very possibly) of the other two epigrams quoted by Herodotus.

The claim of the Thespians to one of the five memorials mentioned by Strabo is generally regarded as overwhelming; they not only fought in the last stand with Leonidas, but subsequently refused to submit to the Persians (which resulted in the destruction of their city and the flight of the inhabitants to the Peloponnese), and they eventually fought on the Greek side at Plataea.[32] An impressive array of opinion holds that a couplet quoted by Stephanus of Byzantium as an "*epigramma* on those killed by the Persians", and ascribed by him to an otherwise unknown poet Philiadas of Megara, belongs to the presumed Thespian memorial at Thermopylae;[33] but Page inclines to follow Boas' view that the preservation of the author's name means that the lines are not inscriptional. The general assumption that the name of the author of an inscription could not have been preserved, even in the odd exceptional case, is perhaps somewhat over-confident. However in this instance a good reason for scepticism about Philiadas' authorship of an inscription for the Thespians at Thermopylae is the difficulty of imagining the Amphictyons commissioning this obscure figure for one isolated epitaph among the several inscriptions on the polyandrion at Thermopylae, despite the known association of Simonides with Thermopylae through the Megistias epigram and the lyric encomium — an association which rather suggests that, if any inscription for the Thespians stood on a memorial at Thermopylae, it is likely to have been the work of Simonides. Possible alternative explanations of Philiadas' couplet which might seem plausible are that it could belong to an inscription or elegy for the Thespian dead of the entire war (including Plataea) commissioned by the Thespians themselves; or, if his poem mentioned other states besides Thespiae, that it celebrated the role played in the whole campaign, or in some particular battle, by various cities, including perhaps Philiadas' own city of Megara. However a simple objection to all such hypotheses is that it again seems to have been Simonides who was chosen to celebrate the Megarians' role in the Persian Wars;[34] it is unlikely that an obscure Megarian, whom his own city did not choose to employ, would be sought out and commissioned by the Amphictyons, Thespians, or others. All these factors point to the conclusion that Philiadas was not a contemporary poet commissioned to celebrate the events at the time of their occurrence, but a late composer of either a demonstrative epigram or an elegy on some aspect of the Persian Wars.

The only other relevant epigrams are two poems which the Palatine Anthology refers to Thermopylae, but which Bergk, followed by Page, assigns to Plataea.[35] The argument (on which Page appears to rely) that there is no place for these two epigrams among the five implied by Strabo, is open to some doubt, in view of the diversity of opinion on how to account for Strabo's five memorials. Of more weight is Bergk's point that these two epigrams, unlike the three Thermopylae inscriptions quoted by Herodotus, do not identify the people honoured, and therefore imply a different kind of monument, on which the identification was made in some other way, for example by means of a separate prose inscription.

Discussion of the possible claims of other states, such as the Phocians or Thebans, to one of Strabo's five memorials, would seem to be more appropriate to a history of the Persian Wars than to a study of Simonides, even though it may be thought likely that Simonides may have been the author of the inscriptions on all the memorials.

Any inscriptions carved at Thermopylae must be dated after Plataea.[36] Until then the Persians were no doubt in control of the Thermopylae area,[37] and Diodorus[38] explicitly states that the epigrams on the Peloponnesians and the Spartans were inscribed after Plataea.

Finally the famous lyric encomium on Thermopylae, which is quoted by Diodorus, must be considered:[39]

> In general terms, they alone[40] of men up to their time passed into immortality because of their outstanding valour. Therefore not only the writers of history but many of the poets too have dwelt on their heroic exploits. Among these was Simonides the lyric poet, who composed an encomium befitting their valour, in which he says:
>
>> "Of those who died at Thermopylae, glorious is the fortune and noble the doom. For a tomb they have an altar; instead of lamentation, remembrance; and for pity, praise. And such an offering (?) neither decay nor all-conquering time shall obscure. This precinct of heroes has received as its guardian-deity (?) the glory of Greece. To this, even Leonidas, the king of Sparta, bears witness, who has left behind a great ornament of valour and everlasting renown." [41]

Our discussion must be limited (in view of the scope and aims of the present study) to matters relevant to the occasion and date of the poem; and conclusions even on these matters will have to be stated more briefly and dogmatically than would be the case in a commentary.

The Thermopylae dead have been the sole topic of discussion in Diodorus' text for several paragraphs[42] up to the point where he introduces this poem with the remark that Simonides composed "an encomium befitting their valour". This can only mean that the Thermopylae dead are the principal theme of the poem; we must reject all theories[43] which hold that the Thermopylae dead in the opening lines, and Leonidas in the closing lines, are merely used as an illustration of the fame of some other group of war-dead, to whom the central section of the fragment,[44] and the poem as a whole, refers.

In the central section, that reading should be accepted which produces the meaning "this σηκός (precinct) of noble men";[45] and this phrase should be interpreted literally and deictically of an actual physical *sekos* or precinct at which the poem was performed, not anaphorically[46] ("this (literal) *sekos* referred to in the preceding lines"), nor metaphorically[47] ("this figurative 'shrine' which the honours referred to in the preceding lines may be said to constitute"). These points, if accepted, exclude the possibility that the poem was written in honour of one man, Leonidas,[48] or that the poem, though honouring the Thermopylae dead collectively, was sung not on a public occasion at the consecration of a *sekos* but on some more private occasion, perhaps in the men's messes in Sparta.[49]

The opening phrase "those who died at Thermopylae" does not mean that the poem cannot have been performed at Thermopylae itself; if the lines are intended as a permanent tribute to the dead, the site of the battle would naturally be specified, even if the poem was originally performed there. Again, the fact that Leonidas "bears witness" to the poet's assertions does not necessarily mean that he is not among those being honoured; it may mean merely that the undoubted fact of Leonidas' immortal glory proves that the whole Thermopylae band, of which he was one, are assured of a like fame.

All those who believe that the poem was written in honour of the Thermopylae dead assume that it was written for Sparta. Thus Bowra[50] argues persuasively that it was sung at a shrine dedicated at Sparta to the Three Hundred, and that Leonidas "witnesses" from his own shrine nearby and testifies to the glory of his fellow-combatants. Another possibility is that the poem was sung at Thermopylae,[51] perhaps before a *sekos* dedicated to the Thermopylae dead, or at the tomb here regarded as a *sekos*; in this case, while it could have been written in honour of and commissioned by the Spartans alone, it is perhaps more likely that it celebrated all those who died in the last stand, Spartans and Thespians alike, or perhaps all those who died at Thermopylae, including the dead (from many states) of the earlier engagements in the pass. If this is so, it may have been commissioned, like the Thermopylae epigrams and their *stelae*, by the Amphictyons.

If the poem was performed at Sparta, it would seem reasonable to date it conjecturally to the autumn of 480. The Spartans, being exempt from the immediate distractions and dangers confronting Athens, might reasonably be expected to build and dedicate a *sekos* in honour of their dead as soon as was practically possible. We need only allow them time to construct the *sekos* (and, if Bowra's theory is accepted, to have already consecrated a memorial to Leonidas); the performance of the poem, which may or may not have involved a visit of Simonides to Sparta, could thus be dated within two or three months of the battle of Thermopylae (which took place in August 480). If the place of performance was Thermopylae, the poem must be dated after Plataea; it has already been noted, in connection with the inscriptions, that until then the Persians were in control of the Thermopylae area.

2. Salamis

Simonides' work on Salamis apparently included poems for several of the states which took part in the battle. His work for the Athenians may be considered first.

There is clear evidence for a Simonidean poem entitled *The Sea-Fight at Salamis*,[52] but unfortunately it is not known whether it was a melic or an elegiac poem (a question of obvious importance when considering what fragments can be assigned to it). The Suda states that Simonides wrote *The Sea-Fight at Artemisium* in elegiacs and *The Sea-Fight at Salamis* as a melic poem; but, as has already been noted, the existence of melic fragments from *The Sea-Fight at Artemisium* shows that the first part of this statement is incorrect. Some scholars have accepted Bergk's suggestion[53] that "elegiac" and "melic" have been transposed in the Suda's text, so that *The Sea-Fight at Salamis* was elegiac;

others accept the Suda's statement that it was melic; others are non-committal. If the question is approached from the other direction, by keeping an open mind on the question of metrical form and considering what fragments can be most plausibly assigned to this poem on the basis of other criteria, it emerges that Bergk's view, that it was elegiac, is likely to be the correct one.

Nothing is known for certain about the content of *The Sea-Fight at Salamis*; but the general assumption that Plutarch[54] is referring to it in the following passage is no doubt correct:

> But the rest of the Greeks, their numbers now matching those of the barbarians within the narrow strait, routed the enemy who advanced against them in detachments and collided with each other, even though they (the enemy) held out until evening, as Simonides has said, thus winning that noble and famous victory, than which no more glorious deed has ever been accomplished at sea by either Greeks or barbarians, (an achievement won) by the bravery and zeal of all those who fought in the battle, but also by the counsel and skill of Themistocles.

Though some editors[55] do not make clear their position on the matter, it is important to try to determine how much of this passage constitutes the Simonidean quotation. It seems most natural to assume that the quotation consists of the phrase immediately preceding "as Simonides has said", viz. "holding out until evening" (μέχρι δείλης ἀντισχόντας). These are probably either Simonides' actual words,[56] or very close to them; Plutarch no doubt meant to echo the poet's phrasing here, for there would be little point in quoting Simonides' authority merely to vouch for the approximate duration of the battle, which must have been common knowledge. Others however carry the Simonidean quotation further. Boas[57] clearly believes that the Simonidean quotation (with at least close echoes of Simonides' actual words) extends as far as "that famous and noble victory'';[58] and it is possible that Boas means to include the following words down to ''accomplished...by Greeks or barbarians''.[59] Podlecki regards the Simonidean quotation as extending, in paraphrase at least, down to the end of the Plutarch passage as quoted above.[60] It seems to me, however, that the whole of the latter part of the sentence[61] is pure prose; and I can scarcely believe (and the less so, the longer the quotation is alleged to be) that Plutarch would have obliterated Simonides' poetic phrasing so effectively. Admittedly this is a highly subjective impression; more importantly, there is perhaps some evidence of an alternative source on which Plutarch could have been drawing at this point. It has been pointed out[62] that the Troezen inscription bears witness to a tradition (echoed in Herodotus and Thucydides) according to which Athens and Greece owed their salvation to Themistocles; moreover, there is a fragment of Ctesias[63] which bears a strong resemblance to the closing words of this passage of Plutarch. It seems likely therefore that the direct source of Plutarch, in the latter part of the sentence quoted, was some prose tradition favourable to Themistocles, rather than a poem of Simonides. This does not rule out the possibility that such a prose tradition may have had something in common, in theme if not in wording, with Simonides; but it would mean that the present passage of Plutarch does not provide any actual evidence of Simonides' involvement in Themistoclean propaganda on Salamis.

Of the attempts to identify other fragments of this poem, the most convincing is Lobel's proposal to assign to this poem an elegiac papyrus fragment[64] which appears to contain references to a naval battle and to Medes (?), Phrygians, and Phoenicians; Lobel's reason is that Simonides is known to have written elegiac pieces about battles of the Persian Wars and that there are choral lyric fragments, probably by Simonides, in the same hand.[65]

Wilamowitz[66] believes that the following two elegiac couplets,[67] on the exploits at Salamis of Democritus of Naxos, though designated as an *epigramma* by Plutarch, are from an elegy:

190 SIMONIDES

> Democritus was the third who led the fight, when the Greeks clashed with the Medes by sea at Salamis. He captured five ships of the enemy, and rescued a sixth ship, a Greek one, as it was falling into the hands of the barbarians.

It is possible that Wilamowitz means to identify the elegy in question with *The Sea-Fight at Salamis* (Page, on Simon. 31/536, is quite confident that this is Wilamowitz' meaning). Barigazzi[68] firmly assigns the lines to *The Sea-Fight at Salamis*, and Podlecki[69] is sympathetically disposed to this suggestion. However, Page may be right to insist that the lines are a complete poem;[70] at least they would constitute an odd opening to an elegy on the battle of Salamis; and if they occurred in the middle of such an elegy, the words "at Salamis" (πὰρ Σαλαμῖνα, line 1) would be superfluous.

Podlecki[71] assigns frag. 9 West, which was quoted above in connection with Marathon,[72] to *The Sea-Fight at Salamis*, and argues that what "the *demos* of the Athenians accomplished alone" (line 2 of the fragment) was the victory of Salamis, such a claim being in harmony with Athenian propaganda on the battle. I do not find this suggestion attractive. Even though it may be over-fastidious to be unwilling to ascribe such a crude and explicit falsification to Simonides, or naive to object that in other poems Simonides apparently gave appropriate recognition to the role of other states at Salamis,[73] the fact remains that no adequate parallel to such distortion is quoted by Podlecki. He does indeed cite Pindar *Pythian* 1.75-7 for the mention of the Athenians alone in connection with Salamis, and Aeschylus' *Persae* for the distortion of the relative significance of the battles in the Persian Wars; but both these instances involve a far smaller degree of falsification than an explicit claim that one state won single-handed a battle in which a dozen states took part.[74] Moreover, Podlecki's readiness to admit, in connection with the proposed attachment to *The Sea-Fight at Salamis* of the lines on Democritus of Naxos, that Simonides may have "given some attention to describing the achievements of individual contingents and their commanders on the Greek side" seems at variance with his own suggestion that the same poem claimed Salamis as a uniquely Athenian achievement.

Bowra's suggestion that the almost certainly melic fragment 30/535 Page, which is sometimes assigned to *The Sea-Fight at Artemisium*, belongs to *The Sea-Fight at Salamis*, was discussed and rejected above.[75]

The Sea-Fight at Salamis is universally assumed (that is, by scholars who discuss the point at all) to have been written for Athens. This assumption is entirely reasonable, in view of the prominent part played by Athens in the battle, and becomes virtually imperative, if the Simonidean quotation in Plutarch is thought to include the reference to Themistocles.

The date of the poem no doubt depends on the nature of the occasion; the more formal and elaborate the occasion is assumed to be, the less likely it becomes that the poem was performed by the Athenians either in their temporary habitat on Salamis or during their (possible) temporary return to Athens in the interval between Salamis and Plataea. It is known, however, that the Athenians celebrated Salamis with a paean of victory, apparently very soon after the battle, and presumably on the island of Salamis;[76] and it is therefore possible that Simonides' poem (*The Sea-Fight at Salamis*) was performed in similar circumstances, or is even to be identified with the paean of victory to which our source refers.[77] Bergk, on the other hand, suggests that the poem, which he believes to have been elegiac, was written "cum Athenienses...iusta persolverent civibus, qui in bello ceciderant"; if this was some simple funeral ceremony, the date must again have been very soon after the actual battle.

If the poem, whatever its nature, was written very soon after Salamis, it may lend some slight support to the conjecture that Simonides was with the Athenians at the time of the battles of Artemisium and Salamis. On the other hand, it remains possible that the poem belongs to a more elaborate occasion of the kind which can have been resumed at Athens only after Plataea.

192   SIMONIDES

Turning now to Simonides' poems on Salamis for other states, we find ascribed to him a number of epigrams on the Corinthians' role in the battle. The epitaph on the Corinthians buried on Salamis runs:

> O stranger, once we dwelt in the well-watered city of Corinth, but now Salamis the isle of Ajax holds us (lines 1-2); here, by defeating the Phoenician ships and Persians and Medes, we saved holy Greece (lines 3-4).

Fragments of the first couplet appear on a stone found near the ancient city of Salamis; literary sources quote the two-couplet version, stating that the inscription was carved on a gravestone "near the city" and adding the Simonidean ascription.[78] It has usually been thought that this is yet another instance of the expansion of an inscription in the literary tradition;[79] but it has recently been pointed out that a second couplet could have stood beneath the first on a worn section of the stone;[80] and Page accepts it as probable that in this exceptional instance the longer version represents the original inscription.

A cenotaph at the Isthmus is said to have carried the following epigram, which appears in the literary sources in a shorter and a longer version:

> We lie, having with our own lives rescued the whole of Greece, when it stood on the razor's edge (lines 1-2), from slavery; and we afflicted the hearts of the Persians with all manner of woes, to remind them of the grievous sea-fight (lines 3-4). Salamis holds our bones; but Corinth, our native city, raised this memorial to us for our services to her (lines 5-6).[81]

Page accepts only the first couplet as a genuine inscription, rejecting the other two on grounds of wording and style; but he considers that some supplement, similar in content to the last couplet, must have stood on the monument to explain the unusual use of "we lie" (κείμεθα) on a monument which did not stand over the actual grave. The erection of such a memorial in the home city, to honour the dead who were buried near the scene of the battle, is normal and natural; Jacoby's suggestion[82] that the memorial was not erected until after the outbreak of war between Athens and Corinth in 461, when the Corinthian dead lay in hostile territory (Salamis and Plataea), seems unnecessarily elaborate.

A dedication of arms in the temple of Leto by the crew of the Corinthian trierarch Diodorus is thus recorded:

> The sailors of Diodorus dedicated these arms (captured) from the Persian enemy, in memory of the sea-fight.[83]

The following dedicatory epigram was apparently inscribed in the temple of Aphrodite at Corinth, accompanying a painting which depicted the women of Corinth who prayed to the goddess to inspire their men with zeal for battle:

> These women stood praying their inspired prayer to the Cyprian on behalf of the Greeks and their close-fighting fellow-citizens; for divine Aphrodite did not wish to hand over the citadel of the Greeks to the bow-carrying Medes.[84]

Neither the text of the epigram nor the accounts of the dedication specify the Salamis campaign; though Plutarch in the relevant chapter is chiefly concerned with refuting charges of Corinthian cowardice at Salamis.

Finally there is the epitaph on the Corinthian admiral Adeimantus:

> This is the grave of that (famous) Adeimantus, through whom the whole of Greece put on a crown of freedom.[85]

This is in a different category from the other epigrams considered. It is not an epitaph on a war-grave; Adeimantus was not killed at Salamis, and "must have survived the battle for quite a long time, if it is true that he had four children to whom he gave names which reflected his glory at Salamis".[86]

As regards the date of the other four epigrams, the inscription over the dead (XI) and the dedication of booty (XIII) are probably to be dated very soon after the battle. The inscriptions for the cenotaph at the Isthmus (XII) and for the Corinthian women (XIV) might be somewhat later; the latter (which does not specify Salamis) is perhaps to be dated after the end of the war, as the Corinthians fought at Plataea and Mycale also.

Even though the sources for the Simonidean ascriptions are not completely reliable, Simonidean authorship of some or most of these epigrams would seem to be not merely possible but intrinsically probable, in view of his known connection with Salamis and other battles of the Persian Wars. The only exception is the epitaph on Adeimantus, who may have died after the traditional date of Simonides' death (468/7); the ascription of this epigram, which looks back to Adeimantus' role at Salamis, could have been prompted by knowledge of Simonides' contemporary poems on the battle. It is likely that the jealousy between Athens and Corinth was already manifest during the Persian War;[87] and certainly there had been a flare-up of personal animosity between Themistocles and Adeimantus before Salamis;[88] but, in view of Simonides' skill in exploiting the lyric poet's "diplomatic immunity", his connections with Athens and Themistocles cannot be regarded as an argument against his authorship of poems for Corinth.

To accept the authenticity of any Simonidean epigrams is always open to criticism for excessive credulity; and it is not made easier in the case of the Corinthian epigrams by passages of Aristotle and Plutarch which have been regarded as proof of hostility between the Corinthians and Simonides. Wilamowitz considers that these passages prove that the Corinthian epigrams are not by Simonides;[89] and it must be admitted that at first sight there is a real difficulty here. However I believe that these passages do not provide reliable evidence of hostility between the Corinthians and Simonides, though the reasons for this belief can only be stated briefly here. The passage of Aristotle states that the Corinthians were offended by Simonides' line "Troy has no fault to find with Corinth", which is an allusion to the distinguished part played on the Trojan side by the Corinthian-descended Glaucus and his followers. However the fact that Pindar also alludes to Glaucus' role at Troy, in a complimentary fashion, in an ode written for a Corinthian,[90] suggests that he knew of no occasion when such an allusion by his predecessor Simonides had given offence, and that therefore Aristotle's statement should be regarded with scepticism. It may be that Aristotle remembered Simonides' line out of context, and that his conception of the likely reaction of the Corinthians was prompted by his own train of thought in the passage in question, where he is discussing the generalisation that "those whom their enemies do not blame are worthless"; here "not being blamed" by one's enemy is an indication of worthlessness, in that one has not acted with due vigour against one's enemy; but this is inapplicable to the peculiar dual role of the Corinthians on both sides in the Trojan War, to which Simonides was referring. The Plutarch passage concerns a remark of Themistocles, who is reported to have said, "jestingly" or "mockingly" (ἐπισκώπτων), that Simonides showed a lack of sense in abusing (λοιδοροῦντα) the Corinthians, who dwelt in a great city, while commissioning portraits of himself though ugly. It is likely that Plutarch regarded the exchanges between Simonides and Themistocles, and Simonides and the Corinthians, as no more than some kind of joke or friendly banter; he assigns to Simonides works for both Themistocles and the Corinthians at the time of the Persian War,[91] thus implying that he knew of no estrangement at least up to that date. In any case, even if the passages of Aristotle and Plutarch were accepted as evidence of hostility, they would count against Simonidean authorship of the Corinthian epigrams only if the episodes could be dated before 480/79; but the fragment on the Corinthians' role at Corinth cannot be dated at all; and although the context in Plutarch might seem to set Themistocles' remark on Simonides and Corinth before 480,[92] it is disputed whether the distribution of sayings and anecdotes within the narrative framework of Plutarch's *Lives* is chronologically significant.[93] Simonidean authorship of poems for Corinth on the Persian Wars should be regarded as entirely possible.

It is likely that Simonides also wrote for the Naxians. The epigram XIX (a) Page, describing the part played at Salamis by Democritus of Naxos, was quoted above,[94] where the suggestion that it was part of *The Sea-Fight at Salamis* did not commend itself. If the lines are a complete poem, they might be an inscription, presumably carved at Naxos to commemorate some dedication by Democritus, or (as Page believes) a short non-inscriptional poem or skolion for recitation at symposia; however it is quite possible that they are a fragment of an elegy, not on Salamis, but on the role of the Naxians in the Persian Wars as a whole, that is at Salamis, Plataea,[95] and (presumably) Mycale. If the piece is non-inscriptional, and so had no anonymous existence on stone, there is a fair chance that the Simonidean ascription represents the preservation of a genuine tradition of authorship. Page, disregarding this principle, states that "nobody but a Naxian would have any interest in celebrating the actions of Democritus"; to which one might fairly reply "except a professional poet commissioned by Democritus or the Naxians — Simonides, for instance". If the poem was intended for inscription or performance at Naxos, its date would depend on the position of the islands after Salamis. From Herodotus it seems that the Greeks were in command of the islands as far east as Delos and the Persians unwilling to venture farther west than Samos.[96] Presumably, then, Naxos was free from Persian control, and our poem could be dated between Salamis and Plataea, though a date after the end of the war is perhaps preferable. We cannot tell whether or not Simonides himself went to Naxos.

Finally, the possibility that there existed a separate Simonidean poem on the part played by the Megarians at Salamis is mentioned below, in the following section.

3. Plataea and after

Pausanias[97] states that the Athenians and Spartans had separate graves at Plataea, inscribed with *elegeia* by Simonides. The epigrams are not quoted by Pausanias; but mention has already been made of Bergk's suggestion, which is accepted by Page, that they are to be identified with two epigrams connected in our source with Thermopylae.[98] The epigrams are (VIII Page):

> If a noble death is the greatest portion of valour, Fortune has granted this to us above all; for, seeking to confer freedom on Greece, we lie enjoying an ageless fame.

and (IX Page):

> These men, having conferred inextinguishable glory on their dear country, wrapped themselves in the dark cloud of death. But, having died, they are not dead, since Valour, glorifying them, leads them up from the house of Hades below.

Irrespective of the identification of the poems, Pausanias' ascription of the *elegeia* for Athens and Sparta to Simonides is very likely to be correct,[99] in view of his composition of other Persian War poems for both these cities. If correct, it shows that Simonides, after all the disputes between Athens and Sparta,[100] was still being employed by both. If in fact he was now writing for Athens and Sparta at Plataea, it would be reasonable to attribute to him the following lines, which they inscribed jointly on the altar of Zeus Eleutherios there:

> Once the Greeks, having driven out the Persians by the might of Victory and the labour of Ares, set up this altar of Zeus Eleutherios as a common offering on behalf of free Greece.[101]

All these inscriptions were no doubt written within a few weeks or at most a few months of Plataea, that is in autumn 479 or winter 479-8.

The couplet which Pausanias inscribed on the tripod-monument dedicated at Delphi by the Greeks after Plataea is ascribed to Simonides by some sources:[102]

> Pausanias commander of the Greeks, when he had destroyed the army of the Medes, dedicated this monument to Phoebus.

In view of Simonides' close association with the events of the Persian Wars, including Plataea, his authorship of this epigram should be considered highly probable (to what other poet was Pausanias likely to turn?); moreover the anecdotal tradition, though no doubt unreliable in detail, seems to preserve a memory of an association between Pausanias and Simonides.[103] It is probably true that the Spartans were offended by the arrogant tone of the couplet and at once erased it from the monument;[104] but it is doubtful whether Simonides foresaw this reaction or whether the Spartans would extend their annoyance to the poet;[105] the incident occurred before Pausanias received command of the expedition to Cyprus and Byzantium (at the beginning of summer, 478) and therefore at about the same time as Simonides was writing for Sparta at Plataea and in Sparta's honour at Thermopylae.

The elegy in which the Corinthians' part at Plataea is praised[106] is generally, and rightly, accepted as Simonidean, on the well-established principle that the ascription of elegies is more reliable than that of inscriptional epigrams. Plutarch writes:

> One can learn of the Corinthians and the position in which they fought against the barbarians, and the credit which accrued to them from the battle of Plataea, from the words of Simonides in the following lines:
>
> > "(Against the Persians) in the centre (stood) those who dwell in Ephyra with its many fountains, skilled in all kinds of prowess in war...and those who inhabit Corinth the city of Glaucus...made

> (the orb?) of the glorious golden sun (?) in the sky the fairest witness of their labours; and it now spreads abroad the fame of themselves and their ancestors.'"[107]
>
> For Simonides did not tell of these things at a choral performance at Corinth nor in an ode to that city, but has simply recorded those deeds in an elegy.[108]

The poem shows clearly that Simonides was well-disposed to the Corinthians in the period immediately following the Persian Wars, though there is no means of determining its precise date. The nature and occasion of the poem are also obscure; but Plutarch seems to indicate that the poem was not directly commissioned by the Corinthians and to hint that the reliability of Simonides' account is thereby enhanced.

It is likely that Simonides wrote for the Megarians also. A stone of the fourth or fifth century A.D. carries the following inscription:[109]

> Helladios the high priest caused the inscription for the heroes who died in the Persian War and lie here, which had been destroyed by time, to be inscribed in honour of the dead and the city. Simonides composed it.
>
>> "In striving to promote the day of freedom for Greece and the Megarians we received the lot of death, some beneath Euboea and Pelion, where the shrine called after the holy archer Artemis is situated, others on the height of Mycale, others before Salamis..[110] others on the Boeotian plain, they who dared to pit their strength against men on horseback. Our fellow citizens granted us this privilege, round the centre-stone (omphalos) in the thronging agora of the Nisaeans."
>
> The city has sacrificed a bull right down to our day.

It is generally thought that the text of the inscription, and the Simonidean ascription, were derived by Helladios from a literary source. Some have further supposed that we have here yet another instance of the expansion of a short original inscription in the literary tradition, with the late stone representing the expanded version. However Page rightly counters that there is no objection, on grounds of content or style, to supposing that the whole epigram is original. One may add that Helladios' statement that the inscription was "destroyed by time" is most naturally taken to mean that the letters had become too worn to read (he does not say that the stone had been destroyed); thus it would surely be clear to him, from the old stone, whether the original inscription had consisted of two lines or ten. As the wording of Helladios' inscription strongly suggests that he believed himself to be restoring the original version, we may assume that the original inscription consisted of ten lines. If this is correct, the poem, with its allusions to Plataea and Mycale, must be dated after the end of the war.

The Simonidean ascription on this very late stone is no surer guarantee of his authorship than an ascription found in a late literary source; but this does not necessarily mean that it is incorrect. We learn from the scholia to Theocritus that Simonides celebrated the Megarians' naval prowess,[111] which must surely be a reference to a poem on the Megarians' role in the Persian Wars. Bergk's argument,[112] that the poem referred to by the scholiast must have carried a more explicit testimony to such prowess than does our epigram, carries some weight, as the missing pentameter (line 6) could have carried only the briefest of allusions to Megarian sea-power. If Simonides thus celebrated the Megarians' role, at Salamis or in the war in general, in some other poem, it is quite probable that he was also the author of this inscription. Of course, if the Megarians had their own contemporary poet Philiadas, who was prominent enough to receive external commissions for public epitaphs on war graves, their employment of Simonides for this purpose would be unlikely; but the balance of evidence rather favours the view that Simonides was their contemporary poet and that Philiadas belongs to a later period.[113]

Simonides may have written for the Tegeans also. An epigram on the Tegeans states:[114]

> Because of the valour of these men the smoke of broad Tegea on fire did not reach the sky, men who wished to leave to their children a city blooming in freedom, but themselves to die in the front rank.

Page's dismissal of Bergk's suggestion that the lines refer to Plataea, on the ground that the Tegeans who fell in that battle "did not die in the act of saving Tegea from the flames", has a certain ruthless logic about it, but is too dogmatic; after all, the eventual result of a Greek defeat could easily have been the burning of Tegea and other Greek cities, and a memorial erected at Tegea might have reflected local patriotic sentiment rather than a broad Panhellenic view. If the lines do refer to the Persian War, Simonidean authorship is a distinct possibility, so that yet another city would be added to those who sought his services in this connection. Another suggestion which has had considerable support is that the lines refer to the battle at Tegea between the Spartans, and the Tegeans and Argives, which historians usually date to the late seventies or early sixties of the fifth century. It must be admitted that the wording of the epigram is more obviously suited to this local Peloponnesian conflict than to the Persian War, and Simonidean authorship would then be unlikely; he had apparently left mainland Greece for Sicily (476 B.C.) before the date of this battle, and in any case the anti-Spartan overtones of the epigram (if it referred to this battle) would ill accord with his recent praise of Sparta's role in the Persian War.[115]

Also to be dated some time after Plataea is Simonides' poem on Themistocles' restoration of the shrine of the Lycomid family at Phlya, after its destruction by the Persians. It is not clear from Plutarch what type of poem this was; some think it was an inscription, others a hymn. Simonides and Themistocles must still have been on good terms at this time.[116]

4. Conclusions

Stella[117] finds support for her revised Simonidean chronology in two aspects of Simonides' activities in the Persian Wars: firstly in the alleged youthful spirit of his Persian War poetry, and secondly in the sheer amount and intensity of the work involved, which, she claims, would have been an excessive burden for a man in his seventies. (If Stella's chronology were correct, Simonides would be about fifty or a little older at the time of Xerxes' invasion.)

As regards the first point, I feel that the implied distinction between the spirit of the war-poems to be expected from a mature poet in his fifties, and from a poet in his seventies in full command of his powers, is too subtle and subjective for me to make any useful comment. As regards the second point, we have noted perhaps four or five lyric poems or elegies, of indeterminate length, divided between the major battles from Marathon to Plataea; and about twenty short epigrams, some of which may not be genuine. The earliest works of the 480/479 campaign, on Thermopylae and Salamis, were probably written quite soon after these battles, that is, in autumn 480, while the latest can hardly have been earlier than spring 478; the work is thus spread over a period of about eighteen months. It is clear that all these poems together amount to far less than, say, a single tragedy; and the labour of composing them over a period of eighteen months or more would not be too much for an active man in his seventies. It might be argued that the composition of a large number of poems for several different states would involve a great deal of travel and negotiation for commissions; but it is not known how many of these places Simonides actually visited — even choral odes could be sent, and performed in the poet's absence. One might have felt slightly more at ease if Simonides' reputed age had been twenty years younger; but his activity in the Persian Wars is not incompatible with the dating of his birth c. 556 B.C.

References

1. Hdt. 7.228; see Chapter I, section 2, with nn. 6, 38, 41, 43.
2. Page (1975) on eps. XXII (a) & (b).
3. Ἀμφικτύονές εἰσί...οἱ ἐπικοσμήσαντες, Σιμωνίδης...ἐστι...ὁ ἐπιγράψας ("the Amphictyons are...the ones who honoured, Simonides...is...the one who wrote the inscription").
4. Page (1981) on the same two epigrams.
5. Boas (1905) 9.
6. Kaibel (1873) 437-8. Kaibel later added an alternative possibility, that Herodotus was convinced that Simonides did not compose the two inscriptions (1892: 96).
7. Page (1981) ibid.
8. Page rightly adds that it is a natural inference that Simonides personally composed his friend's epitaph.
9. 1905: 12-13.
10. So Kaibel (1892) 96.
11. So Hauvette (1896: 10) and others simply assume that Simonides provided both the inscription and the gravestone for Megistias.
12. This suggestion was advanced by a certain "C.W.B." (*TLS*, Nov. 11, 1939, 655). It might have been more prudent to ignore it, if it had not been accepted and elaborated by W.B.Stanford (*Hermathena* 55 (1940) 99-101). Page apparently does not consider it worth mentioning.
13. Simonides XVII (a) Page; Thuc. 1.132.3.
14. 26/531 Page.
15. Strabo 9.4.2; Simonides XXIII Page.
16. See Page on XXIII.
17. See Page (ibid.).
18. VII Page; *Anth. Pal.* 7.301, assigned to Simonides by the formula τοῦ αὐτοῦ Σιμωνίδου ("by the same author, Simonides"), and with the lemma "on those who died with Leonidas the Spartan".
19. See Chapter VII, section 3, with n. 51.
20. Schneidewin frag. 169. Herodotus' νῦν...ἔστηκε ἐπὶ Λεωνίδῃ (7.225.2) might mean "now stands over the body of

Leonidas", in which case the question whether Leonidas' body was still buried at Thermopylae in Herodotus' day becomes relevant (see Paus. 3.14.1; Macan on Hdt. 7.238; Hignett (1963) 148 n. 3).

21. So Bergk (on Simonides 110); Munro (*CAH* IV 300); Hignett (1963: 147).

22. Bergk 110; Paus. 3.8.2. For the epigram for Cynisca, cf. Paus. 6.1.2; the epigram for Pausanias is XVII (a) Page (138 Bergk).

23. See n. 15 above.

24. Hdt. 8.66.2; 9.31.5.

25. Hdt. 9.81.1; Diod. Sic. 11.33; Meiggs-Lewis (1969) 27.

26. Hdt. 7.218.3; 8.30; 9.17.1; 9.31.5.

27. E.g. the Carystians and Andrians (Hdt. 8.66.2).

28. Hdt. 9.67.

29. Meiggs-Lewis (loc. cit.).

30. Hdt. 8.66.2. However, a Tenian ship had deserted to the Greeks, and it was this which, according to Herodotus (8.82.1), won them a place on the column.

31. Schneidewin (1835) p. 151 n. 9; Bergk 93.

32. Hdt. 8.50.2; 9.30.

33. For references, see Page (1981) p. 78, on Philiadas I. The couplet runs: "(And ?) broad Thespiae takes pride in the spirit of the men who once dwelt beneath the slopes of Helicon". The manuscript reading ἄνδρες θ' οἵ ("and the men who") suggests that the name of some other people preceded that of the Thespians; the emendation ἄνδρες τοί ("the men who"), which is usually accepted, allows the poem to refer to the Thespians alone, but even so most scholars do not regard the couplet as a complete poem.

34. See Section 3 of this chapter, below (with n. 113).

35. VIII & IX Page (100 & 99 Bergk), quoted in Section 3 below (cf. nn. 97-99).

36. Wade-Gery (1933: 72): "at least 18 months" after the battle (this would be about February 478), or "perhaps...a good deal later again". Macan (on Hdt. 7.228) suggests the spring meeting of the Amphictyons in 478 as a possible date.

37. Cf. Hignett (1963) 266.
38. 11.33.2.
39. 26/531 Page; Diod. Sic. 11.11.6. For a judicious survey of scholarly opinion on various aspects of the poem, see the commentary of E. Degani and G. Burzacchini (*Lirici Greci, Antologia* (Firenze 1977) 316-22).
40. Sc. the Thermopylae dead.
41. The interpretation of ἐντάφιον (here translated "offering"), and οἰκέταν (here translated "guardian-deity"), is highly controversial, but cannot be discussed here.
42. From 11.10.4.
43. Such theories are advanced by Bergk (frag. 4); L. Weber (*Phil. Woch.* 47 (1927) cols. 473-8); and Wilamowitz (1897: 323 n. 1; 1913: 140 n. 3).
44. The usual view that the lines are a fragment, not a complete poem, has been challenged, as far as I know, only by F. Cipolla (*Atti del Reale Istituto Veneto*, LX, 1900-1, 513-4).
45. I.e. ὅδε σηκός ("this precinct") should be read, not ὁ δὲ σηκός ("and the precinct"), which causes unnecessary problems of word-order in the Greek text.
46. The deictic use of ὅδε ("this") is much more common than the anaphoric, which however is preferred by Weber here (loc. cit.).
47. A metaphorical interpretation is preferred by Podlecki (1968: 260) and M.L. West (*CQ* N.S. 20 (1970) 210) but convincingly refuted by Page (*CR* N.S. 21 (1971) 317-8).
48. This interpretation is suggested by Kegel (1962: 34), followed by Kierdorf (1966: 28).
49. So Podlecki (1968: 262).
50. *CPh* 28 (1933) 277-81; also Bowra (1936) 362 ff.; (1961) 345 ff.
51. So Schneidewin, frag. 9.
52. 31/536 Page; the title is quoted by the Suda (s.v. Σιμωνίδης 439) and in the Ambrosian Life of Pindar (I p. 2.21 ff. Drachmann).
53. *Anacreontis carminum reliquiae* (Lipsiae 1834) 231-2; cf. his note on Simonides frag. 83.
54. *Vit. Them.* 15.4 (119 f).

206 SIMONIDES

55. E.g. Bergk (83) and Page ad loc.
56. Edmonds, Simonides 91; Bowra (1961) 344 n. 1. These words may well be part of an elegiac couplet (so Edmonds). Bowra regards the poem as melic, but a lyric rhythm is less easily discernible (a comparable succession of *longa* in Simonides 16/521 leads Page to declare the verse "parum numerosus" and to propose emendation).
57. 1905: 52-3.
58. I.e. as far as περιβόητον ἀράμενοι νίκην.
59. I.e. down to ἔργον εἴργασται λαμπρότερον.
60. I.e. down to δεινότητι τῇ Θεμιστοκλέους (Podlecki (1968) 267,271-3).
61. From "thus winning" (i.e. from τὴν καλὴν ἐκείνην) to "skill of Themistocles" (i.e. to τῇ Θεμιστοκλέους).
62. W. den Boer (*Mnemosyne* Series 4, 15 (1962) 225); the Troezen inscription is *SEG* 18 (1962) no. 153.
63. *Persica* 26 (*FGrH* 688 Fr. 13.30), cited by A.Bauer (*Plutarch Themistokles, für quellenkritische Übungen commentiert*, Leipzig 1884 ad loc.) as resembling the closing phrase "by the counsel and skill of Themistocles" (γνώμῃ...Θεμιστοκλέους).
64. E.Lobel, on *P.Oxy.* 2327 frag.31 (ii), vol. XXII (1954) pp. 67 ff.
65. Lobel is apparently referring to the choral lyric fragments which were later to appear as *P.Oxy.* 2430 (vol. XXV (1959) pp. 45 ff.); though when discussing the handwriting of 2430, he does not refer back to 2327.
66. Wilamowitz (1913) 144 n. 2, followed by Diehl (65) and Geffcken (*RE* "Simonides" III A 1 (1927) 195.64).
67. XIX (a) Page, quoted and assigned to Simonides by Plutarch (*Herod. mal.* 869 c).
68. 1963: 67-8.
69. 1968: 268,271.
70. Page on Simonides 31/536 and Simonides XIX (a). The lines are discussed later in the present section, in connection with Naxos.
71. 1968: 269-71.
72. See Chapter VII, section 1 (with nn. 12 & 13.).

73. Simonidean poems on the role of the Corinthians, Naxians, and Megarians at Salamis are considered later in the present section.

74. Any exaggeration of the Athenians' role at Artemisium in XXIV Page (see Chapter VII, section 3, with nn. 45 & 50) is also much less blatant; no other state was involved in the action of the main clause ("the Athenians dedicated this monument"), and modification of the participial clause ("having conquered the Persians"), in order to admit the claims of other states, was hardly to be expected.

75. Chapter VII, section 3 (with nn. 69-70).

76. See above, Chapter VII, section 3, with n. 74.

77. Paeans are among the works attributed to Simonides by the Suda; but on the whole it seems preferable not to make this identification, as it would mean that *The Sea-Fight at Salamis* was melic and that the attempts to identify elegiac fragments from it were misdirected.

78. XI Page; *IG* I² 927; Plut. *Herod. mal.* 870 e; Ps. Dio Chrys. 37.18.

79. From this starting-point, R.Carpenter (*AJPh* 84 (1963) 81-3) argues that the lettering of the first couplet (which does not specify the campaign) points to a date in the late seventh century B.C., the epitaph perhaps honouring the dead of a Corinthian contingent sent to Salamis to aid the Megarians against Athenian aggression. This theory must be left to the epigraphists to judge.

80. A.L.Boegehold, *GRBS* 6 (1965) 185.

81. XII Page; first couplet quoted anonymously by Plutarch (*Herod. mal.* 870 e) and one or two other sources, and as Simonidean by *Anth. Pal.* 7.250; all three couplets quoted by Aristid. *or.* 28.66, II 163 Keil, probably anonymously (see above, Chapter IV, section 2, with n. 24).

82. Jacoby (1945) 172 n. 57, 175 n. 77.

83. XIII Page; Plut. *Herod. mal.* 870 f (anonymous); *Anth. Pal.* 6.215 (Simonidean).

84. XIV Page; Plut. *Herod. mal.* 871 b & Athen. 13.573 c-e (Simonidean), and schol. Pind. *Ol.* 13.32 b (anonymous). See, for a detailed discussion of the testimonia and other matters, Boas (1905) 47-66; and, for a clear summary, Page ad loc.

The testimonia to this epigram are an important item of evidence for the date of the Simonidean Collection; Page's somewhat diverse pronouncements on this matter are discussed above (Chapter I, section 2, with n. 49).

85. X Page; Plut. *Herod. mal.* 870 f & *Anth. Pal.* 7.347 (anonymous), and Ps. Dio Chrys. 37.19 (Simonidean).

86. Page ad loc., with reference to Plut. *Herod. mal.* 871 a.

87. So Grundy (1901) 367-8. It is true that the Athenians allowed the Corinthians to bury their dead on Salamis, but such a request could hardly have been refused in any circumstances.

88. Hdt. 8.59 & 61.

89. Wilamowitz (1913) 144 n. 5; Aristot. *Rhet.* 1.6, 1363 a 14 (= Simonides 67/572 Page, where other relevant testimonia are quoted); Plut. *Vit. Them.* 5.7 (114 d).

90. *Ol.* 13.55-60.

91. For Themistocles, frag. 122/627 Page, ap. Plut. *Vit. Them.* 1.4, 112 a-b (see Section 3 below, with n. 116); for Corinth, ep. XIV Page (already considered) and fr. eleg. 10-11 West (see Section 3 below, with n. 106), ap. Plut. *Herod. mal.* 871 b & 872 d. (The *De Herodoti malignitate* is now generally accepted as Plutarch's: see Ziegler, *RE* "Plutarchos" XXI 1 (1951) 872.11 ff.)

92. As is assumed by Oliver (1935) 199.

93. For a general discussion, see Gomme, *Commentary on Thucydides* vol. I pp. 57-8.

94. See above, this Section, with nn. 66-70.

95. For the Naxians at Plataea, see Diod. Sic. 5.52.3.

96. Hdt. 8.132.2-3. In Hdt. 9.3.1, Mardonius contemplates sending beacon signals to Sardis "across the islands", but it has been suggested that this must mean via Athos and Lemnos (see How & Wells ad loc.).

97. 9.2.5.

98. See above, Section 1, with n. 35.

99. Page, who rarely comments on the authorship of epigrams and even more rarely accepts Simonidean authorship, believes that Simonides did write eps. VIII & IX, in view of their impressive quality of sentiment and expression.

100. On the relations, sometimes strained, between Athens and Sparta in the Persian Wars, see Munro (*CAH* IV 321 f.) and Hammond (1959: 254 f.). According to Plutarch (*Herod. mal.* 42 (873 a); *Vit. Aristid.* 20.1 (331 a)) they were still quarrelling, after Plataea, over the erection of a trophy; but Munro (*CAH* IV 339) is non-committal, and Hignett (1963: 20) is sceptical, about the truth of this story.

101. XV Page; Plut. *Herod. mal.* 42 (873 b) & *Vit. Aristid.* 19.7 (330 f) (anonymous); *Anth. Pal.* 6.50 (Simonidean). The above version ignores the first pentameter, found only in the Anthology; on the unusual metrical form of the version quoted by Plutarch, see Page. Page denies the epigram to Simonides because of its strange metrical form and allegedly poor style, factors which have to be set against the argument for Simonidean authorship which I tentatively advance above.

102. XVII (a) Page; anonymous in Thuc. 1.132.2 and other sources, Simonidean in *Anth. Pal.* 6.197 and Paus. 3.8.2 (who alludes to the epigram but does not quote it).

103. Page describes this epigram as "a model of conciseness and clarity", but rejects Simonidean authorship because of the untrustworthiness of the ascription. I would prefer to accept it as Simonidean for reasons of general probability, as outlined above. (For the tradition associating Simonides with Pausanias see Plato *Epist.* 2.311 a; Plut. *Cons. ad Apoll.* 6 (105 a); Ael. *VH* 9.41.)

104. So Thuc. 1.132.3; but according to Ps. Demosth. 59 (*In Neaeram*) 98, the Spartans took this action only under compulsion, as a result of an action brought by the Plataeans before the Amphictyons.

105. Bowra (1936: 368 f.) once went so far as to suggest that Simonides was deliberately encouraging Pausanias' treasonable self-aggrandisement, in order to aid Themistocles' attempts to weaken Sparta; but this point is omitted from his second edition (1961), where he rightly modifies his former picture of Simonides as closely dependent on Themistocles.

106. Fr. eleg. 10-11 West (84 Bergk, 64 Diehl; not in Page); Plut. *Herod. mal.* 42 (872 d-e).

107. The dots indicate divisions between the excerpts of this poem as quoted by Plutarch; and there is considerable difficulty

in the text at the point where the sun is referred to. However the general sense is clear enough.

108. Lobel (*P.Oxy.* vol. XXII (1954) p. 67) proposes to assign to this poem *P.Oxy.* 2327 frag.27 ii, in which can be detected references to Persians, Spartans, and a land-battle.

109. XVI Page; *IG* VII 53 & *SEG* 13 (1956) 312.

110. The mason has omitted a pentameter at this point.

111. Simonides 124/629 Page; schol. Theocr. 12.17 (pp. 255-6 Wendel).

112. On frag. 199 (followed by Boas (1905) 79 n. 3).

113. See above, Section 1 of this chapter, with n. 33. Page, dismissing the Simonidean ascription of our epigram as fictitious, states that the Megarians had their own contemporary poet, Philiadas; yet in his commentary on Philiadas I he inclines to the view that Philiadas' epitaph on the Thespians is a demonstrative piece (by which he surely means that it is late — a contemporary demonstrative epigram, which pretends to be an epitaph on a (real) war-grave but is not, is surely inconceivable).

114. LIII Page; *Anth. Pal.* 7.512, ascribed to Simonides by the formula τοῦ αὐτοῦ ("by the same author"). On the slipshod lemma "on the Greeks who made Tegea free", see Page. An artificial variation on the theme of LIII is found in LIV Page.

115. W.G.Forrest (*CQ* N.S. 10 (1960) 229 n. 12) places more reliance on a Simonidean epigram than is usual nowadays, when he suggests that it can be inferred from LIII Page (122 Diehl) that the Spartans did not capture Tegea in this battle, and that the Simonidean ascription favours the dating of the battle before 468 (the date of Simonides' death). (He does not claim certainty on either point.)

116. The poem is 122/627 Page; see Section 2 above, with n. 91.

117. 1946: 4, 17.

Chapter 9

Simonides in Italy and Sicily

1. The Ode for Anaxilas of Rhegium

The earliest evidence for this ode is a passage of Aristotle,[1] which illustrates the qualities of covetousness and wit commonly attributed to Simonides in the anecdotal tradition:

> Simonides, when the victor with the mule-car offered him a small fee, scorned to write in honour of mules and refused to compose an ode; but when the victor gave him an adequate fee, he wrote:
>
> "Hail, daughters of storm-footed steeds."
>
> Yet they were also the daughters of asses.[2]

The scholiast on the passage tells the same story at greater length.[3] Simonides is represented as habitually refusing commissions because of inadequate fees, and his reason for refusing on this occasion is quoted verbatim; but there is nothing that could not be extracted from Aristotle's own text. As in Aristotle, the name of the patron is not given.

The following passage of Heraclides Ponticus quotes the same fragment and provides further details of the occasion:[4]

> Anaxilas of Messana ruled over them (sc. the people of Rhegium). Having won an Olympic victory with the mule-car, he feasted the Greeks; and someone in jest said of him: "What would he have been doing if he had won a victory with the horse-chariot?" Simonides composed the epinician:
>
> "Hail, daughters of storm-footed steeds."

Similar in content is the following passage of Athenaeus:[5]

> Alcibiades, having won a victory at Olympia...sacrificed to Olympian Zeus and feasted the whole assembly. And Leophron did the same at the Olympic festival, on the occasion when Simonides of Ceos wrote the epinician ode.

The references to Anaxilas in Heraclides and to Leophron in Athenaeus must surely be connected. In both accounts we have an Olympic victory, a feasting of the assembly, and an ode of Simonides; one account gives us the name of Anaxilas, the other the name of his son Leophron.[6] It would be a strange coincidence if the Leophron named by Athenaeus were an entirely different person and the two incidents quite unconnected.[7] Moreover it seems likely that all these passages refer to only one occasion. It is true that our authorities variously mention Anaxilas and Leophron; but the accounts can easily be reconciled by supposing that Leophron was associated in some way with his father's victory and the resultant celebration. If Leophron represented Anaxilas at Olympia and perhaps drove the car himself,[8] it would scarcely matter whether the victory, the commissioning of the ode, and the entertainment of the gathering, were ascribed to the father or to the son. Other views have however been expressed: that the incident concerns only Anaxilas and has been wrongly transferred by Athenaeus to his son Leophron;[9] that there were two victories (each with a Simonidean ode and an entertainment of the assembly), at the second of which Leophron followed the example set by his father;[10] or that the victory was won by Anaxilas, the ode being addressed many years later to his son Leophron.[11] The view we adopt depends on the date of Anaxilas' victory and on the age and status of Leophron at that time. The evidence on these matters must therefore be considered.

According to Diodorus,[12] Anaxilas died in 476/5 having reigned for eighteen years, that is, from 494/3. That he was tyrant at the time of his victory is proved by the fact that he celebrated it with a special issue of Rhegian coinage stamped with the mule-car.[13] Any Olympic victory won by him must therefore belong to one of the festivals from 492 to 476.[14] Moreover the date can almost certainly be narrowed down further by reference to the issue of the special coinage; 488 would apparently leave too little time for Anaxilas' previous issue of Rhegian coinage c. 489 (492 being, for this reason, totally excluded), so that the date may be narrowed to 484, 480, or (rather less likely) 476.[15]

Can Leophron have participated in one of these festivals? According to the Pindaric scholia[16] Anaxilas' son (here called Cleophron) was old enough, during his father's lifetime, to join with him in threatening war against Locri (in 477 B.C.) and to govern a city as his representative. There is however strong (and older) evidence that Anaxilas died leaving only sons of immature age, and that Micythus, a servant of Anaxilas, acted as regent from 476/5 until 467/6.[17] These accounts can easily be reconciled by the supposition, first advanced by Boeckh and widely accepted since, that Leophron died before his father, leaving Anaxilas with other much younger sons.[18] This seems the most convincing solution, bringing most of our authorities[19] into harmony and allowing the assumption that Leophron participated in his father's victory-celebration in the manner already suggested.

If 484 is the correct date for Anaxilas' victory, it is quite possible that Simonides visited Italy (and perhaps also Sicily) at that time, although he may have gone no further than Olympia. A visit to Italy in 480, after the Olympic festival, is perhaps less likely, in view of Simonides' activity at about this time in commemorating events of the Persian War, but cannot be ruled out entirely. The numismatic evidence suggested that the date 476 is somewhat less likely than 484 or 480; but if the ode is to be associated with an Olympic victory of 476, Simonides could by then have been in the West on his only known visit;[20] the death of Leophron would then have to be set in the short period between the Olympic celebration in 476 and the death of Anaxilas in 476/5.

Clearly the ode is of no help in deciding the dates of Simonides' lifetime. Though it may belong to 476, it could be up to eight years earlier; it cannot therefore count as one of a number of works which, in accumulation, might seem an excessive burden for a man of advanced years.

2. The Ode for Astylus of Croton or Syracuse

Simonides' ode for Astylus is attested by an entry in the lexicon of Photius:[21]

> ...But when athletes began to compete without prizes, those who were linked to them by friendship or kinship used to crown the victors with garlands; of the other spectators, those who were sitting near and were men of means used to present them with things of greater worth, while those who were sitting further back used to pelt them with flowers and leaves as they went round...As a result it became customary for the athletes to parade round in a circle and to gather up and receive the things which were offered to them. Hence Simonides says of Astylus:
>
>> "Who among men of the present day has crowned himself so many times either with myrtle leaves or garlands of roses, after conquering in the contest of the neighbours?"

This version is based on Page's emendation νικάσαις (here translated "after conquering") in the third line of the Simonidean fragment. If the manuscript reading νίκας ("victories") is retained, the meaning must be "who has crowned himself so many times...for victories in the contest of the neighbours?"

In considering the possible occasion and date of the present poem it is necessary to ask what is meant by the term "the contest of the neighbours" (ἀγὼν περικτιόνων); whether there is any means of knowing if the present poem was written for victory in a "contest of the neighbours"; and what are the likely dates of the attested victories of Astylus.

The basic meaning of περικτίονες, which is defined as περίοικοι, γείτονες, πέριξ οἰκοῦντες[22] ("dwelling round, neighbours, those living round about"), is clear enough. But the exact meaning of the apparently simple phrase "the contest of the neighbours" is rather elusive. The most natural meaning seems to be "the contest organised by those living in the region of Astylus' home". Positive support from the context, and probably the plural ἀγῶσι ("contests"), would be needed if we wished to think of local contests of other areas at which Astylus competed as an outsider. "Neighbours" in this type of phrase seems to denote the organisers of the contest rather than the category of eligible competitors,[23] so that such games were probably open to strangers as well as local entrants.[24] In view of the proliferation of such local festivals,[25] and the probable anonymity of most of them, we need not feel bound to show that there were local games at Croton; there is perhaps some evidence for local games at Syracuse,[26] Astylus' adopted home.

A suggestion which has found some favour is that ἐν ἀγῶνι περικτιόνων ("in the contest of the neighbours") refers to the Pythian festival,[27] περικτιόνων here being equivalent to ἀμφικτιόνων ("neighbours" or "Amphictyons"). A possible way of testing this suggestion is to examine the passages in Pindar where these words occur[28] (there is insufficient evidence to conduct this exercise on Simonides or Bacchylides). I have tried to do this, though it is only possible to state a bare conclusion here: that there is no evidence that Pindar felt ἀμφικτίονες alone (and a fortiori περικτίονες alone) to refer especially to the Delphic Amphictyons or to suggest especially the Pythian games; we may therefore assume that the same was true of Simonides. Of course if the phrase "in the contest of the neighbours" was followed, in Simonides' poem, by something like "who hold the festival of Apollo" (or "Zeus" or "Poseidon"), then it could indeed refer to the Pythian games (or any of the great games).[29] But the meaning which we have accepted, viz. local championships, remains the only probable one for this phrase when used without further definition.

We may now ask whether the practice of garlanding the victorious athlete, which in Simonides' lines is part of the "contest of the neighbours", itself offers any clues to the nature of this event, clues which might confirm or contradict the view we have expressed, that local championships are meant.

We owe this Simonidean quotation to the fact that Plato's phrase ὥσπερ οἱ νικηφόροι περιαγειρόμενοι[30] ("like victors going round to collect (gifts)") seemed to the ancient scholars to call for explanation. An explanation of the word περιαγειρόμενοι, and the quotation from Simonides, appear in Didymus, Photius, and the Suda *sub voce* (in each case Plato's phrase is quoted), and eventually in Apostolius (where no mention is made of Plato).[31] An entry in Timaeus' lexicon to Plato[32] gives a short explanation of the word but does not quote Simonides. It is clear, from similarities of content and language, that these explanations derive originally from Eratosthenes,[33] whose account of the custom of φυλλοβολία ("pelting with leaves") is quoted by the scholiast on Euripides to explain Euripides' phrase φύλλοις ἔβαλλον[34] ("they showered (her) with leaves").

Our authorities describe how the spectators would garland the victorious athlete, present him with gifts (which he went round to collect — περιαγείρεσθαι), and shower him with leaves and flowers (φυλλοβολία). They associate the practice with occasions when no formal prize was given; this suggests especially the four great Panhellenic festivals, "festivals of the crown" (στεφανῖται) where only a crown was awarded. Eratosthenes' account is assigned by Jacoby[35] to his *Olympionikai;* he was not, as far as we can tell, explaining any particular reference in any particular author. (The Euripidean scholium which quotes Eratosthenes refers especially to Olympia, but does not mention Plato nor quote Simonides.) So Gardiner[36] mentions the *phyllobolia* as part of the Olympic festival. However it would be rash to assume, and impossible to prove, that some such practice as Simonides describes could not be found at almost any athletic festival, whether Panhellenic or local, and whether formal prizes were awarded or not.[37]

If Simonides' words refer, as appears to be the case, to the unofficial acclaim received from the spectators and not to crowns officially awarded to the victor, it is reasonable to suppose that the specification of two types of flower would not indicate the venue, even if those flowers happened to be associated with certain festivals as constituting the official crown. Therefore the fact that myrtle crowns were officially awarded at a number of minor festivals[38] is not, I think, of any significance; and in any case I cannot find any evidence that roses formed the official crown at any athletic festival.

It seems then that the garlanding of the athlete, to which Simonides alludes, sheds no further light on the nature of his "contest of the neighbours".

We must now consider whether the present poem is likely to have been written for a "contest of the neighbours".

If the manuscript reading νίκας ("victories") is retained, Simonides is saying "Who has won so many victories in the contest of the neighbours?" If this means, as seems most likely, "...so large a total number of victories, at separate celebrations of the contest of the neighbours", the present victory may belong to this kind of festival, but need not—

Simonides may be listing his patron's previous triumphs at other festivals of a kind different from the present occasion. If it means "who has won victory in so many events at a single celebration of a contest of the neighbours?", it would seem natural to supply "as he has now" and therefore to suppose that the present occasion is a "contest of the neighbours".

If νικάσαις ("having conquered") is read, so that Simonides is saying "who has crowned himself so often, after conquering...?", the meaning is probably the same as with the reading νίκας, viz. "who has won so many victories?"; and the choice (mentioned in the previous paragraph) between the interpretations of such a phrase is still open to us. But the meaning of νικάσαις κτλ. could be "who has received so many garlands by way of acclamation after a single victory in the contest of the neighbours?"; in this case there might be a fair presumption that the present occasion is a "contest of the neighbours", as such a vivid and detailed description of the victor's acclaim would not be expected if the reference were to a triumph in his past career.

It is thus clear that whichever reading (νίκας or νικάσαις) we adopt, there are three possibilities for the occasion of the present poem. The present occasion may be a "contest of the neighbours", Astylus having now won his first victory in such a competition; or the present occasion may be a "contest of the neighbours", Astylus having already won victories in several such competitions; or the present occasion may be an entirely different type of competition (perhaps a Panhellenic festival), the poet referring to Astylus' past successes in the "contest of the neighbours" (whether on one, or more than one, occasion).

The evidence for the attested victories of Astylus may now be considered. Dionysius of Halicarnassus tells us that Astylus of Croton won the stadion at Olympia in 488 B.C. (Ol. 73) and that Astylus of Syracuse won the stadion in 484 (Ol. 74).[39] Diodorus reports that Astylus of Syracuse won the stadion in 480 (Ol. 75).[40] Eusebius agrees with these authors in ascribing stadion victories in the same three Olympiads to Astylus.[41] Pausanias mentions that the statue of Astylus of Croton stood at Olympia; he records that Astylus won three successive victories at Olympia in the stadion and diaulos,[42] that on the last two occasions he called himself a Syracusan in order to please Hieron, and that the people of Croton took retaliatory measures against him for this.[43] Pausanias gives no dates. It was once generally assumed that he refers to the victories of 488, 484, and 480 known from Dionysius and Diodorus, and that he mentions Hieron (whose reign at Syracuse did not begin until 478) simply in mistake for Gelon.[44]

The picture was slightly complicated by the publication of the fragmentary papyrus list of Olympic victors,[45] which gives the following data for the years from 480 B.C. (no information is given about earlier years):

B.C. 480: [stadion winner not given]
[diaulos winner not given]
winner in the hoplite-race, Astylus of Syracuse
[αστ]υλος συρακοσιος οπλειτην
B.C. 476: [stadion winner given — not Astylus]
[diaulos winner given — not Astylus]
winner in the hoplite-race, Astylus (?) of Syracuse
[αστ]υρος[46] συρακοσιος οπλειτ...
B.C. 472: winner in all three of these races given: none is Astylus.

Grenfell and Hunt[47] think that Pausanias should have said "hoplite-race" instead of "diaulos", and they date Astylus' victories at 488, 484, and 480 in the stadion, and 484, 480, and 476 in the hoplite-race. It is true that Pausanias' language seems to imply that Astylus won three double victories in three successive Olympiads; but the discrepancy is slight and does not form a serious obstacle to Grenfell and Hunt's suggestion. Robert[48] on the other hand conjecturally supplements Pausanias' text to include a reference to the two hoplite victories attested by the papyrus, and dates Astylus' victories thus: 488, 484, and 480 in the stadion and diaulos, and 480 and 476 in the hoplite-race. These explanations at least agree in restoring Astylus' name opposite 476 in the papyrus and so in dating his victories over four Olympiads, from 488 to 476; and the inclusion of 476 means that Pausanias was partly justified in connecting Astylus' self-designation as a Syracusan with complaisance towards Hieron. Moretti[49] however rejects the emendation "Astylus" for the year 476, and dates Astylus' victories to 488 (stadion and diaulos), 484 (stadion and diaulos), and 480 (stadion, diaulos, and hoplite-race), adhering to the old theory that Pausanias has mentioned Hieron in mistake for Gelon. The emendation is also rejected, it seems, by a number of scholars who, without giving their reasons, date the victories from 492 to 480.[50]

On the whole it seems best to accept the dates 488, 484, 480, and 476 for the Olympic victories of Astylus, while admitting some doubt about the precise pattern of the categories of events in which the victories were won. The present poem of Simonides could have been written for a success, early in Astylus' career, in some local competition, which he would have entered, no doubt, before his run of successes at Olympia; but it could equally well have been written when he was at the height of his fame, for one of these Olympic victories, the poet referring to an earlier success or successes in the "contest of the neighbours". It is possible, but not necessary, to suppose that Simonides wrote the ode on a visit to Italy or Sicily before his only known visit in 476 B.C. The ode is clearly of no help in establishing Simonides' dates.

3. Simonides and Gelon

The evidence for any association between Simonides and Gelon is very flimsy. No lyric poetry is firmly attested; however there is some possibility that the Aetna poem[51] was written for Gelon as ruler of Gela (491-85 B.C.) or of Syracuse (485-78). Severyns[52] seems to suggest that Simonides may have written for Gelon's Olympic chariot victory of 488 B.C.,[53] on the ground that Simonides is said to have written an epigram for Gelon in 480 (or later) and could have been in Sicily earlier than this, and that Gelon could hardly have afforded to let such a victory go uncelebrated; this is a reasonable, though very tenuous, hypothesis.

The main evidence connecting Simonides and Gelon is a dedicatory epigram quoted by the Pindaric scholia:[54]

> They say that Gelon, acting with good will towards his brothers, dedicated gold tripods to the god, with this inscription:
>
> > "I say that Gelon, Hieron, Polyzelus, and Thrasybulus, the sons of Deinomenes, dedicated the tripods (lines 1-2), having conquered the barbarian tribes, and that they provided a great force of allies for the Greeks in support of their freedom (lines 3-4)."

The epigram is assigned to Simonides by the Palatine Anthology,[55] which refers in the first couplet to only one tripod, and offers an alternative version of the second couplet, describing the value of the dedication in terms which Page (ad loc.) pronounces "unintelligible".[56]

The difficulties which normally surround "Simonidean" epigrams are in this case compounded by the amount and complexity of the relevant literary, archaeological, and epigraphical evidence. The lines have been discussed by commentators on Sicilian history, on Simonides' epigrams, and on Bacchylides' poems, as well as by Delphic archaeologists and by numismatists.[57]

The archaeological evidence, in brief, is as follows. There were found at Delphi two tripod-pedestals mounted on a common base, one pedestal (A) bearing a prose inscription showing that Gelon dedicated the tripod and a Nike, the other pedestal (B) bearing a mutilated prose inscription showing that it was dedicated by (apparently) a son of Deinomenes (perhaps Hieron).[58] Two smaller tripod-pedestals (C & D) were also found, of similar shape to those already mentioned, but with no inscriptions on them, and with no common base preserved; it has generally been thought that these smaller pedestals (or perhaps only one of them)[59] are to be associated in some way with the Deinomenids and with the first two tripod-pedestals mentioned above.

Next a brief summary of the literary evidence. As regards Gelon, the Pindaric scholium referring to his dedication of gold tripods with a verse inscription has already been quoted. Diodorus[60] mentions a gold tripod dedicated by Gelon at Delphi after the battle of Himera (480 B.C.); and Athenaeus[61] mentions a gold tripod and Nike dedicated by Gelon at Delphi "at the time of Xerxes' invasions". As regards Hieron, Bacchylides,[62] in an ode addressed to him for his Olympic chariot victory of 468, refers to gold tripods set before the temple at Delphi; clearly this is a tribute to Hieron's munificence, but Bacchylides does not state the number of the tripods nor the date or occasion of their dedication. Athenaeus (in the passage just cited) mentions, besides the tripod and Nike of Gelon, a similar offering made at Delphi by Hieron (clearly at a different time from Gelon's offering), and he further quotes Theopompus to the effect that Hieron's offering was of refined gold, which for a long time he had scoured Greece to procure.

One view of modern scholars is that our epigram, or part of it, commemorates some dedication made by Gelon (perhaps in association with his brothers) at Delphi between 480 (the date of the battle of Himera) and 478 (when Gelon died). There are many variants of this view. For instance, Homolle[63] thinks that Gelon dedicated tripod (A) after Himera, and Hieron dedicated tripod (B) to claim parity with Gelon; and that Gelon dedicated tripods (C) and (D), perhaps with our epigram on a common base, to reprove Hieron and to associate his younger brothers, Thrasybulus and Polyzelus, in his triumph. Gentili[64] thinks the lines celebrate a re-dedication by Gelon of a single tripod (tripod (A)) originally dedicated after Himera, Gelon having decided for reasons of family prestige to associate his brothers with him. (Gentili associates tripods (B) and (C) with later dedications made by Hieron to celebrate the victory of Cumae in 474 and his Pythian chariot victory of 470; he believes that tripod (D) has no connection with the Deinomenids.) Another body of opinion refers Simonides' lines to some dedication made by Hieron after Gelon's death. Thus Reinach[65] thinks that a dedication planned by Gelon may have been completed by Hieron, but he is vague about possible occasions for the dedication. Sitzler[66] supposes that the lines celebrate the dedication of tripods (B), (C), and (D) by Hieron after Cumae for himself and his brothers, these tripods, with Gelon's earlier one (tripod (A)), making up a monument of all four Deinomenids.

Page (ad loc.) adopts a sceptical attitude, claiming that the epigram cannot be reconciled with the archaeological data and is therefore a late literary exercise. He maintains that there is no place for the inscription of our epigram on the principal monument, which already had its prose inscriptions; but some of the theories mentioned above seem to provide a reasonable explanation by suggesting an addition to the original monument or a re-dedication, and in any case the combination of a simple prose inscription with a more elaborate verse epigram is not unlikely. Page's other main objection is that there is no apparent subject of φημί ("I say that Gelon...dedicated") in the first line of the epigram, as it would be absurd to make the figure of Nike speak of the tripods but not of itself; but one might ask whether it is likely that Page's supposed Hellenistic composer arbitrarily introduced this rare form of first-person statement into his demonstrative epigram. On the whole it seems preferable to allow that the lines may have been an inscriptional epigram associated in some way with the Delphic monument.

If the lines are really by Simonides, he could have written them for Gelon between 480 and 478. We could hardly assume a visit to Sicily in these crowded years; but the dedication was made at Delphi, and Gelon could easily have commissioned Simonides, the acknowledged "laureate" of the Persian Wars, to celebrate his victory over Carthage. Or the lines could have been written for Hieron, some time after Simonides' arrival in Sicily (476); his acquaintance with Hieron at this time is well known. This epigram is of no help in deciding the question of Simonides' dates.

4. Simonides and Hieron

A fairly strong tradition, mainly of an anecdotal nature, connects the names of Simonides and Hieron, though traces of actual works by Simonides for Hieron are extremely meagre. Plato[67] refers in general terms to Simonides' association with Hieron; and anecdotes concerning the poet's covetousness and connecting him with Hieron are found in several sources.[68] Cicero quotes Simonides' reply to Hieron's question on the nature of the gods, and Athenaeus reports a witticism by the poet at Hieron's court.[69] These anecdotes are worth little individually, but taken together indicate the strength of the tradition; the same tradition is also reflected in Xenophon's choice of Simonides as Hieron's interlocutor in the *Hieron*.

The most significant event which the tradition records is Simonides' reconciliation of Hieron and Theron. Different versions of the story occur in the scholia to the second *Olympian* ode, in which Pindar, writing for Theron, alludes obliquely to certain troubles which have passed and are best forgotten. The most frequently quoted version[70] first mentions Aristarchus' view, that Pindar is referring to the troubles of Theron's ancestors, but then expresses a preference for Didymus' account which is said to be based on Timaeus' *Sicilian History*.[71] This account, which need not be set out in full here, tells of a quarrel between Hieron and Theron that brought them to the point of war; but the war did not come about, "for they say that Simonides the lyric poet came along and reconciled the kings' quarrel". Simonides is also named in another version of the scholia.[72] A version of the quarrel and reconciliation is found in Diodorus,[73] who dates these events to the archonship of

Phaedon (476/5 B.C.), but no mention is made of Simonides. The different versions are compared and evaluated by Freeman,[74] who thinks that a place can be found for Simonides' role in Diodorus' account.

The account of the reconciliation by Simonides is usually accepted.[75] It is sometimes rejected on grounds of date; thus Wilamowitz[76] states that Simonides was still in Athens in 476, and that he went to Sicily in 475. But the last firm date we have for Simonides' presence in Athens is spring 476, when he won a dithyrambic victory at the Dionysia during the archonship of Adeimantus (477/6);[77] and he could, as Farnell shows,[78] have been in Sicily by autumn 476.[79] It is true that the quarrel and reconciliation of Hieron and Theron must have occurred before the composition of *Ol*.2, if Pindar is indeed referring to these events in lines 15-18 of that poem; but *Ol*.2 may have been composed some little time after Theron's victory (won in late summer 476), so that several months are left in which Simonides (after his victory at Athens in spring 476) could have come to Sicily and reconciled the tyrants.

A better reason for scepticism is the anecdotal nature of this part[80] of the scholiast's account. Scholarly reaction to such items of the anecdotal tradition seems to oscillate between extremes, the prevailing general trend at present being towards total scepticism. Indeed the present attitude towards Greek biography might not unfairly be summarised as: "Nothing ever happened; even if it did, no one could have known about it; even if they did, they could not have communicated it". In this instance a more moderate course would be to allow that the story could be true in essentials, and to consider what its implications would be if it were true. It might be argued that the tyrants' submission to Simonides' mediation implies that he was an old and trusted friend and had therefore visited Sicily before;[81] and there are some other indications (though no actual proof) that he could have visited the West earlier.[82] But it is not hard to believe that Simonides' reputation and personal qualities were sufficient to achieve this task after only a short acquaintance.

The scanty evidence for actual poems written by Simonides for Hieron may now be surveyed briefly. Evidence of a lyric *propemptikon* or valedictory ode is provided by Himerius in the following extract from a valedictory oration to Ampelius:[83]

> For the Cean poet Simonides also, when seeing Hieron off from Sicily for another land, touched his lyre and as he did so mingled tears with the notes.

The occasion of Hieron's voyage is not known. Himerius' words do not suggest a departure for a campaign; so the occasion was probably not Hieron's departure on the campaign, apparently commanded by Hieron in person, which culminated in the battle of Cumae (474 B.C.). Wilamowitz[84] supposes that Himerius has invented the Simonidean poem, but as he gives no reason for this suggestion, it can be ignored; he would not, presumably, base anything on Hieron's complaint, in Xenophon's *Hieron*,[85] that despots dare not go abroad. There is thus no indication of the date of the ode, though it would be reasonable to date it to 476 or later, when Simonides is known to have been in Sicily.

It is possible that one of a pair of epigrams, which are attributed to Simonides in the Palatine Anthology, may belong here:[86]

> (a) Once while these men were bringing an offering of spoils from Sparta to Phoebus, one sea, one night, and one ship interred them.
>
> (b) While these men were bringing an offering of spoils from the Tyrrhenians to Phoebus, one sea, one ship, one grave interred them.

It is generally agreed[87] (at least by those who formulate the question in these terms) that we have here, not one epigram with some variations of text, but two epigrams, one of which is an imitation of the other (so that the two epigrams are to be attributed to different authors). The question of which was the primary version can be approached by reference either to the alternatives of "Sparta" and "the Tyrrhenians" in the first line, or to the alternative versions "one sea, one night, one ship" and "one sea, one ship, one grave" in the second line.

Boas, followed by Page, starts from the second line and argues that the version of (a), with "one night, one ship", makes good sense, whereas the version of (b), with "one ship, one grave" is a clumsy "correction" (or, according to Page, a "copy") of this. They make out a convincing case for preferring the version of the second line found in (a); even so, the question of which is the primary version of this line is less important,[88] in my view, than the question of the relationship between "Sparta" and "the Tyrrhenians" in the respective versions of the first line. Thus Wilamowitz, taking the first line as his starting point, argues that the familiar name "Sparta" is much more likely to have replaced the unfamiliar "Tyrrhenians" than vice versa, so that version (b), with "from the Tyrrhenians", is the original one. This seems to show that Wilamowitz regarded one version as an "imitation" of the other in the sense of a literary variation on a theme, composed with reference to nothing but the text of the primary version. If imitation in this sense has occurred, Wilamowitz is surely right to regard version (b) as the original. "Sparta" would be an easy conjectural replacement for "the Tyrrhenians", devised perhaps by someone who did not understand the use of "from the Tyrrhenians" in the sense of "spoils from the victory over the Tyrrhenians" and who could not imagine the Tyrrhenians themselves bringing offerings to Apollo;[89] whereas no literary adapter would have conjured up the name "Tyrrhenians". Moreover the name "Tyrrhenians" in the primary version could only be a reference to some real event involving the Tyrrhenians; their name would never have suggested itself to the composer of an original (non-derivative) literary epigram on the general theme of shipwreck. On the other hand, "imitation" in a rather different sense might have occurred, in that an epigrammatist, writing about a real shipwreck, may have borrowed the form and wording of an earlier poem which had also commemorated an actual shipwreck; it is clear that Page, in describing (b) as an inferior copy of (a), is thinking of imitation in this sense, for he describes the epigrams as epitaphs for men lost at sea and thinks they may be copies of old inscriptions.[90] If imitation of this kind has occurred, the "Sparta" version could be the original and the "Tyrrhenians" version the imitation. At any rate, whichever kind of "imitation" may have occurred, the essential conclusion is that the unfamiliar name "Tyrrhenians" can only be explained as a reference to some real event concerning them.

If this event was some well-known historical event, two explanations of the origin of the epigram are possible: either it was a genuine sepulchral inscription, composed at the time of the event; or it was a later epideictic epigram, in the form of a sepulchral inscription, written in reminiscence of the event. The only major historical event which has been suggested (or, as far as I am aware, could be suggested) in this connection is Hieron's victory over the Etruscans at Cumae in 474;[91] and the supposition is that the lines commemorate the crew of a ship which was lost while taking offerings from the spoil of this victory from Sicily to Delphi. This is an extremely persuasive suggestion. Hieron is known to have made an offering at Olympia[92] as a result of his victory at Cumae. Further, as we have seen, it is sometimes supposed that one of the Delphic tripods discussed in connection with the epigram XXXIV Page was dedicated by Hieron for his victory at Cumae; and our epigram might well refer to an earlier but abortive mission to make some such offering to Apollo. Though no reliance can be placed on the Simonidean ascription in the Palatine Anthology, Simonidean authorship of the epigram, if in fact it refers to events consequent upon Hieron's victory, is quite possible, in view of Simonides' known acquaintance with Hieron. The ill-fated mission to Delphi was presumably despatched very soon after Hieron's victory (won in 474), a date which accords well with the other evidence connecting Simonides with Hieron.

An alternative suggestion by Wilamowitz, that the spoil dedicated had been taken from Etruscan pirates, seems less attractive. If it is correct, there is nothing to connect the lines with Hieron or with any other known patron of Simonides, and no means of dating them. If the lines do refer to some such event, the natural assumption must be that they are a genuine sepulchral inscription contemporary with the event, as Wilamowitz supposes; a later literary reminiscence of a comparatively trivial occurrence seems unlikely.

Evidence of another Simonidean poem for Hieron may perhaps be found in the following extract from the Theocritean scholia:[93]

> Aetna is a mountain in Sicily, called after Aetna the daughter of Ouranos and Ge, as Alcimus says in his History of Sicily.[94] Simonides says that Aetna judged between Hephaestus and Demeter, when they contested possession of the land.

It is possible that the poem was written in praise of Demeter and merely mentioned Sicily among the places where she was worshipped; but the emphasis on Aetna rather suggests that the poem had some special connection with Sicily. Schmid[95] offers the attractive suggestion that the poem concerns Hieron's founding of the town of Aetna in 476/5;[96] and a specific occasion might even be sought in the games which Hieron appears to have instituted to celebrate the founding of Aetna.[97] According to Alcimus' account "Aetna" is the personification or eponym of Mt. Aetna, and "she" would no doubt fill the same part for Hieron's newly-founded city; Pindar, of course, personifies cities quite freely. It may also be noted that according to some sources[98] Aetna was the mother of the Gelon who was the eponym of Gela, home of Hieron and Gelon. There is no means of knowing whether the key role of arbiter given to Aetna in the myth is Simonides' invention; but it would be a fitting compliment to the new city. The contest was presumably decided in favour of Demeter, in view of her close connection in cult with Sicily. One of the centres of this cult was Syracuse, where temples to Demeter and Core are said to have been founded by Gelon from the spoils of Himera[99] and where Hieron is said to have held a hereditary priesthood of Demeter and Core;[100] thus the reference to Demeter might be regarded as a compliment to Hieron.

An alternative possibility, consistent with many of the facts already noted, is that the poem was addressed to Gelon as ruler of Syracuse. Simonides' main emphasis in this part of the poem would then presumably be on Demeter rather than Aetna. Gelon's temple to Demeter, dedicated after Himera, has already been mentioned; and he must surely have held the hereditary priesthood of Demeter which is attested for his younger brother Hieron. Aetna, though less prominent than in a poem to Hieron, would still be appropriately included as mother of Gelon the eponym of Gela; moreover, Diodorus[101] notes that after dedicating his temple to Demeter in Syracuse, Gelon planned to build a temple to Demeter on Mt. Aetna, though he died before he could fulfil his plan. There would be a range of possibilities for such a poem to Gelon. If it was associated with the temples dedicated after Himera or with the plan for a temple on Aetna, it would belong to the years 480-478, between Himera and the death of Gelon. However in this period Simonides would be heavily engaged with commissions from the Persian Wars, and a visit to Sicily would be unlikely; it would therefore be preferable to assign the poem to that period of Gelon's rule at Syracuse between 485 and 480, when a visit of Simonides to Sicily would be perfectly possible. Finally, it may be observed that the hereditary priesthood of Demeter and Core held by the family, and the connection of the personified Aetna with Gela, would make Simonides' reference appropriate enough (we cannot guess on what occasion) to Gelon or Hieron as ruler of Gela. The date could then be 491-485 (the period of Gelon's rule at Gela) or 485-480 (between the beginning of Hieron's rule at Gela and the Persian War); the remaining years of Hieron's rule at Gela (480-478) should be excluded for the reason already given.

Finally, it is possible that Simonides wrote for Chromius, the brother-in-law of Gelon and Hieron. The name Chromios was tentatively restored by Lobel in *P.Oxy.* 2430 (Simonides 14/519 Page) frag. 84.1. Podlecki[102] points out that the Apolline epithet χρυ]σοκόμα ("with golden hair") occurs at line 9 of the same fragment; draws attention to Chromius' victory in games for Apollo at Sicyon celebrated (c.473 B.C.?) by Pindar in *Nem.* 9; and speculates on the possibility of a Simonidean ode for some such victory of Chromius. The date of Chromius' other attested victory, in the Nemean games, celebrated by Pindar in *Nem.* 1, was probably 477 B.C. or later.[103] Thus Podlecki is probably right in dating any Simonidean poem on a victory of Chromius to the period of Simonides' acquaintance with Hieron (rather than with Gelon, who died in 478 B.C.).

The evidence for the dates of Simonides' acquaintance with Hieron may now be summarised, and its relevance to the general question of Simonidean chronology considered. There is no definite indication that Simonides visited Sicily before 476. His mediation between Hieron and Theron is dated to 476/5. The Aetna poem (47/552 Page), if it is for Hieron, may well belong to the period from 476/5 onwards; the epigram LXXVI Page, if it refers to a dedication made by Hieron after his victory at Cumae, must be dated to the year 474 or soon afterwards; any poem for Chromius (14/519.84 Page) would probably belong to the period from c.476; and the lyric *propemptikon* for Hieron (75/580 Page) cannot be dated. Occasionally an anecdote connecting Hieron and Simonides makes special mention of Syracuse[104] and so dates itself to the period of Hieron's rule in that city (478-67).

An earlier acquaintance with Hieron, presumably before the Persian Wars, when Hieron was tyrant of Gela (485-78), is however just possible, as was noted above in connection with the Aetna poem. Schmid, it is true, argues against any association between Hieron and the professional poets before 476; he cites in support a passage of Aelian, where it is said that Hieron, once as uncultured as his brother Gelon, began to employ Pindar and the Cean poets after a spell of illness had afforded him the leisure to listen to recitations.[105] Schmid dates Hieron's conversion to culture, or rather his realisation that poets could enhance his prestige, only from 476 onwards, pointing out that his earlier victories in the games, in 482 and 478,[106] were not celebrated. But Aelian dates Hieron's "conversion" from his illness; Severyns[107] rightly says that this cannot be dated, and that the uncelebrated early victories offer no clue, as victories after 476 were also uncelebrated (e.g. Hieron's Olympic victory with the single horse in 472).[108] There is then no evidence against an acquaintance between Simonides and Hieron before 476. The strong tradition connecting him with Hieron suggests that he stayed in Syracuse for most of the time he spent in Sicily.

Stella[109] twice mentions Simonides' mediation between Hieron and Theron in support of her revised chronology, arguing that such diplomatic activity would not be expected of an old man of eighty. Stella does not claim that this point is anything like conclusive, and rightly so — a personal mediation between two autocrats does not imply the bustle and activity which would have been necessary in, say, negotiations between ambassadors. Stella also remarks[110] that Xenophon in his *Hieron* does not seem to depict Simonides as an old man, but (as is only right) she uses this argument with great reserve. There is in fact very little support, in what we know of Simonides' relations with Hieron, for Stella's chronology; indeed one or two points may be made which seem to support the traditional dating. Firstly, we may notice that several anecdotes[111] connecting Simonides and Hieron concern the poet's covetousness. Some other anecdotes[112] about this covetousness concern the poet's old age. (Of the rest of the anecdotes about this trait, I do not know of any that are precisely datable.) It may be that tradition connected this foible with Simonides' old age; if so, the fact that many of the anecdotes about it name Hieron might suggest that Simonides was an old man when he knew Hieron.

The second point is this. We have noticed that Simonides wrote for Hieron occasionally and that there was a tradition of a close and apparently long-lasting association between them. This friendship does not suggest that Hieron slightingly rejected Simonides in favour of Pindar, still less in favour of Simonides' own nephew Bacchylides; yet Hieron's major poetic commissions did in fact go to Pindar and Bacchylides, Hieron apparently regarding Simonides rather as a confidant and counsellor. These facts would be quite consistent with, and indeed might well suggest, the view that Simonides regarded himself as a poet emeritus — that, though in full command of his powers, he was so secure in his reputation and his position of trust with Hieron that he was content to leave Hieron's major commissions to his fellow poets; and that he now regarded Pindar not so much as a rival as a successor.

5. Simonides and the Emmenidae of Acragas

The following passage of the Pindaric scholia provides evidence of the only known Simonidean ode for the Emmenidae, an epinician for Xenocrates the brother of Theron:

> This Xenocrates not only won an Isthmian victory in the chariot race, but also a Pythian victory in the twenty-fourth Pythiad (490 B.C.), as Aristotle records. And Simonides, praising him, sets forth (κατατάσσει) both his victories.[113]

This form of wording must surely mean that Simonides in a single ode mentioned both the Pythian and Isthmian victories of Xenocrates.[114] Some have taken the passage to mean that Simonides wrote two separate epinicians, one for each victory; thus we are often told[115] that Simonides wrote an official epinician for the Pythian victory of 490; and Pindar's sixth *Pythian* ode, written for this victory, is represented as an unofficial personal tribute from Pindar to Thrasybulus, Xenocrates' son. But as I see it, this Pythian epinician of Simonides is a fiction, based on an unnatural interpretation of the Pindaric scholium, and so no evidence can be sought here for a visit of Simonides to Sicily about 490 B.C.

The single Simonidean ode, in which both victories were mentioned, could have been an epicinian written on the occasion of the second victory (the Isthmian victory), or a more general ode in honour of Xenocrates, which could have been written some time after the actual victory, perhaps even after Xenocrates' death, though it might still be classed as an epicinian.[116]

The date of the Isthmian victory of Xenocrates is clearly of interest for Simonides' dates. It is mentioned by Pindar in the second *Olympian* ode;[117] and as this poem celebrates an Olympic victory of summer 476, the Isthmian victory must have been either in the Isthmian festival of spring 476 or earlier. It can hardly have been before the sixth *Pythian* ode (490 B.C.), which does not mention it, so that the earliest possible date would be the Isthmian festival of spring 488. The victory can thus be dated with some confidence to the period 488-476, in any one of the years in which the biennial Isthmian festival occurred.[118] Wilamowitz[119] thinks that the Isthmian victory of Xenocrates occurred soon after the Pythian victory of 490, on the ground that the same driver, Nicomachus, won both races. It is true that Nicomachus is said by the scholiast on the sixth *Pythian* ode[120] to have won the Pythian race in 490; but although he is mentioned in the second *Isthmian* ode[121] as having won races at Athens and (apparently) in the Pythian games of 490, it is not clear that Pindar means he won the Isthmian victory to which the second *Isthmian* ode refers. In any case, since it is known that Nicomachus won Theron's Olympic victory of 476 B.C.,[122] Wilamowitz' reason for dating the Isthmian victory close to the Pythian victory of 490, that races won by the same driver must be close together in time, is invalid. (Despite his early dating of the Isthmian victory, Wilamowitz is inclined to date Simonides' ode c. 475-2, thinking that Simonides took his time in composing it.) Freeman's view[123] that there were two Isthmian victories of Xenocrates, one won in 476 and celebrated in *Isthmian* 2, the other won earlier and mentioned in *Ol.* 2.49 f., is rightly dismissed by Bury,[124] on the ground that Pindar in *Isthmian* 2 would not have failed to mention both Isthmian victories. It is not clear when Stella would date the victory; her reasons for dating this ode of Simonides at 470,[125] and Pindar's *Isthmian* 2 at "467-66" or "466",[126] are not stated.

We are thus unfortunately left with a fairly wide range of dates for Simonides' ode, which could have been written at any time from 488 until some years after 476. An early date would provide an occasion for a visit to Sicily in the 480's B.C., which some like to assume, on the ground that Simonides' reconciliation of Theron and Hieron in 476/5, soon after his arrival in Sicily on his only known visit, seems to imply a previous acquaintance. The date of the ode is at any rate too vague to help decide the central question of Simonidean chronology; this ode cannot even be thrown into the scale as one of the works of Simonides' extreme old age, the accumulation of which is one of Stella's arguments against the traditional dating.

It would be interesting to know how much time Simonides spent at Acragas during the period when he is known to have been in Sicily, from 476 onwards.[127] If the reference to the "chattering crows" in Pindar's second *Olympian* ode is to Simonides and Bacchylides,[128] it may be that he was active at Acragas in 476, whether for the Xenocrates ode or for some other purpose. Apart from this ode, no other works for the Emmenidae are attested; nor do any anecdotes connect him with them, unless one counts the story of his reconciliation of Theron with Hieron. The tradition that he was buried at Acragas[129] is usually accepted but variously interpreted. Wilamowitz[130] implies that he lived at Acragas for most of his stay in Sicily, but this clashes with the strong tradition of his intimate, and presumably long, acquaintance with Hieron, a tradition which we need not reject. We cannot explain why, in the lifetime of Hieron (who died in 467/6), and after the fall of the Emmenidae (472/1), Simonides should have gone from Syracuse to Acragas, where he died (in 468/7); but it would not be hard to imagine circumstances which might have prompted such a visit. Schmid[131] suggests that he may have outlived Hieron, gone from Syracuse to Acragas after Hieron's death, and died there in 466. This makes a tidier picture, but it is not an adequate reason for rejecting the date 468/7 given by our authorities for Simonides' death.

References

1. *Rhet.* 3.2, 1405 b 23; Simonides 10/515 Page.
2. The literary aspects of this fragment are discussed by Marzullo (1984: 145-56), who sees in the lines an ironical jibe by Simonides against the pretensions of Anaxilas. This affects the question of the relationship between Simonides and Anaxilas (cf. below, Chapter X, section 3, n. 114), but not the date of the ode (for Marzullo's view on this, see n. 14 below).
3. Schol. Anon. p. 174 Rabe.
4. Heraclid. Pont. *Pol.* 25.5, *FHG* II 219.
5. 1.3 d-e.
6. Anaxilas' son is named as Leophron by Dion. Hal. *Ant. Rom.* 20.7.1 and Justin 21.3.2, but as Cleophron by schol. Pind. *Pyth.* 2.38 (II 38 Drachmann).
7. Though Obst (*RE* "Leophron" XII 2 (1925) 2057.58 f.) states that it is not known from what city Athenaeus' Leophron came; and A.M. Desrousseaux (*Athénée, Les Deipnosophistes* I & II (Paris 1956) p. 6, n. 4) and Moretti (1957: p. 93, no. 247) explicitly claim that the Leophron mentioned by Athenaeus has no connection with Anaxilas' son Leophron.
8. Compare Thrasybulus' role in the Pythian victory which prompted Pindar's *Pythian* 6 (Farnell 1930-2: I 248 & II 183).
9. Bergk ad loc. (frag. 7); Beloch (1912-27: II 2 176).

10. Förster (1891-2: nos. 173 & 223).

11. Wilamowitz (1922: 312).

12. 11.48.2.

13. Aristot. frag. 568 Rose, ap. Pollux *Onomast.* 5.75; B.V.Head, *Historia Numorum*[2] (Oxford 1911) 108.

14. Thus the year 496 B.C., the upper limit given by Severyns (1933: 74) ("entre 496 et 476"), must be excluded. It is apparently based on the fact that the mule-race was not instituted until 500 B.C., when the first winner was Thersias (or Thersius?) (Paus. 5.9.1). (Severyns cites Förster (1891-2: no. 173), who in fact dates Anaxilas' victory as "zw[ischen] 500 u. 476". Förster must be reckoning exclusively; he knows that Thersias was victor in 500.) Marzullo (1984: 145 n. 1) approvingly cites the dating of Schmid (1929: 507 n. 4) as "tra il 496 ed il 476", though Schmid's wording "nach 496" rightly excludes that year. Cf. n. 20 below.

15. See Head (loc. cit.), who dates 480; E.S.G.Robinson (*JHS* 66 (1940) 17), who prefers 480 on the basis of the numismatic evidence, and tends to exclude 476, on the ground that there would not be time for the issue of the coinage between Anaxilas' victory and his death; T.J.Dunbabin, *The Western Greeks* (Oxford 1948) 398 & n. 4 (480 or 476, with preference for 480); Moretti (1957: p. 89, no. 208) (480); G.Vallet, *Rhégion et Zancle* (Paris 1958) 366 (484, 480, or 476, with preference for 480); C.M.Kraay *Greek Coins* (London 1966) 312 (484 or 480).

16. Loc. cit. (above, n. 6). Justin (loc. cit., above, n. 6), telling of a similar threat against Locri, mentions only Leophron; but his account is not incompatible with the Pindaric scholiast's account of a joint operation by Anaxilas and Leophron ruling simultaneously in different cities. Therefore it is not necessary to follow Beloch (1912-27: II 2 p. 176) in seeing in Justin's account a reference to an independent campaign by Leophron some years after the death of Anaxilas (see Woodbury (1978) 288-9, 290 n. 15).

17. Hdt. 7.170.4; Diod. Sic. 11.48.2 & 66.1-3; Justin 4.2.5.

18. Boeckh (1811-21: II 2 p. 241); Freeman (1891-4: II 241, 490-1); Holm (1870-98: I 215); Dunbabin loc. cit. (above, n. 15); Vallet op. cit. (above, n. 15) 370; A.Schenk von Stauffenberg, *Trinakria: Sizilien und Grossgriechenland in archaischer und frühklassischer Zeit* (Munich & Vienna 1963) 216; and

Woodbury (1978: 289-90), who also suggests the alternative possibility that Leophron may have been debarred from the succession, and Micythus installed as regent, by Hieron.

19. Except Dionysius, whose statement (*Ant. Rom.* 20.7.1) that Anaxilas "left power to his son Leophron" is inconsistent with the account of Herodotus and others of the regency of Micythus and should be rejected for that reason. The suggestion of Woodbury (1978: 289) that Leophron succeeded Anaxilas, but lived or remained in power for only a short time afterwards, does not formally reconcile the accounts of Herodotus and Diodorus with that of Dionysius, but perhaps comes as close as one can get to doing so.

20. See below, Section 4 of this chapter, with nn.75-79. Marzullo (loc. cit., n. 14 above) wrongly states that Anaxilas must have been already dead at the time of Simonides' arrival in Sicily in 476. (He cites Schmid (1929: 514 n. 1) to this effect; but Schmid's own wording is more cautious.)

21. Simonides 1/506 Page; Phot. *Lex.* s.v. περιαγειρόμενοι (II 77 Naber). Versions of Photius' article also appear in the Suda s.v., and in Apostolius *Cent.* 14.18 (II 610 Leutsch & Schneidewin). The oldest version is that of Didymus (E. Miller, *Mélanges de Littérature Grecque* (Paris 1868) 403), where the Simonidean quotation appears in a mutilated form.

22. Hesychius s.v., III 315 Schmidt.

23. The phrase would thus be akin to Pindar's ἀγῶνες Βοιωτίων, "the games held by the Boeotians" (*Ol.* 7.84, where the context makes it clear that the participants were not limited to the Boeotians), rather than to ἀγὼν πρεσβυτέρων, "the contest in which older men compete" (*Ol.* 9.90).

24. Gardiner (1930: 39) implies that practically all local festivals had at least some events open to strangers.

25. A list of such festivals is given by Severyns (1933: 35). Gardiner (1930: 39) says that every state had at least one athletic festival.

26. Cf. Farnell (1930-2) II 119.

27. Urlichs (1885: 5), tentatively followed by Förster (1891-2: nos. 176-7), Kirchner (*RE* "Astylos" II (1896) 1869.18-20), and apparently Christ (1941: 27).

28. περικτίονες: *Nem.* 11.19-21; *Isth.* 8.69-71. ἀμφικτίονες: *Pyth.*4.66 f., 10.8 f.; *Nem.* 6.39-41; *Isth.* 4.7 f.; frag. 94b (= *Parth.* II) Snell-Maehler, lines 41-9.

29. The context in *Nem.* 6.39-41, with the references to the Isthmus and Poseidon, shows that ἀμφικτίονες here means those who live near the venue of the Isthmian games and supervise them (i.e. the Corinthians).

30. *Resp.* 10.621 d.

31. For references, see n. 21 above.

32. C.F.Hermann, *Platonis Dialogi* VI p. 405, s.v.

33. So G.Bernhardy, *Eratosthenica* (Berolini 1822) 249; Wilamowitz (1913) 153 n. 1.

34. Eratosth. frag. 14 (*FGrH* II B p. 1015), ap. schol. Eur. *Hec.* 573 (I 53 Schwartz).

35. *FGrH* II C-BD p. 712.

36. 1910: 206.

37. Hug (*RE* Φυλλοβολία XX 1 (1941) 1025.31 ff.) does not associate the custom with any particular festival; nor does Blech (1982: 112 f.), who further points out that the practice was extended from victorious athletes to successful statesmen, generals, and others. The practice is alluded to by Pindar in connection with a local contest in Libya in the time of his patron's ancestors (*Pyth.* 9.123-5: cf., on this passage, Burton (1962: 59), who refers to an illustration of the φυλλοβολία on a vase by Oltus).

38. See Blech (1982: 140 & nn.158-9); Bury on Pind. *Isth.* 7.74 (= 8.67).

39. Dion. Hal. *Ant. Rom.* 8.1.1 & 8.77.1.

40. Diod. Sic. 11.1.2, where the mss. give the name as Ἄσυλος (Asylos) or Ἄσταλος (Astalos).

41. Euseb. I 204 Schoene, where the name appears as Ἀστύαλος Κροτωνιάτης (Astyalos of Croton).

42. 6.13.1: τρεῖς δὲ ἐφεξῆς Ὀλυμπίασι σταδίου τε καὶ διαύλου νίκας ἔσχεν.

43. Podlecki (1979: 12) discusses the historical events which may have caused friction between Hieron and the people of Croton, and suggests that this factor may have made Astylus' action doubly offensive to the Crotoniates. His suggestion (ibid.) that Simonides may have met Astylus at Hieron's court is attractive, if the ode is to be dated to 476 or later.

44. So Förster (1891-2) nos. 176-7, 181-2, 187-8; Kirchner, *RE* "Astylos" II (1896) 1869.12 ff. However Urlichs (1885: 5) thinks the reference to Hieron is correct and dates the victories 480, 476, 472.

45. *P.Oxy.* no. CCXXII, vol. II (1899) 85 ff.

46. Grenfell and Hunt (*P.Oxy.* ad loc. p. 91, on line 17) emend to [Ἀστ]υλος (Astylos).

47. *P.Oxy.* ad loc., p. 90.

48. C.Robert, *Hermes* 35 (1900) 163-4.

49. 1957: p. 82, nos. 178-9; p. 84, nos. 186-7; p. 87, nos. 196-8; cf. p. 90, no. 219.

50. Maas (*RE* "Simonides" III A 1 (1927) 187.10 f.) and Stella (1946: 10 n. 1) date the victories at "492-480" (without specifying the type of victory); Bowra (1961: 314) dates them at 492, 484, and 480 (mentioning only the diaulos); Kegel (1962: 69) dates the victories in the "wedren" (stadion?) at "492-480" (but at 488, 484, and 480, p. 69 n. 2). I have not yet found out who proposed the date 492, or how it was arrived at; possibly Pausanias' notice of three successive double victories in the stadion and diaulos was accepted, and these victories dated to the three Olympiads (492, 488, 484) before the occasion of the victory in the hoplite-race in 480 (as attested by the papyrus), on the ground that, if any double victory in the stadion and diaulos had been accompanied in the same year by a third victory (in the hoplite-race), Pausanias would have mentioned the fact. However it is conceivable that Maas' "492-480" is a slip for "488-76" and has been copied by other scholars.

51. 47/552 Page; see Section 4 below, with nn. 93-101.

52. 1933: 75-6.

53. Paus. 6.9.4.

54. XXXIV Page; schol. Pind. *Pyth.* 1.152 b (II 26 Drachmann).

55. *Anth. Pal.* 6.214.

56. However Podlecki (1979: 6) regards this alternative version of the second couplet, with its facts and figures, as "workaday" and probably authentic (though he does not translate or otherwise interpret it). He prefers it to the "palpably propagandistic" first version (as quoted above from the Pindaric scholia); but is not propaganda to be expected in a tyrant's dedication?

57. For bibliography, see Meiggs-Lewis (1969) no. 28; Page ad loc.
58. These two inscriptions are *SIG* nos. 34 & 35 C.
59. Pedestal (C) was found next to (A) and (B), pedestal (D) in a different spot.
60. Diod. Sic. 11.26.7.
61. Athen. 6.231 e-f, on the authority of Phaenias (frag. 11 Wehrli) and Theopompus (frag. 193, *FGrH* II B p. 576).
62. 3.17-21.
63. *Mélanges...H.Weil* (Paris 1898) 220.
64. 1953: 205-6.
65. *REG* 16 (1903) 20.
66. Bursian, *Jahresb.* 133 (1907) 200; similarly Pomtow, *SIG* 35 C.
67. *Epist.* 2.311 a.
68. Aristot. *Rhet.* 2.16, 1391 a 8; *P.Hib.* 17.1-8 (Part I, Grenfell & Hunt, 1906, p. 64); Athen. 14.656 d-e; Ael. *VH* 9.1.
69. Cic. *ND* 1.60; Athen. 14.656 c-d.
70. Schol. Pind. *Ol.* 2.29 d (I p. 68.18 ff. Drachmann).
71. Timaeus frag. 93, *FGrH* III B pp. 627 ff.
72. Schol. *Ol.* 2.29 c.
73. 11.48.3-8.
74. 1891-4: II 527-30. Freeman (followed by Podlecki (1979: 9)) rightly regards the scholiasts' alternative version (n. 72 above) as corrupt and barely intelligible; it attributes to the poet a role which naturally belongs, as in Diodorus' account (n. 73 above), to the scheming tyrant, Hieron.
75. E.g. by Holm (1870-98: I 214, 217); Lenschau (*RE* "Hieron" VIII 2 (1913) 1497.60-65); Schmid (1929: 513); Bowra (1961: 359). Hackforth (*CAH* V 146) and Maas (*RE* "Simonides" III A 1 (1927) 188.41 ff.) are non-committal.
76. 1913: 147 & n. 2; 1922: 242; so also Schachermeyr (*RE* V A 2 (1934) s.v. "Theron" no. 1, 2451.18 ff.). Podlecki (1979: 9 n. 14) seems inclined to agree.
77. Simon. XXVIII Page; *Marm. Par.* ep. 54.
78. 1930-2: II 12 & 22.

242 SIMONIDES

79. It is stated by Syrian (*In Hermog.* I p. 86.10 Rabe), echoed by Tzetzes' scholia (on *Chil.* 1.619), that Simonides departed for Hieron's court after this victory and died in Sicily soon afterwards. Aelian (*VH* 9.1) refers to him as leaving for Hieron's court in his old age.

80. Introduced by φασί ("they say"), as Jacoby remarks (*FGrH* III B, Kommentar (Text) p. 580). But Jacoby (ib., Kommentar (Noten) p. 342 n. 472) does not reject the story out of hand.

81. Stella (1946) 14.

82. See the other four sections of the present chapter.

83. 75/580 Page; Himerius *Or.* 31.2 (p. 135 Colonna).

84. Wilamowitz 1913: 153 n. 2. Wilamowitz is followed by Podlecki (1979: 9; cf. id. 1984: 200), whose suggestion that the tale was "fabricated by the late pseudo-biographical tradition on the basis of Simonides' much-acclaimed ability to rouse τὸ συμπαθές" hardly seems to provide an adequate reason for the wholesale invention of ode, recipient, and occasion. We may note that elsewhere Podlecki (1968: 264-5; 1984: 193; cf. above, Chapter VII, section 3, with nn.68 & 70) accepts Himerius' testimony on a lyric poem of Simonides.

85. *Hieron* 1.12.

86. LXXVI (a) & (b) Page: (a) *Anth. Pal.* 7.270, with the lemma "on those from Sparta who were shipwrecked"; (b) *Anth. Pal.* 7.650, "on some men who were shipwrecked in Tyrrhenia".

87. Boas (1905) 243-4; A.Wifstrand, *Studien zur griechischen Anthologie* (Lund 1926) 70; Page ad loc.

88. Some scholars (e.g. Wilamowitz, 1913, 213 n. 2) combine elements of versions (a) and (b) in the second line. This seems a legitimate procedure, compatible with the view of the separate identity and origin of the two epigrams, as there may have been some contamination of the text of the two versions in the course of transmission.

89. The possibility of a dedication by the Tyrrhenians, which is mentioned though not accepted by Schneidewin (frag. 168), cannot be entirely excluded, as there is evidence of Delphic treasuries of the Etrurian cities of Agylla (later Caere) and Spina (Strabo 5.2.3; 5.1.7 & 9.3.8), and of a consultation of the Delphic oracle by Agylla (Hdt. 1.166-7);

though it is uncertain whether these Delphic associations belong to the original Greek or the later Etruscan stage of these cities' existence.

90. However Page says nothing about Sparta, the Tyrrhenians, or the occasion of the dedication to Apollo.

91. This explanation of the epigram was hinted at by Schneidewin and adopted with varying degrees of confidence by Bergk (frag. 109) and others (e.g. Hauvette (1896) no. 36, p. 97; Pomtow, *SIG* 35B (b); Meiggs-Lewis (1969) no. 29).

92. The offering comprised, or included, the famous helmet found at Olympia (*SIG* 35B (a)).

93. Simon. 47/552 Page; schol. Theocr. 1.65/66a (p. 56 Wendel). The phrase ἐν τῷ περὶ Σικελίας ("in his work on Sicily") follows the name of Simonides in the ms., but was transposed by Bergk (Simon. frag. 200B) to follow that of Alcimus.

94. *FGrH* no. 560 frag. 5, III B p. 571.

95. 1929: 512 n. 2.

96. Diod. Sic. 11.49.1; cf. Pind. *Pyth.* 1.29 ff. & 3.69.

97. For these games (the *Aitnaia*) see schol. Pind. *Ol.* 6.162a (I p. 192 Drachmann).

98. Hellanicus (*FGrH* no. 4, frag. 199, vol. I p. 152); Proxenus (*FGrH* no. 703, frag. 4, vol. III C p. 557).

99. Diod. Sic. 11.26.7.

100. Schol. Pind. *Ol.* 6.158 (= 93) a (I p. 191 Drachmann), with the relevant lines of Pindar. Cf. also Hdt. 7.153.1-2 for a hereditary priesthood, apparently of Demeter and Core, held by Gelon's family.

101. 11.26.7.

102. 1979: 12-13.

103. *Nem.* 1.19-24 seems to suggest that Pindar was present in Sicily for the performance of the ode (he went there in 476 B.C.).

104. E.g. Athen. 14.656 d, on Simonides' miserliness. Of course such anecdotes are of doubtful value.

105. Schmid (1929) 511 & n. 5, 512; Ael. *VH* 4.15.

106. For these Pythian victories with the single horse, see schol. Pind. *Pyth.* 3 Inscr. a (II p. 62 Drachmann).

107. 1933: 75 n. 15, 77.

108. Schol. Pind. *Ol.* 1 Inscr. a (I pp. 15-16 Drachmann); *P.Oxy.* no. CCXXII col. I 32 (vol. II, 1899, p. 89).

109. 1946: 4, 14-15.

110. 1946: 3-4.

111. Cited above, n. 68.

112. Aristoph. *Pax* 697-9; Plut. *An seni* 5 (786 b); Stob. *Ecl.* 3.10.61, III 423 Hense.

113. Simonides 8/513 Page; schol. Pind. *Isth.* 2 Inscr. a (III 212 Drachmann). Podlecki (1979: 6-7) suggests that the scholiast's words were prompted by a reminiscence of Pindar's mention of Xenocrates' victories in *Ol.* 2.49-51, and that he mistakenly substituted Simonides' name for Pindar's; but this would surely be a very odd lapse on the part of a scholiast commentating on *Isth.* 2, where the two victories are (naturally) mentioned again (lines 12-19).

114. So Schneidewin (apparently: frag. 14); Bergk (frag. 6); Maas (*RE* "Simonides" III A 1 (1927) 187.26 ff.).

115. Gildersleeve (1885) p. 315; Bury (1892) p. 27 & n. 4; Gaspar (1900) 45-6; Farnell (1930-2) II 183; Severyns (1933) 73. Cf. also Burton (1962) 15; Nisetich (1980) 194; Verdenius (1982) 12.

116. Some of Pindar's "epinicians" (e.g. *Pyth.* 3) did not celebrate any recent victory; this applies to *Isth.* 2, which all agree to have been written after the death of Xenocrates.

117. *Ol.* 2.49-51.

118. Cf. Gaspar (1900) 119.

119. 1901: 1304 n. 3; 1922: 140.

120. Schol. *Pyth.* 6.15 (II 196 Drachmann).

121. *Isth.* 2.18 ff.

122. *Isth.* 2.23 ff.; schol. *Isth.* 2.28 b (III 217-8 Drachmann).

123. 1891-4: II 534-5.

124. 1892: p. 30 n. 2.

125. Stella (1946: 10 n. 1) dates Simonides' epinician for Xenocrates "470...(oppure 490?)". This I cannot understand. It is a possible view (though, I have argued, an incorrect one) that there were two such epinicians by Simonides, one in 490 and one later; I believe myself that there was only one (later) ode; but how could one assume that there was only one (earlier) ode (in 490)?

126. Stella (1946) 15 n. 2, 16. On the date of *Isth.* 2, see below, Chapter X, section 2 (with nn. 55-56).

127. Podlecki (1979: 15-16; 1984: 200) maintains that the evidence for Simonides' continuous presence in Sicily from 476 until his death in 468/7 is weak. But the evidence for his presence elsewhere at any time during this period is weaker still, consisting as it does (a) of the doubtful ascription to Simonides of poems which certainly or probably concern events in Greece proper during this period (see above, Chapter VIII, section 3, with n. 115 on the epigram for Tegea; and below, Chapter XI, section 2, on the Eurymedon epigrams); or (b) of the conjectural association of a definitely Simonidean poem with events in Greece during that period (see above, Chapter V, section 5, n. 87 for Podlecki's view of the Theseus poem, 45/550 Page).

128. *Ol.* 2.83 ff.; see below, Chapter X, section 2.

129. Callim. frag. 64 Pfeiffer; Ael. frag. 63 Hercher (= Suda Σιμωνίδης 441).

130. 1913: 138 f.; 1922: 248.

131. 1929: 514 & n. 1.

Chapter 10

Simonides' Relations With Pindar

1. The argument based by Stella on the relationship of Simonides and Pindar; methodology of the interpretation of Pindar.

An important part of Stella's case against the traditional dates of Simonides is the alleged rivalry of Simonides and Pindar, in Sicily, in the years from 477/6. Stella[1] argues from certain passages of Pindar that Pindar regards Simonides as a flourishing rival, and that therefore Simonides was still at the height of his powers, so that the traditional dates of Simonides' life, according to which Simonides would have been very old or already dead when the Pindaric passages were written, are incorrect.

We are at once confronted with an important question of principle concerning the interpretation of the odes of Pindar. Whatever her particular interpretation of individual passages may be, Stella is at least on common ground with traditional Pindaric scholarship in seeing personal references to, or attacks on, contemporary personalities at certain points in Pindar's odes. However, Bundy and his school, whose methods have largely dominated Pindaric scholarship in recent years, see such an approach as misguided, and interpret such references as part of the encomiast's stock-in-trade, aimed at achieving the greater glory of the patron by distinguishing Pindar from the general class of less adequate *laudatores*.

While the outstanding value of Bundy's contribution to the understanding of Pindar is beyond dispute, it may nevertheless be thought that his methods occasionally run the risk of obscuring the individuality of passages which he does not select for detailed treatment.[2] In one or two of the passages discussed in the following pages, it seems to me that Bundy omits to mention some important point which weakens his contention that no specific or personal reference is intended. In other cases his methods are clearly of value in suggesting that what could be taken as specific personal references may be generalising conventional utterances. In cases where there is no clear indication either way, it seems best to try to confront Stella's arguments on her own terms, while tacitly acknowledging that the methodology of such debate is itself in dispute among Pindaric scholars.

2. Pindaric passages quoted as evidence by Stella: Ol. 2; Isth. 2; Ol. 9.

The first passage in which Stella finds evidence of rivalry between Simonides and Pindar occurs in the second *Olympian* ode:[3]

> Within my quiver beneath my arm I have many swift shafts which speak to those with understanding; but as for the masses, they need interpreters [or (?) "and they (= my themes) thoroughly crave oracular announcers (= poets to express them)"].[4] Wise is he who knows much by nature; but those who have learnt, wild in their babbling, chatter vainly, the pair of them, like crows against [or "in comparison to"][5] the divine bird of Zeus.

The scholia on the passage identify the pair of chatterers as rival poets; according to one version, Pindar "hints at Simonides and Bacchylides, calling himself an eagle and his rival artists crows".[6] The scholia are not however unanimous in this view.[7] The opinions of scholars best qualified to judge are almost evenly divided as to whether we should accept the scholiasts' explanation that Pindar is referring to Simonides and Bacchylides.[8] Stella, it should be said, does not claim that there is an unmistakable reference to Simonides here.

There can be virtually no doubt that the verb in the crucial clause[9] is dual. The reading γαρύετον is unanimously attested by manuscripts, scholia, and testimonia; and this form can only be a dual[10] ("you two chatter" or "those two chatter", indicative; or "you two, chatter!", imperative). Bergk's proposed reading γαρυέτων,[11] which hardly counts as an emendation, would be an acceptable alternative, and must surely be interpreted, as Bergk intended, as third person dual imperative ("let those two chatter"); the notion that γαρυέτων should be interpreted as third person *plural* imperative is based on a curious misinterpretation of Bergk's intention,[12] and is surely unjustified in view of the fact that no such plural form is attested for -ω verbs, in inscriptions or literature, from any period.[13] A number of other proposed emendations, designed to avoid the implications of the dual, may be found in the editions of Pindar, but they are unconvincing, in that none of them seems likely to have been corrupted to γαρύετον. On the assumption, then, that the verb is unmistakably dual, it is necessary to ask whether the dual idea lies in the main statement, or in the simile, or in both. Kirkwood cites an impressive array of examples in which two κόρακες ("ravens" or "crows") are referred to, and argues that the dual lies primarily in the simile.[14] I would prefer to use Kirkwood's examples as a basis for arguing that the dual may well *continue* into the simile or that it makes the simile especially apt; for it seems to me that the dual lies in the main statement, not primarily in the simile. Pindar's sentence should surely be construed as follows: μαθόντες λάβροι παγγλωσσία ἄκραντα γαρύετον, κόρακες ὥς (= ὡς κόρακες γαρύουσι or γαρύετον), meaning "those who have learnt, wild in their babbling, chatter vainly, the pair of them, like crows (= as crows in general chatter or as a pair of crows chatter)"; that is, γαρύετον is the main verb of the sentence, and its subject is two specific individuals, who are compared either to the general class of crows, or to a pair of crows. It seems much more difficult to take γαρύετον as the verb of a subordinate clause and to supply a verb for the main clause, on the following lines: μαθόντες λάβροι παγγλωσσία ἄκραντα (γαρύουσιν), ὡς κόρακες γαρύετον, "those who have learnt, wild in their babbling, (chatter) vainly, as a pair of crows chatter". The grammatical awkwardness of this, and the rhetorical imbalance (with the meagre and verb-less main clause), is in striking contrast to the satisfying structure of the first version. Moreover, even if the second of these versions were to be accepted, so that the dual was explicit only in the simile, it would still point strongly to a dual main subject. A sentence such as "those boys are as mischievous as a pair of monkeys" would almost inevitably be understood to mean "those *two* boys"; and on the assumption that such a basic principle of discourse is valid for ancient Greek, the same must surely apply to Pindar's sentence. In short, the conclusion seems almost inevitable that Pindar in this passage is referring to some particular *pair* of individuals, whom he chose for some reason to designate as chattering crows. Bundy's claim[15] that types, not individuals, are meant in this passage (as in many others) is completely undermined by his failure to discuss or even mention the dual verb and its implications.

On the assumption that a particular pair is meant, we must ask whether there is any means of deciding if this pair is likely to be Simonides and Bacchylides. Conflicting a priori assumptions, that the scholiasts are likely to have been drawing on an accurate tradition of hostility between Pindar and the Cean poets, or alternatively that they relied solely on the text of the odes and on their own imagination, should be disregarded. Nor can it be safely assumed that the status of Pindar and Simonides as major poets necessarily excludes the possibility of disputes of a personal or even petty nature.

A more promising line of approach is to consider the circumstances in which the ode, which celebrated a chariot-victory of Theron, was written. Gildersleeve (ad loc.) implies that, as Simonides was on good terms with Theron, whom he had reconciled with Hieron, Theron was not likely to take kindly to scurrilous attacks on Simonides. It is true that Pindar would hardly find in Theron a ready audience for a gratuitous expression of contempt for Simonides; on the other hand, if it is supposed that the chattering of the crows refers not only to the poetic standards of the Ceans but also to some form of innuendo against Pindar,[16] he would presumably feel entitled to reply in kind, before Theron or anyone else. This point may well suggest the conclusion that if the reference is to Simonides and Bacchylides, it must be a topical one, reflecting a recent dispute. Therefore the question whether Simonides or Bacchylides was present in Sicily when Pindar's ode was performed, or had been present shortly before its performance, is of some importance.

The victory celebrated in *Ol.* 2 is dated Ol. 76, 1 (476/5 B.C.), the Olympic festival occurring in late summer 476. The exact date of the ode cannot of course be determined, but some little time could have elapsed since the victory; for *Ol.* 3 is likely to be later than *Ol.* 1 (which was written for Hieron's victory in this same festival of 476), echoing as it does (3.42) the famous proem of *Ol.* 1; and *Ol.* 2 is probably later again than *Ol.* 3, for *Ol.* 3 (written for the same victory of Theron as *Ol.* 2) seems to be more directly related to the actual victory.

There seems little doubt that Simonides could have been in Sicily at this time. Wilamowitz[17] indeed refuses to admit any reference to Simonides and Bacchylides in our passage, on the ground that neither was yet in Sicily; but Farnell, as we have seen,[18] shows that Simonides could have been in Sicily by autumn 476.

The case of Bacchylides is not so clear. His fifth ode celebrates that Olympic victory of Hieron in 476 which is the subject of Pindar's *Ol.* 1. Bacchylides' words at lines 10-12 of Ode 5 ("your guest-friend sends a hymn from the holy island to your famous city") are usually (and I think rightly) taken to mean that he sent the ode from Ceos and so was not present in Sicily for its performance.[19] Wilamowitz[20] and Farnell[21] conclude from this that he was not present in Sicily when Pindar's *Ol.* 2, which celebrated a victory of Theron in the same Olympic festival of 476, was performed, and therefore that the reference in *Ol.* 2 cannot have been to him. But Bowra,[22] though accepting that Bacchylides was not in Sicily when he wrote Ode 5, suggests that he could have gone to Sicily in autumn 476 after writing it, so that all three poets may have been at Acragas when *Ol.* 2 was performed; another possibility is that he had been in Sicily earlier in 476 but had left shortly before his own ode, and Pindar's *Ol.* 2, were commissioned. It is at any rate clear that we cannot exclude the possibility that Bacchylides may have been in Sicily near the date of the composition of Pindar's *Ol.* 2, so that this poem could have contained a topical reference to him.

We may next ask whether there is any internal evidence, in other passages of *Ol.* 2, which may help to decide whether Pindar in our passage is attacking Simonides and Bacchylides. At lines 15-18 of this ode Pindar says:

> Not even Time, the father of all, could render undone the issue of deeds accomplished in justice and contrary to justice. But, with a happy fortune, forgetfulness may come about.

These lines suggest two points. Firstly, Pindar's language here is strongly reminiscent of Simonides' phrases "that which has been accomplished will never be undone" (an undatable fragment)[23] and "all-conquering time" (from the Thermopylae poem,[24] which is almost certainly earlier than *Ol.* 2, so that if direct influence is assumed, Pindar would be the borrower). Of course borrowing cannot be proved, and in any case could be quite unconscious. But if Pindar was consciously echoing Simonides, we could not accept that he proceeded to attack him later in the ode. Secondly, Pindar's words on the vicissitudes of fortune have been thought[25] to refer to the recently averted armed clash with Hieron which had threatened Theron's security; and the scholiasts (ad loc.) tell us that the two tyrants were reconciled by Simonides.[26] Admittedly reflection on the vicissitudes of fortune is common in Pindar, and in Bundy's view[27] it is used as foil "to highlight victorious achievement or merit in general" or "to emphasise the need to praise it". However, if Pindar was referring specifically in this instance to recent events, and if the story about Simonides' reconciliation of the tyrants is true, it is reasonable to suppose that Pindar would not have reminded Theron of Simonides' services if he intended to attack him later in the same poem.

The other passage of *Ol. 2* which may be relevant to our enquiry occurs at lines 95-8:

> But envious satiety (κόρος) overtakes praise (or: has overtaken my praise of him?), not consorting with justice, but, under the influence of frenzied men, seeking to obscure the fair deeds of noble men with babbling.[28]

There is some similarity between this passage and the *korakes* passage (with λάβροι,...γαρύετον compare μάργων,...λαλαγῆσαι). There is no clear indication whether these lines constitute a specific reference,[29] or, as Bundy[30] inevitably maintains, a generalisation. If a specific reference is intended, the question arises whether, in view of the similarities of language, the reference is to the same individuals as in the *korakes* passage; for if this were the case, we should have here an argument against the identification of the *korakes* with Simonides and Bacchylides, who, though they might have attacked Pindar, are not likely to have attacked Theron (it is Theron's praise which is the object of the activities of the *margoi* here). But it must be admitted that there is no necessity to assume that the same individuals are meant in both passages, and that therefore there is no serious obstacle here to the identification of the *korakes* as Simonides and Bacchylides.

Finally it may be appropriate to consider some of the solutions which have been offered as alternatives to the identification of the *korakes* as Simonides and Bacchylides. Freeman seems disposed to accept the scholiasts' statement that Pindar's words at lines 95-8 of our ode refer to a rebellion against Theron by his cousins Capys and Hippocrates; Freeman then goes on to suggest that the crows of our passage may also refer to Capys and Hippocrates and the eagle ("the divine bird of Zeus") to Theron (an eagle appears on the coins of Acragas). This explanation of the *korakes* passage is also urged by Lavagnini, who claims to have arrived at it independently of Freeman.[31] It may be that Pindar, in the same immediate context as the *korakes* reference, contrasts wise and ignorant hearers ("those with understanding" and "the masses"),[32] so that the phrase "wise is he who knows much by nature" might at first sight seem to particularise Theron as one of "those with understanding". But the whole theory collapses in ruins as soon as one asks why two aristocratic rebels against Theron should be described as two babbling *mathontes* whose superficially acquired knowledge contrasts with his intuitive wisdom — a question which Freeman does not pose, and which Lavagnini, with his explanation that Theron was an initiate and his rebellious kinsmen were not, conspicuously fails to answer. The suggestion that democratic opponents of Theron are meant[33] is more in accord with Pindar's (possible) reference to "the masses"; but even so it remains more likely that the *mathontes* slur is aimed at artistic inferiors than at political agitators. Farnell's suggestion that the "crows" are "two local critics" of Pindar at Acragas meets this condition, but has received short shrift from the commentators.[34] It is true that there is no other evidence for the existence of these critics; at the same time, there does not seem to be any positive objection to Farnell's suggestion (as there is against some alternative solutions). Farnell may be justified in citing the fourth *Nemean* ode[35] for a reference by Pindar to the carping of some Aeginetan critic, whose identity was not known to the ancient commentators and is of course unknown to us. In these occasional odes, there is always the possibility of thinly-veiled topical references which would be easily understood by Pindar's hearers but which are inexplicable to us, who lack their knowledge.

We may now sum up on this passage. γαρύετον (or γαρυέτων) must almost certainly be understood as dual; and it must surely constitute the main verb of the sentence (that is, it is not confined, syntactically, to the "crows" of the simile). If this is correct, Pindar must be referring to two particular persons. The most likely identification yet proposed is "Simonides and Bacchylides"; we do not know, nor did the ancient commentators know, of any other pair who would be so obviously suitable, and other attempts at identification are open to various objections. Nevertheless, a certain residue of doubt must remain, for two reasons. Firstly, it is possible that Pindar is alluding to events and personalities known only to his hearers, at Acragas, at the time of performance, but unknown to any extant ancient author, so that the problem is insoluble to us. Secondly, some of the points discussed above seem to count against the identification with Simonides and Bacchylides, though none of these points is as cogent as the arguments against some other identifications that have been proposed.

The second passage cited by Stella as evidence for the relationship of Simonides and Pindar is *Isthmian* 2.1-13:

> The men of old, Thrasybulus, who mounted the car of the golden-crowned Muses, accompanied by their glorious lyre, swiftly shot forth their sweet-voiced hymns in honour of boys, for whoever was handsome and had the sweet bloom which brings to mind the fair-throned Aphrodite.
>
> For then the Muse was not yet a lover of gain nor a hireling; nor were sweet-voiced songs sold by honey-toned Terpsichore with their faces covered in silver. But now she bids us observe the saying, which comes closest to very truth, of the man of Argos,

Who said "it is money, and money alone, which makes a man", when bereft of his possessions and friends together. Enough, for you have understanding. I sing of the well-known Isthmian victory with the horse-chariot...

The scholia offer different interpretations of Pindar's words. One version[36] quotes Callistratus' explanation, that Pindar had received an inadequate fee from Xenocrates, father of Thrasybulus, and is asking Thrasybulus for his proper reward. Another version, quoting some lines of Callimachus[37] on Simonides' mercenary Muse, says that Pindar is referring to Simonides' introduction of the practice of charging fees for poetry and is rebuking Simonides for covetousness.

Scholars cannot agree on whether the explanation which sees an allusion to Simonides should be accepted or not.[38] Stella[39] thinks that an allusion to Simonides is highly probable here, so that this passage is of some importance to her case. I myself feel sure that Pindar is not referring to Simonides.

It is true that one or two points might be made in favour of understanding an allusion to Simonides here, though none is conclusive. Simonides had a reputation (whether deserved or not) for covetousness,[40] and those who accept that Pindar attacks Simonides in other passages[41] might suppose that he is doing so here. It seems likely that Callimachus, whose reference to Simonides' "hireling Muse" echoes Pindar's wording, understood Pindar thus; on the other hand, Callimachus may have been merely naming Simonides as the most notorious exponent of a mercenary muse while quoting Pindar for the most vivid description of this. In any case, even if Callimachus did understand Pindar as referring to Simonides, we are not bound to follow him. Stella[42] makes much of the fact that Pindar's phrase "the car of the Muses" in the opening lines seems to echo Simonides' "chariot of Victory" in the epigram XXVII Page; but this metaphor is almost commonplace; it is not certain that Simonides invented it, and even if he did, Pindar borrows it so often that its use in *Isthmian* 2 could have little special significance.

The difficulties of understanding an allusion to Simonides are overwhelming, and are set out with complete cogency by Farnell.[43] It cannot possibly be said that the opening lines contrast the practice of Pindar and Simonides — that Pindar, like "the men of old", does nothing but compose (gratis) "hymns in honour of boys", whereas only Simonides' songs are "sold". Farnell compares *Pythian* 11 (41 ff.), where Pindar admits quite candidly that his Muse is hired.[44] Of course, as Farnell says, a charge of profiteering, or demanding excessive payment, might have been levelled at Simonides by Pindar; but whatever differences there may have been between Simonides and Pindar in their character or in their attitude to their patrons, their profession was the same.[45] One might also ask what such an attack on Simonides would be doing at the opening of Pindar's ode. The ode is mainly concerned with a eulogy of Xenocrates, including his Pythian and Isthmian victories; and we know that Simonides also, in an epinician or encomium, eulogised Xenocrates and made mention of his victories.[46] There is no reason to think that Thrasybulus would welcome, or even understand, a gratuitous attack on the poet who had served his father.

A number of acceptable alternative explanations have been proposed, which makes the explanation by reference to Simonides superfluous. Farnell[47] may be right in accepting, from the scholia, that Pindar is delicately asking for a fee; or the suggestion of Fennell and others, that Pindar means he has been prevented by professional duties from writing earlier, seems quite possible.[48] Pavese[49] believes that Pindar is praising Thrasybulus for his liberality, just as he often mentions a patron's hospitality. Thummer [50] argues that in this passage and in others Pindar mentions possible difficulties in the way of composition (here, the mercenary nature of the muse) as foil to enhance the importance of the ode (for the production of which the "difficulties" have had to be surmounted) and thus enhance the value of the tribute to the victor. Woodbury[51] thinks that Pindar is congratulating Thrasybulus on his use of wealth in commissioning the ode and entertaining his friends to hear it, thus perpetuating the fame of Xenocrates' victory. Nisetich[52] sees in the passage an ironic over-emphasis of the mercenary nature of epinician poetry, a feature which (Pindar hints) will not prevent someone of Thrasybulus' discernment from perceiving the superiority of this kind of poetry over erotic song.

I discuss elsewhere[53] the date of the Isthmian victory of Xenocrates mentioned in *Isth.* 2, which Simonides himself celebrated in an ode. The view of most commentators, that this victory was won at the Isthmian festival of spring 476 (Ol. 75,4) or earlier (possibly as early as spring 488), seems correct. The date of *Isth.* 2 itself is not so certain, the only clues being Pindar's reference to, or silence about, various members of the Emmenid house in this ode. It has long been observed that as lines 23 ff. allude to Theron's Olympic victory of Ol. 76 (476 B.C.), the ode must have been written after 476. The historical facts which further help to date the ode are the death of Theron (brother of Xenocrates) in 472/1 and the expulsion from Acragas of his son Thrasydaeus later in the same year.[54] All commentators (that I have seen) agree that *Isth.* 2 was written after the death of Xenocrates (the date of which is not, apparently, known); and as Pindar does not mention Theron by name, and seems to allude (in lines 43 ff.) to some misfortune which has befallen the family, most commentators believe that it was written after the death of Theron and the fall of the Emmenid house.[55]

Stella alleges that Fraccaroli dates *Isth.* 2 to 468 at the earliest; and she perhaps fancies she is following Fraccaroli when she herself, giving no reason, dates *Isth.* 2 at "467-66" or "466". In fact, Fraccaroli dates *Isth.* 2 to Ol. 77,1 or Ol. 77,2 (472/1 or 471/0 B.C.), or "not before Ol. 77".[56] I know of no good reason for dating *Isth.* 2 as late as does Stella. It is very probable, as we have seen, that *Isth.* 2 was written, or could have been written, well within the lifetime of Simonides (according to the traditional Simonidean dating, which places his death in 468/7).

Stella, as has been noted, thinks that an allusion to Simonides in this ode is highly probable. Dating this ode after the traditional date of Simonides' death, she argues that this probable allusion to Simonides means that Simonides must have died later. As there are no grounds for Stella's dating of the ode, the argument can be rejected.

As I have said, I do not believe that there is any allusion to Simonides in *Isth.* 2. If it were admitted, for the sake of argument, that there might be one, and if we were to date *Isth.* 2 (with most scholars) c. 472 or a little later, the same argument in favour of Stella's Simonidean dating might be based on *Isth.* 2 as Stella bases on *Ol.* 2 (an argument based on the fact that the traditional dating of Simonides would make him an old man at the time when Pindar's ode was written). I attempt to sum up on this matter in the final section of this chapter.

The last of the three Pindaric passages mentioned by Stella is the brief aphorism found at *Ol.* 9.48-9: "Praise old wine, but the bloom of newer songs". The evidence for the relationship of Simonides and Pindar is found in the scholia[57] on the passage, where a Simonidean fragment is quoted:

> This seems to have been said in answer to Simonides' remark; for he, when worsted by (pronounced inferior to?) Pindar (ἐλασσωθεὶς ὑπὸ Πινδάρου), wrote abusive words against Agathonidas (?) who had passed this judgement.[58] Since Simonides had said,
>
>> "Wine when still new does not yet put to the test last year's gift of the vine; this empty-headed saying[59] is fit only for boys"[60] (Simonides 97/602 Page),
>
> Pindar for this reason praises old wine.

There are difficulties in the text of the scholium and in the text of the Simonidean fragment quoted there; the meaning of Pindar's aphorism on old wine and new poetry is disputed; and there is the usual question of the reliability or otherwise of the scholiasts. On this last question, we may simply observe that the notion of a link between the remarks of the two poets on "old wine" does not seem intrinsically unlikely, and then attempt to interpret the scholium on the assumption that it could be based on fact.[61]

Despite the difficulties in the text of the scholium, two things emerge clearly: that Pindar in *Ol.* 9.48-9 is alluding to the words of Simonides quoted in the scholium, and that Simonides himself, in the words quoted, was attacking someone who had passed an adverse judgement on his poetry as compared with Pindar's. The main difficulties of interpretation are the meaning of ὅδε μῦθος (translated above as "this saying") and the identity of the critic.

Boeckh[62] thinks that ὅδε μῦθος is some new story or myth (*nova fabula*) of which Simonides disapproved. If this was a myth told by Pindar, Simonides was referring to Pindar in offensive language ("fit only for boys", etc.). But according to the scholiast, Simonides directed his "abuse" against some critic of his own (and Pindar's) poetry; there is no hint of any attack on Pindar himself, and the moderate and courteous tone of Pindar's reply, in which he grants Simonides' point about old and new wine but perhaps refuses to apply it to poetry,[63] suggests that there had been no such attack. If the *nova fabula* was told by someone other than Pindar, the scholiast's statement that Simonides delivered his attack when "worsted by Pindar" (ἐλασσωθεὶς ὑπὸ Πινδάρου) is inexplicable. The interpretation of ὅδε μῦθος on the lines suggested by Boeckh cannot be accepted.

I assume that *mythos* means "saying"; but what is this "saying" which is foolish and fit only for youths? The saying is not, surely, anything like "new wine is often better than old," as Bergk[64] alleges; if this were the saying, Simonides would be using poetic language ("last year's gift of the vine") merely to clothe his *opponent's* remark before proceeding to deny its truth by prefixing a negative, or he would be quoting verbatim an opponent's poetically-worded maxim, and merely prefixing a negative to it. Simonides' words are surely a clear and eloquent statement of his *own* position by means of an obvious example from everyday life — "old wine is superior to new". The saying or *mythos* which this is meant to refute is presumably some general statement to the effect that "the new supersedes or excels the old".[65] But whether or not one follows Bergk on this issue, it is so far agreed that Simonides is defending the old against the new.

The dispute is presumably between the new and the old in poetry, turning on Pindar's retelling or invention of myths (compare Pindar's praise of "newer songs" in our passage). Simonides means that new wine does not yet (until it's no longer new) put to the test, or bear comparison with, the old; and so new myths must stand the test of time before they can replace the older versions.[66]

I do not agree with Bergk that old and young *poets* are being contrasted. Bergk emends the text of the Simonidean fragment so that it reads: "the new wine of youths does not put to the test last year's gift of the vine, and the saying is foolish".[67] "The new wine of youths" would mean "the productions of young poets", and Bergk expands on Simonides' meaning thus: *nondum ita confectus sum senio, ut mei labores superentur adolescentium rudimentis...Simonides, cum adolescentulo poetae posthabitus esset, non sine acerbitate castigat Agathoclem eiusque discipulum Pindarum*. It is not clear when Bergk imagines Simonides' remarks to have been made. He dates Pindar's ode at 454,[68] which might suggest that he could hardly have placed Simonides' remarks very long before his death in 468/7 (even a fourteen-year gap between Simonides' remarks and Pindar's reply strains one's credulity). In that case, Simonides' alleged suggestion that Pindar was a new and untried poet at this time would be absurd, as Pindar (who was born in 518 B.C.) would be about fifty; and though we are supposing Simonides to have been of an advanced age, we should prefer not to imagine him sunk in the senility which regards all under sixty as *kouroi*. On the other hand, if (as Bergk seems to be suggesting) Pindar really was *adolescens* at the time of Simonides' remark, the gap between it and Pindar's reply in *Ol.* 9 would (on Bergk's dating of *Ol.* 9 at 454) be forty years or more; we need hardly ask if this is likely.

Who is "the person who passed the judgement" (τοῦ κρίναντος), against whom Simonides' abuse was directed? It was surely not, as Schmid believes, Pindar himself, even though emendations which leave τοῦ κρίναντος unnamed would formally permit this conclusion;[69] the phrase more naturally refers to the person responsible for Simonides' being "defeated" (ἐλασσωθείς) by Pindar. Drachmann's Ἀγαθωνίδου is the most widely accepted emendation; and we may follow Wilamowitz in conjecturally identifying this Agathonidas with an *eromenos* of Pindar's whose name is restored by Wilamowitz as Agathonidas in a passage of Athenaeus.[70] If this identification is correct, the scholiast's reference to a judgement and a defeat cannot be taken as evidence of a formal competition between Simonides and Pindar, whose *eromenos* could never have been judge in such a competition; and the same applies to Bergk's identification of the person who passed the judgement as Agathocles, Pindar's teacher. Perhaps the scholiast has distorted an informal comparison of Simonides and Pindar by an interested party into a formal competition.[71] If on the other hand the one who passed the judgement is someone who has no personal connection with Pindar, Simonides' "defeat" could refer to a formal competition (perhaps at Athens?).

There is surely no evidence, in Simonides' fragment and Pindar's reply, of any animosity between them. Simonides' abuse of "the person who passed the judgement" (whoever he was) for an inane and easily refuted generalisation need not mean hostility to Pindar himself; and Pindar's reply is courteous in tone.[72] The dispute over the merits of the new and the old in poetry concerns a question of principle; no doubt there were many supporters of either view; and though Pindar's remark in *Ol.* 9 probably echoes Simonides, it is not merely a personal reply but a public statement of Pindar's position.

Pindar's *Ol.* 9, which in lines 11-18 mentions a Pythian as well as an Olympian victory, is probably to be dated 466 B.C. The scholia give contradictory information; some[73] give Ol. 73 (488/4 B.C.) for both victories (which would mean 488 for the Olympian and 486 for the Pythian victory); for the Pythian victory, some[74] give Pythiad 30 (466 B.C.) or Pythiad 33 (454 B.C.). The date of the Olympic victory has now been fixed at 468 B.C. by the papyrus list of victors, and it seems reasonable to emend the scholiasts' date for the Olympian and Pythian victories from Ol. 73 (488/4 B.C.) to Ol. 78 (468/4 B.C.)[75] and so to accept the scholiasts' version which dates the Pythian victory at 466 B.C. (Pythiad 30); for Pindar's language at lines 1-18 implies that the two victories were won fairly close together. It is strange, but not unbelievable, that the ode should have been delayed until two years after the Olympic victory.

Thus Stella is probably right in dating *Ol.* 9 after the traditional date of Simonides' death.[76] She concludes that the certain reference to Simonides in the ode means that Simonides must have died later than is commonly supposed. This argument is discussed in my summary in the concluding section of the present chapter.

3. Other evidence for the relationship of Simonides and Pindar

It is now necessary to consider what further evidence there is for the relationship of Simonides and Pindar, evidence which might affect our views on the passages discussed in the preceding section. Clear evidence of their relationship at any time would be welcome, though evidence from earlier years would have to be used with caution in the assessment of the vital period from c. 476 B.C. If we were to find any items of evidence for certain hostility after 476, these might not merely influence our interpretation of the passages quoted by Stella and discussed above but might even be added to Stella's passages and used in the same way in her support, that is, to argue that Simonides and Pindar must have been near-contemporaries.

Some passages from Pindar may first be considered in which scholars ancient or modern have seen evidence of hostility between the two poets. Apart from the passages discussed in the preceding section, the only other passage of Pindar where the ancient scholiasts allege that he is criticising Simonides occurs in the fourth *Nemean*:[77]

> But the rules of my art and the hastening hours prevent me from telling a long tale, and my heart is beguiled

to touch upon the new-moon festival. At any rate, even if the deep salt sea holds you around the waist[78] (?) (καίπερ ἔχει βαθεῖα ποντιὰς ἅλμα/ μέσσον), resist the plotting against you; then we shall be seen to step forth in the light far superior to our foes. But another man, with envy in his look, in darkness ponders his vain purpose, which falls to the ground.

The scholiasts comment:[79]

> Resist those who plot against you; that is to say, do not yield to rivals in your craft and those who slander you, do not give them grounds for saying that you have digressed. For we shall be seen to step forth far (superior)[80] to the rival poets and rival artists who make war on us and to pass on our way in triumph, if we do not digress. This seems to refer to Simonides,[81] since he is accustomed to employ digressions.

It is clear that the meaning of the scholiasts is that Pindar is cautioning himself against digression here, deprecating excessive digression in general, and so glancing at Simonides (who "is accustomed to employ digressions"); and that he is warning himself that digression and the resultant delay in completing the ode will provoke attack from a certain envious enemy, whom the scholiasts do not name. It is sometimes wrongly alleged (for example, by Jebb and Farnell)[82] that according to the scholiasts the "man with envy in his look" (line 39) is Simonides. In fact the scholia on this line[83] simply paraphrase Pindar's wording at length, and say nothing about the identity of the jealous man. It may well be that the scholiasts regarded the jealous man (line 39) as the same person who is "plotting" (line 37); but there is no ancient authority, and no a priori grounds, for saying that this person is Simonides. It seems that Jebb and Farnell have misunderstood the reference to Simonides in the scholium on line 60 (= 37) (quoted above) as if it were to Simonides' "plotting" instead of his "digressions"[84] — which imputes to the scholiasts the absurd notion that Pindar regarded himself as liable to criticism for digression by the jealous Simonides, who is accustomed to employ digression!

It is true that neither Jebb nor Farnell accepts what they allege the scholiasts to be saying; Farnell, like Wilamowitz,[85] supposes that the jealous man is some local Aeginetan critic.[86]

To turn to what the scholiasts do in fact say: it is very unlikely that they are right in seeing in the passage some innuendo against Simonides for his tendency to digress. Whether Pindar's digressions are to be regarded as real departures from his main theme, or as exercises introduced with the sole intention of highlighting, by comparison or contrast, the main theme of the victorious patron,[87] no one digresses more frequently or more brilliantly than Pindar; there is no reason why he should think especially of Simonides in this connection; and it is scarcely conceivable that he could be attacking Simonides, or any other poet, for this tendency. There is thus no evidence in this passage for the relationship between Simonides and Pindar.

Two Pindaric fragments and an *apophthegma* may next be considered, in which there is a probable or certain reference to Simonides.

The fragment referring to Pisistratus has already been discussed.[88] It was noted that when Simonides used the term "Siren" of Pisistratus, he may have intended a compliment, and that Pindar may have been using Simonides' term ironically in a poem praising an opponent of Pisistratus. But even if this is so (and it is far from certain), I do not think there is certain evidence of hostility between the poets here. Their obligations to their patrons, Simonides' to the Pisistratids, Pindar's to the Alcmeonidae, may have led to a clash of views, but we need not suppose that this amounted to a difference of political principles or to a disdain of each for the other and for the masters he served. Both poets wrote at times for the Thessalian feudal aristocrats, democratic Athens, the Sicilian tyrants, and oligarchic Sparta.[89] Personal animus, though it cannot be discounted, cannot be proved by their disagreement over Pisistratus, any more than by their difference on poetic methods.[90]

In a fragment of Pindar's Paean for the Ceans to Delos, at a point where the attributes of Ceos are being listed, occurs the phrase "I am also known for providing the muse in sufficient measure".[91] This could mean "affording ample material for poets", but is usually thought to mean something like "furnishing the poet's handiwork in fair measure",[92] i.e. "producing good poets". Those who accept the latter interpretation hold widely-varying opinions about the significance of Pindar's remarks. Farnell states[93] that it is rather a cold admission and remarks that "generosity towards his rivals is not known to have been a trait of Pindar". For Farnell this is a purely negative conclusion, for elsewhere[94] he shows himself highly sceptical of any positive hostility between Pindar and the Cean poets. Wilamowitz[95] goes much further and remarks that Pindar's words are so condescending as to amount to an insult. Bowra[96] however thinks these lines show that Simonides and Pindar were "on friendly enough terms"; and Snell[97] rejects Wilamowitz' view that Pindar intended a sneer. For our purpose it is enough to note that there is no positive evidence here of hostility between Simonides and Pindar.

The *apophthegma* in question is quoted by Eustathius:[98]

> It is said that Pindar, when asked why Simonides went to live with the tyrants in Sicily but he himself did not wish to do so, replied: "Because I wish to live for myself, not for another".

The authenticity of such *apophthegmata* is of course very doubtful. Even if it is allowed that there may be some factual basis to the story, its implications are slight. The incident would no doubt be dated after Simonides' arrival in Sicily in 476 and after Pindar's own return from Sicily.[99] Pindar has himself consorted with the Sicilian tyrants and praised them in glowing terms (as he continues to do in later odes).[100] It may be that Pindar would not make a "successful courtier";[101] but any implied reproach to Simonides for continuing to tolerate what Pindar himself could no longer tolerate can only have been of the mildest. There is no evidence here of any hostility between the two poets.

Next, there are three passages of Pindar in which modern scholars have seen unfriendly allusions to the Cean poets.

In the course of a difficult and disputed passage in the seventh *Nemean* (written for Sogenes of Aegina) Pindar says:

> Allow me. If I uttered something in excessive zeal, I am not over-reluctant, as a favour to the victor, to set it aside (or: "to pay the victor the favour owed"? νικῶντι χάριν καταθέμεν) (lines 75-6). To weave garlands is an easy matter. Begin the song...(line 77).

It is disputed whether there is any element of personalia here. It has often been thought that in this and other passages of the ode Pindar is apologising for offensive references to Neoptolemus[102] in Paean 6 (frag. 52f. Snell-Maehler), though Bundy and others deny any such reference.[103] Schmid, dating the poem to the mid 480's, sees evidence in line 77 of hostility between Pindar and the Cean poets at this earlier period.[104] This suggestion can be confidently dismissed; the ancient commentators did not notice, nor does the text itself suggest, any such thing.

Schmid sees another reference to the Cean poets in Pindar's words at *Pythian* 1.92:[105] μὴ δολωθῇς, ὦ φίλε, κέρδεσιν εὐτράπλοις. It is uncertain whether these words are addressed to Hieron himself or to his son Deinomenes, and whether κέρδεσιν refers to the love of "gains" (perhaps in the sense of stinting on poets' fees) or the "cunning arts" of flatterers. In order to understand a reference to the Ceans, it must first be assumed that the "arts of flatterers" are meant. Next some evidence must be sought that the flatterers are rival poets; but there is no such evidence, either elsewhere in the ode or in the scholia. This passage is clearly valueless as evidence for any hostility between Pindar and the Cean poets.

The last passage for consideration under this heading is *Pythian* 2.76 f.:[106] "The purveyors of slander are an irresistible evil to both parties, exceedingly like foxes in disposition." Wilamowitz[107] implies that at this point the scholiasts identify the foxes as Simonides and Bacchylides. In fact the scholiasts do not mention either Simonides or Bacchylides in connection with these lines. The scholiasts do indeed see hostile references to Bacchylides at other points in this ode;[108] but the scholia on this ode do not mention Simonides at all. Wilamowitz must have been misled by a recollection of schol. *Ol.* 2.157a & 158d,[109] the only places in the ancient scholia where Simonides and Bacchylides are mentioned together.[110] Severyns[111] reports the scholia correctly, but he too is inclined to see hostile allusions to Simonides, as well as to Bacchylides, in this ode. The question whether Pindar was hostile to Bacchylides, and the relevance of this matter to an assessment of Pindar's relations with Simonides, are discussed later in the present section of this chapter. It is at least clear that there is no direct evidence in this ode for hostility between Pindar and Simonides.

Thus the passages discussed so far in the present section provide no clear indication of the relationship between the two poets, and therefore shed no light on the passages cited by Stella and examined in Section 2.

The question may next be raised whether there were circumstances in the careers of Simonides and Pindar which make rivalry or hostility between them a probable assumption. Their way of life was very similar, in that both wrote poems on commission for patrons who rewarded them for their services. If ever they were active, then, in the same place at about the same time, it could be expected that a certain rivalry might develop. Their paths may have crossed in this way in Thessaly, at about the time of Pindar's composition of *Pythian* 10 for a Thessalian patron (498 B.C.). They may have met (perhaps in competition) at Athens; Simonides' poems on the Persian Wars include some for Athens, while many of his numerous dithyrambic victories (in the period up to 476 B.C.) must have been won there; and Pindar's dithyrambic fragments for Athens, though they cannot be dated,[112] could belong to the same period. They were almost certainly in Sicily together for some time from 476.

But there is no certain evidence of a head-on collision of the kind which seems to have occurred between Pindar and Bacchylides. The idea that Simonides and Pindar both wrote an ode for Xenocrates' Pythian victory of 490 proved to be groundless; and some years may have separated Simonides' celebration of Xenocrates' Isthmian victory from Pindar's ode (*Isthmian* 2) addressed to Xenocrates' son Thrasybulus, in which this victory is mentioned.[113] The most likely battleground might appear to be the courts of Hieron and Theron, but again real evidence of any clash is wanting. In 476 B.C. both poets seem to have enjoyed the favour of Theron, for whom Pindar wrote *Olympian* 2 & 3, and whom Simonides is said to have reconciled with Hieron, but little is known of their relations with Theron (and so with each other as regards his favour) after this. Pindar enjoyed Hieron's favour from 476 (*Ol.* 1) to at least 470 (*Pyth.* 1), though he seems to have been ousted by Bacchylides by the year 468 (Bacchylides, Ode 3). Simonides' supposed reconciliation of Hieron with Theron (in 476), and the number of anecdotes connecting him with Hieron, suggest an easy relationship between them for some time after this, but there is not much evidence that Hieron employed Simonides as a poet. I have suggested that Simonides may well have been content for Hieron's major commissions to go to Pindar (or Bacchylides), and that the fact that they did so implies no coolness between Simonides and Hieron. If this is true, there is no cause here for hostility between Simonides and Pindar.

I have argued that it is not possible to differentiate clearly between Pindar and Simonides by the political cast of their respective patrons, though it is possible that obligations to mutually hostile parties (the Pisistratids and the Alcmeonidae) may have led to an occasional clash of views. Again, there may have been a clash in their attitude to Aegina. Pindar's affection for Aegina is very apparent from the large number of odes for Aeginetan athletes; but it seems that Simonides attacked Crius of Aegina for purely political motives on behalf of an Athenian, thus making an exception to his policy of remaining on good terms with mutually hostile parties. Other examples of this kind of clash are very dubious,[114] but the examples we have just mentioned would be enough to cause some strain between the two poets.

Pindar's temperament makes it unlikely that he would be on cordial terms with Simonides. He is proudly confident of his own superiority, disdainful to rivals, and wont to lecture even his tyrant patrons. His devotion to the old aristocratic societies and the heroic and anthropomorphic mythology of Greece gives him little common ground with the more sceptical and rationalistic Simonides.[115]

There is thus some evidence for a clash of temperament, a clash of loyalties in certain cases, disagreement on the poet's art, and a possibility of rivalry as both moved in similar orbits, engaged in the same profession. But no evidence has emerged of a direct confrontation of interests in a struggle for the favour of one patron. (And there is one example of a courteous reply by Pindar to a saying of Simonides.) There is reason to suppose that there might be a certain coolness and reserve between the two poets; it is not possible to disprove that there was active hostility strong enough to make Pindar include sneering references to Simonides in his poems; but the circumstances of their careers (as far as they are known) do not seem to provide any definite evidence of such hostility.

Another line of approach might be to enquire whether there is any evidence of a friendly or respectful relationship between Simonides and Pindar; more specifically, to ask whether such evidence might be found in quotations of one poet by the other, or in the tradition which associates them as teacher and pupil.

Two passages where Pindar appears to echo Simonides, with the probable intention of disagreeing with him, have already been discussed; in a third passage, it was noted that if Pindar were echoing Simonides, it would be with hostile intent, but that no deliberate imitation need be assumed.[116]

The common type of literary quotation in which one poet echoes another's words without any intention of countering an argument or developing a point can normally be regarded as a mark of respect or affection (though it may of course be unconscious borrowing). If any such quotation of Simonides by Pindar (or vice versa) could be demonstrated, it would provide an argument against the existence of hostility between them. Possible cases of this type of quotation have already been noted from (a) *Ol.* 2 and (b) *Ol.* 9.[117] A list of further alleged parallelisms is quoted by Michelangeli, apparently in support of his contention that no hostility existed between the two poets. Michelangeli's passages, in addition to the passage of *Ol.* 2 just referred to, are as follows (the Simonidean extract is quoted first in each case): (c) "for not even the demigods reached old age having achieved a life without toil" and "a life free from danger did not befall either Peleus son of Aeacus or godlike Cadmus"; (d) "in a short time comes toil upon toil" and "the gods allot mortals two woes for one good"; (e) "what life is desirable without pleasure?" and "do not blot out enjoyment in life"; (f) "no-one achieves *arete* without the gods" and "men become *agathoi* according to divine will"; (g) "such an offering neither decay nor all-conquering time shall obscure" and "a treasure which neither the winter's rain nor the wind will sweep into the depths of the sea".[118] The only other example that I have noticed is (h) "who has crowned himself so many times with myrtle leaves or garlands of roses, after conquering (or "for victories") in the contest of the neighbours?" and "victories among the neighbours garlanded him...having crowned his hair with wreaths".[119]

In most of these cases the Simonidean fragment cannot be dated and (if borrowing is assumed) there is no means of knowing who borrowed from whom. However, in one case ((g) above) Simonides would be the borrower, as his Thermopylae poem (26/531 Page) is later than Pindar's *Pyth.* 6 (490 B.C.). In two cases Pindar would be the borrower: one of these, item (a), was discussed above; in the other case (item (h)) it would be helpful if imitation could be regarded as certain, as Pindar's *Nem.* 11 is not only much later than Simonides' ode for Astylus but comes towards the end of Pindar's own life, so that the development of hostility to Simonides after it would be impossible.

In none of these instances can borrowing be regarded as certain. In (a), (b), (c), (e), (f), and (h), there is parallelism of thought and expression; in (d) and (g) parallelism of thought but hardly of expression. In at least four[120] of the six cases where there is parallelism of both thought and expression, a similar passage from an earlier author can be quoted which might have prompted the corresponding thought in Simonides or Pindar or both, and which would thus obviate the need to assume borrowing between these two poets. In (h) it must be borne in mind that both poets were often called upon to celebrate the same circumstances of athletic victory in language which could not be varied indefinitely. There is thus no compelling evidence of deliberate quotation; nevertheless, the accumulation of so many possible examples from the meagre remnants of Simonides' poetry may be thought to be of some significance.

The tradition which represents Pindar as a pupil of Simonides[121] cannot be regarded as evidence of friendly relations at a later stage of their careers. In the first place its accuracy is highly suspect; the source is very late, and in any case the ancient scholars were fond of constructing fictitious "genealogies" representing famous poets as teacher and pupil. In the second place, even if the information were correct, rivalry and hostility between an aging master and a mature and successful "pupil" challenging his position would be quite possible.

The fact remains that no certain indication of hostility between Simonides and Pindar has emerged from the evidence so far considered. The Pindaric scholiasts never suggest any convincing motive for Pindar's alleged attacks on Simonides (their suggestions that he attacks Simonides for making money by his poetry, or for employing digression, are not convincing); and in the one case where we suspended judgement on their allegation, they offered no motive for Pindar's attack.[122] In thus concluding that the scholiasts, on some occasions at least, wrongly alleged attacks by Pindar on Simonides, we are forced back on the question whether the scholiasts' statements are arbitrary inventions, perhaps a manifestation or extension of the tendency of ancient scholars to postulate competitions or contests between poets; or whether there may be some more concrete reason for these incorrect allegations of hostility.

Some such reason may perhaps be found in the relationship of Pindar and Bacchylides. The scholiasts often see attacks on Bacchylides in the odes of Pindar; what is more, in the case of Bacchylides (unlike that of Simonides), the scholiasts offer reasonable causes for this alleged hostility, viz. that Bacchylides slandered Pindar before Hieron and that Hieron preferred Bacchylides' poems to Pindar's.[123] To say that they are reasonable is not to claim that they must be true; but at least the second one seems verifiable — we know that at the end of *Ol.* 1 (108-111) Pindar hopes that he will celebrate an Olympic chariot victory of Hieron but that when that victory came in 468 it was celebrated by Bacchylides (Ode 3). Furthermore, we know of two occasions when Bacchylides and Pindar were both commissioned to celebrate the same victory of the same patron,[124] a circumstance where it would be hard not to imagine an intense personal rivalry. The limited facts at our disposal thus offer some confirmation of the allegations of hostility between Bacchylides and Pindar. It is possible, therefore, that the ancient scholars may have been led, by a knowledge of hostility between Pindar and Bacchylides, and a knowledge or assumption of certain disagreements between Pindar and Simonides, into classing Simonides and Bacchylides together as active enemies of Pindar.[125]

We may now finally sum up on the evidence for the existence of hostility between Simonides and Pindar. The material discussed in the present section has provided no definite evidence to confirm or deny such hostility and thus illuminate the controversial passages discussed in Section 2 above (from *Ol.* 2, *Isth.* 2, and *Ol.* 9). The strongest single item of evidence was the passage from *Ol.* 2, where a hostile allusion to Simonides and Bacchylides appeared to be a possibility. If it were accepted that *Ol.* 2 contained a hostile allusion, this would naturally colour our view of many passages which, when regarded in isolation, were inconclusive; it might cause us to allow that the rivalry, to which the careers of Simonides and Pindar could have given occasion, developed into open hostility, to suppose that the scholiasts did possess knowledge of such hostility, and to be sceptical about supposed quotations of Simonides by Pindar. On the other hand, we insisted that some doubt must remain about the interpretation of *Ol.* 2; so that the final verdict on the entire body of evidence must be "not proven".

4. Assessment of Stella's conclusions

The relevance of the material discussed above to the question of Simonidean chronology may now be considered.

The passages from *Ol.* 2 and *Isth.* 2 may be taken together, for *Ol.* 2 was certainly written, and *Isth.* 2 was probably written, before the traditional date of Simonides' death. I have suggested that *Ol.* 2 possibly, though not certainly, contains a hostile allusion to Simonides; and that no hostile reference to Simonides can be read into *Isth.* 2. Suppose, however, that for the sake of argument we were to accept as certain a hostile reference to Simonides in either or both of these odes; would it then be necessary to accept Stella's conclusions from them, that Pindar regarded Simonides as a flourishing rival, and that therefore the traditional Simonidean chronology, which makes Simonides almost forty years older than Pindar, is incorrect?

In *Ol.* 2 Pindar would be denouncing Simonides not merely as an inferior poet, but also, it seems, as one who had been slandering or attacking him in some way.[126] In *Isth.* 2 he would be attacking Simonides' covetousness. It is difficult to see why slanders against oneself, or mercenary greed, should be any less open to denunciation in an old man of eighty or more than in a flourishing rival and contemporary. It would not be a question of either earnest argument or professional rivalry, only of rather petulant attacks on rather unpleasant characteristics. Thus neither of these passages of Pindar (if a reference to Simonides were admitted) would suggest that Simonides must have been younger than the traditional dating allows.

The case of *Ol.* 9 is rather different, as there is a strong probability that it was written in 466, after the traditional date of Simonides' death (468/7). I do not admit any hostility *to Pindar* in Simonides' words (frag. 97/602 Page); and I do not see how any hostility or even discourtesy[127] can possibly be read into Pindar's reply; Pindar admits there is some truth in Simonides' words, and the point on which he disagrees concerns the art of poetry, not his personal relations with Simonides. It surely could not be regarded either as impossibly bad taste, or as a useless waste of words, to express moderate and courteous disagreement with the tenets of a fellow poet, who had died a year or two earlier, on a matter that was still of as much interest and concern to poets and their audiences as it had ever been. The conclusion must be that here again there are no grounds for supposing that the traditional date of Simonides' death is too early.

References

1. 1946: 15-17.
2. Cf. G.M.Kirkwood, *Gnomon* 35 (1963) 131, 133; Crotty (1982) vii-ix.
3. *Ol.* 2.83-8. (Stella, p. 15 n. 1, gives the line numbering as 72-77.)
4. This interpretation of ἐς δὲ τὸ πὰν ἑρμανέων/χατίζει is proposed by Most (1986: 304-16).
5. Most (1986: 314 & n. 60) prefers to understand πρός thus.
6. Schol. *Ol.* 2.157a (I 99 Drachmann). Schol. 158d also mentions Simonides and Bacchylides; schol. 158c, Simonides alone.
7. Schol. 158b states that the dual is out of place here.
8. Among those who accept the scholiasts' explanation are Schmid (1929: 513 n. 2), Bowra (1961: 361), and van Leeuwen (1964: I pp. 245-52); those who do not accept it include Wilamowitz (1922: 248) and Farnell (1930-2: ad loc.). Most (1986: 304 n. 1) allows that Simonides and Bacchylides may be meant; Race (1986: 25) is sceptical. Nisetich (1980: ad loc., p. 91) does not translate the dual at all.
9. μαθόντες δὲ λάβροι/παγγλωσσίᾳ κόρακες ὣς ἄκραντα γαρύετον/Διὸς πρὸς ὄρνιχα θεῖον.
10. The only suggestion to the contrary is made by J.Wackernagel, that γαρύετον can be regarded as a survival of an otherwise obsolete third person plural present imperative (in a letter to Schroeder in 1898: see Schroeder (1900) ad loc.).
11. Pindar ad loc. (*PLG* I 67).
12. Bergk surely intended his emendation γαρυέτων to be interpreted as dual; but he then went on to admit that this

was a very rare dual form, and quoted some examples from εἰμί (sum) where the -των form could be plural, not dual. However, Schroeder (1900: ad loc.) wrongly supposed Bergk to be quoting these examples in support of a proposal to take γαρυέτων as plural; and this misunderstanding (to which, it must be admitted, Bergk laid himself open) has been echoed or repeated by a series of scholars from Wilamowitz (1901: 1302) to Lloyd-Jones (*JHS* 93 (1973) 126-7, 127 n. 105). Occasionally one sees Bergk's views correctly reported (e.g. by Jebb (1905) 17). The first report known to me of Schroeder's misunderstanding of Bergk appears in Kirkwood's article (1981: 240-1) (q.v. for a full discussion of the linguistic points).

13. The only attested examples are from -μι verbs (ἔστων from εἰμί, *sum*; and ἴτων, from εἶμι, *ibo*).

14. Kirkwood (1981) 240-3; id (1982) 76. So Race (1986: 17, 25) translates as if the dual belonged only to the simile ("learners... are like a pair of crows that vainly cry...").

15. 1962: I 3 n. 11, I 13 & n. 36, I 29 n. 71, I 32 n. 78, II 71 n. 91.

16. If Most (above, n. 5) is right in arguing that πρός means not "against" but merely "in comparison to (the divine bird of Zeus)", the passage contains no evidence for any attack by the Ceans on Pindar. On the other hand, the argument advanced above, that an unprovoked attack by Pindar on Simonides would be unwelcome to Theron, might suggest that πρός does after all refer to attacks "against" Pindar by the Ceans.

17. 1922: 248.

18. See above, Chapter IX, section 4, with n. 78.

19. Tedeschi (1985: 29-54) argues, both in general terms and with special reference (p. 40) to this passage of Bacchylides, that the poets' allusions to the "sending" of an ode should be taken literally.

20. 1922: 248, 313-4.

21. 1930-2: II 22.

22. 1936: 386-7.

23. 98/603 Page.

24. 26/531.5 Page.

25. E.g. by Farnell (1930-2: II 12), following the scholiasts.

26. On this episode, see above, Chapter IX, section 4, with nn. 70-75.

27. 1962: I 7. (Bundy does not, I believe, mention this particular passage.)

28. More literally "satiety...seeking to make babbling a cause of concealment for the fair deeds of men" or "...to set babbling as a cause of concealment upon the deeds..." (τὸ λαλαγῆσαι θέλων κρυφὸν τιθέμεν ἐσλῶν καλοῖς/ἔργοις). Minor variations of text produce "satiety...seeking to babble and to set concealment upon the deeds..." (...κρυφόν τε θέμεν); or "satiety...consisting in babbling that seeks to set concealment upon the deeds..." (θέλον, neuter participle modifying τὸ λαλαγῆσαι). A radically different interpretation of the text is referred to in n. 30 below.

29. Kirkwood (1982: ad loc.) comments: "perhaps Pindar has in mind some specific dissatisfaction against Theron, but this hardly matters, since it is in his view a recurrent and inevitable concomitant of excellence".

30. On Bundy's interpretation (1962: I 29 & n. 71) the μάργοι are not envious detractors, but *laudatores* of the kind who do not know when to stop and would produce *koros* in the hearers by recounting Theron's praise ad nauseam. This does not really seem to fit phrases like οὐ δίκᾳ συναντόμενος and θέλων κρυφὸν τιθέμεν (*Ol*. 2.96-7). It seems more likely that they are the kind of resentful men who have heard enough of Theron's praise and wish it to be drowned in babbling.

31. Freeman (1891-4: II 529), citing schol. *Ol*. 2.173g, I 102 Drachmann; Lavagnini (1933: 5-14). The relevant lines of Pindar (*Ol*. 2.95-8) were quoted above (this section, with n. 28).

32. On Most's interpretation of lines 85-6 there is no reference to "the masses" (see above, this section, with n. 4).

33. So Fennell (1893: ad loc.). Hubbard (1985: 151) entertains the idea as a possibility.

34. Farnell (1930-2: II 22). The suggestion is dismissed by Bowra (1961: 361 n. 1) and van Leeuwen (1964: I 250).

35. *Nem*. 4.39-40: see Section 3 below, with nn. 77 & 86.

36. Schol. *Isth*. 2 Inscr. a (III p. 213.4 Drachmann).

37. Frag. 222 Pfeiffer; schol. *Isth.* 2.9a (III 214 Drachmann).

38. Among those who see a certain or possible reference to Simonides are Jebb (1905: 22), Wilamowitz (1922: 312), Puech (ad loc.: vol. IV ed. 2 (1952) 27), and Gentili (1984: 225). Some alternative explanations of other scholars are cited later in this section.

39. 1946: 15-16, 16 n. 1.

40. References in Page *PMG* Simonides 148/653 II; discussion in Bell (1978: passim) and Lefkowitz (1981: 50-3).

41. The passages in Pindar where ancient or modern scholars have claimed to detect attacks on Simonides are discussed in Section 3 below. It should be noted that nowhere except in *Isth.* 2 do the Pindaric scholiasts, as far as I can find, understand Pindar to be attacking Simonides for covetousness. Zuntz' statement (1935: 5 n. 14) that Simonides' covetousness "is often commented on in our scholia to Pindar" is incorrect.

42. 1946: 15-16, 16 n. 1.

43. 1930-2: I 249-50. See also Woodbury (1968) 529-30.

44. Bowra (*Problems in Greek Poetry* (Oxford 1953) 86-7) sees a similar admission at *Pyth.* 2.56. Other relevant passages are cited by Verdenius (1982: 13 & n. 38).

45. For development and refinement of this point see Woodbury (1968) 533-5, and Privitera (1982) on *Isth.* 2.6.

46. On Simonides' ode, see Chapter IX, section 5 above.

47. Farnell (1930-2) I 250; similarly Bowra (1964: 126) and Verdenius (1982: 11-15). There is on the other hand a substantial body of opinion in support of the opposite view, that Pindar is offering the ode free (Bury (1892) p. 34; Freeman (1891-4) II 536; Simpson (1969) 471 n. 65; and others cited by Verdenius (1982) 11 n. 33).

48. Fennell (1899) ad loc., following some earlier scholars (references in Nisetich (1977) 152 n. 5). Pindar appears to apologise in *Ol.* 10.3 ff. & 84 ff. for being late with an ode.

49. 1966: 108-11; so also Privitera (above, n. 45).

50. 1968-9: I 82, II 37.

51. 1968: 540-2.

52. Nisetich (1977) 133-56 (especially 141-2); cf. id. (1980) 50.

53. In Chapter IX, section 5 above.

54. Diod. Sic. 11.53.1 & 5.

55. However Fennell (ad loc., p. 155) dates the ode before Theron's death; and Pavese (1966: 103-4) expresses a cautious preference for this view. Woodbury (1968: 527 n. 2) seems to think that the ode was written after the end of Theron's tyranny, but his interpretation of the poem means that Thrasybulus is still prosperous and influential.

56. Stella (1946) 15 n. 2, 16; G Fraccaroli, *Le odi di Pindaro* (Verona 1894) 20, 655.

57. Schol. *Ol.* 9.74, I 285 Drachmann (cod. A).

58. κατὰ τοῦ κρίναντος Ἀγαθωνίδου. This name is restored by Drachmann in his apparatus criticus (for the unintelligible ἀγαθῶν εἰδέου of the ms.) and is accepted by Wilamowitz (*Hermes* 40 (1905) 128-9) and Page (Simonides ad loc.). Other suggestions include ἀγαθῶν ᾠδῶν (Boeckh) ("against the one who had passed judgement on good poems" (?)); and Ἀγαθοκλέους (Bergk) ("Agathokles", who is named as Pindar's teacher in the *Vita Ambrosiana*, I p. 1.11 f. Drachmann).

59. The "saying" is not quoted and has to be inferred; on the pattern of thought, see n. 65 below.

60. This translation of the last clause of the Simonidean fragment reflects Page's tentative restoration proposed in his apparatus criticus, κούρων δ' ὅδε μῦθος κενεόφρων (for the unintelligible ms. version which he obelises in his text). Instead of ὅδε μῦθος ("this saying"), ὁ δὲ μῦθος ("and the saying") is sometimes read. This need not radically affect the interpretation of the fragment; and it might seem to have the advantage of eliminating ὅδε ("this") in its rarer sense of referring back to what has preceded. See however n. 65 below for an apparent example of this sense of ὅδε in a Simonidean fragment structurally similar to the present one.

61. For a suitably cautious assessment of these issues, see Bernardini (1983) 139-40.

62. 1811-21: II 2 p. 190.

63. Lattimore suggests (*CPh* 41 (1946) 232) that Pindar does not mean "praise old wine, but new poetry" but rather "praise

the old wine (poetry), surely, but praise the younger poetry, too". This has certain advantages related to Pindar's handling of an age-old myth in the relevant part of *Ol.* 9; see Bernardini (1983) 140.

64. Simonides frag. 75.

65. The pattern of thought is no doubt the same as in 76/581 Page. Simonides quotes the opinion with which he disagrees (76/581.2-4; not quoted in our present fragment); he then refutes it (76/581.5-6; from "wine when still new" to "gift of the vine" in our fragment); he then concludes "this is a fool's notion" (ἅδε βούλα, 76/581.7; ὅδε μῦθος in our fragment).

66. It is conceivable that Simon. frag. 138/643 Page indicates that Simonides had tried to introduce new myths but had failed to put them across.

67. κούρων δ' ἐξελέγχει νέος/οἶνος οὐ τὸ πέρυσι δῶρον/ ἀμπέλου, ὁ δὲ μῦθος κενεόφρων (Simon. frag. 75).

68. Bergk, *PLG* I 107-8.

69. Schmid (1929) 513 n. 2. For some emendations, see n. 58 above.

70. Athen. 10.427 d-e (= Pind. frag. 128 Snell-Maehler).

71. So, apparently, Wilamowitz (above, n. 58).

72. Lattimore (*CPh* 41 (1946) 231-2) detects other verbal reminiscences of Simonides in *Ol.* 9, comparing lines 103-4 ("without a god, each thing is none the worse for being shrouded in silence") with Simon. 77/582 Page ("the privilege of silence is without risk") and lines 107-8 ("the heights of wisdom are hard to scale") with Simon. 74/579 Page (in which Arete is said to dwell on inaccessible rocks). If Pindar were consciously echoing Simonides, this would confirm that he felt no hostility towards him at this time. See further Section 3 below, with nn. 117-119.

73. Schol. *Ol.* 9.17c, I 271-2 Drachmann, with Drachmann's app. crit.

74. Schol. a on line 17, I 271 Drachmann, with Drachmann's app. crit.

75. *P.Oxy.* CCXXII, col. I line 37 (vol. II, 1899, p. 89). The emendation was proposed by Grenfell and Hunt (*P.Oxy.* ad loc., p. 92), and is accepted by most commentators on Pindar.

76. She dates it (1946: 16) to "467-66".

77. *Nem.* 4.33-41. The date of the ode, written for Timasarchus of Aegina, is uncertain; Gaspar (1900: 116 ff.) and Bowra (1964: 409) date it to 473, Farnell (1930-2: II 263; cf. I 177) apparently between 473 and 460, Jebb (1905: 22) between 467 and 463.

78. Similarly Nisetich (1980: 52, 247) and others. This would be a metaphorical expression indicating some difficulty confronting Pindar (for various possibilities, see Farnell (1930-2) II 266). But some (including Farnell, loc. cit., and Crotty (1982) 148 n. 30) prefer to understand literally as "even though the deep salt sea intervening keeps me away" (i.e. separates Pindar from his patron).

79. Schol. *Nem.* 4.60b (III 74-5 Drachmann). (Line 60 = line 37, ἀντίτειν ' ἐπιβουλίᾳ.)

80. The text of the scholium clearly echoes Pindar's language at this point; it retains the genitive plural in its expansion ("rival poets") of his δαΐων ("foes", line 38), but seems to lack a word (corresponding to his ὑπέρτεροι, "superior") which would govern this genitive.

81. Or "he (Pindar) seems to be directing this against Simonides"? (δοκεῖ δὲ ταῦτα τείνειν εἰς Σιμωνίδην).

82. Jebb (1905) 22; Farnell (1930-2) II 267.

83. Scholia on line 64 (= 39) a-e (III 75 Drachmann).

84. Lefkowitz (1981: 57), citing the scholium on line 60 (= 37), appears to make the same mistake.

85. 1922: 402-3.

86. For Crotty (1982: 59) the plots are laid by jealous men who would denigrate the victory. Nisetich's view (1980: 52-3) of the plotters as "enemies of the victor" is similar; but the jealous man is Pindar's "poetic rival", whose poetic function is to act as a "foil for Pindar" (though Nisetich seems to leave open the question of whether such enemies and rivals existed actually or potentially). As usual, Bundy (1962: I 3 n. 11) insists that the φθονερὰ ἀνὴρ βλέπων is not an individual but a type, the kind of "stinter" (not "jealous" person) who, in contrast to Pindar himself, would celebrate the patron with inadequate praise; so also Miller (1983: 202-11). Here again Bundy seems to me to ignore certain specific features of the passage in question; vigorous language like "plotting" and "foes" rather suggests that enemies or rivals (actual or potential) are meant.

87. So Bundy passim. Bundy (1962: I 4 n. 13) regards Pindar's self-admonition on his tendency to digress as a rhetorical device to mark transitions between topics.
88. Pindar frag. 339 Snell-Maehler: see above, Chapter III, section 2, with n. 19.
89. On Pindar's work for Sparta, see Wilamowitz (1922) 321-5.
90. See Section 2 above, on Pindar's *Ol.* 9.
91. μοῖσαν παρέχων ἅλις, *Paean* 4 (frag. 52d) lines 23-4 Snell-Maehler. In these lines "the leader of the chorus speaks as if representing the island" (Farnell (1930-2) I 301 n. 1). The date of the poem is uncertain, though most scholars tend to date it after Simonides' death (Wilamowitz (1922) 325; Farnell (1930-2) II 334; Snell-Maehler ad loc., p. 21).
92. Farnell (1930-2) I 301.
93. 1930-2: I 303.
94. 1930-2: II 22 & 262.
95. 1922: 325.
96. 1961: 359.
97. Bacchylides, ed. 8 p. 122, *Testimonia* no. 7.
98. Eustath. *Prooem.* 26 (III p. 297.21 Drachmann).
99. Dated at 474 by Farnell (1930-2: I 367), a date which is supported by the very probable dating of an ode for a non-Sicilian patron (*Pyth.* 9 for Telesicrates of Cyrene) to 474 (cf. Bowra (1964) 408).
100. Cf. *Ol.* 6.93 ff.
101. Jebb (1905) 20.
102. Or claiming that his references to Neoptolemus were not offensive.
103. Bundy (1962) I 4. For a full discussion and citation of scholars' views, see Most (1985) 203-10.
104. Schmid (1929) 513 n. 2 (and, for the date, p. 555). Schmid is here following Wilamowitz (1922: 167), who, without giving any line reference or quoting any Greek, claims to detect an attack on the Cean poets in this ode.
105. Schmid (1929) 513 n. 2. The ode was written for Hieron (470 B.C.).

106. For Hieron; date and event uncertain. For a summary of opinions on the date and occasion, see T.N.Gantz (*Hermes* 106 (1978) 14-26) and Most (1985: 61-8); suggested dates range from 477 to 468.
107. 1922: 293.
108. See n. 123 below.
109. See above, Section 2 & n. 6.
110. That is, if Drachmann's indexes (III 312 ff.) are complete and accurate. I disregard those places in the scholia where Simonides and Bacchylides are mentioned together merely as belonging to the nine lyric poets or as being respectively older and younger than Pindar.
111. 1933: 84 & n. 47.
112. Frags. 75-7 Snell-Maehler. Farnell (1930-2: I 324) reasonably dates them c. 470 or earlier. Bowra (1964: 408) dates them "after, but not long after, the Persian Wars", perhaps after the capture of Eion by Cimon and so "in the spring of 474".
113. See Chapter IX, section 5, and Section 2 of the present chapter (with n. 55). The fragments of Pindar's encomium on the Emmenidae (frags. 118-9 Snell-Maehler) presumably cannot be dated.
114. For instance, it may be true that Pindar in *Pyth.* 2.18-20 (of uncertain date: see n. 106 above) shows himself hostile to Anaxilas of Rhegium because of the latter's recently thwarted aggressive designs against Locri (see Farnell (1930-2) II 118); but Simonides' employment by Anaxilas could be many years earlier than Pindar's *Pyth.* 2 — there is no evidence of a conflict of loyalties at any given time between Simonides and Pindar in their attitude to Anaxilas.
115. Evidence for these characteristics of Simonides may be sought in the extant fragments (cf. especially the poem to Scopas, 37/542 Page, and the papyrus fragment 36/541 Page), and also in the memory of him which was preserved in the anecdotal tradition (e.g. in Cic. *ND* 1.60).
116. The two passages were *Ol.* 9.48 f. and frag. 339 (see above, Section 2, with nn. 57 ff.; and the present section, with n. 88); the third passage was *Isth.* 2.1-13 (see above, Section 2, with n. 42).
117. *Ol.* 2.15 ff. (above, Section 2 and nn. 23 & 24); *Ol.* 9.103-4 & 107-8 (above n. 72).

118. Michelangeli (1897) 43. The passages are: (c) Simon. frag. 18/523 & *Pyth.* 3.86 ff.; (d) 15/520 & *Pyth.* 3.81 f.; (e) 79/584 & frag. 126 Snell-Maehler; (f) 21/526 & *Ol.* 9.28 f.; (g) 26/531 & *Pyth.* 6.8 ff.

119. The passages in (h) are Simonides' ode for Astylus (1/506) (see above, Chapter IX, section 2) and *Nem.* 11.19-29, which is perhaps to be dated 446 B.C. (see Bowra (1964) 413).

120. For passage (a) cf. Hom. *Il.* 9.249 ff., cited by schol. Pind. ad loc. (schol. *Ol.* 2.31); for (b) cf. Hes. *Op.* 289 ff., cited by Diehl (Simon. frag. 37); for (d) cf. Hom. *Il.* 24.527 f., cited by schol. Pind. ad loc. (schol. *Pyth.* 3.141a); for (e) cf. Mimnerm. frag. 1.1 West, cited by Diehl (Simon. frag. 57).

121. Eustath. *Prooem.*, III p. 297.13 Drachmann; cf. also *Vita Thomana*, I p. 7.13 Drachmann.

122. The passages in question were: *Isth.* 2.1-13 (Section 2 above); *Nem.* 4.33-41 (this section, above); *Ol.* 2.83-8 (Section 2 above).

123. Schol. *Pyth.* 2.97 (Pindar slandered); 131 b-c; 132 c-f; 166 d & 171 c (Bacchylides preferred to Pindar); schol. *Nem.* 3.143.

124. Pind. *Nem.* 5 and Bacc. Ode 13 (for Pytheas of Aegina, in 485 or 483); Pind. *Ol.* 1 and Bacc. Ode 5 (for Hieron, in 476).

125. Bowra (1961: 361) thinks that Pindar himself may have been influenced, by his contempt for Bacchylides, into associating Simonides with Bacchylides; I find this idea less attractive.

126. It was argued in Section 2 above that any attack on Simonides in this ode to Theron, who was apparently on good terms with Simonides, would be difficult to explain except as a response to some provocation by Simonides.

127. Stella herself (1946: 16) admits that Pindar replies "non senza cortesia".

Chapter 11

Late Simonidean Epigrams

1. The argument based by Stella on epigrams referring to events after 468/7 B.C.; the principles involved.

There is a small group of epigrams, each ascribed to Simonides by at least one ancient source, which refer (or may refer) to events after 468/7, the traditional date of the poet's death. As long as this date was regarded as certain, any "Simonidean" epigrams which referred to later events could automatically be dismissed as spurious. But Stella proposes to lower the date of Simonides' death to about the mid fifth century, though without claiming the same certainty on this point as for her revised date of Simonides' birth. One of her arguments in favour of this proposal is that whoever included such epigrams in the Simonidean collection must have remembered that Simonides was still alive about the mid fifth century.[1] (She does not argue that the epigrams must be authentic.) The epigrams which she specifies are XLIX Page (117 Diehl), which she assigns to Tanagra (457 B.C.), and XLV Page (103 Diehl), which, she thinks, may refer to the events of "449-8", by which she means Cimon's campaign in Cyprus. I include in the present discussion other epigrams which could be placed in the same category and which might be thought to support her argument, viz. XLVI Page (which definitely concerns the

Eurymedon) and XLVII Page (which may refer to the Eurymedon).

Stella's argument provides a striking example of the assumption that the ancient ascription of an epigram to Simonides, though it may be erroneous or based partly on guesswork, must always have been consistent with or prompted by historical facts, and not due to lack of historical awareness on the part of the ascribing authority or to some accident in the course of transmission in the manuscripts or to deliberate fraud. I have already suggested briefly that this is not an acceptable principle, and indicated in general terms the steps that should be taken when one finds this principle applied to epigrams whose Simonidean authorship would be incompatible with evidence on Simonides obtained from other sources.[2] One or two such instances have already come up for discussion;[3] but there the clash between the Simonidean ascription and the other evidence was not so unmistakable, nor the bearing on the main theme of this study so important, as in the present instance. The matter is therefore discussed rather more fully here.

In putting forward her argument, Stella makes no attempt to identify the authority who "included [these epigrams] in the collection",[4] and on whose presumed reliability she bases so much. We might feel tempted to reduce her argument *ad absurdum* by applying the same argument to (say) the "Simonidean" epigram on the death of Sophocles.[5] But this would be to indulge in the same kind of over-simplification of which Stella herself is guilty when she fails to name the ascribing authority or discuss its reliability. Rather, we must briefly survey some of the demonstrably false Simonidean ascriptions which are found in various sources, in order to have a basis for judging what degree of error may reasonably be imputed to a given authority when it becomes necessary to choose between a Simonidean ascription found in that authority and other evidence incompatible with the ascription.

The hazards to which epigrams and their titles were exposed in the course of transmission from Meleager's

Garland to the Palatine and Planudean Anthologies are well known.[6] An ascription found only in one or both of these Anthologies, though it could represent the truth, is of very little value; and some Simonidean ascriptions there are patently absurd[7] (e.g. the epigram on the death of Sophocles mentioned above; or LVIII Page, on the Colossus of Rhodes). Probably no errors as gross as these can be demonstrated in earlier writers, whether of the Classical, Alexandrian, or Roman period. (The grossness of an error depends not only on the number of years involved in a misdating which connects Simonides' name with some late event, but also on the nature and familiarity of that event — for instance, whether it is a famous historical landmark or obscure athletic victory.) However there is at least one definite error in a comparatively early writer. Hephaestion attributes to Simonides an epigram[8] for Aristodemus, an athlete who won in Ol. 98 (388 B.C.).[9] Boas[10] thinks that this epigram acquired Simonides' name in Meleager's *Garland*, so that the error did not originate either from Boas' Collector of Simonidean epigrams or from Hephaestion himself. Hephaestion, of course, is still guilty of carelessness in passing on the false ascription, though the misdating of an obscure athlete is a minor error compared with the gross misdatings just noted from the Anthology.

Apart from these demonstrable errors, scholars sometimes show themselves willing to impute careless errors of ascription to comparatively early writers. For example, Boas supposes that his Collector (whom he believes to have been a Peripatetic living towards the end of the fourth century B.C.) carelessly ascribed to Simonides epigrams on events which happened after the poet's death;[11] that he arbitrarily ascribed to Simonides epigrams plainly ascribed to Empedocles in the source from which he drew them;[12] and that he carelessly ascribed to Simonides the epigram XLI Page (163 Bergk) (anonymous in two passages of Aristotle) because he found the Archedice epigram (XXVIA Page, 111 Bergk) ascribed to Simonides in the second passage of Aristotle.[13] It is, indeed, usual for those who postulate a collection or collections of Simonidean epigrams at various dates from the fourth to the second century B.C. to assume that some of the obviously false Simonidean ascriptions originated in such collections.[14]

We can now apply to our group of "late" epigrams the method of enquiry outlined in general terms in Section 2 of the introductory chapter. Firstly we must consider the date and importance of the events referred to, and ask how serious is the error involved in the ascription of these epigrams to Simonides, if the traditional date of Simonides' death is correct. Secondly, we must consider whether the authorities who ascribe these epigrams to Simonides are such that we ought not to impute such an error to them, but ought rather to assume (with Stella) that the Simonidean ascriptions must be consistent with historical fact (even though they may happen to be mistaken) and that the traditional date of Simonides' death is therefore wrong.

For an epigram to qualify as relevant material for our discussion, it must fulfil two conditions. The first is that it must refer unmistakably to some definite event. Or alternatively, if the actual wording of the epigram does not indicate the event, the epigram must be assigned to a definite event by the same ancient authority as ascribes it to Simonides; Stella's argument, that the ancient authority remembered that Simonides was alive at the time of that event, would then still apply. The same point holds good, when, of two ancient scholars working on the Palatine manuscript, one (the Lemmatist)[15] connects the epigram with some definite event, while the other (the Corrector) ascribes the epigram to Simonides. In such cases, the Corrector (if he took the Lemmatist's annotation into account)[16] is connecting Simonides' name with the event. The second condition is that the event must be one which can be definitely dated after 468/7, the traditional date of Simonides' death.

2. The epigrams cited by Stella, and other epigrams in the same category.

Some epigrams which certainly or possibly refer to the battle of the Eurymedon may now be considered.[17] An unambiguous example is XLVI Page:[18]

> These men once lost their lovely youth by the Eurymedon, fighting as spearmen with the front ranks of the bow-carrying Medes, both on foot and on the swift ships; and having died they have left a most fair memorial of their valour.

Here the text refers explicitly to the Eurymedon. The main point of doubt is the date of this battle. Diodorus[19] gives the date as 470/69, which certain modern scholars have accepted.[20] A later date is usually preferred, but there is no agreement on an exact date, and it is still not clear whether the battle occurred before or after the traditional date of Simonides' death (468/7). Several scholars date it to 468;[21] some to 467 or 466,[22] or even to 465.[23] Opinions on the possibility of Simonidean authorship of the epigram vary accordingly. Bergk and Hauvette date the battle shortly before Simonides' death, but reasonably argue that he is unlikely to have composed the lines (whether sending them from Sicily or visiting Athens) in the few intervening months;[24] others deny the lines to Simonides on the ground that the battle occurred after his death.[25] But most scholars ignore the question of Simonidean authorship, and concentrate on the question of whether the lines were a genuine inscription for the Eurymedon dead or a late literary exercise. Page inclines to the belief that the epigram was a genuine inscription;[26] he does not explicitly discuss Simonidean authorship (which his dating of the battle to 468 would allow), but apparently thinks that the epigram was the work of an inferior poet of Cimon's circle.

It seems, therefore, that epigrams on the Eurymedon do not obviously and necessarily belong to the period after the traditional date of Simonides' death, and therefore should not be grouped with those which Stella cites, nor used to reinforce her argument. The battle could have occurred before 468/7; or (and this is all we really need say) the ancient authority who ascribed any Eurymedon epigrams to Simonides may well have had reason to believe, as Diodorus believed, that the battle occurred before that date. Therefore the ascription of Eurymedon epigrams to Simonides

290 SIMONIDES

need not be at variance with the traditional date of his death; and we need not proceed to the second stage of our enquiry (which would have been to consider the reliability of the ascribing authority or its source, and to decide whether we preferred to impute errors of dating to this authority or to accept its statements and adjust the dates of Simonides).

The text of the following epigram contains no clue to its occasion, but it is assigned to the Eurymedon by the Lemmatist:[27]

> Once impetuous Ares washed the long-barbed arrows in red drops in these men's breasts. And, instead of the living men, who were accustomed to bear the assault of spears (?), now that they have died this dust conceals the lifeless relics of them.[28]

Some suspect the Lemmatist of indulging in guesswork in assigning the lines to the Eurymedon.[29] Boas[30] counters that the epigram echoes the language of XLVI Page (105 Bergk), which is definitely on the Eurymedon, in its contrast of archers and spearmen, and regards the subject-lemma as reliable and based on ancient authority; he thinks the lines are a composition by Mnasalces (*floruit* c. 250 B.C.) on the Eurymedon theme. Wade-Gery[31] also regards the lines as a Hellenistic composition on the Eurymedon, whether a literary exercise or a genuine inscription on a late memorial at the Eurymedon. Pritchett[32] goes so far as to argue, on the basis of the lemma in the Anthology, that the epigram is the genuine epitaph of the Eurymedon dead. Yet the alleged contrast between archers and spearmen depends on the interpretation of the disputed word ἀκοντοδόκων ("struck by the javelin" or "armed with the javelin"?) in line 3;[33] moreover, Boas himself shows that the contrast between Persian archers and Greek spearmen occurs in XIV Page (137 Bergk) (on Salamis) and that our epigram also has some phrases which recall IX Page (99 Bergk) (of uncertain subject, but assigned by the Anthology to Thermopylae); and it is possible that these lines were intended by their author to refer to some event of the Persian Wars other than the Eurymedon.

Nevertheless, though the epigram itself does not indicate the event, and its author's intentions are uncertain, it fulfils in a sense the first of the conditions we prescribed for the admission of an epigram to this discussion, viz. that it must refer to some definite event: the Lemmatist assigns it to the Eurymedon, and the Corrector, coming to the same manuscript, connects the epigram, thus assigned, with Simonides — it is, in this sense, a Simonidean epigram on the Eurymedon. But then it fails to fulfil the second condition we laid down, that the event in question must be datable after the traditional date of Simonides' death; for it is apparent that the battle of the Eurymedon cannot with certainty be thus dated.

Of this group of epigrams, the one that has provoked most debate is ep. XLV Page, which is quoted by a number of sources. Among these is Diodorus, who, after describing the Eurymedon campaign, proceeds:

> The Athenian people, taking a tithe from the spoils, dedicated it to the god, and carved the following inscription on the monument which was erected:
>
>> "Ever since the sea divided Europe from Asia and the impetuous Ares has held sway over the cities of men, never yet has such a deed of mortal men been done on land and sea at the same time (lines 1-4). For these men, having destroyed many Medes in Cyprus, captured at sea one hundred ships of the Phoenicians together with their crews; and Asia lamented greatly, smitten by them with both hands in the mighty deeds of war (lines 5-8)."[34]

Diodorus does not name the author. The lines are twice quoted, again anonymously, by Aristides; in one passage[35] he connects the lines with the Eurymedon campaign, but does not say for what type of monument they were intended; in the other,[36] he quotes them with no indication of the occasion. The lines are ascribed to Simonides by Aristides' scholiast, commenting on a passage in which Aristides, without citing our epigram, discusses the Eurymedon campaign.[37] An important textual variant is that in line 5 Aristides and his scholiast say "on land" (ἐν γαίῃ) for Diodorus' "in Cyprus" (ἐν Κύπρῳ). Finally, the Palatine Anthology[38] quotes the lines and ascribes them to Simonides, with the lemma "on the Athenians who campaigned with Cimon in Cyprus, when he captured the hundred Phoenician ships"; here "in Cyprus" is read in line 5, as in Diodorus.

Many difficult problems surround this epigram, and the variety of the answers to them may be inferred from the existence of an extensive literature on the subject; nevertheless, a reasonably confident answer can, I believe, be given on the matter with which the present discussion is mainly concerned, that is, the bearing of the epigram on Simonides' dates. A full discussion of the wider range of problems is not called for here; but at least a sketch of them is necessary if we are to say what the epigram was about — or what our ancient authorities thought it was about. Moreover, for any discussion of this epigram to be intelligible, it seems necessary to outline the main versions of the two campaigns with which our authorities connect it (or have been thought to connect it), viz. the Eurymedon (so Diodorus and Aristides) and the campaign in Cyprus c. 450-49 B.C. (if this is what is meant by the subject-lemma in the Anthology.)

Firstly, the Eurymedon campaign. According to Diodorus,[39] Cimon first defeated the Persian fleet off Cyprus, capturing over a hundred ships; he then sailed for Pamphylia the same day, landed his troops (whom he had disguised as Persians) at the mouth of the Eurymedon, and defeated the Persian army on land. (Diodorus then quotes our epigram in connection with this campaign.) According to Plutarch,[40] Cimon first won a sea-victory at the mouth of the Eurymedon, driving the Persian ships aground; he then landed and routed the Persian army, and finally won another sea-victory against eighty Persian ships which had arrived as reinforcements from Cyprus.

These accounts of Diodorus and Plutarch are the only reasonably full accounts of the Eurymedon campaign. However Diodorus' account is usually dismissed as confused and contradictory; thus it is said to be impossible for Cimon to have won a victory off Cyprus and at the mouth of the Eurymedon on the same day.[41] The reason for this confusion is often said to be that Ephorus, Diodorus' source, was led to include a sea-fight off Cyprus in his account of the Eurymedon campaign simply because he had before him the epigram with the reading ἐν Κύπρῳ ("in Cyprus") and because he thought the epigram referred to the Eurymedon campaign (though it really referred to the Cyprus campaign of c. 450-49).[42] At any rate, Plutarch's account is, by common consent, the only full account which can be used with any confidence to reconstruct the campaign. An important question for the assessment of the accuracy of our epigram (and, therefore, of its status as a contemporary inscription) is the order of events at the Eurymedon. Plutarch's account indicates unmistakably that a victory at sea was the earliest event, followed by a victory on land (though this is followed by yet another sea-victory). Other authorities which definitely put a sea-victory first are Nepos and Aristodemus.[43] There are other sources[44] which, though they mention the sea-victory before the land-victory, do not use a form of words which necessarily means that the sea-victory came first.

There are also a number of sources[45] which, in referring to the Eurymedon, mention the land-battle first. But there is no ancient authority (as far as I am aware) whose form of words indicates unambiguously that the land-battle preceded the sea-battle. (It is true that our epigram, XLV Page, does clearly indicate that a land-battle came first; but whether or not this epigram refers to the Eurymedon is part of the present enquiry.) The prior mention of the land-battle in the sources just cited may merely mean, as Meyer suggested,[46] that the land-battle was regarded as more important, although the sea-battle occurred first.

Next, the Cyprus campaign of c. 450-49. According to Thucydides,[47] Cimon sailed for Cyprus and laid siege to

Citium but died during the siege; the Greeks then raised the siege because of lack of provisions, sailed to Salamis in Cyprus, won a double victory by sea and land[48] against the allies of the Persians, and returned home. According to Diodorus,[49] Cimon (in 450/49) reduced Citium and Marium in Cyprus; he then put to sea and defeated some Cilician and Phoenician ships, capturing a hundred of them with their crews, pursued the rest to Phoenicia, won a land victory in Cilicia against the Persians who had fled there, and sailed back to Cyprus. During the following year (449/8) he "sought to reduce"[50] (?) the cities of Cyprus. While the outcome of the Greeks' siege of Salamis was undecided, the Persians offered peace terms and the peace of Callias was concluded; the Athenians then withdrew from Cyprus. Cimon died during his stay in Cyprus. According to Plutarch,[51] Cimon sailed to Cyprus and defeated some Phoenician and Cilician ships at sea; he then "sought to win back"[52] (?) the cities round about, but died while besieging Citium, whereupon the Athenian fleet withdrew.

Thus our authorities do not give any clear and unmistakable account of the order of events. Thucydides mentions the sea-battle first, but does not indicate unmistakably that it preceded the land-battle. (The use of ἅμα[53] ("at the same time") by Thucydides need not mean that the sea-battle and land-battle were exactly simultaneous; at least our epigram, XLV Page, which uses the same word in line 4, nevertheless indicates a definite sequence of events.) Diodorus appears to place a sea-victory first, a land-victory second (the reduction of Citium and Marium hardly constitutes a land-battle); but the land-victory was won in a different locale; and in any case Diodorus' account of the Cyprus campaign, as of the Eurymedon campaign, is generally considered unreliable, in that it similarly crowds together, in a short space of time, operations in widely separated locations (Cyprus and Cilicia, with a pursuit as far as Phoenicia); indeed, his account may be no more than "a confused repetition of his own account of Eurymedon".[54] Plutarch's brief account puts a sea-victory first, but does not include mention of any definite land-victory.

The problem of deciding what events the epigram was intended to commemorate is complicated by the fact that its status as a single eight-line poem has sometimes been doubted: some[55] have divided the epigram into two separate poems, referring the first four lines to the Eurymedon and the last four lines to the Cyprus campaign; others[56] have referred the first four lines to the Eurymedon, rejecting the last four as a late supplement. The objections to such procedures have been stated most recently by Page (ad loc.); the argument that the last four lines cannot be an independent epigram because of the presence of γάρ ("for") in line 5 seems conclusive; the argument that the first four lines are too imprecise and unspecific to stand alone carries some weight, but should be based on the absence of any particularising phrase such as "these men" or "this dedication", rather than on the fact (stressed by Page) that the participants and the location of the battle are not named; the frequently stated argument, that an epigram must not be denied to be a contemporary inscription merely because it does not state the occasion, as the occasion would be made clear by the monument *in situ*, seems to be a valid one.[57] However that may be, it will be assumed in the present discussion that the lines constitute a single poem.

Of those who accept the lines as a single poem, some refer them to the Eurymedon, usually with the reading "on land" (ἐν γαίῃ) in line 5;[58] Boas[59] is an exception, in that he reads "in Cyprus" (ἐν Κύπρῳ) but still refers the lines to the Eurymedon. Others, invariably reading "in Cyprus", refer the lines to the campaign in Cyprus c. 450-49 B.C.[60]

Although it is not immediately obvious how the events as summarised in this epigram (whether Κύπρῳ or γαίῃ is read) are to be harmonised with any of the explicit accounts of either the Eurymedon or the Cyprus campaign, many of the scholars who assign the epigram to one or other of these campaigns say nothing of this problem. It is true that, for those who regard the first four lines as a separate epigram, this problem scarcely exists, as these lines give little detail of the event.

Among those who refer the entire epigram to the Eurymedon, there are some who do at least face up to this problem; but their solutions are hardly satisfactory. Bergk unconvincingly attempts to evade the epigram's reversal of what he believes (following Plutarch) to be the true order of events at the Eurymedon (sea-battle, then land-battle), by stating that ὀλέσαντες ("having destroyed") (line 5) need not be prior in time to ἕλον ("(they) captured") (line 6). Uxkull-Gyllenband[61] rejects Plutarch's account; considering the epigram to be a genuine contemporary inscription, he treats it as a primary historical source, and regards its account of the order of events (land-battle, then sea-battle) as correct and as confirmed by the sources which (in fact) merely *mention* the land-battle first. But as the epigram is the object of our enquiry, it is not open to us to proceed on the assumption that the epigram concerns the Eurymedon and that it constitutes a contemporary and accurate record.

In short, the epigram (if the last four lines are accepted as part of it) seems to conflict with Plutarch's account of the Eurymedon, which is the only full and explicit account with a fair claim to credibility. The majority of modern historians (who assess the situation without taking the epigram into account) seem to accept Plutarch's version.[62] If they are right (as seems probable), it would appear that the epigram is not likely to be a contemporary record of the Eurymedon campaign, and is therefore not to be accepted as evidence that Simonides wrote on the Eurymedon.

Those who assign the epigram to the Cyprus campaign occasionally raise the problem of the sequence of events. Weber[63] says that ἅμα ("at the same time") (line 4) does not mean that there were victories by land and sea on the same day (an interpretation which caused the epigram to be wrongly associated by the ancients with the Eurymedon); he claims that the word merely has the force of "both...and". He refers ἐν ἠπείρῳ ("on land") (line 4) to "the land-victory in Cyprus over the Medes", and κατὰ πόντον ("by sea") to "the sea-victory over the Phoenician fleet", but he does not particularise further or state which ancient account of the Cyprus campaign he is following. Wade-Gery,[64] who refers lines 5-8, as a separate epigram, to events in Cyprus, states in the course of his discussion that "in Cyprus, the defeat of the land-force was preliminary to the sinking of the reinforcing fleet". But he does not quote any authority for his account. He is not, apparently, following Diodorus, for he refers the epigram to "the Battles of Cyprian Salamis, fought after Kimon's death by the Athenians in Cyprus", whereas according to Diodorus the victories at Cyprus were won *by* Cimon.

As the ancient accounts of the course of the Cyprus campaign are either imprecise or unreliable, we lack a yardstick against which to test the accuracy of our epigram's account. We must therefore allow that the epigram may well give an accurate account of the Cyprus campaign, and that therefore it may have been inscribed, as has often been supposed,[65] on some memorial to that campaign.

The general picture, then, is fairly complicated; but it is not too difficult to isolate those points which are essential to our discussion. For while we should like to know the answers to the many problems surrounding this epigram, the essential question for our purpose is this: What opinion about the occasion of the epigram may we reasonably presume to have been held by the ancient scholars who first ascribed it to Simonides? For it is on their association of Simonides' name with a given event that Stella's argument depends. They may have either (1) referred the lines, with the reading γαίῃ ("(on) land"), to the Eurymedon, as did Aristides; or (2) referred the lines, with the reading Κύπρῳ ("(in) Cyprus"), to the Eurymedon, as did Diodorus; or (3) referred the lines, with the reading Κύπρῳ, to the Cyprus campaign of c. 450-49.

The earliest ascription of this epigram to Simonides is by the scholiast to Aristides; here γαίῃ is read, and the scholiast indubitably refers the lines to the Eurymedon. Apart from the title in the Palatine Anthology, this is the only extant Simonidean ascription of the epigram. It might seem, then, that we have no evidence that any authority earlier than the Anthology (if we may postpone for a moment our discussion of the Anthology) associated the epigram, under Simonides' name, with anything but the Eurymedon; so that the remarks already made about the relevance of Eurymedon epigrams to our discussion would apply here.

Boas[66] however argues persuasively that there is a common source, viz. Meleager's *Garland*, behind the Simonidean ascription in the scholia to Aristides (the scholiast reads γαίῃ, as does Aristides) and the Simonidean title in the Anthology (where Κύπρῳ is read); and that in Meleager's *Garland* Κύπρῳ (the common reading of Diodorus and the Anthology) was read. Boas thinks, therefore, that his Collector, on whose *Sylloge Simonidea* Meleager drew, ascribed the epigram to Simonides *with the reading* Κύπρῳ.

But even if this is right, it is still entirely possible, and Boas himself certainly seems to assume, that the Collector believed that the lines referred to the Eurymedon. The Eurymedon is the only event with which the lines, with the reading Κύπρῳ (or of course with any other reading), are unmistakably connected in any ancient source, viz. in Diodorus' account, which is presumed to be based on Ephorus. What Ephorus-Diodorus did, the Collector may have done. And if the Collector assigned the lines to the Eurymedon, they do not support Stella's argument. For them to do so, it has to be assumed that the Collector assigned the lines to a Cyprus campaign which he knew to be distinct from the Eurymedon campaign and which he knew to be dated c. 450-49 (or at least, later than 468/7, the traditional date of Simonides' death), and that he ascribed the lines to Simonides not in a moment of carelessness, but with these historical facts, and the dates of Simonides' life, consciously before his mind.

The assumption that the Collector assigned the lines to the Cyprus campaign rather than the Eurymedon, though possible, is totally unnecessary; this, I think, is the main objection to allowing the lines to count for much in Stella's favour. *If* the Collector assigned the lines to the Cyprus campaign, the error of connecting with Simonides an event occurring some twenty years after the traditional date of his death would be a serious one (it might be thought more serious, for example, than Hephaestion's apparent misdating of an obscure athlete by four times that number of years),[67] and the assumption that the Collector's dates were right and our dates of Simonides wrong might seem to be a reasonable way out. Nevertheless, such an assumption in favour of the Collector's historical knowledge and care in working is not one which we are obliged to make (we have seen that Boas imputes some careless errors to his Collector). All in all, the Collector's supposed ascription of this epigram to Simonides is of very little help to Stella.

The testimony of the Palatine Anthology must be considered separately. The Simonidean title here, which we owe to the Corrector, probably has some ancient authority, as it is supported by Aristides' scholiast, who also ascribes the epigram to Simonides. The subject-lemma is in all probability based on the wording of the epigram itself;[68] but we are concerned not so much with what the Lemmatist meant by this lemma, as with what the Corrector, adding the Simonidean title to the manuscript, understood by it. It is clearly possible that, just as Ephorus-Diodorus referred the epigram with the reading Κύπρῳ to the Eurymedon, so the Corrector understood the epigram and lemma, both containing the words ἐν Κύπρῳ, to refer to the Eurymedon. There is no need to suppose that the Lemmatist meant, or the Corrector understood, this lemma to refer to a different campaign from that which is named in the lemmata to XLVI and XLVII Page (viz. the Eurymedon). If the Corrector thought the Eurymedon was meant, the remarks we have made on the relevance of Eurymedon epigrams still apply. For the Simonidean title of this epigram in the Anthology to be of any help to Stella, we should again have to make the same assumptions about the Corrector of the Palatine manuscript that we discussed above in connection with Boas' Simonidean Collector, viz. that he connected the lines with a campaign several years after 468/7 and that his accuracy and care were such that his testimony can overrule the evidence for Simonides' death c. 468/7: again, these assumptions are not justified.

The other epigram (in addition to XLV Page) which Stella cites in support of her later dating of Simonides is XLIX Page:[69]

> Farewell noble warriors, having great glory in war, sons of the Athenians, outstanding in horsemanship, who once in defence of your native city with its fair dancing-floors lost your youth fighting against most of the Greeks.

The few letters of this epigram which were discovered on stone were enough for Wilhelm[70] to identify the inscription with the lines found in the Palatine Anthology, where they are ascribed to Simonides, with the lemma "on the champions of the Athenians". Thus the subject-lemma gives no clue to the occasion of the poem, and the lines themselves only the slight clue of "against most of the Greeks"; but the form of the letters has reduced the choice of dates to the mid fifth century or soon after. Wilhelm himself, followed among others by Stella and (tentatively) Page, assigned the lines to the battle of Tanagra (457 B.C.); a slight variation of this theory is to suppose that the lines commemorate this battle but were not actually carved until c. 451.[71] The other main body of opinion refers the lines to the cavalry engagement near Athens during Archidamus' first invasion of Attica (431 B.C.).[72]

If one makes the obvious assumption that the events commemorated, and the composition of the epigram, are at least roughly contemporary with the carving of the inscription,[73] the epigraphical evidence seems to prove that the lines could not have been composed by Simonides before 468/7 B.C. But the use which Boas and Stella make of this fact is open to criticism. Boas,[74] who thinks that this epigram was in his Collector's *Sylloge Simonidea*, classes it among those epigrams which refer to events after Simonides' death and which therefore convict the Collector of carelessness in including them among the *Simonidea*. But the lines are dated for us not by their content or context, but only by the form of the letters on the stone; and it is very difficult to say what means the Collector (or whoever first assigned the lines to Simonides) had for dating them. If he found them in a literary source, can it be regarded as certain that that source made the context clear? If he found them on stone, can we be sure that he was capable of dating the lines by their lettering, or that the monument made the occasion unmistakably clear? We have already accepted as valid, in general terms, the claim that the occasion of an epigram, even if not revealed by the wording of the text, may sometimes have been made clear by the monument *in situ*.[75] But does this mean that the occasion would necessarily have been clear to someone (like our Collector) seeing the monument and inscription perhaps centuries after the event? If a monument stood on the actual site of a battle, the occasion would remain self-evident. But whether the occasion of a monument erected at Athens would remain clear long after the event would often have depended on the degree of precision with which the event was described in the verse-epigram or in any prose-inscription that may have accompanied the verse-epigram, or on whether the inscription was accompanied by any sculpture signifying the event. In short, the epigram, though datable for the epigraphist, may not have been datable for the ancient scholar who ascribed it to Simonides. Boas is therefore hardly justified in accusing the Collector of carelessness, if by this he means that the Collector ignored the context of the epigram and failed to correlate it with Simonides' dates; for the Collector may have been simply ignorant of the occasion of the poem.

Stella similarly assumes that the ancient scholar who ascribed the epigram to Simonides had access to information on the dating of the events to which it refers; but, as we have seen, she draws what is virtually the opposite conclusion to Boas, namely that the ascription to Simonides could be correct and that the traditional date of Simonides' death is therefore wrong. However, the point just made, that the epigram may not in fact have been datable for an ancient scholar, means that it does not adequately fulfil the conditions we imposed,[76] viz. that it must refer unmistakably to an event which can be definitely dated after the traditional date of Simonides' death. Therefore Stella's argument, that the epigram counts in favour of her later dating of Simonides, cannot be allowed to stand.

References

1. Stella (1946) 17-18, 18 n. 1.
2. See Chapter I, section 2.
3. See Chapter III, section 2, on the tyrannicide epigram; Chapter IV, section 3, on the epigrams for Aeginetans.
4. Stella (1946) 18.
5. LI Page.
6. Cf. Gow (1958) 34-44.
7. The same is true of ascriptions to other authors (e.g. Anacreon XVII Page, on a sculpture by Myron).
8. LII Page.
9. Eusebius I 206 Schoene. The date is confirmed by Pausanias' naming (6.3.4) of the artist Daedalus who made the athlete's statue.
10. 1905: 91-2.
11. Boas (1905: 231), on the "Eurymedon" epigrams XLVI & XLV Page (105 & 142 Bergk), and an epigram from the mid fifth century (XLIX Page, 108 Bergk).
12. Boas (1905: 124-6, 231) on Emped. frags. 156 & 157 Diels-Kranz (= Emped. frags. 2 & 1 Bergk).
13. Boas (1905: 70-2, 230); Aristot. *Rhet.* 1.7, 1365 a 24; ib. 1.9, 1367 b 18-20.
14. For the view of Gow & Page on ep. LI, see Chapter I, section 2, with n. 50.
15. On the identity of the Lemmatist, see Gow (1958) 11; Gow & Page (1965) I pp. xxxiv-v.
16. C. sometimes corrects or criticises L. (Gow (1958) 11 & n. 6).

17. These will include ep. XLV, which (as already noted) is referred by Stella to the campaign in Cyprus c. 450-49, but which some scholars connect with the Eurymedon.

18. *Anth. Pal.* 7.258, assigned to Simonides, with the lemma "on those who distinguished themselves with Cimon at the Eurymedon". For the extensive literature on this epigram, see Peek (1955) no. 13 (cf. Page ad loc., p. 269 n. 2).

19. 11.60-61.

20. E.g. Meritt, Wade-Gery, and McGregor (*ATL* III (1950) 160) date the battle to 469. For further references to scholars who accept this date, see *RE* "Kimon" XI 1 (1921) 445.16 ff.

21. E.g. Busolt (1885-1904) III 1 143 n. 2; Page *FGE* (1981) ad loc. (though in *EG* (1975) on ep. XLV Page dated c. 468/7 and doubted whether the battle occurred before or after Simonides' death).

22. Walker (*CAH* V 53). For references to scholars who accept one or other of these dates, see *RE* ib. 445.7 ff.

23. P. Deane, *Thucydides' Dates* (Don Mills, Ontario 1972) 11-13. Cf. Peek (1955: no. 13), who dates these lines "nach 469/8 (465/4)".

24. Bergk, *PLG* III p. 446; Hauvette (1896) no. 32, p. 90.

25. E.g. Boas (1905) 231; Bowra (1938) 187; Pritchett (1960) 166.

26. Page finds some support for this view in the assumption (for which, see Boas (1905) 180) that the epigram derives from the Collection of Simonidean epigrams (the *Sylloge Simonidea*) on which Meleager drew.

27. Simon. XLVII Page; *Anth. Pal.* 7.443, assigned to Simonides, with the lemma "on the Greeks who fell by the river Eurymedon".

28. On the difficult and contorted forms of expression in this epigram, see Page's commentary.

29. Stadtmüller, *Anth. Pal.* ad loc. (following Jacobs); Page.

30. 1905: 213 ff.

31. 1933: 81.

32. 1960: 166.

33. See Boas loc. cit. and Page ad loc.

34. Diod. Sic. 11.62.3-63.1. For bibliography on this epigram, see Page ad loc., p. 266 n. 1.

35. *Or.* 46.156.

36. *Or.* 28.63 f.

37. Schol. (III 209 Dindorf) on Aristid. *Or.* 13.152.

38. *Anth. Pal.* 7.296.

39. 11.60-2.

40. *Vit. Cimon.* 12-13.

41. See, for example, Busolt (1885-1904) III 1 146 n. 5.

42. Meyer (1892-9) II 10 & n. 1; Beloch (1912-27) II 2 162; Walker, *CAH* V 55 & n. 1.

43. Nep. *Vit. Cimon.* 2.3; Aristodemus (= no. 104) frag. 11.2 (*FGrH* II A p. 500).

44. Frontin. *Strat.* 2.9.10; Aristid. *Or.* 13.152 & 46.156.

45. Thuc. 1.100.1; Lycurg. *in Leocr.* 72; Paus. 1.29.14 (cf. 10.15.4); so also the epigram XLVI Page (cited above).

46. 1892-9: II 20-2.

47. 1.112.2-4.

48. ἐναυμάχησαν καὶ ἐπεζομάχησαν ἅμα, καὶ νικήσαντες ἀμφότερα... ("they fought a sea-battle and a land-battle at the same time, and having conquered in both..."), Thuc. 1.112.4.

49. 12.3-4.

50. ἐχειροῦτο τὰς κατὰ τὴν Κύπρον πόλεις, Diod. Sic. 12.4.1.

51. *Vit. Cimon.* 18-9.

52. ἀνεκτᾶτο...τὰς ἐν κύκλῳ πόλεις, Plut. *Vit. Cimon.* 18.6.

53. N. 48 above.

54. Gomme (*Commentary on Thucydides* I p. 330), following Busolt (1885-1904: III 1 343 n. 4) and Meyer (1892-9: II 18).

55. Wade-Gery (1933: 82-7), following Domaszewski.

56. E.g. Schwartz, *Hermes* 35 (1900) 117-20.

57. See for example Schneidewin (1835) pp. 154-5; Wilamowitz (1913) 193; Shefton, *Annual of the British School at Athens* 45

Late Simonidean Epigrams 305

(1950) 149 & n. 29. For further consideration of this matter, see the discussion of ep. XLIX (below, this Section).

58. Bergk (ep. 142); Hauvette (1896) no. 66, p. 127; Uxkull-Gyllenband (1927) 55.

59. 1905: 107-8.

60. Meyer (1892-9) II 9-10; Weber (1917) 248 ff.; Peek (1955) no. 16; Page.

61. 1927: 53-8.

62. E.g. Busolt (1885-1904) III 1 149; Meyer (1892-9) II 2-7; Swoboda, *RE* "Kimon" XI 1 (1921) 445.31 ff.; Walker, *CAH* V 55 & n. 1.

63. 1917: 256 n. 2.

64. 1933: 84 n. 53.

65. E.g. by Meyer (1892-9) II 12; Weber (1917) 254; and (apparently) Page (ad loc.).

66. 1905: 97, 105, 108 & n. 46, 111, 247 n. 3.

67. See above, Section 1, with n. 8.

68. Cf. Gow (1958) 18.

69. *IG* I² 946; *Anth. Pal.* 7.254.

70. 1899: 221 ff.

71. Wade-Gery (1933) 79; similarly Bertelli, *QUCC* 6 (1968) 52-98.

72. Domaszewski (1917) 18; Hiller von Gaertringen (*IG* I² ad loc.); Raubitschek, *Hesperia* 12 (1943) 25 f.

73. It is just possible that the lines have been re-inscribed from an earlier monument (for certain or possible instances of this, see the discussion of eps. III, XX (a) & (b), and I, in the present study); if that were so, the epigram could not be dated at all.

74. 1905: 180, 231.

75. See above, this Section, with n. 57.

76. See Section 1 of this chapter.

Chapter 12

The Ancient Testimonia on Simonides' Dates

1. The ancient testimonia and the orthodox modern interpretation

An important item of evidence for Simonides' dates is the Simonidean epigram which indicates that he was ὀγδωκονταέτης ("eighty years old") at the time of his dithyrambic victory in 477/6; depending on the way in which the figure eighty was reckoned, this puts his date of birth at about 557/6 B.C. The epigram is quoted by the fifth-century Neo-Platonist philosopher Syrian, who is commenting on a passage in which the rhetorician Hermogenes of Tarsus discusses the term δεινός ("skilled") as applied to Simonides by Theocritus.[1] Syrian writes:

> "Unless the skilled bard of Ceos."[2]
>
> You must know that in the works of Theocritus now in circulation, "unless the divine bard" is found in the text. But "skilled" (δεινός) is by far the most appropriate term in that context. For this man (Simonides) was so well versed in every poetical and musical art, that from his youth until the age of eighty

he won victories in the competitions at Athens, as the epigram makes clear:

> "Adeimantus was archon over the Athenians, when the Antiochid tribe won the well-wrought tripod (lines 1-2). And a certain son of Xenophilus, Aristides, was choregus for the chorus of fifty men who had learnt their part well (lines 3-4). And the glory for training the chorus fell to Simonides, the eighty-year-old son of Leoprepes (lines 5-6)."

And they say that after his victory he sailed away to Hieron's court and died in Sicily soon afterwards.

This passage of Syrian is closely echoed, and the epigram is quoted, by Tzetzes in his scholia on his own *Chiliades*;[3] also modelled on Syrian is a scholium on Hermogenes by Planudes,[4] who again quotes the epigram, but omits the sentence about Simonides' voyage to Sicily. Aelian[5] is apparently quoting from the same set of data when, without mentioning the epigram, he says that Simonides went to Hieron when "weighed down with old age". Plutarch[6] quotes the last two lines of the epigram as evidence that Simonides was victorious with dithyrambic choruses in his old age. Valerius Maximus[7] must be referring to this epigram when he writes: *Simonides vero poeta octogesimo anno et docuisse se carmina et in eorum certamen descendisse ipse gloriatur*; this is the only explicit testimony that Simonides himself composed the epigram.

Nothing further is known of the choregus named in the epigram, Aristides son of Xenophilus, except that he is said[8] to have been one of the only two persons named Aristides to have won a choregic victory between the Persian Wars and 403 B.C. The archonship of Adeimantus is firmly dated to 477/6 B.C.[9] It is generally assumed that the epigram refers to a victory in the Great Dionysia, which would have occurred in March 476. Wilamowitz[10] thought that the victory may have been won in either the Dionysia or the Thargelia (which was celebrated in May or June); but as we are told that at the Thargelia two tribes competed jointly,[11] and only one tribe is mentioned in this epigram, the Thargelia seems to be excluded.

Further evidence for Simonides' dithyrambic victory in 477/6 is provided by ep. 54 of the Parian Marble,[12] though the Marble does not, in this entry, state Simonides' age:

> Since Simonides the son of Leoprepes, the Cean, the one who discovered the art of memory, won a victory in training the chorus at Athens, and the statues of Harmodius and Aristogeiton were set up, 213 (?) years,[13] in the archonship of Adeimantus at Athens.

Ep. 57 of the Marble does give information on Simonides' age:

> Since the stone fell at Aegospotami and Simonides the poet died, having lived (βιούς) 90 years, 205 years, in the archonship of Theagenides at Athens.[14]

Simonides' death is thus dated to 468/7, the year of the archonship of Theagenides. As his life-span is given as ninety years, this puts his date of birth at about 558/7 B.C. (depending on how the figure ninety was reckoned), and thus confirms, to within a year or two, the date of birth implied by the epigram XXVIII Page.

The following passages of Cicero and the Suda, which are thought to derive from Apollodorus' *Chronicle*, confirm for the most part the dating of Simonides' lifetime to approximately 556-468 B.C. as attested by the epigram and the Parian Marble:

Cicero *De Rep.* 2.20[15]

> For Stesichorus was not his (Hesiod's) grandson by his daughter, as some have said. For in the very year in which Stesichorus died, Simonides was born, in the fifty-sixth Olympiad (556/5 B.C.).

Suda s.v. Σιμωνίδης 439

> ...He (Simonides) was later in time than Stesichorus...He was born (γέγονε) in the fifty-sixth Olympiad (556/5);

but others have said Olympiad 62 (532/1). And he survived until the seventy-eighth Olympiad (468/7), having lived (βιούς) 89 years.

The meaning of the term γέγονε (which here must be rendered "was born"), the reason for the alternative date of birth (as it appears) in the Suda, and the method of calculating his life-span as eighty-nine years, are discussed later in the present section of this chapter, as is the question whether the naming of a given Olympiad is intended to refer to the first year of the Olympiad (as assumed in the equivalent dates B.C. given above) or more generally to the four-year period of the Olympiad.

There are three sets of entries on Simonides in various works which derive from the *Chronicle* of Eusebius; these works include the Latin version of Hieronymus, the Armenian version, and the seventh-century Greek chronicle known as the *Chronicon Paschale*. The entries on Simonides in the Greek chronicle of Syncellus (c. 800 A.D.) echo the wording of these other sources but are undated, and are therefore not quoted here. For various reasons, only approximate dates can be assigned to Eusebius. The quotation of dates from the version of Hieronymus is complicated not only by the selection of different manuscripts by various editors, but also by the intrinsic difficulty, caused by vagaries in aligning historical entries against columns of figures, of deciding what the manuscripts of Hieronymus report. In the entries on Simonides at least, the dates given by the Armenian version always fall within the range of dates offered by the various manuscripts of Hieronymus; but the dates given by the *Chronicon Paschale*, in the relevant entry on Simonides, are half-a-dozen years outside this range. However, the fact that Eusebius' datings can only be approximately recovered does not substantially affect the overall interpretation of the ancient evidence on Simonides' dates.

The first set of entries on Simonides belongs to approximately the same date as the date of birth (c. 556 B.C.) stated or implied by the sources already quoted; but the event assigned to this date is not Simonides' birth, but his *floruit*;[16] the significance of this discrepancy is discussed later in the present section. (A similar reference to Simonides' *floruit*, based on Eusebius and dated to Ol. 56 (556/5 B.C.) is found in Cyril of Alexandria.)[17] The second set of entries again gives Simonides' *floruit*,[18] this time in company with Phocyllides and Xenophanes, at a date corresponding approximately with the alternative date of birth (c. 532 B.C.) given by the Suda. The third set of entries dates the *floruit* of Simonides and Pindar together at about 486/5 B.C.;[19] this date does not directly correspond with any statement of Simonides' dates in any other source, though it falls within the life-span (c. 556-468) implied by the sources already quoted.

There are a number of passages which, though not giving Simonides' dates, are evidence of the ancients' belief that he lived to an advanced age. Some of these passages link the theme of Simonides' old age with that of his covetousness.[20] One or two other passages are potentially of rather more interest. A passage of Aristides refers to the boast made by Simonides about his powers of memory in old age, in the lines:[21]

> And I say that no one equals Simonides in memory,
> the eighty-year-old son of Leoprepes.

The connective particle indicates that this is a fragment of a longer poem; the content does not suggest an inscription, and Boas[22] believes that the couplet was not in the *Sylloge* of Simonidean epigrams. The lines could well be a fragment of an elegy, in the sense of a non-inscriptional, personal, elegiac poem. If that is so, the poem may have been preserved with a genuine tradition of Simonidean authorship; at least, Aristides' firm insistence on Simonides' authorship ("no one else says this about Simonides, but he has written it about himself") would seem to indicate that he is not merely relying on the occurrence of Simonides' name in the couplet itself, as Boas would have us believe.

The following passage of Hieronymus similarly testifies to Simonides' vigour in old age:[23]

> ad Poetas venio, Homerum, Hesiodum, Simonidem, Stesichorum, qui grandes natu, cygneum nescio quid, et solito dulcius, vicina morte, cecinerunt.

This reference to Simonides' swan-song in old age is probably based simply on the biographical tradition of Simonides' longevity (here extended into the pseudo-biographical allusions to the earlier poets); but it is just possible that it indicates an awareness, based on a corpus of surviving Simonidean poems (some of them datable), that much of Simonides' poetic activity was concentrated in his old age. This point will be taken up again in the concluding chapter.

Finally, two passages may be quoted which date Simonides in relative terms, by making him older than Pindar and Aeschylus; Stella, it will be remembered, regards Simonides as a near-contemporary of these poets.[24] The Pindaric *Lives* contain a number of statements to the effect that Simonides was older than Pindar, of which the following is typical:[25]

> He (Pindar) overlapped with (or "came after"? ἐπέβαλλε) Simonides in time, as a younger man in relation to an older man (ἢ νεώτερος πρεσβυτέρῳ).

The phraseology of this sentence is entirely in keeping with the traditional dating of Simonides, which makes him thirty-eight years older than Pindar; a biographical notice about Democritus,[26] which states that he was forty years younger than Anaxagoras, uses similar language (νέος κατὰ πρεσβύτην Ἀναξαγόραν, "in his youth during the old age of Anaxagoras"). As regards Aeschylus, a papyrus fragment from a treatise on metres, composed between the time of Callimachus and the end of the first century A.D., says:

> I once thought that I had been the first to discover this metre, and I prided myself upon the discovery of a new

metre. I subsequently found that it had been used by Aeschylus, and still earlier by Alcman and Simonides.[27]

We may now turn to the interpretation of these testimonia and the question of the relationship between them. As early as the seventeenth century, scholars were working their way towards an understanding of the methods of ancient chronographers, and were beginning to interpret some individual items of evidence about Simonides' dates in ways which are now regarded as correct; indeed Bentley, discussing the dating of Simonides, anticipates many of the essentials and some of the details of the orthodox modern account. The most authoritative and detailed modern account of the dating of Simonides is to be found in the numerous works of Jacoby;[28] and it is on his account that the following statement of the orthodox modern position is based, with supplementation from the work of Rohde[29] and Maas.[30]

First of all, it is assumed that the epigram (Simonides XXVIII Page), which states that Simonides was ὀγδωκονταέτης ("eighty years old") in 477/6, is a genuine composition of Simonides and provides a starting point for the ancient scholars' attempts to date the poet's life. Although the possibility is occasionally mentioned that "eighty" may be a round figure, Jacoby in most of his discussions assumes that it is to be taken literally, and deals in exact arithmetic.

Simonides' date of birth is given as Ol. 56 (556/5) by Cicero and the Suda, both of whom are thought to derive their information ultimately from the *Chronica* of Apollodorus,[31] Cicero through the *Chronica* of Cornelius Nepos, and the Suda through the *Chronike Historia* of Hesychius of Miletus (sixth century A.D.). The Suda's notice that he died in Ol. 78 (468/7), βιούς ("having lived") 89 years, is also referred to Apollodorus. The Parian Marble (ep. 57) gives the same year of death as Apollodorus (468/7), but makes him one year older (βιούς 90 years), thus apparently placing his birth one year earlier at 557/6. Jacoby argues that Apollodorus and the Parian chronicler both calculated Simonides' year of birth from the epigram XXVIII Page

(Simonides ὀγδωκονταέτης in 477/6), reaching slightly different results (556/5, and 557/6 respectively) through different means of reckoning, a topic to which we shall briefly return presently. The same conclusion on the relationship of the epigram, the Parian Marble, and the Suda, had already been reached, in a brief but masterly discussion, by Bentley,[32] who, as far as I am aware, was the first to use this epigram as evidence for Simonides' dates. He first showed that the victory mentioned in the epigram (where Simonides' age is given as 80 in 477/6 B.C.) is the victory recorded against that year in *Marm. Par.* ep. 54 (where Simonides' age is not given), and that therefore ep. 54 must refer to the same Simonides as ep. 57 (where Simonides' age is given as 90 in 468/7 B.C.), a point on which earlier scholars had not been agreed.

Jacoby is not so explicit about the notices of Simonides' death, which is dated alike by Apollodorus and the Parian Marble at 468/7. At one point he merely remarks that the date of death was either known to the ancients or obtained "durch kombination"; the meaning of this last phrase may be sought in an earlier work, where he suggests that as Simonides died in Sicily and is not mentioned in connection with anyone later than Hieron, the chronologers may have dated his death to the year before Hieron's (which occurred in Ol. 78,2, 467/6).[33] Jacoby does not seem to offer any suggestions as to the source from which the notices about Simonides' death may have originated, but he is confident that 468/7 is at least approximately correct, as no item of evidence for Simonides' life nor any fragment of any genuine Simonidean poem refers to events after this date.

The entries on Simonides in Eusebius are also thought to derive from Apollodorus, through the *Chronographiai* of Julius Africanus. Those entries in Eusebius which (with the varying manuscript readings) set Simonides' *floruit* c. Ols. 59-61, are at least partially consistent with the dating of Simonides' life just cited from Apollodorus and the Parian Marble; although the earliest date given by the manuscripts (Ol. 59,3, 542/1 B.C.) is far too early, by Ol. 61,4 (533/2)

Simonides would be about twenty-three, old enough to have begun his poetic career. No difficulty is caused, either, by the entries which date his *floruit* with Pindar c. Ols. 71-73 (c. 494/485), by which time Simonides would be aged about sixty to seventy. Of course, if both these sets of entries are to be accepted, it must be assumed that *clarus habetur* and equivalent phrases may refer not only to a particular period about the age of forty, but more loosely to any part of an adult working life, but this presents no problem; it is generally allowed[34] that some elasticity in the use of these phrases is a feature of ancient biographical notices.

The two dissonant testimonies, viz. the Suda's alternative date of birth, Ol. 62 (532/1), and one of Eusebius' dates for the *floruit*, c. Ols. 54-6 (c. 561-554), are reasonably explained as errors. It is thought that in Apollodorus, the ultimate source for the entries of both the Suda and Eusebius, γέγονε[35] was used twice with different meanings, firstly for the poet's birth (Ol. 56) and secondly for his *floruit* (Ol. 62). These complementary entries were then misunderstood by Hesychius of Miletus, who thought that they were contradictory and represented alternative dates for the same event; and his error appears in the Suda's entry, which rightly gives "γέγονε Ol. 56" as the date of birth, but wrongly gives Ol. 62 as an alternative date of birth. Eusebius has made a similar error but in reverse, understanding both instances of γέγονε in Apollodorus as *floruit*. His first (incorrect) entry of the *floruit* c. Ols. 54-6 corresponds just about exactly with the date of birth given by Cicero and the Suda. His second entry of Simonides' *floruit* c. Ols. 59-61 (γέγονε now being correctly interpreted) corresponds closely with the "Ol. 62" which appears (though wrongly referred to the date of birth) in the Suda. It is thought that the date "Ol. 62" (532/1) for the *floruit* may represent either Simonides' first competition[36] or a synchronism with Anacreon, whose *floruit* is dated by Eusebius to about this date.

We may now briefly return to the question of the methods of calculation used by the ancient writers in determining Simonides' dates. One or two preliminary observations may be in order at this point. Firstly, as regards the Parian Marble, it is generally agreed that most of its fifth-century dates (stated in terms of the number of years from the chronicler's own time) appear to be one year too early according to our knowledge of the archon-years. But it is disputed whether they actually are a year early (the chronicler being presumed to have inserted an extra archon between Laches, whom we date 400/399, and Aristocrates, whom we date 399/8); or whether they are to be regarded as correct by our standards of knowledge, having been worked out by a different method of calculation from that used for the Marble's fourth-century dates, or else from a different year as starting point.[37] In the present discussion I simply quote the Marble's dates as given by Jacoby, who believes that its fifth-century dates are generally correct. Fortunately the only aspect of the Marble's archon-dates which affects our discussion is the number of years by which it separates the archonships of Adeimantus (ep. 54) and Theagenides (ep. 57); it does not matter whether its dating of these archons is correct when measured by Olympiads or number of years B.C. Secondly, the calculations discussed here are based on the assumption that the ancient writers interpreted ὀγδωκονταέτης of the epigram (XXVIII Page) as an exact figure, not a round number. Thirdly, it is assumed that phrases like "in the fifty-sixth Olympiad", as used by the Suda in its article on Simonides, denote an exact year, viz. the first year of the Olympiad, not a four-year period. This cannot be taken for granted in all cases; thus Cadoux,[38] discussing the meaning of the phrase "in the n'th Olympiad" in ancient writers, concludes that, except in annalistic contexts where the Olympiad number is given only every four years, one cannot be confident that the first year of the Olympiad is meant; and indeed there are instances elsewhere in the Suda where the reference cannot be to the first year of the Olympiad.[39]

The slight discrepancy between Apollodorus (represented by the Suda) and the Parian Marble in their calculation of Simonides' age at the time of his death is explained as follows. Apollodorus and the Parian chronicler both had access to the epigram (XXVIII Page) which makes Simonides ὀγδωκονταέτης in 477/6, and also to a source which placed his death in 468/7. Apollodorus worked out the year of Simonides' birth by reckoning back 80 years from 477/6 by the system of "inclusive" reckoning (according to which, in calculating the interval between two numbers, both the numbers are counted in the total); he thus arrived at 556/5 as the date of birth. He also used "inclusive" reckoning (from 556/5) to calculate Simonides' age as 89 ("βιούς 89 years") at the time of his death in 468/7. Another way of expressing the same point might be to say that Apollodorus understood ὀγδωκονταέτης as meaning "in the 80th year" (79 years old), and used "βιούς 89 years" in the same way to mean "in the 89th year" (88 years old). The Parian chronicler, on the other hand, reckoned back 80 years from 477/6 by "exclusive" reckoning (the normal modern method, by which only one of the two numbers is counted when reckoning the interval between them), and thus (it is presumed) arrived at 557/6 as the year of birth; but in calculating Simonides' age in 468/7, the chronicler used inclusive reckoning (from the year 557/6) and so stated Simonides' age at the time of his death as 90. In other words, the chronicler (unlike Apollodorus) understood ὀγδωκονταέτης as meaning "80 years old" (in the 81st year); but (like Apollodorus) he used "βιούς n years" to mean "in the n'th year", so that his "βιούς 90 years" means "in the 90th year" (89 years old).

It may at first seem odd that the Parian chronicler, knowing (it is assumed) from the epigram that Simonides was ὀγδωκονταέτης at the time of the victory recorded in *Marm. Par.* ep. 54, should have apparently added 10 years to his age (βιούς 90 years) when recording his death in ep. 57, and yet separated ep. 54 and ep. 57 by an interval of no more than 9 years (ep. 54: "214" (?) years since..."; ep. 57, "205 years since..."); but there is no discrepancy if ὀγδωκονταέτης and "βιούς so many years" had different kinds of meaning for the chronicler, as described above. But if the true reading in ep. 54 is "213 years", so that there is a difference of only eight between the figures by which the chronicler dates ep. 54 and ep. 57, the picture becomes more complicated. The solution of Jacoby, who does in fact tend to accept the figure "213" for ep. 54, is that this figure and the figure "205" in ep. 57 are arrived at by different methods of reckoning, "213" by exclusive reckoning from the chronicler's own time (viz. 264/3 B.C.) and "205" by inclusive reckoning—so that, though there is a difference of only eight between the figures, they are intended to mark an interval of nine years (and the chronicler's relative dating of the archonships of Adeimantus, ep. 54, and Theagenides, ep. 57, is correct by our standards of knowledge). But Jacoby's theory of the chronicler's methods of reckoning is not always accepted. If it is thought both that "213" should be read in ep. 54, and that the chronicler intended an interval of only eight years between ep. 54 and ep. 57, Jacoby's arithmetically exact account of the chronicler's dependence on the epigram breaks down, the difference between ὀγδωκονταέτης (at the time of Simonides' victory) and βιούς 90 years (at the time of his death) being too great. It would still be possible, of course, to argue that the epigram is genuinely Simonidean and was known to the chronicler, but that he regarded ὀγδωκονταέτης as a round figure and based his statement of Simonides' age (ep. 57) on another source.

2. Stella's treatment of the ancient evidence

One of the fundamental pieces of evidence for Simonides' chronology has always been the epigram, XXVIII Page. Stella[40] challenges the authenticity of this epigram in three ways, by considering the sources where the epigram is found, its style and spirit, and its claim to be regarded as a fifth-century choregic inscription.

Although the epigram is not found on stone, nor in any author before the first century A.D., the majority of modern scholars have accepted it both as a genuine inscription and as a composition by Simonides himself. Others admit to some sort of doubt about this epigram when they claim VI Page (on Megistias) as the only definitely genuine Simonidean epigram; but I know of only one scholar (before Stella) who has rejected the epigram outright.[41] One can only agree with Stella that it is very strange that the authenticity of this epigram has been so little doubted; apart from the testimony of late authors, which has been regarded as an inadequate guarantee of the genuineness of many epigrams, there is no obvious reason why it should be regarded as Simonidean or even of the fifth century. The fact that it contains Simonides' name proves nothing. This epigram, then, must be subjected to the same doubts and queries as most other "Simonidean" epigrams.

Stella then proceeds to argue that our epigram is different in general style and spirit from the more restrained and concise epigrams of the fifth century, though she only quotes one fifth-century epigram (XVII (a) Page) by way of comparison. I think that this question is too subjective to be worth pursuing further here. We have already noted that extravagance of ideas, verbosity, and sheer length, are commonly regarded as indications of the late origin of an epigram, but that there is some disagreement as to how rigorously these criteria should be applied.[42]

The most important part of Stella's case against the epigram is her specific challenge of its claim to be regarded as a fifth-century choregic inscription. One point which she emphasises is that τις ("a certain person"), attached to the name of the choregus in line 3, would be an impossible insult to a contemporary choregus, but a plausible stopgap by a late writer interested only in Simonides himself. She is obviously right to argue that τις is unacceptable in a contemporary inscription; but it is less certain whether she is right in rejecting the possibility of emendation and so regarding this word as clear proof of the epigram's late origin (a procedure in which she is followed by Page). τις seems such a clumsy stopgap, even for a late, demonstrative epigram, that the possibility of corruption in the text at this point should probably be allowed.

The main criterion for the status of the epigram is a comparison with other choregic dedications; and Stella is surely right to accept only inscriptions as firm evidence for the nature of these. Page, though agreeing with Stella in rejecting the epigram because of the presence of τις, is unimpressed with her argument that it does not follow the pattern of choregic dedications, and cites, as evidence for choregic dedications in verse in the time of Simonides, the twelve-line epigram Antigenes I, which purports to be an inscription on a tripod-base celebrating a dithyrambic victory of Antigenes for the Acamantid tribe at the Dionysia. However, the common belief that this epigram is a copy of a fifth-century inscription is merely an assumption (no better supported than similar assumptions about our Simonidean epigram XXVIII Page). The poet Antigenes is otherwise completely unknown, as is the choregus named in the epigram (Hipponicus) and the flute-player (Ariston). The epigram is found only in the Palatine Anthology; and its only link with the fifth century is the ascription there to "Bacchylides or Simonides", which must be open to the same doubt as all ascriptions in the Anthology and which Page himself regards as absurd. It is very strange that Page, who shows extreme scepticism about the authenticity and fifth-century origin of so many "Simonidean" epigrams, should simply accept Antigenes I as a model from which inferences can be drawn about the nature of fifth-century choregic dedications. The correct course is surely to regard Antigenes I and Simonides XXVIII as being in the same category, that is, as the object of enquiry into their possible status as fifth-century dedications.

Using the epigraphical evidence, Stella seeks to show firstly that our epigram is unlike fifth-century choregic inscriptions and is therefore neither Simonidean nor fifth-century; and secondly that it is similar to late choregic inscriptions and therefore belongs to their period.

As far as fifth-century choregic inscriptions are concerned, there seems to be little doubt about the facts. Known examples are in prose, with a brief and simple formula. Stella quotes the famous example

Ἀντιοχὶς ἐνίκα, Ἀριστείδης ἐχορήγει, Ἀρχέστρατος ἐδίδασκεν[43]

"The tribe Antiochis was victorious; Aristeides was choregos; Archestratos trained the chorus."

This inscription was referred by Panaetius,[44] because of its lettering, to the late fifth century B.C.; and modern scholars follow Panaetius. With this, Stella[45] compares a number of further examples of fifth-century choregic inscriptions, though only one[46] of these is (on Meritt's restoration of the text) exactly parallel to the example just quoted. The others are very similar, but show slight differences: one quotes the name of the choregus first and names two tribes (and so belongs to the Thargelia); another adds the patronymic and deme of the choregus; while a third adds the patronymic of the choregus and adds ΠΑΙΔΟΝ ("in the boys' contest") to qualify the victory.[47] It is, at any rate, true that none of the inscriptions quoted in this section of *IG* I² (nos. 768-772: choregic monuments, before Eucleides) is at all similar to our epigram, and the variations of wording which they show are slight; no. 772 is formulated somewhat differently,[48] but Wilamowitz' suggestion that a hexameter can be read there is very daring.

Stella[49] also cites five, mainly later choregic inscriptions[50] (from the late fifth to the early third centuries B.C.), in which the name of the archon appears as well, though one[51] of these belongs to the Thargelia, where two tribes competed jointly, and two[52] are dedications of *agonothetai*, with the demos as "choregus". The flute-player is often named, so that a typical fourth-century choregic inscription of the Dionysia is:

Λυσικράτης Λυσιθείδου Κικυννεὺς ἐχορήγει.
Ἀκαμαντὶς παίδων ἐνίκα.
Θέων ηὔλει. Λυσιάδης Ἀθηναῖος ἐδίδασκε.
Εὐαίνετος ἦρχε.[53]

"Lysikrates son of Lysitheides of the deme Kikynna was choregos. The tribe Akamantis was victorious in the boys' contest. Theon was the flute-player. Lysiades of Athens trained the chorus. Euainetos was archon."

These items sometimes appear in a different order; sometimes one item (the name of the archon or the flute-player) is omitted; sometimes the artist who made the monument is named.[54] Occasionally the wording is different.[55] On the whole, though, the variations, whether in content or wording, are small; in the numerous examples in *IG* II² 3027-3062 (choregic inscriptions from the Dionysia, after Eucleides),[56] there is no inscription resembling our epigram, and probably no trace of verse.[57] Stella then is right in claiming that there is no attested choregic inscription similar to our epigram, from the fifth century or for some time afterwards. However one or two points may be added to Stella's statement of the facts. Firstly, the formulae are not quite so rigid as one might gather from Stella. Secondly, private verse dedications having some connection with choregic victories seem to be occasionally attested, both for the fifth century (for the men's chorus) and for the fourth (for comedy at the Rustic Dionysia).[58] Thirdly, verse inscriptions associated with dedications of a somewhat similar kind are occasionally found.[59]

It is not certain how these facts should be interpreted. Stella's statement[60] that if the epigram were by Simonides it would be "una vera e propria iscrizione coregica", inscribed in the usual way on the tripod base, could not be proved; Simonides or the choregus might have made some special dedication requiring its own inscription. And it is not impossible that the lines could be the actual choregic inscription, representing a departure from the usual prose formula, or even that the lines were inscribed on the stone underneath a short prose formula, as seems occasionally to have been done later.[61] (These considerations also mean that the epigram Antigenes I Page, which was discussed above, may be a genuine, fifth-century choregic inscription.) It is even possible that Simonides' lines are an example of a purely literary epigram, not intended by him to be an inscription at all. I do not think therefore that any firm conclusions can be drawn from the negative demonstration that it is not a normal early choregic inscription; for either some modification of the usual formula might have been allowed, or this epigram might have been written for a different purpose.

Stella next tries to show that certain features of our epigram mark it out as late[62]—more particularly, that it has the characteristics of authentic choregic verse-inscriptions of a later period (in fact, the Roman Imperial period). This is a weightier argument than the one we have just been considering. If our epigram can be shown to conform to the pattern of late inscriptions, the natural conclusion is that it was written late, after the fashion of contemporary inscriptions; it would be less likely that the resemblance was due to coincidence or that late inscriptions suddenly began to imitate a Simonidean epigram of much earlier date.

Against Stella's argument, however, the following considerations may be set. Firstly, although there is indeed some resemblance between our epigram and late metrical choregic inscriptions, it is not so complete or consistent as one might gather from Stella. The phrase ἦρχεν Ἀθηναίοις ("was archon over the Athenians") (line 1 of our epigram) may (as Stella claims) not be found in any classical Attic inscriptions, and does indeed occur (as Stella says) in a late choregic inscription;[63] but it occurs nowhere else in the other late choregic inscriptions assembled in the relevant section of *Inscriptiones Graecae*.[64] Stella's argument that this phrase has real significance in the Roman period, "quando di 'arconti' non c' erano più solo quelli d'Atene", perhaps carries some weight; though one might reply that Simonides sought to perpetuate his achievement in the minds of the Greeks at large, and, though in an Athenian inscription, addressed them rather than the Athenians alone. There is little point in Stella's comparison of the word κῦδος ("glory") (line 5 of our epigram) with an inscription in which the tripod declares that it (the tripod) is the κῦδος of the choral art.[65] Two of Stella's comparisons depend on conjectural restorations of the text of the inscriptions: these are ἀμφὶ διδασκαλίῃ...ἕσπετο κῦδος ("for the training of the chorus...glory accompanied") (line 5 of our epigram) compared with ἀμφὶ δὲ Νίκα/[ἕσπετο][66] ("and Victory [accompanied]"); and ὅτ' ἐνίκα ("when (so and so) won") (line 1 of our epigram) compared with ὅτ' ἐχορήγεε⁶⁷ ("when (so and so) was choregus"). Oddly enough Stella does not mention a similarity which was observed long ago; the actual phrase ἕσπετο κῦ[δος] ("glory accompanied") is found in one of these inscriptions,⁶⁸ but in circumstances which mean (as we shall see) that it hinders rather than helps Stella's case. Most of these resemblances then, in so far as they are valid at all, are odd ones culled from various late inscriptions. If we compare, say, the inscription *IG* II² 3118 as a whole with our epigram, we notice some resemblances: the inscription is in verse, contains the phrases ἄρχεν Ἀθαναίοις ("was archon over the Athenians") and ἀμφὶ δὲ Νίκα/[ἕσπετο?] ("and Victory [accompanied?]"), names the choregus and the poet-didaskalos, and mentions the tripod. But there are many differences: the archon, choregus, and didaskalos, are named in a different order; in the inscription, several tribes are named, and the flute-player and the praecentor (Tryphon) are named; and the inscription is nearly twice as long as our epigram. A glance at the other late choregic inscriptions in the relevant section of *IG* II² (3112-21) reveals no consistent pattern. Some are in elegiacs (3117, 3118), some in iambics (3120 a & b; and part of 3115?); some apparently in prose (3119); some are preceded by a prose inscription (3113, 3114), or followed by a prose inscription (3115?); they vary in length (3117 twelve lines; 3118 ten lines; 3113 six lines), and, obviously, in the amount of information given. If the class of late choregic inscriptions shows no regular pattern, it is hard to demonstrate that our epigram belongs to this class. It remains true, of course, that our epigram has more in common with these late inscriptions than with those of Simonides' time.

Secondly, although the evidence is admittedly slender, there are perhaps some positive grounds for supposing that, in the case of one of the resemblances which we have just mentioned, the late choregic inscription has borrowed from the Simonidean epigram (and not vice versa). In *IG* II² 3117 there is a correspondence not only of ἕσπετο κῦ[δος] ("glory accompanied") (line 7) with line 5 of our epigram, but also of the phrase οὐκ ἔλαθεν Χάρι[τας] ("he did not escape the notice of the Graces") (line 12) with another Simonidean epigram (οὐκ ἔλαθες Χάριτας, "you did not escape the notice of the Graces", in line 2 of the epigram on Leocrates son of Stroebus, 150 Bergk).[69] These resemblances were noticed by Wilhelm.[70] They could perhaps be coincidental; but if Wilhelm is right in thinking they are not, we know that in writing οὐκ ἔλαθεν Χάρι[τας] the author of *IG* II² 3117 was the imitator; for the first couplet of 150 Bergk was found on stone, in letters of the first part of the fifth century B.C. Boas[71] offered an ingenious explanation of why these two Simonidean epigrams should be echoed in the one inscription. Noticing that 150 Bergk[72] is immediately preceded in the Anthology by the other choregic epigram of Simonides (145 Bergk),[73] he argued that our choregic epigram (147 Bergk, XXVIII Page) had stood between them in an earlier version of the Anthology (viz. Meleager's *Garland*), the order being 145, 147, 150 Bergk; and that the author of *IG* II² 3117 (the late choregic inscription), using Meleager's *Garland*, worked into his inscription phrases from two Simonidean epigrams which stood side by side in the Garland.[74]

If Boas is right, our epigram (XXVIII Page, 147 Bergk), though not proved genuinely Simonidean, is at least earlier than the Roman Imperial period, and cannot have been modelled on the inscriptions of that period; we will have to assume that the stray resemblances between our epigram and other choregic inscriptions of the Imperial period are due either to coincidence or to sporadic use of the Simonidean epigram as a model by late writers of choregic inscriptions. Boas' argument does not amount to a demonstration. It was at least worth Stella's consideration; but she seems to be unaware of it.

To sum up: Stella has not demonstrated conclusively that our epigram cannot belong to the fifth century or that it must be a late composition. But she has at least deflated our confidence in its authenticity, leaving us instead with the suspicion that it may be contemporary with those late inscriptions with whose form and occasional phrasing it has certain things in common.

Stella's account of the other sources may now be considered. She claims, of course, not merely that the epigram is spurious, but also that it reports Simonides' age incorrectly, so that the other ancient authorities which Jacoby believed to depend on it are inaccurate as well. We should expect Stella to suggest a reason for this error in dating, and to offer an alternative to Jacoby's account by suggesting where the error may have first appeared and how it was transmitted. Unfortunately Stella's article proves deficient on both these counts.

She does not explicitly suggest a reason for the error. There is indeed a hint; as we have seen, she supposes that a true tradition of the attendance of Simonides' grandfather and namesake at Hipparchus' court was wrongly attached to Simonides himself, and she would presumably argue that this mistake caused Simonides to be dated too early. It was apparent, however, that the evidence for this particular theory was very feeble.[75] We shall consider presently whether any other reason suggests itself for the "erroneous" early dating.

Nor does Stella give any convincing or even coherent account of the source and transmission of the dating 556-468. To support this criticism it is necessary to quote some of the relevant sentences from her article. After saying that the epigram (XXVIII Page) is spurious, she concludes:[76] "È un epigramma fittizio, come amavano scriverne i dotti ellenistici, composto in età post-classica sopra una autentica notizia storica, ma calcolando l'età del poeta in base alla cronologia di Apollodoro o di qualche altro cronografo". Later, arguing that rivalry between Pindar and Simonides can be shown to have existed after the traditional date of Simonides' death, she concludes:[77] "Questa indiretta testimonianza di Pindaro[78] ha per la cronologia di Simonide un' importanza di primo ordine, che è strano non sia stata rilevata: smentisce, con tutto il peso di un autentico, inoppugnabile documento contemporaneo, la notizia della morte di Simonide nel 468; e viene indirettamente ad infirmare la cronologia 556-468[79] sulla quale tale data era più o meno approssimativamente calcolata, da Apollodoro o da qualche altro cronografo". Apparently, then, Stella attributes the traditional chronology to Apollodorus (or "some other chronographer(s)"), but it is not clear what calculation Apollodorus is supposed to have made. In the second extract quoted, Stella seems to say that the date of death 468 ("tale data") was calculated on the chronology 556-468—but such a statement would be meaningless. In an equally puzzling reference to Jacoby, Stella states:[80] "Secondo l' Jacoby la data della morte è calcolata sulla nascita alla 56ᵃ:[81] cfr. Apollod., 244 F.337 Jacoby (= Cic. *de rep.* II 20)". I see no statement by Jacoby that could be interpreted as does Stella;[82] nor can the date of death be said, strictly speaking, to be "calculated" on the date of birth, with no other datum mentioned, except in the general sense that a date of birth in 556 would make a date of death later than about 468 unlikely. Perhaps Stella's meaning in these passages is that the date of death, 468, was calculated by Apollodorus from the poet's supposed birth in 556 and lifespan of 88 years (though she does not say how Apollodorus arrived at this "incorrect" date of birth). If this is her meaning, it is strange that she should ascribe the date of death to Apollodorus, for she knows that this date appears already on the Parian Marble.

Surprisingly Stella seems to overlook the fact that the traditional chronology appears in full (i.e. date of death plus age at death, and therefore in effect date of birth) on the Parian Marble (ep. 57), a century before Apollodorus. This criticism, almost inevitable in that Stella ascribes the traditional dating to "Apollodorus or some other chronographer(s)" without mentioning the Marble, is upheld by two references which she *does* make to the Marble. When listing the ancient authorities for the poet's dates, she states:[83] "Invece il Marmo di Paro riporta la morte del poeta alla data del 468, già riferita da Suida; e ricorda una vittoria del 477-6, senza precisare peraltro l'età del poeta in quell' anno"—which would suggest to the casual reader that the Marble does not give Simonides' age at all. Secondly, we have seen that she confidently accepts from the Marble (ep. 49) an allusion to Simonides' grandfather for the year 489/8, without mentioning that the Marble itself (ep. 57) gives a date for Simonides' birth[84] which would make it practically impossible for his grandfather to be alive in 489/8.

Stella's handling of the evidence is thus easy to assail and compares unfavourably with Jacoby's exact account. But such deficiencies as we have noted do not necessarily invalidate Stella's whole case. We should therefore try the experiment of making good these deficiencies in a way that leaves her main argument unchanged, and only then compare this reformed account with Jacoby's for general probability.

The reason for the "erroneous" early dating will have to remain obscure. Stella's implied reason, that a true tradition of Simonides' grandfather at Hipparchus' court was wrongly attached to Simonides himself, seemed inadequate. On the basis of the evidence available, only two other possible theories (neither of them convincing) suggest themselves: either that Simonides' birth was made to coincide with the known date of Stesichorus' death (an inversion of the usual view that Stesichorus' death was dated by Simonides' birth);[85] or that the second line of 14 West (describing Simonides as eighty years old) was wrongly attached to the epigram (XXVIII Page) celebrating the victory of 477/6, and that XXVIII Page then led to the traditional chronology in the way described by Jacoby. (Stella of course gives no hint of any such theories; she does not mention Stesichorus; and she dates XXVIII Page too late for it to have originated the "erroneous" early dating of Simonides.) There might of course be some good reason for the "erroneous" early dating which is entirely hidden from us.

The main correction to be made is that the "erroneous" early dating must be ascribed in its entirety not to Apollodorus but to some authority at least as old as the Parian

Marble. (It does not matter in what form this information appeared: dates of birth and death; date of birth or death, and life-span; date of death, and age at victory in 477/6.) Apollodorus and the Marble would then be presumed to have drawn either on the same source (the slight discrepancy between the Suda and the Marble on Simonides' life-span resulting from different calculations from the same data), or on different sources giving almost identical information.

How then does Stella's account, when its errors have been repaired, compare with Jacoby's? Firstly, it may be noted that Rohde and Jacoby offer a convincing reason (viz. the ambiguous use of γέγονε for both birth and *floruit*) for the alternative date of birth which appears in the Suda. This explanation is all the more convincing in that it is not an isolated hypothesis put forward to explain discrepancies in Simonides' dates alone, but is applicable to other passages where ancient chronographers are thought to have made similar mistakes.[86] Stella on the other hand offers no convincing reason for the "erroneous" early dating. This tends to predispose us in favour of Jacoby, though it must be admitted that neatly coherent theories can be delusive and that the lack of an explanation could be due to our defective knowledge.

Secondly, Jacoby gives a precise account of the transmission of the evidence at every point, but Stella does not explain how the "correct" chronology (Simonides born c. 532, Ol. 62), which was ousted at an early date and is absent from the Marble and Apollodorus, reappears very late in the Suda (and perhaps in Eusebius, where, however, the corresponding date, c. Ol. 61, refers to the *floruit*). Again, this argument is not decisive, but one feels that Stella should have mentioned the problem and advanced some tentative hypothesis (it could be no more than that).

Thirdly, a more telling point. One reason for Jacoby's confidence in accepting the traditional dating as approximately correct is that the ancient scholars who accepted it possessed Simonides' works and found in them nothing to contradict it. Indeed, the poems of Simonides, who had relations with important political figures, and wrote

330   SIMONIDES

at the commission of states about important historical events, and for athletic victors at the great games, must have contained ample material for establishing dates. And it is quite likely that the datable Simonidean poems known to the ancient world covered a sufficient span of time to enable the approximate period of his lifetime to be determined from them without much doubt; thus it is likely that there existed poems for Hipparchus, written between 527 and 514, and poems for Hieron, written between 478 and 468. Moreover Apollodorus, from whom the Simonidean dating in the Suda and Eusebius is thought to derive, is known to have used the method of dating literary figures against political figures whose dates were approximately known, and also to have used the actual works of poets and other writers as a basis for dating.[87] More specifically, Apollodorus is known to have written about Simonides;[88] and he is thought to have used Simonides' actual works for the synchronism with Stesichorus[89] and for the genealogy of Lycurgus.[90] If however Stella is right, and Simonides was born c. 532, the ancient scholars must have possessed a corpus of Simonides' works belonging to the period from c. 510 (no earlier) to 468/7 or even later, yet have had no hesitation in dating his life from 556/5 (so believing that he wrote nothing till his mid forties) to 468/7 (perhaps carelessly disregarding works written after that date).

3. A possible modification of the orthodox account

One of the strongest parts of Stella's case was her attack on the authenticity of the epigram XXVIII Page. If we allow to Stella that the epigram may be spurious and too late to be a common source for the Parian Marble and Apollodorus, but continue to assume that the traditional chronology is correct, the orthodox account, as represented by Jacoby, must be modified. But the change need not be drastic; all we need do is to assume some common source (or similar sources) from which the Marble and Apollodorus drew the dates of Simonides' life, and a source (which could well be the same one) from which the Marble drew the account of Simonides' victory in 477/6. The epigram could then be fitted into the scheme at almost any point—either deriving all its information from the common source of the Marble and Apollodorus, or taking the details of the victory from some historical record, and the dates of Simonides' life from the Marble or from Apollodorus or from their common source. The picture from Apollodorus onward would remain unchanged. Jacoby's account would retain its advantages over Stella's, except that the transmission of evidence in the early stages cannot be traced so clearly, nor the slight discrepancy between Apollodorus and the Marble on Simonides' life-span accounted for so precisely.

There can be no doubt that Jacoby's account is more convincing than Stella's, even if the errors are eliminated from Stella's and Jacoby's is modified on the assumption that the epigram (XXVIII Page) may be late. Thus a study of the ancient sources and their relationship tends to favour the traditional chronology. This fact will count in the final decision for or against Stella; though Stella's arguments on other grounds are examined on their own merits, and if strong enough could turn the scale.

References

1. Simon. XXVIII Page; Syrian. *in Hermog.* I p. 85 f. Rabe (on Hermog. π. ἰδεῶν (*On Qualities of Style*) 2.9., pp. 369 f. Rabe). On Syrian's reference to Simonides' frequent victories, see above, Chapter V, section 2.

2. Theocr. 16.44: "unless the skilled bard of Ceos had made them (the Scopadae etc.) famous"; on this passage of Theocritus, see above, Chapter VI, section 1, with n. 4.

3. Tzetz. schol. ad Tzetz. *Chil.* 1.619, *Anecd. Oxon.* III 353 Cramer.

4. Max. Plan. schol. in Hermog., Walz, *Rhet. Graec.* V pp. 543 f.

5. *VH* 9.1.

6. *An seni* 3 (785 a).

7. 8.7. *Ext.* 13.

8. By Panaetius ap. Plut. *Vit. Aristid.* 1.6 (319 a).

9. *Marm. Par.* ep. 54; Diod. Sic. 11.41.1.

10. 1922: 314.

11. Aristot. *Ath. Pol.* 56.3.

12. *FGrH* no. 239, A 54, II B p. 1000.

13. Some scholars prefer to read "214" years; see the final paragraph of the present section.

14. *FGrH* ibid. Ps.-Lucian (*Macrob.* 26 (228)) also gives Simonides' life-span as "over (ὑπέρ) ninety years".

15. This passage appears as Apollodorus (= no. 244) frag. 337, *FGrH* II B p. 1121. The text of Cicero is badly mutilated at this point; the translation given is based on the text, as restored by various hands, which appears in *FGrH* loc. cit.

16. *Simonides clarus habetur* (Hieron.), Σιμωνίδης ἐγνωρίζετο ("Simonides was well known") (*Chron. Pasch.*). Hieronymus' date (Fotheringham's edition) Ol. 55,2 (559/8); range of dates in Fotheringham's mss. of Hieron., Ol. 54,4 (561/0)—56,2 (555/4); Armenian Ol. 55,4 (557/6); *Chron. Pasch.* Ol. 53,1-3 (568/7-566/5).

17. *Adv. Iulian.* I 13 (vol. 76, col. 521 Migne).

18. Hieron. (Fotheringham) Ol. 60,2 (539/8); range of dates in mss. of Hieron. (Fotheringham) Ol. 59,3 (542/1)—61,4 (533/2); Armenian reported as Ol. 60,2 (539/8) (Karst) and 60,4 (537/6) (Aucher, Schoene). The corresponding entry in *Chron. Pasch.* refers only to Xenophanes.

19. Hieron. (Fotheringham) Ol. 73,3 (486/5); range of dates in mss. of Hieron. (Fotheringham) Ol. 71,3 (494/3)—73,3 (486/5); Armenian Ol. 73,2 (487/6). The corresponding entry in *Chron. Pasch.* refers only to Pindar.

20. Cited above, Chapter IX, n. 112.

21. Simon. 14 West (146 Bergk); Aristid. *Or.* 28.60 (II 161 Keil). The second line of the couplet is identical with the last line of the epigram XXVIII Page.

22. 1905: 111.

23. Hieron. *Epist.* 52.256 (vol. 22, col. 529 Migne).

24. Stella (1946) 24.

25. *Vit. Pind. Ambr.*, I p. 2.21 f. Drachmann. Cf. *Vit. Pind. Thom.*, I p. 5.4 f. Drachmann; Eustath. *Prooem.* 25, III p. 297.13 f. Drachmann; ib. 26.

26. Diog. Laert. 9.41.

27. P. *Oxy.* no. CCXX, col. V lines 1-8 (vol. II, 1899, pp. 44-5, 49); quoted in Grenfell and Hunt's translation (cf. 147/652 (iv) Page).

28. For Apollodorus (and his successors) see Jacoby, 1902 (= *Apollodors Chronik*) pp. 196-203, on Apollod. frag. 19 (= Cic. *De Rep.* 2.20) & 20 (= Quintil. 11.2.14); these fragments appear in *FGrH* as Apollod. (= no. 244) frags. 337 & 67 (with Jacoby's commentary in *FGrH* II C-BD pp. 805 & 749); cf. also Eratosthenes (*FGrH* no. 241) frag. 34 (= Quintil. loc. cit.), with commentary in II C-BD p. 714. On the Parian Marble see Jacoby, 1904 (= *Das Marmor Parium*) pp. 112-4 (on ep. 49), 176 (on synchronism with Stesichorus), 180 (on eps. 54 & 57), 182 (on ep. 57); also *FGrH* II C-BD pp. 693-4 (on eps. 49, 54, 57).

29. Rohde (1878) 187 f. (on Simonides) and 198 ff. (on Stesichorus), from a long article on γέγονε ("was born" or "flourished") in the Suda; id. (1881) 567 ff. (on Stesichorus).

30. *RE* "Simonides" III A 1 (1927) 186.38-53.

31. Jacoby believes, however, that Apollodorus derived some biographical information on Simonides (perhaps without exact dates) from Eratosthenes.

32. Bentley (1699) pp. 41-3 (pp. 103-6, Wagner, 1874). (Bentley's argument is not made any easier to follow by the different sets of misprints in the numbering of Olympiads in these two editions.)

33. Jacoby (1904) 180 and (1902) 203 & n. 12.

34. E.g. by Rohde (1878) 199, apropos of Stesichorus.

35. Jacoby (unlike Rohde) thinks that the term γέγονε was not used by Apollodorus himself but by later compilers of synchronistic tables summarising Apollodorus' biographical notices (Jacoby (1902) 49-51). But, for the argument we are quoting, it does not matter whether the ambiguous γέγονε was derived from Apollodorus himself or from some intermediary.

36. See above, Chapter V, section 2, with n. 40.

37. Viz. 263/2 B.C., as against 264/3 for the calculation of fourth-century dates. On the controversy see Laqueur in *RE* "Marmor Parium" XIV 2 (1930) 1886-8.

38. *JHS* 68 (1948) 87.

39. Thus Plato is said by the Suda (s.v.) to have been born in Ol. 88 and to have died in Ol. 108, having lived 82 years, though the first years of these Olympiads (428/7 and 348/7) are only 80 years apart.

40. 1946: 5-10.

41. Meyer (1909) 242 n. 4; (1939) 344 n. 3. The statement of Wilamowitz (1897: 319 & n. 2; 1901: 1283 n. 1; 1913: 205 & n. 2), who is followed by Boas (1905: 111 n. 54), that this epigram (= 147 Bergk) was rejected by Bergk, is incorrect; it is apparently based on a misunderstanding of Bergk's comments on eps. 145 & 146 (XXVII Page & 14 West).

42. See Chapter I, section 2, with nn. 51-53.

43. Plut. *Vit. Aristid.* 1.2-3 & 6; cf. *IG* II² 3027.

44. Panaetius ap. Plut. (loc. cit.), against Demetrius of Phaleron (ibid.), who referred it to the great Aristides.

45. 1946: 8 n. 1.

46. Now *SEG* 10 (1949) 322 (cited by Stella from *Hesperia* 8 (1939) 49).

47. These three inscriptions are: *IG* I² 770; 771; 769 (cited by Stella as *CIA* I 336). (Stella's citation of *IG* I² 777, which is not a choregic inscription, is apparently an error.)

48. Ἀριστοκράτης Σκελίο ἀνέθηκεν νικήσας [χορηγὸν] κτλ. ("Aristokrates son of Skelios, having won a victory as choregos, dedicated...etc."). This was classed under the heading of "private" inscriptions in *IG* I (422); but *IG* I² does not classify "public" and "private" choregic dedications separately.

49. 1946: 8 & n. 2.

50. *IG* I² 770a (415/4 B.C.); *IG* II² 3065 (365/4 B.C.), 3042 (335/4), 3081 (c. 280-70), 3078 (early third century B.C.) (these last four inscriptions are cited by Stella from Dittenberger *SIG* ed. 2, 704, 707, 710, 711).

The Ancient Testimonia on Simonides' Dates   335

51. No. 3065.
52. Nos. 3081, 3078.
53. No. 3042.
54. See, respectively, *IG* II² 3043, 3045, 3039, 3038.
55. *IG* II² 3055 is similar to *IG* I² 772 (above, n. 48), but adds (amongst other things) the title of the dithyramb.
56. All except 3027 (n. 43 above) are from the fourth century according to Kirchner ad locc. (though no date is offered for 3062).
57. Koehler (*IG* II 1249), following Keil, thinks it is possible to detect a (choregic?) inscription of the third century B.C. written partly in verse; but the arrangement of Kirchner (*IG* II² 3038), who dates to the fourth century, means that this inscription does not contain verse.
58. *IG* I² 673; II² 3101.
59. *IG* II² 3089 (c. 200-150 B.C.) is a dedication in elegiacs, perhaps by a victorious actor. *IG* II² 3022, the prose dedication of a gymnasiarch (fourth century), is followed by an elegiac couplet drawing attention to the victory-dedication as a stimulus to *arete*.
60. 1946: 7.
61. *IG* II² 3113-4 (Imperial Period). Cf. also n. 59 above.
62. Stella (1946) 9-10.
63. *IG* II² (cited by Stella as "I.A. II-III") 3118.7.
64. *IG* II² 3112-3121 (*Tituli Choregici Imperatorum Aetatis*): all these inscriptions are dated to the first or second century A.D.
65. *IG* II² 3120 b.
66. *IG* II² 3118.9-10 (restored as [ἔπλετο] ("came about") by Wilamowitz ap. Kaibel (1878) 928).
67. ὅτε ("when") is conjectural in Kaibel's text (1878: 929); Dittenberger's restoration (ap. *IG* II² 3113) is different. However ἦρχε...ὅτε ("was archon...when") does occur in *IG* II² 3120 a.
68. *IG* II² 3117.7.
69. 150 Bergk = Anacreon XV Page. For the sake of clarity in

presenting the arguments of Wilhelm and Boas, I retain Bergk's enumeration of the epigrams at this point.

70. 1899: 232 & n. 32.
71. 1905: 153 f.
72. Found in *Anth. Pal.* 6 between nos. 213 and 214, and sometimes referred to as "*Anth. Pal.* 6.213*". It first occurs at *Anth. Pal.* 6.144.
73. XXVII Page; *Anth. Pal.* 6.213.
74. Some support for Boas' suggestion is perhaps to be found in the other examples which he quotes (pp. 222 ff.) of resemblances between Simonidean epigrams and inscriptions of the Roman period, especially the instance of an inscription apparently echoing four epigrams (ascribed to Simonides and other authors) which are found in close proximity in the Anthology.
75. See Chapter III, section 1.
76. Stella (1946) 10.
77. P. 17.
78. Stella is referring to Pindar's reply to Simonides in *Ol.* 9.48 f.; see Chapter X, section 2.
79. The figures appear on Stella's page as "456-68", an obvious misprint.
80. Stella (1946) 2 n. 3.
81. I.e. Ol. 56 (556/5 B.C.).
82. The statement on the method of calculating the date of *Simonides'* death, which Stella here attributes to Jacoby (citing, as she does, Apollod. frag. 337 Jacoby), bears a suspicious resemblance to Jacoby's view (stated in his commentary on this very fragment of Apollodorus, *FGrH* II C-BD p. 805) that Apollodorus dated *Stesichorus'* death by Simonides' birth (see also n. 85 below); thus the possibility that Stella has misunderstood or imperfectly remembered Jacoby's point cannot, perhaps, be entirely excluded. For the reason which Jacoby does, in fact, give for the ancients' dating of Simonides' death, see above, Section 1 of this chapter, with n. 33.
83. Stella (1946) 2.
84. Actually the date of death and age at death are given. See above, Chapter III, section 1.

85. The dating of Stesichorus' death by Simonides' birth is thought to have been based on Simonides 59/564 Page, where Simonides cites Stesichorus and is therefore shown to be later than him: see Rohde (1878) 198; Jacoby (1902) 197; id., *FGrH* II C-BD pp. 749, 805.

86. See Rohde (1878: 190 & n. 1) and Jacoby (1902: 159 n. 8), on Anacreon; Jacoby (1902: 244, 246-7), on Anaxagoras.

87. Jacoby (1902) 56 & 52-3.

88. Quintil. 11.2.14.

89. Simon. 59/564 Page; see n. 85 above.

90. Simon. 123/628 Page; Jacoby (1902) 55, 110.

Chapter 13

Conclusions on Stella's Revised Simonidean Chronology

Before attempting to pass a verdict on Stella's proposed dating of Simonides, it may be in place to indicate how her suggestion has been received up to the present time. The reaction to Stella's article has been, to say the least, somewhat muted.

To a large extent, her article has been ignored. General histories of Greek literature continue to quote the traditional dates of Simonides' life without comment,[1] as also do works of a narrower scope in which Simonides features rather more prominently,[2] and some editions or studies of lyric or elegiac poetry which include selections from Simonides.[3] It would be possible, but pointless, to list other miscellaneous works (written after Stella's article) which refer briefly to Simonides and quote the traditional dating.

Some scholars refer without explicit comment to Stella's work, but continue to accept the traditional dating of Simonides. Bowra[4] mentions Stella's suggested date for

Simonides' birth without direct comment, though it is clear that he himself accepts the traditional date for this event. Fogelmark refers to Stella's article for her discussion of one specific point (the identity of the "grandfather" of Simonides mentioned in ep. 49 of the Parian Marble), but he retains the traditional date of Simonides' birth, which is crucial to one of his main arguments.[5] Gerber accepts the traditional dating of Simonides and the status of the epigrams XXVII & XXVIII Page (79 & 77 Diehl) as evidence for that dating; but he cites Stella's entire article in his bibliography, apparently as one of the works which he regards as "of importance for further study".[6]

I have seen only one explicit rejection of Stella's thesis, by Kegel, who dismisses her dating of Simonides by claiming that Simonides can be dated by Scopas; but I cannot accept that Scopas provides a firm dating.[7]

The following three references may be grouped together, in that the authors concerned do not commit themselves to the traditional dating, and seem in their different ways to provide some indication that they regard Stella's theory as worthy of consideration. Page agrees with Stella in dismissing as a late composition the epigram XXVIII, which states that Simonides was eighty in 477/6; and he seems to regard the dating of Simonides as an open question.[8] Gentili seems to offer a veiled hint that he thinks Stella's case worth consideration, though he does not refer to her explicitly. At the end of his discussion of the epigram XXXIV Page, on the Deinomenid dedication,[9] he refers to "la necessità di risolvere, prima di dimostrare l'autenticità dell' epigramma, l'altro problema, non meno discusso, riguardante la morte di Simonide".[10] He then cites Gaspar's work on the chronology of Pindar,[11] and states that Gaspar "forse non a torto, ritiene che il poeta sia morto prima, e non dopo il 466". In fact Gaspar, as one would expect, simply quotes the traditional date of Simonides' death, 468/7, without comment and without any suggestion of an alternative possibility. Gentili's words seem to me to suggest that he thinks that Simonides' dates are, since Stella wrote, open to some doubt. D'Agostino, in an article on Simonides' mnemonic technique,[12] states that the chronology of Simonides is "oggetto di discussione" and cites Stella's article. These last two references to the dating of Simonides, by two fellow-countrymen of Stella's (Gentili and d'Agostino), are the closest thing I have seen to an acknowledgement that Stella has undermined the former universal confidence in the traditional dates of Simonides. I have nowhere seen either a tacit acceptance of her revised dating or an explicit statement of agreement with her.

We may now go on to state our conclusions on Stella's thesis. It must be admitted at the outset that there is much to be said for Stella's case. There is a strong ancient tradition that Simonides' life was long, and that he was still poetically active in old age. But the definitely datable works are confined to a surprisingly short period, the earliest belonging to c. 500 B.C.[13] and the latest to c. 476.[14] This is something of a difficulty whichever chronology we adopt; but the difficulty is the greater if the traditional chronology is correct (Simonides born c. 556), for there is then a lack of definitely datable fragments until comparatively late in Simonides' life (about fifty-six years old), while many of his datable works[15] belong to a period when he was either approaching or well past seventy. If Stella's chronology is correct (Simonides born c. 532-29), the datable works at least belong to the middle period of his life (from about the age of thirty to about sixty), when a man's greatest activity may be expected.

Nevertheless, I believe that the balance of evidence is against Stella.

In Chapter XII above, I examined the ancient testimonia on Simonides' dates, and concluded that, on this evidence considered by itself, the traditional dating remained the more probable, the strongest argument being that the ancient scholars who accepted it must surely have possessed Simonides' works to guide them.

In Chapters II-XI above, I examined the datable fragments and references, looking especially for any clues that might confirm or refute Stella's arguments. The evidence here is multifarious and cannot be summed up in a sentence; the best one could do would be to recapitulate one's conclusions point by point.[16] I think that here again Stella's attack on the traditional chronology fails on balance, the most important points being these: she does not convincingly dispose of the tradition connecting Simonides with the Pisistratids; she does not demonstrate active professional rivalry between Simonides and Pindar near the traditional date of Simonides' death; she does not prove that the literary works and general activity of Simonides c. 480 B.C. or later would be too heavy a burden for so old a man, for although the traditional chronology certainly credits Simonides with a remarkably vigorous old age,[17] it is not possible to demonstrate an excessive concentration of work within any particular year; and the late ascription to Simonides of some epigrams dealing with events after 468 is of very doubtful significance. There were also several other instances in Chapters II-XI where the evidence, though less decisive than the points we have just mentioned, seemed, if anything, to favour the traditional dating.[18] Taken together, these considerations must outweigh both the general considerations in favour of Stella and the occasional instance where the balance of evidence on some particular point seemed to be marginally in her favour.[19]

Moreover, the "blank" period (c. 556 to c. 500) which the traditional dating seems to involve, though it lacks any definitely datable fragments, is not a complete vacuum. There is, of course, the tradition of his association with Hipparchus, which may have begun at any time between 527 and 514; the date of c. 520 for the Glaucus ode[20] could be right; the epigram for Milo's statue,[21] admittedly of doubtful authenticity, may belong to the year 516 B.C.; and the works for Eualcides[22] and for Thessalian patrons could extend back several years into the sixth century. The vacuum is then reduced to the first thirty-five years or so of Simonides' life, from c. 556 B.C.; in other words, to the first fifteen years or so of his potential career as a poet, i.e. from

c. 536 B.C., when he would be about twenty, to c. 520. The gap is still regrettable, but less surprising (especially in view of our fragmentary knowledge) than it at first appeared.

It might be argued that Stella's dating offers similar difficulties. Stella is inclined to accept the tradition of Simonides' longevity, and therefore to date his death about the middle of the fifth century.[23] She also seems to think that Simonides remained active until quite a late age; at least she refers to "il fervore della sua attività poetica negli anni tra il 490 e il 470";[24] describes him as being "ancora nell'*acmè*, certo...in piena attività poetica..."[25] c. 475 B.C.; considers that the reply by Pindar in *Ol.* 9, which Stella dates 467-66, is addressed "ad un uomo ancor nel pieno vigore della sua attività poetica";[26] and dates the dirge to Antiochus between 475 and 460.[27] These remarks suggest that Stella thinks that Simonides was probably active until some years after 466, and we begin to ask where are the traces of poems from this period; the absence of any fragments or historical references for this period, when Simonides was at the height of his reputation, in the better-documented fifth century, would be more surprising than a similar lack (which we must assume if the traditional chronology is accepted) for the earlier years of his life, when he was comparatively unknown, in the more remote sixth century. But we must not press this point too hard, for Stella finally insists only that Simonides "è vivo e scrive versi ancora intorno al 466".[28]

Stella rightly saw that the traditional chronology does pose problems; but in my view she does not make out a convincing case for her own alternative theory, which raises as many problems as it solves.

Stella's real service, in a sense a negative one but valuable nonetheless, has been to remove complacency and to shake confidence in opinions long taken for granted, by probing, exploring and questioning. Though I accept the traditional chronology as substantially correct, it is hard to feel quite so confident in it as before. Perhaps there can be no absolute certainty until fortune provides us with a Simonidean fragment definitely datable at 530 or 460 B.C.

References

1. E.g. A.Lesky, *Geschichte der griechischen Literatur* (Bern 1957/8) 174 f.

2. Fränkel (1962) 391, 417; Treu (1955) 296.

3. Campbell (1982) 377 f. & (1983) 295; West (1971-2) II 112.

4. 1961: 309 n. 7.

5. Viz. that the word χρύσαιγις ("with golden aegis"), in a Cean inscription of c. 525-500 B.C., was borrowed from the poetry of Simonides, who must already have been famous enough to make the dedicator of the inscription prefer a Simonidean to a Homeric epithet (Fogelmark (1975) 34).

6. Gerber (1970) 309, 329 (on the epigrams), & 404, 428 (bibliographical references).

7. Kegel (1962) 1 n. 12, 22 n. 4 (on the dating of Scopas, see above, Chapter VI, section 5). Podlecki (1979: 5 & n. 2) refers to Stella's dating of Simonides in somewhat sceptical terms.

8. Page (1981), commentary on ep. XXVIII.

9. See Chapter IX, section 3, with n. 64.

10. Gentili (1953) 208.

11. Gaspar (1900) 184.

12. D'Agostino (1952-3) 126 n. 7.

13. Poems for Eualcides (13/518 Page); and perhaps poems for Aleuas (above, Chapter VI, sections 1 & 5). These works are "definitely datable" in the sense that the *terminus ante quem* can be established with some confidence; the *terminus post quem* cannot be determined.

14. Perhaps the latest definitely datable work is the dithyramb which won the victory (476 B.C.) recorded in the epigram XXVIII Page. However it is very likely that 75/580 Page (for Hieron) belongs to 476 or after; and ep. LXXVI, if it is connected with Hieron's victory at Cumae, must belong to 474 or later. The ode for Anaxilas (10/515 Page) could be as late as 476; those for Xenocrates (8/513) and Astylus (1/506) could be later. The latest datable *reference* (apart from the notices of his death in 468/7) is to his reconciliation of Hieron and Theron in 476/5 (above, Chapter IX, section 4).

15. On Marathon (aged c. 66); other Persian War poems (aged at least 76); dithyrambic victory (aged 80); works for Hieron (aged presumably over 80); works for Xenocrates, Anaxilas, Astylus (age might range from mid sixties to over 80).
16. Here it must suffice to refer back to the separate chapters (II-XI) where these conclusions are stated (usually in the final paragraphs of the relevant chapter or section of a chapter).
17. As already noted (Chapter XII, section 1, with n. 23), Hieronymus' reference to Simonides' swan-song may reflect an informed awareness of his intense activity in old age.
18. See Chapter II, section 3; Chapter IV, sections 1 & 2; Chapter V, section 2; Chapter VI, section 5.
19. See Chapter V, section 1 (on the kinship of Simonides and Bacchylides).
20. 4/509 Page.
21. XXV Page.
22. 13/518 Page.
23. Stella (1946) 23-4.
24. P. 17.
25. Ibid.
26. P. 16.
27. P. 13 (but "470-60", p. 23). (The dirge is 23/528 Page.)
28. P. 24.

Bibliography

The titles of most standard collections, works of reference, and periodicals, are abbreviated in the present study in accordance with the list in *The Oxford Classical Dictionary*² (ed. N.G.L.Hammond & H.H.Scullard, Oxford, 1970) pp. ix-xxii, supplemented in the case of periodicals by the lists in the volumes of *L' Année Philologique*. Other abbreviated titles of modern works are, it is hoped, full enough to be self-explanatory.

Items in the Bibliography below are for the most part identified in the main text by author and date. A few of them are occasionally identified in the text by an abbreviation of the title, which in the Bibliography is cited in brackets after the relevant item (e.g. *PLG* for Bergk's *Poetae Lyrici Graeci*).

Aucher, P.J.B., 1818: *Eusebii Pamphili Chronicon Bipartitum, nunc primum ex Armeniaco textu in Latinum conversum* (Venetiis).
Barigazzi, A., 1963: "Nuovi frammenti delle elegie di Simonide (Ox. Pap. 2327)", *MH* 20, pp. 61-76.
Bell, J.M., 1978: "Κίμβιξ καὶ σοφός: Simonides in the Anecdotal Tradition", *QUCC* 28, pp. 29-86.
Beloch, K.J., 1912-27: *Griechische Geschichte*² (Strassburg; Berlin & Leipzig).
Bentley, R., 1699: *A Dissertation upon the Epistles of Phalaris* (London). Also edited by W. Wagner (Berlin 1874).
Bergk, T., 1878-82: *Poetae Lyrici Graeci*⁴ (Lipsiae), especially vol. III (1882) containing Simonides (*PLG*).

Bernardini, P.A., 1983: *Mito e Attualità nelle Odi di Pindaro* (Rome).
Blech, M., 1982: *Studien zum Kranz bei den Griechen* (Berlin & New York).
Boas, M., 1905: *De Epigrammatis Simonideis, Pars Prior: Commentatio Critica de Epigrammatum Traditione* (Groningae).
Boeckh, A., 1811-21: *Pindari Opera* (Lipsiae) (*Pindar*).
Bowra, C.M., 1936: *Greek Lyric Poetry*[1] (Oxford).
  1938: *Early Greek Elegists* (Oxford).
  1961: *Greek Lyric Poetry*[2] (Oxford).
  1964: *Pindar* (Oxford).
Brussich, G.F., 1975-6: "Laso d'Ermione. Testimonianze e frammenti", *Quaderni triestini per il lessico della lirica corale greca* 3, pp. 83-135.
Bundy, E.L., 1962: *Studia Pindarica* (Berkeley & Los Angeles).
Burn, A.R., 1962: *Persia and the Greeks* (London).
Burton, R.W.B., 1962: *Pindar's Pythian Odes* (Oxford).
Bury, J.B., 1892: *The Isthmian Odes of Pindar* (London).
Busolt, G., 1885-1904: *Griechische Geschichte* (Gotha).
Buttmann, P., 1829: *Mythologus* (vol. II) (Berlin).
Campbell, D.A., 1982: *Greek Lyric Poetry*[2] (Bristol).
  1983: *The Golden Lyre* (London).
Christ, G., 1941: *Simonidesstudien* (Freiburg, Schweiz).
Costanzi, V., 1906-7: "Saggio di Storia Tessalica, Parte I", *Annali delle Università Toscane* 26 (1906) 1-74 & 27 (1907) 77-158; also issued separately with continuous pagination (pp.75 ff. = 78 ff.).
Crotty, K., 1982: *Song and Action: The Victory Odes of Pindar* (Baltimore & London).
D'Agostino, V., 1952-3: "Simonide inventore della mnemotecnica in Cicerone e in Quintiliano", *Rivista di Studi Classici* 1, pp. 125-7.
De Boissi, M., 1788: *Histoire de Simonide et du siècle où il a vécu*[2] (Paris).
Diehl, E., 1936-42: *Anthologia Lyrica Graeca*[2] (Lipsiae), especially vol. II, fasc.1 (1942) containing Simonides.
Domaszewski, A. von, 1917: "Der Staatsfriedhof der Athener", *Sitzungsberichte der Heidelberger Akademie der Wissenschaften, Philosophisch-historische Klasse*, Abhandlung 7.
Edmonds, J.M., 1928-40: *Lyra Graeca*[2] (London), especially vol. II (1931) containing Simonides.
Farnell, L.R., 1930-2: *The Works of Pindar* (London).
Fennell, C.A.M., 1893: *Pindar: the Olympian and Pythian Odes*[2] (Cambridge).
  1899: *Pindar: The Nemean and Isthmian Odes*[2] (Cambridge).
Flach, H., 1883-4: *Geschichte der griechischen Lyrik* (Tübingen).
Fogelmark, S., 1975: *Chrysaigis: IG XII,v,611* (Lund).

Fornara, C.W., 1966: "Some Aspects of the Career of Pausanias of Sparta", *Historia* 15, pp. 257-71.
Förster, G.H., 1891-2: *Die Sieger in den olympischen Spielen* (Programm des Gymnasiums zu Zwickau).
Fotheringham, J.K., 1923: *Eusebii Pamphili Chronici Canones, Latine vertit...S. Eusebius Hieronymus* (Londinii).
Fränkel, H., 1962: *Dichtung und Philosophie des frühen Griechentums²* (München).
Freeman, E.A., 1891-4: *History of Sicily* (Oxford).
Friedländer, P. & Hoffleit, H.B., 1948: *Epigrammata: Greek Inscriptions in Verse, from the beginnings to the Persian Wars* (Berkeley & Los Angeles).
Gardiner, E.N., 1910: *Greek Athletic Sports and Festivals* (London). 1930: *Athletics of the Ancient World* (Oxford).
Gaspar, C., 1900: *Essai de chronologie Pindarique* (Bruxelles).
Gentili, B., 1953: "I Tripodi di Delfi e il Carme III di Bacchilide", *La Parola del Passato* 8, pp. 199-208.
  1960: "Studi su Simonide, I: I nuovi frammenti papiracei (P. Oxy. 2431)", *Rivista di Cultura Classica e Medioevale* 2, pp. 113-23.
  1984: *Poesia e pubblico nella Grecia antica* (Bari).
Gerber, D.E., 1970: *Euterpe: An Anthology of Early Greek Lyric, Elegiac, and Iambic Poetry* (Amsterdam).
Gildersleeve, B.L., 1885: *Pindar: The Olympian and Pythian Odes* (New York).
Gow, A.S.F., 1958: *The Greek Anthology: Sources and Ascriptions* (London).
Gow, A.S.F. & Page, D.L., 1965: *The Greek Anthology: Hellenistic Epigrams* (Cambridge).
Grundy, G.B., 1901: *The Great Persian War* (London).
Hammond, N.G.L., 1959: *A History of Greece to 322 B.C.* (Oxford).
Harris, H.A., 1964: *Greek Athletes and Athletics* (London).
Hauvette, A., 1896: *De l' authenticité des épigrammes de Simonide* (Paris).
Hignett, C., 1963: *Xerxes' Invasion of Greece* (Oxford).
Hiller von Gaertringen, F., 1890: "Das Königtum bei den Thessalern im sechsten und fünften Jahrhundert", in *Aus der Anomia: Archaeologische Beitraege, Carl Robert* (Berlin) pp. 1-16.
Holm, A., 1870-98: *Geschichte Siciliens im Alterthum* (Leipzig).
Hubbard, T.K., 1985: *The Pindaric Mind* (Leiden).
Huxley, G.L., 1978: "Simonides and his world", *Proceedings of the Royal Irish Academy* 78, Section C, pp. 231-47.
Jacoby, F., 1902: *Apollodors Chronik. Philologische Untersuchungen*,

hrsg. A. Kiessling & U. von Wilamowitz-Moellendorff, Heft 16 (Berlin).

1904: *Das Marmor Parium* (Berlin).

1923-: *Die Fragmente der griechischen Historiker* (Berlin & Leiden), especially vol. II B (1927-9) & II C-BD (1926-30) (*FGrH*).

1945: "Some Athenian Epigrams from the Persian Wars", *Hesperia* 14, pp. 157-211.

Jebb, R.C., 1905: *Bacchylides* (Cambridge).

Junghahn, A.A., 1869: "De Simonidis Cei epigrammatis quaestiones", *Vierter Jahresbericht über das Luisenstädtische Gymnasium in Berlin* (Berlin) pp. 3-41.

Kahrstedt, U., 1924: "Grundherrschaft, Freistadt und Staat in Thessalien", *NGG*, pp. 128-55.

Kaibel, G., 1872: A review of Junghahn (1869) in *Neue Jahrbücher für Philologie und Paedagogik...herausgegeben...J.C.Jahn... Fleckeisen* (= *Iahnii Annales*, or *Fleckeiseni Annales*, or *Fleck. Jb.*) 105, pp. 793-802.

1873: "Quaestiones Simonideae", *RhM* N.F. 28, pp. 436-60.

1878: *Epigrammata Graeca, ex lapidibus conlecta* (Berolini).

1892: A review of T.Preger's *Inscriptiones Graecae Metricae* (Lipsiae 1891) in *GGA*, pp. 89-104.

Karst, J., 1911: *Eusebius Werke* (fünfter band) *Die Chronik, aus dem armenischen übersetzt* (Leipzig).

Kegel, W.J.H.F., 1962: *Simonides* (Groningen).

Kierdorf, W., 1966: *Erlebnis und Darstellung der Perserkriege: Studien zu Simonides, Pindar, Aischylos und den attischen Rednern* (Göttingen).

Kirkwood, G.M., 1981: "Pindar's Ravens (*Olymp.* 2.87)", *CQ* N.S. 31, pp. 240-43.

1982: *Selections from Pindar* (Chico, California).

Klee, Th., 1918: *Zur Geschichte der gymnischen Agone an griechischen Festen* (Leipzig-Berlin).

Lavagnini, B., 1933: "Gerone e Terone nelle due prime Olimpiche di Pindaro", *Archivio Storico per la Sicilia Orientale* 29 (= Seconda Serie 9), pp. 5-14.

Lefkowitz, M.R., 1981: *The Lives of the Greek Poets* (Baltimore).

Marzullo, B., 1984: "Simonides fr. 515 Page", *Philologus* 128, pp. 145-56.

Meiggs, R., 1972: *The Athenian Empire* (Oxford).

Meiggs, R. & Lewis, D.M., 1969: *A Selection of Greek Historical Inscriptions to the end of the Fifth Century B.C.* (Oxford).

Meyer, E., 1892-9: *Forschungen zur alten Geschichte* (Halle).

1909: *Theopomps Hellenika* (Halle).

1939: *Geschichte des Altertums*³, vol. IV 1 (Stuttgart).

Michelangeli, L.A., 1897: *Della vita di Bacchilide e particolarmente delle pretese allusioni di Pindaro a lui ed a Simonide* (Messina); also in *Rivista di Storia antica e Scienze affini* 2 (1896-7) nos. 3-4, pp. 73-118.

Miller, A.M., 1983: "N. 4.33-43 and the Defense of Digressive Leisure", *CJ* 78, pp. 202-20.

Molyneux, J.H., 1971: "Simonides and the Dioscuri", *Phoenix* 25, pp. 197-205.

Moretti, L., 1957: *Olympionikai, I Vincitori negli Antichi Agoni Olimpici* (Roma).

Morrison, J.S., 1942: "Meno of Pharsalus, Polycrates, and Ismenias", *CQ* 36, pp. 57-78 (especially section II, "Thessaly down to 400 B.C.", pp. 59-65).

Most, G.W., 1985: *The Measures of Praise. Structure and Function in Pindar's Second Pythian and Seventh Nemean Odes* (Göttingen).

1986: "Pindar, O. 2.83-90", *CQ* N.S. 36, pp. 304-16.

Nisetich, F.J., 1977: "Convention and Occasion in *Isthmian* 2", *CSCA* 10, pp. 133-56.

1980: *Pindar's Victory Songs* (Baltimore).

Oates, W.J., 1932: *The Influence of Simonides of Ceos upon Horace* (Princeton).

Oliver, J.H., 1935: "The Marathon epigrams", *AJPh* 56, pp. 193-201.

Page, D.L., 1951: "Simonidea", *JHS* 71, pp. 133-42.

1962: *Poetae Melici Graeci* (Oxford) (*PMG*).

1975: *Epigrammata Graeca* (Oxonii) (*EG*).

1981: *Further Greek Epigrams* (Cambridge) (*FGE*).

Pavese, C., 1966: "XPHMATA, XPHMAT᾽ ANHP ed il motivo della liberalità nella seconda Istmica di Pindaro", *QUCC* 2, pp. 103-12.

Peek, W., 1955: *Griechische Vers-Inscriften:* Band I, *Grab-Epigramme* (Berlin).

Pickard-Cambridge, A.W., 1962: *Dithyramb, Tragedy, and Comedy*² (revised T.B.L. Webster) (Oxford).

Podlecki, A.J., 1966: "The Political Significance of the Athenian 'Tyrannicide'-Cult", *Historia* 15, pp. 129-41.

1968: "Simonides: 480", *Historia* 17, pp. 257-75.

1975: *The Life of Themistocles* (Montreal & London).

1979: "Simonides in Sicily", *La Parola del Passato* 34, pp. 5-16.

1980: "Festivals and Flattery: The Early Greek Tyrants as Patrons of Poetry", *Athenaeum* 58, pp. 371-95.

1984: *The Early Greek Poets and Their Times* (Vancouver).

Pritchett, W.K., 1960: "Marathon". *University of California Publications in Classical Archaeology* IV 2, pp. 137-90.

Privitera, G. A., 1965: *Laso di Ermione nella cultura ateniese e nella tradizione storiografica* (Rome).

1982: *Pindaro, Le Istmiche* (Milan).

Puech, A., 1922-: *Pindare* (Paris).

Race, W.H., 1986: *Pindar* (Boston).

Rohde, E., 1878: "Γέγονε in den Biographica des Suidas", *RhM* N.F. 33, pp. 161-220.

1881: "Zur Chronologie der griechischen Litteraturgeschichte", *RhM* N.F. 36, pp. 524-75.

Rose, H.J., 1933: "Simonides and Glaukos", *CR* 47, pp. 165-7.

Rutgers, I., 1862: *Sexti Iulii Africani* Ὀλυμπιάδων Ἀναγραφή (Lugduni-Batavorum).

Schmid, W., 1929: *Geschichte der griechischen Literatur* (W. Schmid & O.Stählin): Erster Teil, *Die klassische Periode der griechischen Literatur* (W.Schmid), Band I.

Schneidewin, F.G. (= F.W.), 1835: *Simonidis Cei carminum reliquiae* (Brunsvigae).

Schoene, A., 1866-75: *Eusebi Chronicorum Libri Duo* (Berolini).

Schroeder, O., 1900: *Pindari Carmina* (Lipsiae) (= *Poetae Lyrici Graeci*, T.Bergk, ed. 5, Part I vol. I, recensuit O.Schroeder).

Sealey, R., 1976: *A History of the Greek City States ca. 700-338 B.C.* (Berkeley, Los Angeles, & London).

Severyns, A., 1933: *Bacchylide: Essai Biographique* (Liége).

Simpson, M., 1969: "The chariot and the bow as metaphors for poetry in Pindar's odes", *TAPA* 100, pp. 437-73.

Slater, W.J., 1972: "Simonides' House", *Phoenix* 26, pp. 232-40.

Smyth, H.W., 1904: *Greek Melic Poets* (London).

Sordi, M., 1958: *La Lega Tessala* (Roma).

Stella, L.A., 1946: "Studi Simonidei I. Per la cronologia di Simonide", *Rivista di Filologia Classica* Nuova Serie 24, pp. 1-24.

Tedeschi, A., 1985: "L'invio del carme nella poesia lirica arcaica: Pindaro e Bacchilide", *SIFC* ser. 3, 3, pp. 29-54.

Thummer, E., 1968-9: *Pindar, Die isthmischen Gedichte* (Heidelberg).

Treu, M., 1955: *Von Homer zur Lyrik* (München).

Urlichs, L. von, 1885: *Archaeologische Analekten (18 Programm des von Wagnerschen Kunstinstituts*, Würzburg).

Uxkull-Gyllenband, W., 1927: *Plutarch und die griechische Biographie* (Stuttgart).

Van Leeuwen, J., 1964: *Pindarus' Tweede Olympische Ode* (Assen).
Verdenius, W.J., 1982: "Pindar's Second Isthmian Ode: A Commentary", *Mnemosyne* ser. 4, 35, pp. 1-37.
Wade-Gery, H.T., 1933: "Classical Epigrams and Epitaphs", *JHS* 53, pp. 71-104.
Weber, L., 1917: "ΣΥΚΑ ΕΦ' ΕΡΜΗΙ II", *Philologus* 74, pp. 248-82 (especially section I, "Das Grabepigramm auf die Toten von Kypros (449)", pp. 248-56).
Wehrli, F., 1969: *Die Schule des Aristoteles: Texte und Kommentar*, Heft IX, *Phainias von Eresos, Chamaileon, Praxiphanes* (Basel/Stuttgart).
West, M.L., 1971-2: *Iambi et Elegi Graeci* (Oxonii) (*IEG*).
Westlake, H.D., 1935: *Thessaly in the Fourth Century B.C.* (London).
Wilamowitz-Moellendorff, U. von, 1893: *Aristoteles und Athen* (Berlin).

1897: "Simonides der Epigrammatiker", *NGG*, pp. 306-25 (see also Wilamowitz 1913).

1901: "Hieron und Pindaros", *Sitzungsberichte der königlichen Preussischen Akademie der Wissenschaften zu Berlin*, pp. 1273-1318.

1913: *Sappho und Simonides* (Berlin) (the chapter "Simonides der Epigrammatiker", pp. 192-209, is reprinted with slight modifications from *NGG* 1897, 306-25).

1922: *Pindaros* (Berlin).

Wilhelm, A., 1899: "Simonideische Gedichte", *Jahreshefte des Oesterreichischen Archäologischen Instituts* 2, pp. 221-44.
Woodbury, L., 1968: "Pindar and the Mercenary Muse: *Isthm.* 2.1-13", *TAPA* 99, pp. 527-42.

1978: "The Gratitude of the Locrian Maiden: Pindar, *Pyth.* 2.18-20", *TAPA* 108, pp. 285-99.

Zuntz, G., 1935: "Pindar and Simonides. Fragments of an Ancient Commentary", *CR* 49, pp. 4-7.

Index

Academy, 58 n. 57.

Acragas, 235-6.

Adeimantus (of Corinth), 193-4.

Aeatius, 129-30.

Aegina, 19, 20, 51-4, 90-1, 269.

Aeschylus: in competition with Simonides, 24, 25, 68, 148, 151-2; contemporary of Simonides (?), 26, 27; younger than Simonides, 312-3.

Aetna, 229-30.

Agatharchus, 42, 44-5.

Agathocles, 262.

Agathonidas, 262.

Alcman, 313.

Alcmeonids, 72, 154-5, 156, 265.

Aleuadae, Aleuas, 118-21, 126, 127, 128-9, 130, 134, 136, 137, 138.

Amphictyons, 176-9.

Anacreon: "Simonidean" epitaph on, 15; at Abdera, 20; in Thessaly, 20, 129; at Hipparchus' court, 25, 65, 67, 69; earlier than Simonides, 27; synchronism with Simonides, 113 n. 40, 315; chronologers' dates of, 337 n. 86.

Anaxagoras, 312, 337 n. 86.

Anaxilas, 211-4, 283 n. 114.

Antenor (tyrannicide group), 72.

Antiochus (of Thessaly), 24, 27, 118 & n. 5, 125-6, 127-9, 134-7, 343.

Archedice, 19, 20, 70, 74-6.

archon-years, 316.

Aristides, Aelius (as source of Simonidean epigrams), 8.

Aristides (choregus), 308.
Aristides (statesman), 334 n. 44.
Aristodemus (athlete), 287.
Aristodemus (pupil of Aristarchus), 7, 87-9, 91.
Aristophanes, 23.
Aristophanes of Byzantium, 7.
Aristotle (as source of Simonidean epigrams), 7, 11, 12, 75-6, 287.
Artaxerxes, 136-7, 144 n. 119.
Artemisium, 18, 26, 156-66.
Astylus, 214-20.
Athenaeus (as source of Simonidean epigrams), 8.
Athenians, Athens, 51, 54, 70-2, 75-6, 103, 106, 166, 190-1, 194, 197.

— B —

Bacchylides: and Simonides, 24, 25, 97-8;
and Pindar, 24-5, 235, 249-55, 267-9, 272-3;
and Glaucus, 34;
and Hieron, 233, 251, 273.
Bacchylides "the athlete", 97.
Barigazzi, A., 151, 190.
Bell, J.M., 1, 110, 114 nn. 49 & 51, 131, 278 n. 40.
Beloch, K.J., 135, 137, 237 n. 16.
Bennett, H.C., 139 n. 9.
Bentley, R., 313, 314 & n. 32.

Bergk, T., 5 & n. 2, 9-10, and passim.
Bernardini, P.A., 279 n. 61.
Bers, V., 48.
Bertelli, L., 305 n. 71.
Bicknell, P.J., 169 n. 41.
biographical tradition, 124, 225.
Blech, M., 239 n. 37.
Boas, M., 9, 12-3, 14, 31 n. 79, 90, 91, 177-9, 188-9, 207 n. 84, 210 n. 112, 227, 287, 290, 295, 298, 299, 300-1, 311, 325, 334 n. 41.
Boeckh, A., 55 n. 5, 119, 213, 260, 279 n. 58.
Boegehold, A.L., 207 n. 80.
Boeotians, 84.
Boreas, 158-61, 163-6.
Bowra, C.M., 36, 37-8, 98, 100, 106-7, and passim.
Brilessus, Brilissos, 158-61.
Brunn, H., 40.
Brussich, G.F., 94 n. 35, 100, 112 nn. 25 & 26.
Bundy, E.L., 2, 247-8, 250, 253, 267, 281 n. 86, 282 n. 87.
Burn, A.R., 170 n. 47.
Burton, R.W.B., 239 n. 37.
Bury, J.B., 235.
Burzacchini, G., 205 n. 39.
Busolt, G., 141 n. 60.
Buttmann, P., 56 n. 21, 119, 138 n. 2, 139 n. 20.

— C —

Cadoux, T.J., 316.

Callias, 155-6.

Callistratus, 7.

Campbell, D.A., 344 n. 3.

Chaeronea, 151.

Chalcidians, 84, 86.

Chamaeleon (as source of Simonidean epigrams), 7.

Christ, G., 101, 112 n. 30.

Chromius, 231.

Cicero (ascribes epigram to Simonides), 7.

Cimon, 285, 289, 292-4, 297.

Cineas, 131, 134, 135, 136, 137.

Cipolla, F., 205 n. 44.

clarus habetur (significance of), 315.

Cleophron: see Leophron.

collection (of Simonidean epigrams) (see also Collector and *Sylloge Simonidea*), 9, 10, 12, 13-4, 285, 288.

Collector (of Simonidean epigrams), 20, 31 n. 79, 91, 287, 298-301.

Corinth, Corinthians, 19, 192-6, 198-9.

Corrector (of Palatine ms.), 288 & n. 16, 291, 299.

Costanzi, V., 128.

covetousness (alleged, of Simonides), 105, 224 & n. 68, 232 & n. 112, 256 & n. 40, 278 n. 41, 311.

Creon, Creondae, 118 & n. 5, 121 & n. 37, 122-3.

Critius (and Nesiotes: tyrannicide group), 72.

Crius, 19, 47-54, 59 n. 69, 91-2, 269.

Crotty, K., 281 nn. 78 & 86.

Cumae (battle of), 228, 231.

Cyprus (campaign of, c. 450-49 B.C.), 285, 292-9, 303 n. 17.

— D —

D'Agostino, V., 341.

Darius, 102, 144 n. 119.

De Boissi, M., 140 nn. 33 & 34.

Degani, E., 205 n. 39.

Demetrius of Phaleron, 334 n. 44.

Democritus, 312.

Democritus (of Naxos), 189-90, 196.

Diehl, E., 5 & n. 2.

Diodorus (of Corinth), 193.

Diodorus Siculus (as source of Simonidean epigrams), 8.

Dionysia (Great), 113 nn. 37 & 39, 308, 320, 321-2.

Dionysia (Rustic), 322.

Dioscuri, 33, 36-7, 38, 56 n. 21.

diplomatic immunity (of lyric poets), 73, 86, 90, 126, 154, 194.

dithyrambs, dithyrambic competitions, 99-104, 155.

Domaszewski, A. von, 304 n. 55, 305 n. 72.

Dover, K.J., 60 n. 85.

Dyseris, 125, 127, 128, 139 n. 5.

— E —

Echecrateia, Echecratidae, Echecratidas, 24, 122, 125, 127-9, 139 n. 5.

Edmonds, J.M., 56 n. 26, 57 n. 30, 62 n. 96, 156, 206 n. 56.

Eileithyia, 87-9.

elegies, 4, 5, 11-2, 131-2, 196, 311.

Emmenidae, 233-6.

Ephorus, 293, 298, 299.

epigrams, 3, 4-5, 6-23.

Eualcidas (of Elis), 45.

Eualcides (of Eretria), 45-6, 59 n. 69, 86, 342.

Euboea, Euboeans, 46, 86.

Euenus of Paros (elder and younger), 106-7.

Eurymedon (battle of), 286, 288-99.

— F —

Farnell, L.R., 2, 225, 251, 252, 254, 257, 264-5, 266.

Fennell, C.A.M., 257.

Flach, H., 141 n. 60.

Fogelmark, S., 340.

Fontenrose, J., 41-2.

Fornara, C.W., 116 n. 75.

Förster, G.H., 237 n. 14.

Fraccaroli, G., 258.

Fränkel, H., 61 n. 93, 344 n. 2.

Freeman, E.A., 225, 235, 254.

Friedländer, P. (& Hoffleit, H.B.), 58 n. 55.

— G —

Gantz, T.N., 283 n. 106.

Gardiner, E.N., 238 n. 24.

Gaspar, C., 340.

Gelon, 18, 35-6, 40, 94 n. 44, 219, 220-4, 229, 230, 232.

Gentili, B., 130, 145 n. 133, 222-3, 278 n. 38, 340-1.

Gerber, D.E., 55 n. 10, 340.

Gildersleeve, B.L., 251.

Glaucias, 35, 40, 42.

Glaucus (Glaukos) (sea-god), 41.

Glaucus (of Carystus), 33-42, 46, 83, 86, 342.

Glaucus (of Corcyra), 42.

Gow, A.S.F., 14.

Graces, 44.

Grenfell, B.P. (& Hunt, A.S.), 219.

Grundy, G.B., 166, 208 n. 87.

— H —

Hammond, N.G.L., 209 n. 100.

Harris, H.A., 59 nn. 64 & 67.

Index 359

Hauvette, A., 9, 10-11, 16, 30 n. 54, 156, 203 n. 11, 289.

Hephaestion, 11, 74, 287, 299.

Hermann, G., 94 n. 38.

Hermes, 44.

Herodotus, 23; (Simonidean epigrams in), 6-7, 9, 12-3.

Hieron, 24, 25, 106 & n. 51, 153-4, 219, 220, 221-3, 224-33, 235-6, 251, 269, 273, 308, 314, 330.

Hignett, C., 166, 170 nn. 47 & 49, 172 nn. 91 & 92, 204 nn. 20 & 21, 205 n. 37, 209 n. 100.

Hiller, E., 152.

Hiller von Gaertringen, F., 140 n. 47.

Hipparchus, 19, 25-6, 65-8, 69, 70-4, 76, 86, 100, 133, 326, 328, 330, 342.

Hippias, 26, 65, 69, 70-1, 73, 74-6, 133.

Hippocleas, 121.

Holm, A., 237 n. 18, 241 n. 75.

Hubbard, T.K., 277 n. 33.

Huxley, G.L., 55 n. 2, 60 n. 82.

Hypodicus (of Chalcis), 99, 100.

— I —

Ibycus, 27.

Ilissus, 159-61.

— J —

Jacoby, F., 106, 168 n. 16, 193, 313 & nn. 28 & 31, 314, 316, 318, 326, 327-9, 333 n. 35.

Jebb, R.C., 98, 264-5.

Junghahn, A.A., 8-9, 31 n. 59.

— K —

Kahrstedt, U., 137.

Kaibel, G., 9-10, 11, 13, 79 n. 40, 177, 203 nn. 6 & 10.

Kegel, W.J.H.F., 61 n. 94, 205 n. 48, 240 n. 50, 340.

Kierdorf, W., 168 n. 17, 205 n. 48.

Kirkwood, G.M., 249, 275 n. 2, 276 n. 12, 277 n. 29.

Klee, Th., 55 nn. 9 & 10, 57 n. 36.

Koniaris, G.L., 48-9.

Körte, A., 98.

— L —

Lasus, 25, 26, 67, 94 n. 35, 99-102, 106 & n. 52.

Lattimore, R., 279 n. 63, 280 n. 72.

Lavagnini, B., 254.

Lefkowitz, M.R., 1, 141 nn. 60 & 61, 278 n. 40.

Lemmatist (of Palatine ms.), 288 & nn. 15 & 16, 290 & n. 27, 291.

360 SIMONIDES

Leocrates, 42-4, 325.
Leon (of Troezen), 158, 159.
Leonidas, 181-2, 185-7.
Leophron (or "Cleophron"), 212-4.
Leoprepes, 97.
Lobel, E., 189, 210 n. 108.
Locrians, 180, 182-3.
Lycurgus (as source of Simonidean epigrams), 7.
Lysimachus (of Eretria), 46-7, 59 n. 69.

— M —

Maas, P., 40, 45, 168 n. 18, 240 n. 50, 313.
Macan, R.W., 204 n. 36.
Marathon, 24, 26, 68, 70-1, 72, 75, 148-55.
Marzullo, B., 236 n. 2, 237 n. 14, 238 n. 20.
McGregor, M.F., 155, 169 nn. 29 & 30.
Medon: see Meidylus.
Megacles, 155-6.
Megara, Megarians, 184, 196, 199-200.
Megistias, 7, 9, 17, 176-9, 180.
Meidylus (or "Medon"), 97 & n. 3, 98.
Meiggs, R., 168 n. 21.
Meineke, A., 55 n. 14, 56 n. 18.
Meleager (*Garland*), 7, 12, 13, 286-7, 298, 303 n. 26.

melic poems, 3-4.
Meyer, E., 120, 136, 137, 139 nn. 16 & 20, 144 n. 117, 293, 319 & n. 41.
Michelangeli, L.A., 271.
Micythus, 213 & nn. 18 & 19.
Miller, A.M., 281 n. 86.
Miller, S.G., 139 n. 9.
Milo (of Croton), 19, 81-3, 342.
Miltiades, 71, 152, 153, 154-5.
Mnasalces, 290.
mnemonic technique (memory) of Simonides, 311, 341.
Moretti, L., 55 nn. 9 & 10, 220, 236 n. 7.
Morrison, J.S., 137, 139 n. 19, 142 n. 65, 144 n. 117.
Mosshammer, A.A., 139 n. 9.
Most, G.W., 275 nn. 4, 5, & 8, 276 n. 16, 277 n. 32, 282 n. 103, 283 n. 106.
Myres, J.L., 168 n. 22.
myrtle-crowns, 217.

— N —

Naxians, Naxos, 189-90, 196.
Nemeads (dating of), 94 nn. 37 & 38.
Nisetich, F.J., 258, 275 n. 8, 278 n. 48, 281 nn. 78 & 86.

— O —

Oates, W.J., 141 n. 63.

Oliver, J.H., 152, 208 n. 92.

Olympiads (dating by), 310, 316.

Oreithyia, 158-60, 163.

Orpheus, Orphism, 27.

— P —

paeans, 191 & n. 77.

Page, D.L., 5 & n. 2, 13-4, 27 n. 1, 31 n. 63, 38, 48, 50, 52, 54 & n. 114, 63 nn. 109 & 111, and passim.

Palatine Anthology, 7, 8, 14, 23, 287, 288, 299.

Pan, 152, 153.

Panaetius, 321 & n. 44.

Panathenaea, 161-2.

partheneia, 113 n.37.

Pausanias (as source of Simonidean epigrams), 8.

Pausanias (of Sparta), 25, 182, 198.

Pavese, C., 257, 279 n. 55.

Persian Wars, 24, 25, 26, 70, 147-210.

Philaids, 155.

Philammon, 35, 57 n. 34.

Philon (of Corcyra), 42.

Phocians, 182, 184.

Phocyllides, 311.

phyllobolia, 216-7.

Pickard-Cambridge, A.W., 100, 101, 103.

Pindar: relations with Simonides, 24-5, 26-7, 69, 121, 233, 247-75, 326; dating of, relative to Simonides, 26, 27, 247, 258-9, 263, 274-5, 311, 312, 315; pupil of Simonides, 112 n. 27, 272; pupil of Lasus, 99 & n. 16, 112 n. 27; and Glaucus, 34 & n. 5; trends in Pindaric scholarship, 2-3, 247-8.

Pisistratids (see also Hipparchus, Hippias), 65-76, 100, 154, 265, 342.

Pisistratus, 69-70, 265.

Planudean Anthology, Planudes, 6, 7, 83, 287.

Plataea, 43-4, 149, 197-201.

Plato, 23.

Plutarch (as source of Simonidean epigrams), 8.

Podlecki, A.J., 61 n. 91, 79 n. 34, 116 nn. 75 & 87, 138 n. 3, 139 n. 6, 164, 165, 171 n. 68, 189, 190, 205 nn. 47 & 49, 239 n. 43, 240 n. 56, 242 n. 84, 245 n. 127.

Pritchett, W.K., 290.

Privitera, G.A., 100, 101, 102, 278 nn. 45 & 49.

Pythagoreanism, 27.

Pythiads (dating of), 139 n. 9.

— R —

Race, W.H., 275 n. 8, 276 n. 14.

Raubitschek, A.E., 93 n. 20.

Reinach, Th., 223.
Robert, C., 219.
Robertson, N., 115 n. 73.
Rohde, E., 313, 329, 333 nn. 34 & 35.
Rose, H.J., 36-8.
rose-crowns, 217.
Rutgers, I., 56 n. 15, 82.

— S —

Salamis, 149, 161-2, 187-96.
Schmid, W., 59 n. 69, 100, 145 n. 133, 151, 229, 232, 237 n. 14, 238 n. 20, 267.
Schneidewin, F.G. (= F.W.), 8, 120, 156, 168 n. 17, 183, 205 n. 51, 242 n. 89, 243 n. 91.
Schroeder, O., 275 n. 10, 276 n. 12.
Sciathos, 158, 173 n. 95.
Scopadae, Scopas, 24, 33, 118 & n. 5, 121-6, 129, 133, 134, 137-8.
Semonides, 114 n. 46.
Severyns, A., 98 & n. 13, 220, 232, 237 n. 14.
Sicily, 16, 18, 24, 25, 26-7, 116 n. 87, 214-36, 289, 308, 314.
Siebelis, K., 57 n. 30, 81.
Simonides (grandfather of the lyric poet), 26, 67-8, 326, 328.
Simonides (grandson of the lyric poet), 68 & n. 15.

Simpson, M., 278 n. 47.
Slater, W.J., 141 n. 60.
Smyth, H.W., 134, 144 nn. 109 & 114, 145 n. 133.
Sogenes (of Aegina), 87-9.
Sommerstein, A.H., 60 n. 85.
Sophocles, 105 & n. 44, 163, 286, 287.
Sordi, M., 119, 122-3, 137.
Sparta, Spartans, 175-6, 179-80, 186-7, 197-8, 265.
"spirit" of an ode (for assessment of poet's age), 4, 133, 137, 202.
Stanford, W.B., 203 n. 12.
Stella, L.A., 1-2, 3, 19, 20, 22, 23-7, 38, 41, 45, 46, 54, 57 n. 37, 65-8, 70, 72, 73, 76, 82, 83, 86 & n. 27, 97-9, 100, 104, 106, 117, 133 & n. 110, 134, 136-7, 138 & n. 3, 144 n. 119, 153, 202, 232, 235, 240 n. 50, 247-8, 255, 258-9, 263, 274, 285-6, 288, 289, 298, 299, 300, 301-2, 312, 318-31, 339-43.
Stesichorus (synchronism with Simonides), 328 & n. 85, 330, 333 nn. 28 & 29, 336 n. 82.
Stroebus, 43.
Sylloge Simonidea (see also collection and Collector), 91, 298, 300, 303 n. 26, 311.
Syracuse (see also Astylus, Gelon, and Hieron), 236.

— T —

Taccone, A., 97, 98.
Tanagra, 25, 285, 300.
Tedeschi, A., 276 n. 19.
Tegea, Tegeans, 201.
Thargelia (festival), 113 n. 39, 308, 321.
Thargelia (of Miletus), 127-8, 135.
Theagenes, 57 n. 31.
Themistocles, 24, 26, 106, 108-10, 154-5, 166, 189, 194, 195, 201, 209 n. 105.
Theognetus (of Aegina), 89-90.
Theognis, 23, 106-7.
Thermopylae, 149, 158, 175-87, 290.
Theron, 24, 224-5, 234, 235, 251-4, 258, 269, 284 n. 126.
Thespians, 183-4.
Thessaly, 21, 26, 27, 46, 54, 117-38, 342.
Thrasybulus, 234, 236 n. 8, 256-8, 269.
Thucydides (as source of Simonidean epigrams), 7, 12.
Thummer, E., 257.
Timaeus (as source of a Simonidean epigram), 7, 12.
Timocreon, 25, 26, 107-10.
Treu, M., 344 n. 2.
Troezen inscription, 189.
Turner, E.G., 85 & n. 25.

tyrannicides, 26, 70, 72-3.
Tzetzes (scholia of), 62 n. 96.

— U —

Urlichs, L. von, 238 n. 27.
Uxkull-Gyllenband, W., 296.

— V —

Van Leeuwen, J., 275 n. 8.
Verdenius, W.J., 278 nn. 44 & 47.

— W —

Wade-Gery, H.T., 139 n. 20, 204 n. 36, 290, 297.
Weber, L., 205 n. 43, 296.
Wehrli, F., 101.
West, M.L., 5 & n. 2, 113 n. 44, 205 n. 47, 344 n. 3.
Westlake, H.D., 137, 138 nn. 1 & 2, 139 nn. 16, 18 & 24.
Wilamowitz-Moellendorff, U. von, 2, 11-2, 13, 59 n. 69, 61 n. 91, 62 n. 97, 66, 94 n. 37 and passim.
Wilhelm, A., 300, 325.
Woodbury, L., 114 n. 53, 237 n. 16, 238 nn. 18 & 19, 257, 278 nn. 43 & 45, 279 n. 55.

— X —

Xenocrates, 233-5, 257-8, 269.
Xenophanes, 25, 26, 105-6, 311, 332 n. 18.

Xenophon, 23.

— Y - Z —

Young, D.C., 88-9, 92 n. 11.
Zuntz, G., 69-70, 114 n. 48, 278 n. 41.

Index of Passages
A. Fragments of Simonides

(i) Melic fragments of Simonides (plus some miscellaneous references and testimonia), numbered according to Page's *Poetae Melici Graeci*.

1/506	143 n. 95; 214-20; 271 & n. 119; 344 n. 14.	23/528	24; 27; 125 & n. 66; 126; 127 & n. 74; 343 & n. 27.
2/507	19 & n. 73; 47-54; 59 n. 69; 90-2.	24/529	138 n. 5.
3/508	143 n. 95.	25/530	46-7; 86 & n. 28.
4/509	33-42; 86 & n. 28; 342 & n. 20.	26/531	30 n. 58; 180 & n. 14; 185-7; 252 & n. 24; 271 & n. 118.
5/510	54 n. 1; 58 n. 52; 121 & n. 38.	27/532	158 & n. 53.
6/511 fr. 1 (a) & (b)	129 & n. 94; 130.	28/533	158 & n. 53.
		29/534	158 & n. 53; 159-61.
8/513	233-5; 257 & n. 46; 344 n. 14.	30/535	158 & n. 53; 159; 161-2; 191.
10/515	211-4; 344 n. 14.	31/536	161 & n. 69; 187-91.
13/518	45-6; 86 & n. 28; 342 & n. 22; 344 n. 13.	34/539	111 n. 14.
		36/541	283 n. 115.
14/519 fr. 84	231.	37/542	106 & n. 57; 122 & n. 39; 133 & n. 111; 137 & n. 127; 283 n. 115.
15/520	271 & n. 118.		
16/521	122 & n. 41; 124 & n. 59; 125 & n. 66; 206 n. 56.	45/550	116 n. 87; 245 n. 127.
		47/552	220 & n. 51; 229-31.
18/523	271 & n. 118.		
21/526	271 & n. 118.	59/564	337 nn. 85, 89.

366 SIMONIDES

Fragments of Simonides: continued

62/567	27.	102/607	69-70; 265.
67/572	194 & n. 89; 195-6.	122/627	195 & n. 91; 201 & n. 116.
70/575	106 & n. 59.	123/628	337 n. 90.
74/579	280 n. 72.	124/629	200 & n. 111.
75/580	226 & n. 83; 231; 344 n. 14.	130/635	159; 170 n. 53.
76/581	280 n. 65.	138/643	280 n. 66.
77/582	280 n. 72.	146/651	152 & n. 25. (= *Carm. Conviv.* 7/890)
79/584	271 & n. 118.	147/652 (iv)	333 n. 27.
97/602	25; 259-62; 274.		
98/603	252 & n. 23.	148/653 II	278 n. 40.

(ii) Epigrams of Simonides, numbered according to Page's *Further Greek Epigrams*; the numbers in Page's *Epigrammata Graeca* are identical, unless otherwise indicated below. The fragment numbers of Bergk and Diehl (and, where applicable, of West's *Iambi et Elegi Graeci*) are added.

I (131 B. 76 D.)	6 & n. 3; 11 & n. 29; 19 & n. 72; 26; 70 & n. 25; 72-4; 75-6; 305 n. 73.	VII (95 B. 120 D.)	30 n. 58; 181 & n. 18.
		VIII (100 B. 118 D.)	184 & n. 35; 197 & n. 99.
II (89 B. 87 D.)	19 & n. 71; 85-7.	IX (99 B. 121 D.)	184 & n. 35; 197 & n. 99; 290.
III (132 B. 100 D.)	19 & n. 71; 28 n. 8; 84-5; 86-7; 305 n. 73.	X (98 B. 94 D.)	19 & n. 74; 193 & n. 85; 194.
V (133 B. 143 D.)	151; 153.	XI (96 B. 90 D.)	11; 19 & n. 74; 28 n. 17; 192 & nn. 78, 79; 194.
VI (94 B. 83 D.)	7 & n. 6; 9; 12 & nn. 38, 41; 16 & n. 57; 17; 29 n. 43; 147; 176-9; 180-1; 319.	XII (97 B. 95 D.)	19 & n. 74; 28 n. 17; 93 n. 24; 192 & n. 81; 194.

XIII (134 B. 108 D.)	19 & n. 74; 193 & n. 83; 194.	XXV (156 B. 153 D.	19 & n. 70; 81-3; 342 & n. 21.
XIV (137 B. 104 D.)	7 & n. 9; 19 & n. 74; 29 n. 39; 30 n. 49; 193 & n. 84; 194; 195 & n. 91; 290.	XXVIA (111 B. 85 D.)	7 & n. 7; 12 & n. 38; 19 & n. 68; 20 & n. 78; 31 n. 80; 70 & n. 26; 74-6; 287.
		XXVII (145 B. 79 D.)	102-3; 104; 111 n. 14; 256; 325 & n. 73; 334 n. 41; 340.
XV (140 B. 107 D.)	197 & n. 101.	XXVIII (147 B. 77 D.)	19 & n. 69; 24; 102; 103; 104; 111 nn. 5, 14; 241 n. 77; 307-8; 309; 313; 316; 317; 318-26; 328; 330; 332 n. 21; 340; 344 nn. 8, 14.
XVI (107 B. 96 D.)	6 & n. 5; 199 & n. 109; 200.		
XVII (a) FGE (=XVII EG) (138 B. 105 D.)	28 n. 8; 180 & n. 13; 182 & n. 22; 198 & n. 102; 319.		
		XXIX (152 B. 148 D.)	42 & n. 40.
XIX (a) (136 B. 65 D.)	189 & n. 67; 190; 196.	XXX (149 B. 111 D.)	17 & n. 61; 19 & n. 73; 20 & n. 83; 89-90; 91.
		XXXIV (141 B. 106 D.)	18 & n. 67; 221-4; 228; 340.
XX (a&b) (88A&B, D. ed. 2)	148-9; 152-3; 305 n. 73.	XXXVII (169 B. 99 D.)	107 & n. 68; 108; 110.
XXI (90 B. 88 D.)	93 n. 24; 150; 152; 153.	XXXVIII (104 B. 89 D.)	93 n. 24.
XXII (a) (91 B. 91 D.)	12 & n. 38; 28 n. 6; 29 nn. 41, 43; 93 n. 24; 175; 176-9.	XLI (163 B. 110 D.)	28 nn. 8, 12; 287.
XXII (b) (92 B. 92 D.)	7 & n. 14; 12 & n. 38; 28 nn. 6, 8; 29 nn. 41, 43; 150; 175; 176-80.	XLV (142 B. 103 D.)	25; 31 n. 75; 93 n. 24; 285; 291-300; 302 n. 11; 303 nn. 17, 21.
XXIII (93 B. 93 D.	180 & n. 15; 182-3.	XLVI (105 B. 115 D.)	16 & n. 60; 31 n. 75; 285; 288-90; 299; 302 n. 11.
XXIV (135 B. 109 D.)	17 & n. 62; 18 & n. 65; 156-7; 207 n. 74.	XLVII (106 B. 116 D.)	31 n. 75; 286; 290-1; 299.

368 SIMONIDES

XLIX (108 B. 117 D.)	25; 30 n. 54; 31 n. 75; 285; 300-2; 302 n. 11.	LXIX (130 B. 142 D.)	132 & n. 106.
LI (180 B. 127 D.)	14 & n. 50; 31 n. 75; 32 n. 88; 286 & nn. 5, 14; 287.	LXXV (113 B. 84 D. 16 W.)	27 n. 2; 155-6.
LII (188 B. 152 D.)	11 & n. 29; 287 & n. 8.	LXXVI (a) & (b) (109 B. 97 (a) & (b) D.)	226-9; 231; 344 n. 14
LIII (102 B. 122 D.)	18 & n. 66; 201 & nn. 114, 115; 245 n. 127.	LXXXIII (a) & (b) FGE (=LXXXIII EG) (110 B. 141 D.)	157 & n. 51; 158; 181.
LIV (103 B. 123 D.)	18 & n. 66; 210 n. 114.		
LVIII (185B B. 165 D.)	31 n. 75; 32 n. 88; 287.	LXXXVIII (167 B. 67 D. 6 W.)	21 & n. 86; 27 n. 2; 28 n. 12; 130 & n. 98; 131.
LXVI (183 B. 125 D.)	15 & nn. 51, 52.		

(iii) Elegiac or dactylic fragments and epigrams of Simonides, numbered according to West's *Iambi et Elegi Graeci*. (Fragment 17 consists of a dactylic hexameter and a trochaic tetrameter.) The fragment numbers of Bergk and Diehl are added. These items are not in Page's *Epigrammata Graeca* or *Further Greek Epigrams*.

7 (171 B. 68 D.)	7 & n. 10; 131 & n. 102.	14 (146 B. [78] D.)	85; 311 & n. 21; 334 n. 41.
9 (81 B. 62 D.)	150; 151; 153; 190.	17 (170 B. 162 D.)	27 n. 2; 115 n. 71.
10-11 (84 B. 64 D.)	195 & n. 91; 198 & n. 106; 199.		

(iv) Dactylic and elegiac fragments and epigrams of Simonides, numbered according to Diehl's *Anthologia Lyrica Graeca* ed. 2. Bergk's fragment number is added. These items are not in West *IEG* nor Page *EG* or *FGE* (except for 101 Diehl, which Page prints among the epigrams of Anacreon).

63 (82 B.)	27 n. 2; 150-1; 152; 153.	101 (150 B. = Anacreon XV Page *EG* & *FGE*)	28 n. 17; 30 n. 54; 43-4; 325 & nn. 69, 72.
69 (172 B.)	7 & n. 10; 131 & n. 104.		
70 (173 B.)	7 & n. 10; 131 & n. 104.	161 (168 B.)	88.

(v) Epigrams of Simonides numbered according to Bergk's *Poetae Lyrici Graeci* ed. 4.

148 (= Antigenes 1 Diehl, & Page *FGE*; Bacchyl. III Page *EG*)	30 n. 53; 320; 322.	166 (not in Diehl, West, or Page)	17 & n. 61; 19 & n. 73; 20 & n. 83; 28 n. 12; 87-9; 91.

B. Passages in Ancient Authors in which Simonides is mentioned.

Note: Passages where Simonidean poems are quoted are not, as a rule, included here; for these, see index of fragments. For non-specific references to ancient authors in connection with Simonides (e.g. as being sources of Simonidean epigrams), see the general index (pp. 355 ff. above) under the authors' names.

Aelian,		Africanus	314.
VH 4.15	232 & n. 105.	(as source	
8.2	77 n. 4.	of infor-	
9.1	241 n. 68; 242 n. 79; 308 & n. 5.	mation on Simonides)	
9.41	209 n. 103.	*Anth. Pal.*, 4.1.8	see s.v. Meleager.
frag. 63	245 n. 129.		

370 SIMONIDES

Passages mentioning Simonides: continued

Apollodorus (as source of information on Simonides)	24; 25; 309 & n. 15; 313 & nn.28,31; 314-7; 326-31.	Didymus (as source of information on Simonides)	114 n. 48; 224; 238 n. 21.
Aristophanes, *Pax* 696-7	105 & n. 42.	Diogenes Laertius, 2.46	see s.v. Aristot. frag. 75.
697-9	244 n. 112.		
Vesp. 1409 ff.	99; 101; 102.	Eratosthenes (as source of information on Simonides)	333 nn. 28, 31.
Aristotle, *Ath. Pol.* 18.1-2	65-7; 76.		
Rhet. 2.16, 1391 a 8	241 n. 68.		
frag. 75 Rose	107.	*Etymologicum Magnum* 713. 17 ff.	see s.v. Choeroboscus.
Athenaeus, 14.656 c-d	241 n. 69.		
14.656 d	114 n. 47; 243 n. 104.	Eusebius (entries on Simonides)	23; 113 n. 43; 310-1; 314-5; 329; 330.
14.656 d-e	241 n. 68.		
Callimachus, frag. 64 Pfeiffer	124; 245 n. 129.	Eustathius, *Prooem. Pind.* III p. 297.13 f. Drachmann	112 n. 27; 284 n. 121; 333 n. 25.
frag. 222 *Pinakes*	256 & n. 37. 7.		
Callistratus, *Miscellanies*	7; 130-1.	ib. 21 f.	266 & n. 98.
Chamaeleon, frag. 33 Wehrli	105 & nn.47,48; 131 & n. 102.	Herodotus, 7.228	175-9
frags. 33-4 Wehrli	7 & n. 10.	7.228.4	111 n. 5.
Choeroboscus, in *Et. Mag.* 713.17 ff.	114 n. 46.	Hesychius of Miletus (as source of information on Simonides)	313; 315.
Chronicon Paschale (entries on Simonides)	310; 332 n. 16.	Hieronymus, *Epist.* 52.256	312 & n. 23.
Cicero, *De Orat.* 2.351-3	121 & n. 38; 124; 141 n. 53.	Hieronymus, entries on Simonides	see s.v. Eusebius.
De Rep. 2.20	309; 313; 315; 333 n. 28.	Lucian (= Ps. -Lucian), *Macrob.* 26 (228)	332 n. 14.
ND 1.60	241 n. 69; 283 n. 115.	Meleager, (*Anth. Pal.* 4.1.8)	7 & n. 13.
Cyril of Alexandria, *Adv. Iulian.* I 13	311 & n. 17.		

Passages mentioning Simonides: continued

Nepos, *(Chronica)* (as source of information on Simonides)	313.	*P. Oxy* 2430, (cf. Simon. 14/519 Page)	206 n. 65.
Ovid, *Ibis* 511-2	126.	*P. Oxy.* 2535	85.
Parian Marble, eps. 49, 54, & 57 (entries on Simonides)	23; 26; 67-8; 79 n. 34; 111 n. 5; 149; 153; 241 n. 77; 309; 313-4; 316-8; 327-31; 333 n. 28.	Quintilian, *Inst. Or.* 11.2.11-6	33; 34; 36-9; 41; 42; 43; 44; 121 & n. 38; 122; 124; 125; 126; 141 n. 53.
Pausanias, 9.2.5	197 & n. 97.	Schol. Aristoph. *Pac.* 697 (= Xenophanes frag. 21)	105 & nn. 42, 46, 48.
P. Hib. 17.1-8	241 n. 68.		
Plato, *Epist.* 2.311a	209 n. 103; 224 & n. 67.	*Vesp.* 1411 (= 1402)	101; 102 & n. 30.
Hipparch. 228 b-c	65-7; 77 n. 18.	Schol. Pind. *Ol.* 2.29 (= 15)	224 & nn. 70, 72, 74.
Plutarch, *An seni* 5 (786 b)	244 n. 112.	*Ol.* 2.157-8 (= 87)	249 & n. 6; 268.
Cons. ad Apoll. 6 (105 a)	209 n. 103.	*Nem.* 4.60 ff. (= 37 ff.)	264-5.
De aud. poet. 1 (15 c-d)	133 & n. 113.	*Isth.* 2.9 (= 6)	256 & n. 37.
Vit. Them. 5.7 (114 d)	194 & n. 89; 195-6.	Schol. Theocr., 16.34 ff.	118 & n. 5; 127 & n. 73.
ib. 15.4 (119 f)	188-9.	Schol. Tzetz. *Chil.* 1.619	242 n. 79; 308 & n. 3.
Plutarch (= Ps.-Plutarch), *Mus.* 17 (1136 f)	113 n. 37.	Sozomenus, *Hist. Eccles., Praef.* 5	120 & n. 31; 121.
P. Oxy. 220, (cf. Simon. 147/652 (iv) Page)	312-3 & n. 27.	Stephanus Byzantius s.v. "Ioulis"	111 n. 1.
P. Oxy. 2327, frag. 27 ii frag. 31 (cf. Simon. 31/536 Page)	210 n. 108. 189 & nn. 64, 65.	Stobaeus *Ecl.* 3.10.61	244 n. 112.
		Strabo, 10.5.6 (486)	111 n. 1.

372 SIMONIDES

Passages mentioning Simonides: continued

Suda,		Timaeus, frag. 93	224 & n. 71.
s.v. "Bacchylides"	97 & nn. 2-4.		
s.v. "Simonides"		Timocreon,	
439	7 & n. 11; 23; 25; 104 & n. 40; 187 & n. 52; 309-10; 311; 313-6; 329; 330.	frag. 10 West	108 & n. 70.
		Tzetzes,	
		Chil. 1.636-9	112 n. 32.
		ib. 4.487	112 n. 32.
		Valerius Maximus,	
s.v. "Simonides"		8.7 *Ext.* 13	308 & n. 7.
441	245 n. 129.		
s.v. "Simonides"		*Vit. Aeschyl.*	
442	77 n. 15.	p. 332.5 ff. Page	148; 151-3.
s.v. "Timocreon"	107-8.		
		Vit. Pind. Ambr.	
Syncellus		I p. 2.21 f.	312 & n. 25.
(entries on		Drachmann	
Simonides)	310.		
		Vit. Pind. Thom.	
Syrian		I p. 5.4 f.	333 n. 25.
In Hermog.		Drachmann	
I p. 85 f. Rabe	104 & n. 41; 242 n. 79; 307-8.	ib. p. 7.13	112 n. 27; 284 n. 121.
		Xenophanes,	
Theocritus,		frag. 21	105 & n. 44.
16.34-47	118 & n.4; 120; 121 & n.37; 127 & n.73; 129; 307 & n.2.	Xenophon,	
		Hieron	26; 224; 232.
		Hieron 6.7 ff.	153 & n. 26.
Theognis, 1.467-96, 1.677-82, 2.1345-50	106-7.		

C. General Index of Passages

Note: for more general references to ancient authors, see the general index (pp. 355 ff. above).

Aeschines, 3.189	57 n. 34.	Aeschylus, fr. eleg. 1 West	149.
Aeschines Socraticus frag. 22	127 & n. 79.	Anacreon, I Page	20 & n. 76; 31 n. 79.

General Index of Passages: continued

Anacreon,		Herodotus,	
VII Page	20 & n. 81; 127 & n. 75.	6.49 ff.	50; 51-3.
		7.3.6	67 & n. 11.
XIII Page	20 & n. 81; 127 & n. 75.	7.189	158 & n. 54; 163 & n. 77;
XV Page	see Simonides 101 Diehl.	8.11 ff.	164 & n. 85. 163-4.
XVII Page	302 n. 7.	*Inscriptiones*	
Anonymi Tractatus		*Graecae*	
de Mulieribus XI	127 & n. 80; 128; 135.	I² 772	321 & n. 48.
		II² 3027	321 & n. 43.
		3042	321 & nn. 50, 53.
Antigenes I Page	see Simonides 148 Bergk.	3113	324 & n. 67.
Bacchylides,		3117	324 & n. 68; 325.
Ode 3	269; 273.	3118	323 & nn. 63, 66; 324.
3.17-21	222 & n. 62.	3120 b	323 & n. 65; 324.
Ode 5	251-2; 273 & n. 124.		
5.10-2	252.	II-III² 11912	50 & n. 88.
5.11	79 n. 33.	*Lexica Segueriana*	35 & n. 11; 57 n. 32.
Ode 13	273 & n. 124.		
13.224	79 n. 33.		
III Page	see Simonides 148 Bergk.	Ovid, *Ibis* 323-4	120 & n. 27.
Chronicon		Parian Marble ep.46	99 & n. 15.
Paschale		Pausanias,	
I 304	98 & n. 13.	6.10.1-3	34-5; 39; 41-2.
Diodorus Siculus,			
11.60-2	292 & n. 39; 293.	6.14.5 f.	81 & n. 2; 82; 93 n. 14.
12.3-4	294 & n. 49.	Phaenias frag. 14	122; 125.
Empedocles,		Philiadas I Page	183 & n. 33; 184; 200 & n. 113.
frags.156-7 D.-K.	287 & n. 12.		
Eratosthenes,			
frag. 14	216-7.	Philostratus,	
Etymologicum		*Gym.* 34	35; 55 n. 8.
Magnum 582.20	111 n. 3.	Pindar,	
Eustathius,		*Ol.* 1	251; 269; 273 & n. 124.
Prooem. Pind.			
III 296.19-20		1.108-11	273.
Drachmann	111 n. 16.	2	90; 224; 251; 252; 269.
ib. 300.1	111 n. 16.		

374 SIMONIDES

General Index of Passages: continued

Pindar,
Ol. 2.15-8 225; 252-3; 271 & n. 117.
2.49-51 234 & n. 117; 235.
2.50 44 & n. 56.
2.83 ff. 24; 235 & n. 128; 248-55; 272 & n. 122; 273; 274.
2.95-8 253-4.
3 251; 269.
6.93 ff. 282 n. 100.
7.84 238 n. 23.
8.69 51 & n. 98.
9 25; 27.
9.28 f. 271 & n. 118.
9.48 f. 25; 259-63; 270 & n. 116; 273; 274-5; 336 n. 78; 343.
9.90 238 n. 23.
9.103-4 271 & n. 117; 280 n. 72.
9.107-8 271 & n. 117; 280 n. 72.
10.15 f. 56 n. 27.
13.55-60 195 & n. 90.

Pyth. 1 269.
1.29 ff. 243 n. 96.
1.75-7 190.
1.92 267.
2.10 44 & n. 56.
2.18-20 283 n. 114.
2.76 f. 267.
3 244 n. 116.
3.69 79 n. 33; 243 n. 96.
3.81 f. 271 & n. 118.
3.86 ff. 271 & n. 118.
4.66 f. 238 n. 28.
6 234; 236 n. 8.
6.8 ff. 271 & n. 118.
7 156.
8.35-6 90 & n. 41.
8.86 f. 51 & n. 98.
9 282 n. 99.

Pindar,
Pyth. 9.123-5 239 n. 37.
10 119 & nn. 7, 8; 121; 268.
10.8 f. 238 n. 28.
10.64 79 n. 33.
11.41 ff. 257.

Nem. 1 231 & n. 103.
4.33 ff. 254 & n. 35; 263-5; 272 & n. 122.
5 273 & n. 124.
6.39-41 239 n. 29.
7.1 ff. 87-9.
7.75-7 267.
9 231.
11.19-21 238 n. 28.
11.19-29 271 & n. 119.

Isth. 2. 25; 234-5; 244 n. 116; 269.
2.1-13 255-9; 270 & n. 116; 272 & n.122; 273; 274.
2.6 25.
2.18 ff. 234 & n. 121.
2.23 ff. 244 n. 122.
4.7 f. 238 n. 28.
8.69-71 238 n. 28.

frag. 52d 265-6.
75-77 268 & n. 112.
77 26.
94b 41-9 238 n. 28.
118-9 283 n. 113.
339 69-70; 265 & n. 88; 270 & n. 116.

Plutarch
Vit. Cimon.
12-13 292 & n. 40; 293; 296.

P. Oxy. 222 40 & n. 31; 90 & n. 43; 219 & nn. 45, 46, 47; 262; 280 n. 75.

General Index of Passages: continued

Schol. Aeschin.,	
3.189	35; 57 n. 34.
Suda,	
s.v. "Glaukos"	35 & n. 11; 57 n. 32.
s.v. "Glaukos Karystios"	55 n. 8.
s.v. "Lasos"	99 & n. 14; 102.
s.v. "Platon"	334 n. 39.
Thucydides	
1.112.2-4	293 & n. 47; 294 & n. 48.
Timocreon	
frag. 1/727	109-10.
frags. 2/728-3/729	109 & n. 74; 110.
Vit. Pind. Thom.	
I p. 4.14-5 Drachmann	111 n. 16.
Xenophanes,	
frag. 6	105 & n. 50.